NEXT WE SHALL SING

Tony Jasper

About the author

Tony Jasper originally hails from Penzance. Educated in theology and drama at various universities both in the UK and the US, he has some 70 book titles to his name. Tony spent many years in radio both as a DJ and an actor.

In 1992 he formed the Jasperian Theatre Company, writing all its plays and appearing in the productions.

Tony is also an accredited Methodist local preacher, writing a monthly column "Jesus music" in the *Methodist Recorder*.

Other titles by Tony Jasper

Silver Cliff
The Illustrated Family Hymn Book
Worship the King
I Read the News Today
Jesus in a Pop Culture
The Nostalgia Book of Hit Singles
Feel So Real
Moody and Sankey
Johnny Mathis
Worship in Every Event

Cover Photo: Some of the congregation at Gospel Oak Methodist, London NW3

NEXT WE
SHALL SING

Tony Jasper

Highland

First published in the UK by Highland Books Limited,
Two High Pines, Knoll Road
GODALMING, Surrey GU7 2EP

© 2008 by Tony Jasper

Cover design: Inspiration-by-Design, Worthing
ISBN-10: 1 897913 82 6
ISBN-13: 978 1 89791382 6

Printed in Denmark for HIGHLAND BOOKS
by Norhaven Paperback A/S

Contents

Dedication

David and Lynn, two wonderful people who lost their lives in 2007 in a tragic car accident. Both ardent Christians, they were particularly involved in the life and worship of Stithians Methodist Church, Cornwall

Andrew, Jane, Ben and Mark Wade, formerly of the Rectory, Ludgvan and now the parish of Probus, for many kindnesses and welcomes!

Thanks to Major Bruce Tulloch (SA), Douglas Galbraith, Roy Jones and Philip Carter

Preface

Tony Jasper is simply captivated by hymns, and religious music, and has been so since his early teens. In such enthusiasm he empathises with many who belong to the various communions within the Christian world, and a considerable number with no chosen Christian affiliation. He could merely remain an individual in love with some of the most moving and beautiful music that has adorned civilisation, but his other world rests in the practical arena. He has Church commitment. He is a leader of worship. Thus hymns and religious music are seen in a wider context, allied to his own Christian convictions. These convictions have led to his producing numerous books on prayer, music and history. For many years, he appeared in regular slots on the BBC programme *Pause for Thought*, as well as, for a time, introducing 'live' recordings on *Sunday Half Hour*, the long-standing BBC programme featuring hymns linked by Roger Royle. At the same time he has been a DJ, and broadcast on contemporary music for BBC Radio I, Radio Hallam, and both rock and gospel music for British Forces Broadcasting Service; once being voted Europe's number two jock behind John Peel.

The text of this book clearly shows that the writer has enormous enthusiasm for the world of hymnology, and anyone interested in this genre will profit greatly from many sections. He takes the reader through his own hymn journey, how he discovered there is much more to a hymn than singing a particular song, and he opens a wide and varied world for the general hymn follower. While he is an enthusiast for the machinations that surround the 'hymn' as a subject, he is aware that today many Christian people find traditional hymns lacking, and they remain doubtful about much present material often grouped under the term 'praise.' Jasper shares this doubt. He believes this is an opinion held by many in the pew, pushed aside for a number of reasons by those who 'run the ship'. He finds many within the 'praise' world equally unhappy about the fare they are supposed to sing. They consider much of the 'praise' song to be old-fashioned and restrictive as anything that might be loosely labelled 'traditional.'

Jasper says the Christian adventure in recent times has been an unbridled disaster as expressed by the hymns and songs it sings. He asserts emphatically that Christians find it hard to express faith in present contexts because they seem afraid to desert a world which is mostly pre-1940s. Not that he abhors the 'traditional,' neither does he suggest that the past has nothing to say, it is simply that the 'traditional', left to itself, stultifies. In particular he is not deriding the devotional treasures of the golden age of hymn writing between 1700 and 1850. However, if these hymns continue to be sung, rather than being read, if they continue to have a use within meditative areas of church life and personal faith, then those who sing them must know why they should adorn contemporary Christian worship. So he believes much of the music sung by Christians has done more harm than good. He searches in vain for imagery and reference that would indicate to someone from another planet that the Christian faith is alive and well; not just a set of precious memories for a few who find consolation in the past. He asserts that most of the currently used books speak of committees who have shut themselves away from the world in which Faith has to live. Jasper also says that too often the compilation of hymn and songbooks is expressive of a male club; there is a real and dangerous lack of feminine input, and a deafening lack of multi-cultural awareness. He sees this to be particularly true in much of the material served up to youngsters. This he argues, is contributory to their ignoring the Church, and failing to find Faith.

Jasper believes there has been little real evaluation of what has been produced. He finds much of the new music loosely listed under the title of 'praise' dangerously near idolatry with an apparent emphasis on the worshipper's experience rather than any theological content, although he is careful to acknowledge the positive in some charismatic expressions. He holds the view that some current writers of music and song within the independent Christian community display little knowledge of theology, and their lyrics are almost devoid of contemporary reference. That does not prevent them using theological jargon, while their thought patterns resemble a word version of the repetitive and limited music sung to *I am so Glad that our Father in Heaven.*

All is far from lost. Jasper is aware of new composers — often stimulating but simply too few in number. He finds hymns and songs taking shape, new or old, when worship and life's experiences merge together, when sound Christian doctrine is seen taking flesh. This is not a scholarly work giving a systematic history of church music, Jasper sets out his own parameters without showing disrespect for anthems, psalms, and cantatas, and countless other areas of music which have made an invaluable contribution to Christian worship. Jasper's life, so involved in the world of contemporary music, informs his take on his chosen subject. His experience encompasses contemporary music, folk and jazz. Within these musical expressions he has found songs to delight the human soul.

The text will stimulate and provoke disagreement! It may or may not be dismissed, but these are words that should be **read.**

CHAPTER ONE

Journeying off from a Need

I invite you to an adventure, a journey into the world of hymns and songs where the markers may quickly change, and destinations arrived at may suddenly disappear and yet occur again at some other point. Sometimes it is as perplexing as driving down a certain Cornish road where the signpost tells you it is three miles to that place you have in mind. You arrive after driving the seeming distance at a T-Junction to see a further signpost to your destination that simply says it is three miles! While each hymn or song has its own logic, the whole world of music cannot be reduced to an ordered structure: yet the world of hymns continues to fascinate millions across the planet and at the same time both uplift and I believe subconsciously cause much spiritual harm. Thousands have tried their hand at hymn writing, some aware of the fact that Tennyson considered to write a good hymn the most difficult thing in the world.[1]

I come to all this from two apparently diverging paths of thought and experience. First, I have heard thousands of demos and records, been in countless studios with the great and the less so, reviewed so many titles and written thousands of words on rock, pop, folk, jazz, gospel and Jesus Music. Second, I've sung all kinds of religious music, attended more Christian services than perhaps has been good for me; some have been tedious beyond description, second-rate worship run with little thought and inspiration

---

1   Hallam: *Lord Tennyson in Tennyson: a Memoir,*
      11, p.401

---

and in their own little world. Others have been treasures. I take worship for many branches of the Christian family, often using their own hymn books. In preaching I am empowered to relate faith and life, to see God's Word taking shape here and now, but I have to choose hymns and songs. Ask me to name five tracks from the many genres of recorded music, concentrating on subjects of concern to us today, I would be happy to oblige. But when it comes to finding hymns and song to reflect contemporary themes I am at a loss. Too few hymns support my preaching. Sometimes I am deflated, yet aware that to some degree I have to work within the prescribed areas of whatever Christian gathering is kind enough to invite me to lead their worship. I could at risk not choose any hymns! John Wesley was well aware of the value of hymns in public worship.[2] I do not disagree with the great Anglican of the 18th century! Like him I seek the good and the meaningful. John Wesley assiduously edited the outpourings of his brother Charles and not always to the latter's joy! In far less scholarly fashion there are many like myself who find the traditional hymn totally lacking, for whom much of the praise catalogue is nebulous and self-centred; they cry for something real and honest. As you will see in the book, I both agree and disagree with them! Hence my problem when it comes to Sunday, for I love many traditional hymns, and some praise material does radiate a spiritual high. It seems a process of juggling several contradictory impulses at once. Surely something is wrong.

I can find a little chink of light by saying that by choosing time honoured hymns I am reminding myself, and everyone out there in the congregation, that this was how it once was, that these are words that inspired our past brothers and sisters, and along the way we may pick up something vital and real. However I cannot run away from the plain, simple and obvious fact that the world view underpinning most mainstream hymn books no longer has any practical

2   BC Drury, *John Wesley, Hymnologist,*
    Proceedings of the Wesley Historic Society,
    March 1960, Vol.XXXII, part 5, p.102ff

relevance. In part this book is a working out of my own dilemma, and I make the bold claim that it is the same for many other Christians, perhaps even you the reader. At least, I hope you will relate to parts of it. Also the text is not exclusively imbued with these quandaries, for I simply run with what I find, and enjoy letting texts speak for themselves.

But why should I be angry outside of my own inner conflict and uncertainty? Simply this, you can never exaggerate the importance of songs and hymns used week in week out by the Christian community. This applies especially to the 'hymn-prayer sandwich' communities rather than to the more service-order-driven traditions, where speech or visual ritualistic acts can push aside the seeming necessity to sing and sing. It has of course been well said that he who sings prays twice.

For many it is the singing of hymns, and consequent awareness of their words, that formulates their faith, often more so than the preacher and message. I go with those who argue that favourite hymns have taken the place of church catechisms. I would say that most Christian communities have hardly explored what it is to sing 'out there' with faith to the world of today's newspaper and newscast. Usually there is only a token gesture to anything contemporary, nothing radical happens beyond a few texts from a current writer, the rest stays largely untouched and usually placed under conventional themes.

Albert van den Heuvel has said: [3]

> In spite of Lutheran and Reformed emphasis on preaching of the Word – it is the hymns repeated, over and over again, which form the container of much of our faith. They are, probably, in our age, the only confessional documents that we learn by heart. I would have thought that the Christian community could only learn to sing again if we were to find the kairos of our history, the pregnancy of the times in which we live ... Whenever something happens, people start to sing.

---

3   Albert van den Heuvel, *New Hymns for a New Day*, (RISK 1966 WCC).

Neil Dixon, one of British Methodism's most acknowledged experts in the field of worship, liturgy, faith and order, writes:

> I am convinced that hymnody is the element of worship subject to the most abuse at the present time, and because singing fulfils such a significant role in Methodist (as in most nonconformist churches) liturgy and spirituality this is especially dangerous for us.[4]

I hold hands with someone such as den Heuvel, with his Pentecostal roots, plus many years working for the World Council of Churches. Forty years ago he was simply asking why it was that Christian churches engage in experiments with industry, recreation, science, philosophy, hermeneutics and worship formats, and yet our hymns are hardly touched. Hymns are more about restoration than renewal. So yes, we update a bit, remove a few atrocities, but otherwise what we do would be quite acceptable to anyone from the 19th century backwards.

I am acutely aware of my arrogance in penning a book. I say this in the context of reading once more the classic Erik Routley volumes.[5] They were written 50 or so years ago, but are still eminently readable; his scholarship is astounding in its width and breadth of the subject. And for many, his conclusions still hold, such is his knowledge and perception. Within my own Methodist Church there is Ivor Jones whose scholarship and awareness are enough to daunt anyone. I take refuge in the fact that none approach the subject from the perspective of someone who spends

---

4   Neil Dixon, *All-Age Worship; Usage and Abusage,* (Epworth Review Volume 20, Number 2, May 1993), p.52.

5   E.Routley, *Twentieth Century Church Music* (Herbert Jenkins, 1964), then *The Music of Christian Hymnody* (Independent Press, 1957), and *Words, Music and the Church* (Abingdon, USA, 1968) and *I'll Praise My Maker* (Independent Press 1951). There is also a huge number of features which he contributed to various journals, both general and religious.

hours each week listening to the plethora of musical output that is labelled 'contemporary.'

I arrived at page 29 of the *Church Times* for April 13, 2006. Apart from an article mildly critical of Anglicans for not singing more hymns by Albert Bayly, there were reviews of a raft of recent publications, including amongst others, the *Daily Telegraph Book of Hymns* and *Awake My Soul,* [6] expertly put together by a Methodist, Margaret Wallwork. For a moment I wavered, should I continue? I had to sit down and think what might be different about yet another publication on hymns.

Of course the long history of the Christian Church has spawned particular forms and styles that sometimes almost exclusively belong to one tradition; so it is that if I go to a Russian Orthodox service I know I will be taken to the heavens in a musical journey that I will not find elsewhere. I would be stunned if I did not find it. Should I choose to attend evensong at St Paul's, London or Christchurch, Oxford, I would be drawn into choral music of the highest standard that may well transport me outside the tyranny of this present moment.

I am conscious that I know little of the music that drives many Christian traditions of great age. But books can help: I can pick up a book such as *At The Lighting of the Lamps: Hymns of the Ancient Church,* [7] and dip my toes into the Orthodox Church. I learn from his central thesis that embedded in the New Testament are five hymns, and progress into the writings of the early Christian Fathers. Similarly, the non-Anglican groups in which I have spent much of my 'religious' life have mostly ignored the beauty and fascination of the Ancient Office Hymns in *Hymns Ancient and Modern* with their propensity to speak with time, temptation, and the Trinity.

6   'Reflections on Thirty Hymns, and Singing
     With The Saints: Hymns for the Festivals and
     Lesser Festivals of the Church of England.
7   John Anthony McGuckin, (Moorehouse
     Publications, Oxford 1997).

There is of course much more, too much more! There are old English and Scottish psalm tunes, old French psalm tunes and canticles, metrical melodies of the 13th to 16th centuries, and Lutheran tunes, some of the 16th and first half of the 17th century, and those from around the middle of the 17th to the middle of the 18th century, where we can roam with some joy into the exquisite settings of J.S. Bach. More recently there are the hymns, masses, and praise compositions of John Rutter, et al.[8]

I take refuge in the obvious. This is not a book that will take you, the reader, through a history of church music. I refer to certain musical forms, but usually by way of illustration rather than comment on the genre. I would not, for instance, venture a discussion as to whether Bach was a destroyer of the simplicity of the German choral, or the rights and wrongs of harmonising say a 1415 tune in the style of 2006 (although I might have an opinion)! So too I am not willing to take myself into the often confused world of Anglican liturgy, even if Series 3 of the Communion service led to the writing of 'instant music.'

However, I will say something with a positive ring, I can say, I think, with reasonable assurance (you see how doubt easily creeps in) that there are few books of hymnology of the 21st century that mention, let alone cover, such a wide field as this. In this text you will meet old-time gospel, 'pop' and 'jazz' and the already mentioned psalm tunes; there will be a reasonably sympathetic hearing equally of Routley and someone such as Lionel Dakers,[9] both of whom turn their attention to what is happening 'out there' in the wide wicked world. Coming as I do out of the world of music 'biz', I see nothing as untouchable. That is where you may find me different, though it doesn't mean I cease to respect.

In the end I am concerned with relevance, but that doesn't mean a preoccupation with what works or is seen to be useful, even if soon discarded. There are treasures in

8   Carl Jenkins, John Tavener, Bob Chilcott.
9   *Church Music At The Crossroads*, (Marshall Morgan and Scott, London, 1970).

religious music wastefully hidden away from vast swathes of churchgoing people. The horror questions rest in why people neglect such spiritual food. Why do they not continually seek to widen and broaden their soul horizons? When Gregorian music had a brief but useful outing in the popular music charts it was only a pity that pop lovers found it almost impossible to locate. Sadly the Church in general was not able to capitalise on this unexpected happening, although I doubt if many in the Church even knew that the pop world had briefly turned its attention to this form!

Second to relevance comes emotion. Sadly, at times, music heard in Church avoids any kind of emotional commitment, and often is so tedious and uninspiring that it ceases to be a sincere witness to the wondrous message of the God who took flesh in Jesus of Nazareth. A fascinating article on this theme of emotion in music can be found in an issue of *The Franciscan* (don't be put off by its 1968 date). The writer Arthur Wills decries the worship of technical perfection for its own sake instead of its being recognised as merely an instrument for the realisation of the spirit beyond the notes. He says:

> It is unfortunate that the prevalent tradition in English church music is to avoid any kind of emotional commitment.[10]

The writer goes on to contrast the emotion in two popular religious works, once almost mandatory in Holy Week for every Church choir:

> There is the emotion of Stainer's *The Crucifixion* and there is the emotion of *St Matthew's Passion*. The one has but little effect; the other can shake the listener to the core of his being. The great heritage of the church music is rich in emotional power. We must all hope that our performances recreate this power and that the authorities will permit this unique aid to worship to exert maximum sway over the hearts of men.

10   The Franciscan (source unknown)

For many, however, Stainer's work is the more accessible[11] but it remains sentimental, Victorian and indulgent. In this great hymn adventure I expect to find the essence of Mr Wills's article, as also the previous quote from Albert Van den Heuvel, constantly rearing their heads in terms of what some say shall or shall not be sung, and in how some areas it is considered improper to actually sing with heart and soul, and to avoid the horror of enthusiasm.

By the end of this book's text you may wonder whether there is any mainstream hymn book I would use with reasonable happiness. Near the end of 2007, my theatre company found itself in Scotland with the production of Charles Wesley 1707. The most successful show in terms of audience numbers was one presented by the Church of Scotland. This gave me time rather late in the day to realise the many good qualities of *Church Hymnary 4*. The British Methodist Church seeking a new volume would do well to adopt this one. For a greater Wesley contribution the Methodists could continue to use the existing *Hymns and Psalms*.

I want to see Christian song living in the lives of people often from totally differing backgrounds, cultures and perceptions. It is about offering God due praise. It is singing the Faith that emanates from following Jesus. It is being blessed by the Holy Spirit. Singing hymns can be a converting experience. Sometimes the world, and not the Church, sings what is right and good, while the Christian community remains blind to 'signs and wonders' coming down like showers of blessing.

11   (also here to include Maunder's *Olivet to Calvary*)

CHAPTER TWO

Falling in Love – with Hymns, What Else?

So where did it all begin? School, Church and the airwaves, then a powerful threesome. As a *Church Times* editorial succinctly explained:

> Hymns in school overlapped with hymns in church. Church music was strengthened by its cultural proximity to the music in the county school as well as in the choir and voluntary schools.
>
> ... But singing has declined in both together too.[12]

Today the interplay of these three worlds seems rather quaint, and is unlikely to be a formative influence on the young.

Rightly, the writer of the *Church Times* editorial was saddened by the diminishing amount of time devoted to music in state schools, particularly at primary level, with numeracy and literacy ascendant. Yet, with endless schemes, ideas and projects to build bridges between pupils of different backgrounds and cultures, music should be one of the forms most readily available for the pursuance of those aims.

At school in Penzance, Cornwall, an old-fashioned Grammar with an excellent headmaster, that modelled itself on being a day public school where Oxbridge scholarships – and there were many – were seen as the

12   *Church Times*, (January 19th, 2007), p.10.

---

ultimate earthly crown, I grew up with the solid, and to us at the time the never surprising world, of the *Songs of Praise Hymnbook*. Later I would agree with the view that it contains moments of beauty. We did avoid the section 'For Children' with its undue romping through nature. I gathered *Songs of Praise* was favoured for its literary standard.

Later I learned that the renowned Dr Dearmer described the hymnal as:

> the advance guard of a movement which will lead the Englishman of the future to read hymn-books for the poetry that is in them.[13]

I do not think we had any sense of the sentiments expressed by Erik Routley below:

> The hymnbook *Songs of Praise* on the other hand sought to say principally to schoolchildren, 'Secular standards of literary and musical excellence are good enough for the church; there is not a double standard that permits in church what would be regarded by secular eyes as beastly art.' So Shakespeare, Shelley, Traherne and Wordsworth take their place alongside Watts and Wesley, and Bax and Ireland and Howells reinvited to sing hymn tunes.[14]

His expectations were amazing. *Songs of Praise* to most of my fellow pupils represented a morning assembly book that was stuffed into your pocket, dog-eared through misuse rather than study. Still, growing up is a learning process. Later I would learn a little of what it was we were singing. Unfortunately we frequently sang with an incipient boredom that left the Headmaster ill-disposed toward our efforts. We didn't twig that we might be part of a musical tradition, let alone a religious history, and some of that would be hoisted onto a set of rules by which an Englishman should live. I had yet to chase after the distinctive nature of being Cornish.

13   Erik Routley, *I'll Praise My Maker, Studies in English Classical Hymnody*, (Independent Press, London, 1951).

14   Erik Routley, *The Notion of 'Sacred' Music, Christianity in its Social Context*, (SPCK Theological Collections, 1967), p.65.

If only Englishmen would realise that in their blood there is as much French as German, and that the European influence in their culture did not begin with the Restoration of King Charles II, and above all that their own musical heritage is as upstanding as anybody else's, they would realise that they need not go about assuming they had no music in them. [15]

We sang because we were told to sing. Some hymns we ignored, not necessarily because we disliked them, it was simply the way we felt, and our indifference could be protest against whatever we happened to disagree with at the time in the running of the school. When uttering poor levels of volume we were often made to reassemble late afternoon to improve upon our lack lustre performance. The day would not end until we emitted the right spirit. We were lectured on how we had to sing with vigour. It was never explained why, other than there was an assumption that we should see the singing of hymns as some kind of treat. Of course we were a mix of boys, some with voices not broken, others in a kind of gender confusion state, and the rest learning a proud masculine journey of tenor or bass. So it wasn't always easy, and when in the sixth form you always hoped the new boys would carry the flag, their innocence yet to be broached, for they thought it good to sing with heart and be praised in their magnificence.

Some of the less well known hymns which formed part of the repertoire for morning assembly have stayed with me, even though many have been little used in churches; one such is the lovely *Remember O Thou Man* – I push its merit on any occasion I can, though it's not in the non-Anglican orientated hymn books. [16]

15   Erik Routley, *Twentieth Century Church Music*, (Hope Publishing Co. USA, 1984), p.27, reflects on the argument by Ralph Vaughan Williams, National Music and Other Essays, (Oxford U.P., 1963).

16   The tune of *Remember O Thou Man* is crisp and clear with a sense of foreboding, even of the melancholic, and it has a key change to even

We will be looking later at the mystery of what is included and left out of hymn books, such as why the Methodist hymn books of 1933 and 1983 have avoided *Fairest Lord Jesus*. Similarly *Joseph Dearest, Joseph Mine* is a rattling good carol, which never made it into the mainstream hymn books. When in love, you want to tell all, and I was at the outset of my great love adventure with hymns, with no hints of disaffection, let alone thoughts of divorce; I was learning that some things were in and some out, but seemingly nothing could be discarded from *Songs of Praise*. By the time I was in the sixth form, I cannot recall we ever sang anything that was not in *SOP*.

In the mid 1950s the national mood was of austerity with rationing still in place; material possessions were not easy to come by; wages bought little other than basics and it was the process of saving up, although some engaged in the 'never-never' which only drew distaste from my beloved mother.[17] My mother would speak of people living in our road who had a batch of these cards, and they would make payments by either shuffling them or seeing who got to them first.

We sang hymns that spoke of giving and serving, some were popular, particularly when they had a martial air about them, and so seemed less religious. For instance in *I Vow To Thee My Country* we were reminded that the greatest duty of any person was to lay down their life for their country. The Headmaster had a military background, and he seemed to like that one. I was never too sure what to make of:

> better that of *Soll's Sein*, the German tune usually set to John Mason's *How Shall I Sing That Majesty*. It can be sung at Christmas or Lent, 16th century in lyric and set to music in Ravenscroft's *Melismata*.

17   The 'never-never' was where someone paid off their bills by so much each week, but like the modern credit card there was always a little interest to be added on.

> God of our fathers, known of old,
> Lord of our far-flung battle line (SOP 317)

... and of course there was the Edward Carpenter rally cry

> England arises! The long, long night is over,
> Faint in the east behold the dawn appears;
> Out of your evil dream of toil and sorrow,
> Arise o England, for the day is here!
> From your fields and hills,
> Hark! The answer swells!
> Arise, O England, for the day is here (SOP 316)

... with the refrain beginning

> Forth then, ye heroes, patriots, and lovers.
> (SOP321)

... and we could sing to the folkish tune *Sussex*

> Men of England, who inherit
> Rights that cost their sires their blood!
> Men whose undegenerate spirit
> Has been proved on field and flood (SOP)

O God Our Help in Ages Past was reserved for special occasions, as when we were herded together, and lessons ceased, as the Head toured each classroom to announce that King George VI had died, and the school hall became filled with kids glad to be out of lessons, and not totally comprehending the gravitas of the situation. All this was reinforced when the BBC decided the nation must not laugh or sing happy songs; the popular shows of the day were axed, replaced by endless sombre music. It obviously made sense to adults, and those who had survived the war and for whom King and State were symbols of a world seemingly at peace. We also sang *Praise My Soul* to the tune of *Goss* rather than the more energetic *Regent Square*. The former of course has a degree of studied seriousness, while the latter has a jolly edge. We never doubted that all was not well with Britannia as we sang:

> In thee our fathers trusted and were saved
> In thee destroyed thrones of tyrants proud
> From ancient bondage freed the poor enslaved
> To sow thy truth poured out their saintly blood
> *(SOP)*

It might be wondered how any writer could, for instance, write line three, in view of the British role in the money-gathering slave trade that was so much part of the nation in the 18th and early 19th centuries! There was also the music of Gustav Holst for:

> Then let me take thy place
> O England, my country
> Amid the gallant race
> That is thine
> Ready to hear thy call
> Ready to give thee already, what'er befall
> Mother of mine!   *(SOP)*

Time and its passage are always bewildering, I mean did people really sing that? Did we, the brave schoolboys of the mid-late 1950s?

We were also under the misapprehension that Britannia still ruled the waves, and did so with the welfare and benefit of the citizens of distant lands very much in mind. Someone of nonwhite skin was a rarity, only witnessed in the Indian carpet salesman who called with his wares. His appearance provided a tiny chink of light to those 'missionary' services where we learnt how Britain brought decency and goodness to far-off corners of the globe, where people living in the jungle with dark skins still needed to hear the message.

I was too young to hand the stranger who called a tract or two, but he fascinated me. Still we would sing *Remember All the People* with its lines:

> Some work in sultry forest[18]
> Where apes swing to and fro
> Some fish in mighty rivers
> Some hunt across the snow
> (344)

Mostly, as boys with boundless energy, we enjoyed the more racy hymns such as *Onward Christian Soldiers* (the school had a flourishing ATC) and *He Who Would Valiant Be*.

---

18   Congregational Praise, (Independent Press,
     London, 1954),

You could be tempted to bang your feet on the floor to the steady drum beat feel, were it not for the risk of letting others of your year know that you might be interested in this hymn. We did enjoy *And Did Those Feet In Ancient Time*.

Hanover is the tune to *O Worship The King*, and even the stately nature of the *Old Hundredth* had its fans for *All People That On Earth Do Dwell*. We also liked anything that had music by Ralph Vaughan Williams, although I do not recall whether or not we were made aware of his contribution to English hymnody. Ray Palmer's *My Faith Looks Up to Thee* was liked, partly because we sang it to the tune of American Lowell Mason's *Olivet*, and it's one of those tunes that is simple and easy to sing, progressing naturally. [19]

Another favoured hymn was *I Heard The Voice of Jesus Say*. Some hymn books set *Kingsfold* to its words, a tune I appreciate greatly, but *Vox Dilecti* wins if there were to be a contest. We liked the way this hymn sets out its subject for four lines and then answers it; now musically I would add that it runs with a minor key and then changes into a major for the outbursts of faith in response to the call and claims of Jesus, and thus:

> I heard the voice of Jesus say
> 'I am this dark world's Light
> Look unto me, thy morn shall rise
> And all thy day be bright
> I looked to Jesus, and I found
> In him my star, my sun;
> And in that light of life I'll walk,
> Till travelling days are done.

19   In past days it was often the case that the first
      three lines of the original, and the last two were
      set for three voices, and lines 4 and 5 as a duet
      for soprano and alto in parallel thirds. The
      original key was G major, and the first melody
      note of the second line was D (equivalent to
      low B flat in the present key).

Another favourite I picked up in school was the carol *Down In Yon Forest*. It has a folkish air I would later come to recognise, but at the age of 13, I was still learning; I just knew what appealed to me. *My Song Is Love Unknown* was also in my favoured list – I remember being told with some enthusiasm how fortunate it was that we were singing it to the tune *Love Unknown* by John Ireland. [20] Sometime in my teens, as will be recorded shortly, I mixed with the Congregationalists, and when we came to this hymn and the Ireland tune, I could say most importantly that it was *Songs of Praise* that had given this flowing tune to the nation. A brief conversation ensued along the lines of:

Sunday School teacher: 'Why do you say that Anthony?'
Anthony: 'We were told this at school Miss.'
Sunday School teacher: 'You were?'
Anthony: 'Yes, Miss.'
Sunday School teacher: 'Well they're wrong.'
Anthony: 'Teacher wrong Miss?'
Sunday School teacher: 'I'm afraid so.'
Anthony: 'Do I tell the teacher?'
Sunday School teacher: 'We've been singing it for years to that tune, ever since 1887 in the Congregational Church Hymnal.'
Anthony: '1887?'
Sunday School teacher: '1887.'

***

20   I thought *Songs of Praise* was the first hymnbook often sung to give it the chance of becoming 'the' tune to Dean Samuel Crossman's words, and its impressive sound belonged to the culture of the Precincts. Later I would find that the Congregationalists have been singing this hymn since 1887. However, Ireland's tune to those words first appeared in *The Public School Hymnbook* (1887). *The Congregational Church Hymnal* (1887), prints Nazareth from J.W. Elliot and St. John by J.B. Calkin.

(I had never really realised that there was a past so long ago as that).

The next day,

Anthony: 'Sir?'

Teacher: 'What is it now Jasper?'

Anthony: 'My Sunday School teacher says the tune you said we are singing to *My Song is Love Unknown* is not new.'

Teacher: 'Not new?'

Anthony: 'No Sir, she says the Congregationalists have been singing it since (pause) I think 1887.'

Teacher: 'The Congregationalists?'

Anthony: 'Yes. Sir.'

Teacher: 'My dear Jasper, I'm speaking about the true Church, not some break away groups.'

Anthony: 'Yes Sir.'

(But what did he mean by 'break away group'?)

Not that I knew the Congs were under suspicion as wild rascals, and uncultivated – later I learned this was also true of the Baptists. As I walked by their churches I should avert my gaze from their notice board in Clarence Street, or go another way. As for the Methodists, here indeed were the real villains of church unity. The Priest at St Mary's would forbid any Anglican clergyman from stepping across the threshold of Chapel Street Methodist, just one hundred yards away; it was a case of 'enter at your peril' or the black plague would be yours. The Congs would sing a hymn of Henry Mayo Gunn, aptly titled in view of my story and the reaction to it: *Our fathers Were High-Minded Men.* I wondered why it seemed so important.

Eventually I learned the rationale of these extra-ordinary divisions, but I did not understand them at the time, perhaps not even now. How could you sing with vigour and apparent conviction *The Church's One Foundation,* and still doubt that the Foundation is Jesus Christ? We sang this hymn with due passion suggesting we were all bosom pals—the different Churches, Chapels and odd bods. I felt like jumping up and shouting 'rubbish!' These days around the area it is possible to be more chummy, or it was until a priest of more Catholic persuasion announced the need for a Flying Bishop, an odd description that keeps having me imagining Captain Marvel in cleric clothing!

Boys will be boys and there were some hymns we ridiculed. There were those occasions when we found it embarrassing to sing such lyrics as:

> Kindly Spring again is here,
> Trees and fields in bloom appear;
> Hark! The birds with artless lays
> Warble their Creator's praise

The poet was John Newton, no less, but it was plain soppy. So too the same sentiment when asked to sing:

> Hark! A hundred notes are swelling
> Loud and clear
> 'Tis the happy birds are telling
> Spring is here (*SOP*)

Without wishing to disturb your sense of reverence the mere mention of 'birds' was enough to start us off. Glance along the line, someone would start to giggle, then a tremendous effort of self control not to burst out laughing risking a severe caning. It was hard to sing:

> God who created me
> Nimble and light of limb (*SOP*)

Some bright spark would immediately mimic an effeminate movement, and make us all dissolve into laughter.

Although the Welsh traditional melody *Trefaenan* is pleasant enough, it was surely stretching the point to ask growing teenage boys to sing:

> Do you know how many children
> Rise each morning blithe and gay?
> Can you count their jolly voices,
> Singing sweetly day by day?
> God hears all the happy voices,
> In their pretty songs rejoices;
> And he loves them every one. (SOP)

It never occurred to us as children that maybe some hymns were written by young people. I only discovered this on being handed the copy of *Hymns and Human Life*. Perhaps we might have sung with a little more conviction at school had we known someone pretty near to us in age had written a hymn or two. On the other hand this late in life examining the output of the young suggests it might not have been a good thing. Joseph Grigg was 10 when he wrote *Jesus, and Shall It Ever Be*, but it's fairly obvious he was tutored into thoughts of a much older age:

> Jesus! and shall it ever be
> A mortal man ashamed of thee,
> Ashamed of thee, whom angels praise,
> Whose glories shine, through endless days?

Even allowing for a different time period, I don't remember us speaking of 'mortal man' nor of angels. Football yes, girls yes, boring teachers yes, too much homework yes ...

Michael Bruce drowned before he was 21, but fortunately for us, he had dwelt on the Ascension when he put pen to paper and wrote:

> Though now ascended up on high
> He bends on earth a brother's eye;
> Partaker of the human name
> He knows the frailty of our frame

Maybe it's unfair to make too many criticisms, for these young authors wrote hymns for adult consumption; it was never suggested that the young might write for people of their own age. In the 21st century this has only changed in part. Children are still encouraged to do things that please adults in school concerts, and Sunday School presentations. If a child doesn't want to perform, he risks being blamed for letting mummy and daddy down. It takes some children a long time before they realise they might be engaged in some kind of dialogue with others of their age.

I doubt that we would have been so interested to learn that many young hymn writers died in their youth; nor would this have helped us to associate with the words of Thomas Rawson Taylor 1807-35, who when dying at 28 from a painful disease wrote somewhat poignantly:

> What though the tempest rage
> Heaven is my home
> Short is my pilgrimage
> Heaven is my home

However we quite enjoyed singing *Through All The Changing Scenes of Life* without knowing its author George Smart was a mere 19 years old at the time of writing it.

The tear-jerker hymns were the 'limpets' of 333 and 334, stuck together for singing at the end of each academic year: *Lord Dismiss Us with Thy Blessing* and *Lead Us, Heavenly Father*, were sung with considerable emotion, as boys desperately tried not to cry and let down manhood. Girls cry, but not boys. As we bid goodbye to those sixth-form leavers, the Headmaster laid upon us all, even if we were not ourselves leaving, that it was now the big world 'out there' to be met with fortitude, determination, and resolve. His stirring words must have come from his RAF days and you had visions of squadrons taking off into the sky preparing to offload their cargo on Hitler's people, not knowing whether they would return, as 'old boys' occasionally did. The more successful might be seen at the school telling us from the hall stage how they carried the world before them, and how we too could find success if we strove with zeal and application...

My school's excellent music teacher Donald Behenna, organist and choirmaster at an extremely 'high' Anglican church in Penzance, where it was once said they were outdoing Rome when it came to ritual, would have none of 'that free church stuff' of ranting tunes and singers exhausted by endlessly repeated lines and refrains. He would regularly preach to the class an anti-pop diatribe, which in one sense was self-defeating for it made some of us turn a deaf ear to his lessons. I would in my innocence produce one of these noisy affairs, and rather liked the way he dismissed my musical gift. However some things stuck, and for this I will always be grateful, especially the tune I've mentioned as well as the carol *Tomorrow Shall Be My Dancing Day*.[21]

21   It was only later in life that I met Christians who thought dancing was sinful and who were woefully ignorant of how widespread and far reaching into history is the association of

Equally so, we thought the Psalms were laborious and dull. I discovered later on that in their advent they had caused our forefathers to dance and that they were often called 'Geneva jigs.' I think we fell for the old wiles of the devil, that singing like acting does not need discipline and learning. In my arrogance, I did not realise that singing psalms and the great musical movements of the Church is not done by simply picking up a piece of music and proceeding.

As a choirboy in my occasional outings to augment Mr Behenna's musical needs, or to answer the request of someone for extra voices as 'the Bish might be popping by', I sang from the *English Hymnal* and *Hymns Ancient and Modern*. [22] So I was basically an augmenter, asked to sing in a choir for special occasions, as I did at Newlyn and Heamoor, in West Cornwall.

In the choir we were taught to produce a lovely tonal sound, almost ethereal: this spoke of cleanliness and godliness, but no one explained what the words were about (the main subjects seemed to be sin and Heaven). Maybe the audience only wanted the 'choral sound' anyway, and the sight of boys with scrubbed faces looking angelic in their girlish robes.

I had never thought that hymns had anything to do with real life; they were sung in religious places, and in summer they could be heard on the slipway at St Ives or on Penzance promenade as the Sally Army band played invariably *What A Friend We Have In Jesus* to the tune *Converse*. This was long before Alan Price discovered the hymn; some argue that he didn't even know it was a hymn tune until very late in the

religion and dance. These people had been unsettled by the physical dance of club land, and its sexual nature.

22   Here I learned some early French, German and Italian tunes, not that I was told that many of these were considered the 'pop' tunes of their time

filming. [23] Something similar happened with *Morning Has Broken* that was recorded by a disciple of both Buddhism and Christianity, Cat Stevens as he was known then, before converting to Islam. I was there in the office of Tim Blackmore, executive producer of Radio One, the man who compiled the playlist for Tony Blackburn. The everlasting DJ was stunned to find it was a hymn tune he was playing on Radio One's top-rated breakfast show. He didn't want to play it again.

I digress from the horrors of school. Many of the hymns we sang were descriptive of our mortal state, but if we often sang about our sin, we rarely sang polemic hymns that told us of the evils of smoking and drinking. In fact, smoking was considered manly and as for alcohol, I can't recall ever venturing into the intriguing world of the *National Temperance Hymnal*, other than singing *Yield Not To Temptation*. I only ever smoked half a cigarette, and spluttered badly from this first outing. I was never allowed near public houses, and my parents drank little if any alcohol.

My hymn awareness was drastically assailed and given a major input when I defected from the Church of England to the Congregationalists, and sang from their *Congregational Hymnary*. I had been dismissed from the nearest parish church because of my obdurate behaviour, and refusal to learn parrot fashion the creed and catechism. My mother was upset. I had been baptized at St John's Church, and even from an early age it seems she had visions of her son being ordained into the Church of England. At the Congs, I became aware of boisterous and ranting numbers, most of

23   The tune *Converse* is sung in many places to
      What a Friend we Have in Jesus. It became the
      tune adorning an ad for the Volkswagen VW
      Golf in 1988. The ad opened with Alan Price
      singing *Everybody Goes Through Changes* from
      the song entitled *Changes* that was featured on
      the soundtrack of the film 'O Lucky Man'
      (www.youtube.com). At the time few realised
      the music was a hymn tune!

which derived from *Sacred Songs and Solos* and *Golden Bells* or what is often generically called 'Sankeys' to incorporate other songs of similar mould. And Margaret Pengelly of the Market Jew Street branch of the Congs did her best to resist such Sankey associated songs as *Blessed Assurance, Day is Dying in the West* and *Pass Me Not O Gentle Saviour.* Her husband played the organ and was fully appreciative of her efforts – she was a lovely person. I sometimes moved out of the choir to take up position as organ blower. Naturally I could not resist on one occasion letting the air out causing the organ to groan, before I cranked things up. Mrs Pengelly was keen to keep the young people on board, and so swallowed her distaste, as we chose little rousers like *Whosoever Heareth* and *Sound The Battle Cry* at midweek Christian Endeavour.

When the wonderful George Henry Cecil arrived from Newbridge to take up the position of minister it was to usher in tunes from Wales. However this revivalist time would pass, for beckoning on the horizon was a new hymn book. Margaret's great day was the launch of *Congregational Praise*, and with much alacrity the 'order' was placed. The Sunday dawned when its blue cover changed the look of the church. Copies were scattered about the church for people always liked using the entire confine rather than bunching in the centre. I can remember her happiness to this day, seemingly banished forever *Congregational Hymnary* and its inclusion of American chorus hymns. Her most disliked hymn was *Day Is Dying In The West*. But I owe much to her endless moments of kindness. I should add that I was presented with a personally signed copy of the new book.

In good times there were 10 to 12 in the choir with our only really star vocalist, a rather affable Sadie Paul.

The 19th-century hymnody of the mission was almost completely swept away as Routley and Thiman ruled the roost, although surprisingly they retained *Great God of Wonders*, but without either of the two Welsh tunes that are often sung to it. The book sharply separated us from the Methodists who in West Cornwall in the old Primitive and Bible Christian mode loved the ranting tunes. Nevertheless

Golden Bells was used midweek, for a while, before its demise under the slightly spurious reason that the books were falling apart and could not be replaced. So they had to go. Not that I knew too much about the Methodists other than some relations who belonged to them, and there were a great many chapels, seemingly one on every corner.

So you see for a while I was basically a well brought up boy, always inspected by my mother to ensure I looked smart, and rarely guilty of what was then considered disgraceful behaviour, but for a while I blotted my copybook at the Congs whilst singing the children's hymn *Tell Me The Stories of Jesus*. I was moved during the appropriate verse to stand on my chair and pretend I was waving a branch of a palm tree:

> Into the city I'd follow
> The children's band,
> Waving a branch of the palm-tree
> High in my hand;
> One of his heralds,
> Yes, I would sing
> Loudest hosanna,
> Jesus is King!

My youthful rush of drama, or was it rebellion, came to an end quickly, as I was ordered out. I did return. I suppose I was showing off. I was a minor hero for a while.

My only other sign of truculence rested in the regular series of weekday concerts which generally featured everything we considered overblown and pretentious. Warbling contraltos grated most. Made to attend these functions, we could lay out the chairs. We would sit at the back of the hall. If we detected the gathering's indifference to a singer we would clap very loudly at the end of his or her set, mutter the adult yelp of approval and so produce from the artist one or more encores. We became experts at the impassive look for any adults turning in their seats. We always seemed enthusiastic, for the wrong reasons.

School and church singing had brought hymns to my consciousness but I still hadn't a real hot love for them. One evening it all changed, and a big adventure began. We made a trip from Penzance to the Countess of Huntingdon's church, Zion Congregational Church, Fore Street in St Ives for a Christian Endeavour rally. That meant a packed church, hot, sticky and airless, but filled with passionate singing. Here was a first sudden rush of real and lasting love that was not so much for a young girl from the Baptists – although she was rather nice – but from hearing the tune *Diadem*. At that time I had never heard a hymn with a repetitive line; even the Sankeys have none of that, but the Methodists did. I would later learn they had lots of hymns where a second or third line might be sung twice, or a last line three times, or even half a fourth, repeated in whole, and doubling up on the last – enough to make anyone gasp, and sing a line from a famous Charles Wesley hymn – *And Can It Be That I Should Gain?* But, yes! *Diadem* is a tune that slowly works itself up into a frenzy, to hit an almost orgasmic flourish at the end as the 'Crown Hims' came into play, and the bass reverberates from sweating men. We ploughed through six verses and by the seventh, it felt as though we were meeting in the Sahara, hot enough to cook the waiting pasties without an oven!

Later I learnt that this rumbustious tune was the creation of a young musician of Droylsden, in Manchester. None of the mainstream church collections set it as the first tune, that place of honour goes to *Miles Lane* or sometimes *Coronation*. At High Street, Penzance, it was *Miles Lane* that was played in the morning, and with the larger choir and congregation in the evening, it was *Diadem*.

Actually, I do like *Miles Lane*. And on one occasion I heard it sung in such a manner that I forgot I would vote for *Diadem* as the top tune to this hymn. I picked *All Hail The Power of Jesus* one Sunday in London at Harlesden, a mostly black West Indian Methodist Church. I didn't know which tune the organist would play, and somehow assumed because of the size of congregation and choir that it would be *Diadem*. It was *Miles Lane*, but sung in a way I had never heard it sung before. It began slowly, as though the people were looking for the hearse. It slowly gathered momentum, now more like a steam train, straining its innards, moving away from the station, until it became a trot, and then it broke loose, still retaining a stately air, but imbued with passion on the last line and it was struck with a clockwork precision yet seasoned with the inflection and intonation of West Indians. It was another love moment.

That hymn, and its tunes, would hold another memory for me, although not about falling in love. It was in Bridlington. I announced the hymn. The organist struck up *Miles Lane*. There was obvious rebellion out front, and one man in particular was having none of it, and he sang *Diadem* with some vigour. One might have thought that the combination of these two tunes suggested the charismatic movement had reached this popular seaside town. By the time we were into the third verse there was no sign that he was in anything but his own chosen world, with a few half-heard voices lending slight support. It was at this moment that the female organist snapped. Crawling out from her organ stool and tiny space and pushing back the organ curtain that hid her back from the congregation she marched past me with a meaningful walk. She stormed down into the now suddenly silent and apprehensive congregation. Facing our rebellious middle-aged gentlemen, she told him in the manner of an old-fashioned Matron or Headmistress, 'Sing what I'm playing'. Upon which she slowly turned, and made her way back to the organ. *Diadem* was not heard any more.

I had three happy years with the Congs, even becoming a member, and they talked of me going to Mansfield College, Oxford, to study for the ministry. I finally landed with the Methodists when I was 16. Here with the Methodists there were plenty of moments with songs from the Moody and Sankey revivalist era, but also the 'old Methodist' songs many with a folkish air, that could be sung with great gusto, hymns with repeated lines. For the newcomer they could be quite unsettling when of course you didn't know which lines should be sung again, or might be halved. Examples abound, but just two to take the fancy: Charles Wesley's *Come Let Us Anew* set to *Derby*, and the other is *Come On My Partners in Distress*, to a tune called *Praise*. The bases have a whole line to themselves, then a long-sustained top A, whilst the other parts accompany the melody on its way to top F.

Many of these tunes are rarely heard in the 21st century, partly because unison rules the day, also because some were left out of the last Methodist hymnbook in 1983. Methodists can still sing well, but the rallies that drew members of Methodist Churches in one area together have largely ceased. These occasions, apart from a sermon preached by an invited 'special' sometimes from 'up' country, were simply hymn singing times, with each Chapel contributing their favourite. In my younger days at the West Cornwall rallies, Mousehole Mt Zion always contributed *When The Roll is Called Up Yonder*. For some reason I can remember that one, but not the entry of High Street which I attended. Something must have been sung, for it was 'not on' that a Chapel could simply shout 'Pass.' Perhaps I was always fascinated by how joyfully the Mousehole folk sang the Sankey-associated hymn, and I hadn't thought much about heaven.

So it was that services became much more interesting. I would wait for the three hymn boards to be hung, and I could flick through the hymnbook to see what was in store. Sometimes it would go pear-shaped as the preacher arrived late and the boards only got put up, as he climbed into the pulpit. Of course I got to know which preacher would choose a particular style of hymn, and not all favoured the noisy. The new minister went for the poetic.

Even pieces I hadn't known previously sounded 'proper,' as the Cornish like to say. The choir at High Street was huge, and with narrow stairs up to their seats at the back of the large spacious pulpit; it could take the 60-strong choir ten minutes to arrive, sit, compose themselves and, on the note, rise for the introit. With five hundred or more in the congregation, there was always a great sound, thrilling for an impressionable 16 year old.

The time came when I started on the ladder to become a local preacher. In Methodism you start 'On Note', and accompany a qualified person, then if all is well, and your call duly tested, you progress to 'On Trial,' where you can take much or all of the service, and you are evaluated. Written exams follow, services monitored (and in those days it was the sermon that was 'king pin') and suddenly and amazingly, full accreditation. Then you were on your own, and might even be responsible for someone else. It all meant you could choose your own hymns.

My very first chosen hymn, when let loose as a fully-fledged local preacher, was *Let Earth and Heaven Agree, Angels and Men be Joined*. This hymn is hardly heard now; more's the pity, for both words and tune are well matched. It's a good hymn for a young person because it has so much vigour, and it picks up on the Gospel as exciting and imaginative.[24]

Since that first day at Carfury Methodist, a wonderful country chapel largely populated by two farming families, I cannot think how many hymns I've selected. My deliberate policy has been, where possible, to include one unfamiliar choice, either recent or belonging to another church, and different musical idioms found in foreign publications or otherwise brought to my notice.

I go through times and seasons when I think it right and proper in a Methodist context to choose two Wesley hymns per service. They have been labelled 'after the Scriptures the grandest instrument of popular culture that Christendom has produced'[25] and I am reminded of something Erik Routley wrote:

Charles Wesley filtered high culture through to ordinary people by way of Scripture. His mind was stored with all the best in the literature of the English, Latin and Greek languages. By associating this with Scripture, he produced the amazing spate of lyrics by which his people were taught. But the small fraction of his work that Christians now sing largely hides from them the fact that their author was primarily a teacher, and that

---

24   The lyricist is Charles Wesley, and the tune
      Millennium is from an unknown source,
      believed to be of English origin, yet the first
      sight of it is in Beecher's *Plymouth Collection of
      Hymns and Tunes*, (A.S Barnes & Co., New
      York, 1855).
25   Dr Martineau instanced in Henry Bett, *The
      Hymns of Methodism*, (Epworth Press, Norwich,
      1945), p.3.

his hymns were a body of divinity designated to illuminate not only Scripture but the prayer book itself.[26]

Down the years, I suppose I've favoured some hymns more than others, and indulged in those slightly facile exercises of selecting the best and the worst. *Sunday* (BBC Radio 4) ran such an item in the late summer of 2006, and in terms of the least popular it spurred radio reviewer Paul King to write in the *Methodist Recorder* with evident passion:

> The utter uselessness of the exercise was demonstrated by the fact that *Lord of the Dance*, *All Things Bright and Beautiful* and *Shine, Jesus, Shine* were all in the relegation zone. Is it not quite a long time since anyone sang *'The rich man in his castle'* to merit the condemnation of *All Things?*

King then weighed in with the domestic tragedy that could arise if the edict on high forbade the singing of *Lord of the Dance:*

> And this household will continue to find riches in the Sydney Carter (even if *Hymns and Songs* excluded it).[27]

Only the Methodist compilers know why *Lord of the Dance* was deleted – it had appeared in the supplement to the previous hymnbook. Perhaps permission was refused or it was too costly. Some question its theology; others find it too worldly in its overall package when it comes to worship.

After school and church, my third hymn input came from radio, or the 'wireless' as known then. As a young child I occasionally remember listening on a Sunday morning to *Chapel in the Valley* on the BBC, hosted by Sandy Macpherson, an experienced broadcaster, and also an organist of some skill. The programme began four years after the end of the Second World War, and continued through the 1950s. Macpherson says the basic idea started back in 1940. It was all very proper, and very English. We the listeners, were transported each Sunday to an imaginary village church where we were taken through the

---

26   Erik Routley, *The Musical Wesleys*, (Herbert Jenkins Ltd, 1905), p.32.
27   Paul King. *The Methodist Recorder*, (September 7, 2006), p.16.

hymns and songs, lessons and words for the ensuing morning service. There were also request hymns. Macpherson was assisted in this make-believe world by two fictional characters, Mr Drewett and Mr Edwards. The latter worked on a farm and led the hymn singing.

> The little chapel, which, though purely imaginary, was to become more real to millions of listeners than many an edifice of bricks and mortar.[28]

On Sunday afternoons I could pick up the sound of hymn singing from Wales. It was in Welsh with a magic of its own. And to this day I've loved the 'Welsh sound.'[29] These are majestic sounds that have been mostly ignored by English hymnbook compilers partly because of the Calvinistic nature of the thoughts – I am sure this omission widened the communications gap between Welsh and English-speaking Christians. I never really knew the Welsh side of my mother's family except Uncle Edgar who came to stay, usually without much announcement, and who was a fluent Welsh speaker. He spoke hardly any English but seemed content to sit for hours. How I wish he could have told me, among many, about William Thomas, David Jones, Morgan Rhys, William Williams, and especially Anne Griffiths.

> What Paul Gerhardt has been to Germany, what Isaac Watts has been to England, that and more has been William Williams of Pantycelyn, been to the little principality of Wales.[30]

At least I can trawl with pleasure through a book such as *Welsh Hymns and their Tunes*[31] learning about tunes such as *Pen Ucha*, and *Tydi A Roddaist*, and *Arwelfa* with its

---

28 Sandy Macpherson, *Know Our Hymns*, (Coram, 1958), p.10.
29 In my theatre company production of *The Welsh Revival of 1904-5*, it was great to include many evocative and moving Welsh hymns, sung mostly in Welsh.
30 H.Elvet Lewis, *Sweet Singers of Wales: Story of Welsh Hymns and their authors with original translators* , (Tentmaker Publications, Staffordshire, 1994).
31 Alan Luff, (Stainer and Bell, London, 1990).

---

spectacular end just when you might be thinking it was sinking slowly into the abyss. It is well said that the hymn is the folk-song of the Welsh.

An elderly lady Mrs Suzie Francis who lived opposite my parents' house would invite me over to listen to *Sunday Half Hour* on the then BBC Home Service; little did I dream in those days that for a time before Roger Royle became the resident presenter, I would introduce the programme on a number of occasions. She would relish the 'old' hymns, and by that she meant hymns with a mission orientation and located in such books as *Golden Bells*, *Sacred Songs and Solos* and *Alexanders*. These were the boisterous and loudly sung numbers that never attracted much love from the aforementioned Mrs Pengelly of the Congregational Church. We would utter a small but meaningful groan when the announcer said the hymn singing was coming from a parish church: this meant the singing would be very formal – nothing with much gusto, all very self-conscious.

I guess I was less concerned with poetry, imagery and metaphor, let alone theology, than with seeming outbursts of passion, and there was not a great deal of that around on the radio of the 1950s. The visits of *Sunday Half Hour* to less inhibited areas of religious expression were few and far between, and so noticeable when they came, usually from a Salvation Army citadel. Mrs Francis and I would never look at the *Radio Times* to discover in advance the hymns we would hear and at times sing along with.

It has to be remembered that in the mid-1950s there was little music that might be called 'black' heard on BBC radio. Many of us then and into the end of the decade only picked up what is termed R&B (rhythm and blues) and soul music thanks to Radio Luxembourg, the station that was 208 on the Medium Wave and called itself the 'station of the stars'.[32]

---

32   Down in the far West, I was unaware that Paul
      Robeson was bringing the 'spiritual' with some
      vocal force, and finesse, with the Llanelli Male
      Voice Choir to the Eisteddfod in Cardiff.

It was through 208 that I heard a variety of religious programmes beginning at eleven in the evening, an epilogue to the otherwise unadulterated diet of pop music. I had even managed to persuade my parents that I should be allowed to stay up until midnight, to hear *The Hour of Decision* (put out by the Billy Graham Organization) and *The Old Fashioned Revival Hour* (presented by Charles E. Fuller) which I particularly loved, not so much for his too long sermons but the Gospel singing and the motherly voice of his wife, whom he called 'Honey', as she would read out listeners' letters. There was also the sterner *Bringing Christ to the Nations* emanating from the Lutheran Church, which always began majestically with trumpets playing Luther's great tune *Ein' Feste Burg* (*A Mighty Fortress is Our God*).

I heard 'black' gospel music at first on a BBC Home Service programme, and never thought this could infiltrate into Christian worship. But then I had little idea of anyone doing anything other than singing to God the way we sang in Cornwall. I had no awareness of white gospel or black gospel, thriving across the Atlantic and elsewhere in the African nations and the West Indies.

For some religious people, Jazz, R&B and Soul were the pits, only confirmed by the antisocial loud mouth posturing of the famed British group who introduced so many to the rhythms and feel of predominantly black culture through the 208 airwaves. Some say ragtime was brothel music. Such fears and prejudices have made many Christians woefully ignorant of these genres.

Most of what I have said has reached back to school, church and radio roots, but there is one other important influence that remains as strong as ever: the Cornish angle. First, no doubt my Cornishness explains my love of Welsh hymns. More importantly it gives me an empathy towards the stark and the foreboding. People in West Cornwall are shaped in spirit by the North Coast road with its massive granite boulders and the bleakness of the inner land. Pleasure in the tranquil sea cannot prevent the greater awareness that the same waters can throw gigantic fits of protest.

All this means that you grow up with choirs and quartets who sing of life's hardness, of death's nearness, and that means you hear *Lead Kindly Light* or visualise local boats and crews, as the words of *Eternal Father Strong to Save* drive their way home to your consciousness. You knew one, two or more of the Penlee Lifeboat crew who never returned one December day in 1991. One in particular, John Blewett, had been in my form 1B. How was he to know that when we sang *Eternal Father Strong to Save* he would be part of a crew suddenly swallowed like a Jonah's whale, but in this case never to find dry land, for the Eternal Father never answered that day in the way that was desired. Sometimes heard in the far West is *Jesus Saviour Pilot Me*. This was sung at the funeral for one of those lost in the Penlee tragedy. When the local Boys Brigade sings *Will Your Anchor Hold*, the words have very particular meaning.

Today, my taste is pretty eclectic. I can appreciate the nuances of sung worship from a Cathedral choir at evensong; a small hometown Southern American church, and the practice of lining associated with Old Regular Baptists from the coal-mining country in central Appalachia with one of the oldest and deepest veins of the English, Scots and Irish-American melodic tradition. I can worship with Taizé and Iona and Spring Harvest, and lead a Salvation Army meeting, and in a more traditional Corps be moved by the band. I can feel something deep and meaningful in the joyous sound of tambourines. Like most things, it depends on how honest and genuine is the offering, and it can be communicated by the most humble and least educated. A professional interest in hymnody, worship and theatre can be barren indeed if a person has never dug deep into the soul. Although many people stretch beyond one or two genres of music, there is still much resistance in my experience to anything other than the traditional hymn singing the way it was thirty years ago. There are many chapels where a visit would give the impression that time has stood still.

CHAPTER THREE

More Than What Meets the Eye

At first sight the story of the hymn looks simple, there is nothing to it, there is a verse or verses, and more often than not there is a tune. So, from there, a full stop. Well, yes, it can be read or sung, but what else?

I'm afraid you soon realise that adventuring in hymnology and religious song is not a short journey, nor is it for faint hearts. To give an illustration: you could say there is a train and there is a track, but as any rail buff will tell you there are many variations of engine, carriage, underpinning, signalling, crossing, track point, signal box, control centre, stations with their own peculiar layouts. There are numerous erudite rail journals to keep the interested party up-to-date. It is no different when it comes to the world of hymnology. In most general hymn books, there are various kinds of hymns or psalms: Scottish paraphrases, revival items, Silesian folk songs, traditional folk songs, carols, canticles, choruses, chants, Irish melodies, German chorales, Welsh language hymns, and much more. These have been written by people of all spiritualities, even by those who profess to have little or no faith. There is also a group of men and women who decide what shall or shall not be sung by Christians; even publishers who may take risks in issuing a collection or two, although the great heyday has gone.

The obvious starting point with a hymn is its verse. I can sing a particular hymn such as *A Safe Stronghold Is Our God* without realising that if I were doing the same thing with another Christian communion I might be singing a somewhat different version. For example if you consider the version in The Methodist, *Hymns and Psalms*, the Stephen Orchard translation and additions in *Rejoice And Sing*, of the United Reformed Church; some collections add or subtract verses.

The next thing is that the suggested tunes may differ: moreover, all hymn books list a metrical index of tunes, thus allowing an accompanist to choose countless others of the same metre, especially among those with the largest surfeit, the CM and LM formats. The prolific English hymn writer Charles Wesley offers the most horrors, in a choice of tunes, for he sometimes wrote verse employing metres in which few tunesmiths had any interest.

> If song titles are not familiar to you but you have access to the internet, then you have a good chance of finding an MP3 file: try the Australian site: http://smallchurchmusic.com.

It is in tune rather than words that most 'fights' ensue in church pews and choir rooms. The best example of surplus diversity rests with the popular Charles Wesley hymn *O For A Thousand Tongues To Sing* which has over 20 tunes set to it. It always leaves the question of 'why?' – I cannot think that I dislike any of the 20, and I am left wondering why many of these good tunes cannot find some other words of similar metre? Two in particular, do, namely *Richmond* and *University*, which sometimes find themselves set three or more times in a hymnbook to varying words. Along with *Pater Omnium* they might be called the 'utility' tunes of hymnody's world.

Love Divine, All Loves Excelling is another hymn which has collected quite a few tunes. In more general terms it is usually sung these days to a Welsh tune *Blaenwern*, although the Welsh once upon a time sang it to the tune *Moriah*, very much a 19th century Welsh tune. *Blaenwern* sprang out of the 1904-05 Welsh Revival and had its first publication in 1916. It was the British Salvation Army that thought it would serve Wesley's words best and it appeared in the supplement to their general songbook in 1953. Doubtless it was pushed forward because it's a good band tune, sturdy and strong in its melodic form, and well suited to the text. Along the way, the hymn has been set to Stainer's *Love Divine*, then becoming a four-line hymn, and appealing particularly to Anglicans. To their credit the compilers of the 1983 Methodist *Hymns and Psalms* include *Westminster* (Sacred Harmony) with its derivation coming from Purcell's music for the song *Fairest Isle* in Dryden's *King Arthur*. It is said this tune inspired Mr Wesley to write his outstanding lyric. In Baptist circles the tune *Bethany* is sometimes heard, also much used is *Hyfrydol*, a Welsh tune which has never really found a home, but fits a number of hymns admirably. There is *Bithynia*, a tune which has never found real popularity, and its place as the second tune in *The Methodist Hymnbook* of 1933 did it few favours. *Beecher* is sung in American circles, and in Victorian times, an Italian chorale, *Lugano,* made an appearance in some collections. And there are others. Some words never find a good tune, yet here we have two Wesley hymns with a plethora of choice, almost akin to moths fascinated by artificial light.

I have already mentioned *Miles Lane* and *Diadem* for *All Hail the Power of Jesus*. Some hymn books use *Ladywell,* and indeed such is well favoured by the compilers of the 1962 *Baptist Hymnbook* where it takes up four pages of music, and is arranged for both unison and harmony singing. There are also two different tunes that bear the name *Coronation,* these are pretty rousing affairs, especially on the last line. There is also *Crediton*, a tune the organist is commanded to play with dignity. The Welsh can forsake all else for their own tune *Brynhyfryd.*

There are instances where a lively, very singable and splendid tune is ignored because it has never collected good words to its metre. My number one example of this would be the German folk song and melody *Sheltered Dale.* In some sources this has been alarmingly set to *O Little Birds That All Day Long* and is somewhat lost to *Awake, Awake To Love And Work* that is the second half of a Geoffrey Anketell Studdert-Kennedy's poem, *At A Harvest Festival*. This latter hymn suffers badly from the line:

> Awake, awake to love and work,
> The lark is in the sky,
> The fields are wet with diamond dew,
> The world's awake to cry
> Their blessings on the Lord of life
> As he goes meekly by.

I assume 'meekly' when written by the author (the poem was published in 1921) carried the meaning of self-denying obedience, whereas today it denotes submissiveness. Its metre 8.6.8.6.8.6 is the single example in *Hymns and Psalms*. But there is hope found in *Rejoice and Sing*, for that book of the United Reformed Church gives two lyrics in this rare verse structure, and the tune well suits *O Holy City, Seen of John*.[33] The first line is perhaps not the most attractive for the modern day, but the writer has some powerful lines, as he contrasts the splendour of life lived in God's presence with how the world of today functions. His verse two reads:

> O shame to us who rest content
> while lust and greed for gain
> exploiting fear and misery
> wring gold from human pain,
> and bitter lips in blind despair
> cry 'Christ has died in vain!'[34]

Occasionally a tune written specifically for some lyrics loses out because another tune, better known, is also set to the same text by some hymnbook compilers. We can see this in the case of the Welsh tune *Ar Hyd Nos* that has been a good marriage to *For the Fruits of His Creation* by Fred Pratt Green. Yet the writer wrote his words with the tune *East Acklam* in mind *Hymns and Psalms* of the Methodists has tried to ensure that this is sung by giving it as the first tune but by giving the Welsh tune a place on the page many an organist invariably chooses this instead, possibly because they feel it is familiar and known. It all gets rather confusing.

33 Written by W. Russell Bowie (1882-1969), and
    based on Revelation 21.
34 *Rejoice and Sing*, (Oxford University Press,
    Oxford, 1991), no. 627 .

Some hymn writers do get their wish. Percy Dearmer wrote his hymn *Jesus Good Above All Other* specifically for the 14th century German tune *Quem Patores Laudavere*. Most hymn books go with this. However, a greater problem for the writer is whether his or her hymn finds its way into a mainstream hymn book. You would not expect to find Dearmer's hymn in *Mission Praise* or *Songs of Fellowship* but unexpectedly it is not included in *Baptist Praise and Worship* (1991) or even more surprisingly *The Cambridge Hymnal* (1967). Yet it is included in the *BBC Songs of Praise* 'a wide ranging and popular anthology of old and new hymns and songs'.[35]

It might be thought that tune *Crimond* would score constantly across the denominational hymn world by its acknowledged association with *The Lord's My Shepherd*, but there are so many alternatives. On one occasion when I chose this hymn, I recall the organist said something to the effect, 'Oh, let's sing it to something different, anyway people nowadays associate *Crimond* with funeral services.' Perhaps she had a point!

Clearly choices allow worship leaders to suit tunes to mood: if I choose *Praise My Soul*, I prefer the standard tune by Goss when the sun shines, but when it's cold, possibly raining, I go for the more strident Henry Smart tune, *Regent Square* and warm the congregation up! For *Now Thank We All Our God* usually I find the organist plays *Nun Danket* when there are no young people present, and slides effortlessly into Beaumont's *Gracias* when things are supposedly more swinging.[36] But never

35   The 1983 Hymns and Psalms also sets the tune
       to Fred Kaan's *Father, who in Jesus found us*.
       Dearmer was the joint editor of *The English
       Hymnal* (1906),*Songs of Praise* (1925 & 1931) and
       the *Oxford Book of Carols* (1928).

36   As hymn tunes go, *Gracias* is fairly modern,
       and in hymnbook terms it was only in 1962 that
       the Baptists took the plunge, and it ceased
       being merely found in the small booklet *Three
       Hymn Tunes from 20th Century Folk Mass*.

be surprised by comments at the end of the service whatever you choose.

Musically too there are all shades and mannerisms, such as the unusual changes in tonality of tunes by S.S. Wesley, or crotchet beats instead of minims for the tune *Falcon Street* to set the suggested faster tempo. It is fascinating to delve into the history of the Welsh traditional melody *Ar Hyd Y Nos, All Through the Night.* We learn that the setting was in B flat, with harp variations for the respective verses; and more interesting, that the ballad was to be sung by the harpist, with the listeners invited to sing the refrain. *The Companion to Hymns and Psalms* points out that the melody had: 'notes of equal length in the fifth and sixth lines, instead of the present dotted and half notes.'[37]

The source of hymn tunes can also be informative: one of the most absorbing 'pinches' taken from a popular patriotic song to celebrate *Admiral Vernon*'s return from taking *Portobello* in 1739:

> He comes! He comes! The hero comes!
> Sound your trumpets, beat your drums!
> From port to port let canons roar
> His welcome to the British shore.

The tune was a good one, and much too popular to be neglected, so Charles Wesley wrote a parody on the words in the form of a hymn on the Last Judgement, and this new setting of the secular melody was sung heartily for upwards of half a century.[38]

Sometimes one set of words and one tune form the perfect marriage, and that universal peace can reign among the worshipping congregation. Here is a list:

37 *Companion to Hymns and Psalms,* (Methodist Publishing House, Petersborough, 1988), p.221.
38 James T. Lightwood, *Hymn Tunes and Their Story,* (Charles H. Kelly, London, 1905), p.132.

Tune	Words	Comment
Rhuddlan	*Judge Eternal, Throned in Splendour*	Fine Welsh melody has the right timbre of a protest marching feel.
Eisenach	*Father of All, Whose Powerful Voice*	Strong sturdy tune that marries well with John Wesley's excellent words
St. Theodulph	*All Glory, Laud and Honour*	Palm Sunday hymn
St. Denio	*Immortal, Invisible*	Based on the 19th-century song *Can Mylneddi 'awr'*
Hanover	*O Worship the King*	A splendid tune made for singing
Soll's Sein, based on Psalms 104 and 139	*How Shall I Sing That Majesty*	Words by John Mason based on Psalms 104 and 139
St George's Windsor	*Come Ye Thankful People Come*	Tune by Sir G. J. Elvy, organist at the Royal Chapel[39]

But sometimes good tunes are taken a match too far – on this issue much hated argument can take place! The powerful Welsh melody *Ar Hyd Y Nos* already mentioned fails when given some lyrics that are found in Iona, the Abbey services of The Iona Community.[40]

> We have come to stay together
> For a time
> Let us all be one together
> For this time
> Now the evening is approaching
> And the day is almost over

39   It is surely well suited to the harvest hymn, although originally set to *Hark, The Sound of Jubilee.* Even better is its setting to Wesley's *See How Great A Flame Inspires,* a marriage going back to *Wesley's Hymns,* (Wesleyan Conference Office, London, 1877).

40   But the same tune runs fine with Reginald Heber's *God, that Madest Earth And Heaven.*

> So we come to pray, together
> For a time.

To me, at least, it falls down on the short lines. 'For a time' is not strong enough to carry the forceful tune that calls for a stronger statement.[41]

On occasions tune and lyric make a slightly unstable relationship: take the well known Christmas hymn *O Come All Ye Faithful* sung to the tune *Adeste Fideles*. The second stanza sees text that is very much putting the Nicene Creed in verse but to sing correctly there is an inherent problem.

> God of God,
> Light of Light
> Lo! He abhors not the Virgin's womb;
> Very God,
> Begotten, not created;
> O come, let us adore Him, Christ the Lord.

God and Light have to become two syllables, but not the second God in line four. Congregations have their own way of running through a word-music impasse!

The popular Charles Wesley hymn *And Can It Be* seems destined to be forever married to *Sagina*, but it is interesting to note that other tunes ruled for many years. This tune published in 1825 was attached to *Now I Have Found The Ground Wherein* (1905) and it is an interesting and even amusing experience to sing it to those words. Some sources say it was used with *And Can It Be* from the mid 19th-century. The first reference I find is in the *New People's Hymnary* of 1922. Since then it has assumed enormous popularity, including its place among the modern day songs in *Mission Praise*. It is generally sung badly and, obviously, Methodist hymn compilers have attempted to wean people off the tune by including alternatives. In 1933, it was *Lansdown*, and 50 years later, the turn of Cyril Taylor's *Didsbury*, which receives a happy accolade in the Companion volume: 'this fine tune succeeds admirably in

41   Compare 'Darkness and light' in *God, That
      Madest*, or 'Thanks be to God' in Pratt Green's
      hymn.

giving expression to the profound meaning and varying moods of Wesley's lines.' They do not say such effusive things about *Sagina*. James T Lightwood in *Hymn Tunes and Their Story* says it is the only survivor of a large number of tunes by T. Campbell and was initially very popular in the North of England and the Isle of Man. Brian Spinney would remind people of the tune *Cardiff* that Salvationists sing to Wesley's powerful words. He feels the humble wonder of the hymn's first four lines are swamped by the heartiness of *Sagina* (and others see it as a possible cause of angina!)

The wandering Welsh tune *Hyfrydol* once seemed to find a home with *I Will Sing The Wondrous Story*, but for Methodists at least, they are invited first and foremost to sing to it another Welsh tune of some note, *Calon Lan*. Interestingly, the note on this tune in the excellent *Companion to Hymns and Psalms* ends by saying, almost sheepishly, 'an accepted tune for these words is *Hyfrydol* which is suggested as an alternative.' *Calon Lan* does justice to the words but I feel it works best with its Welsh words, albeit translated for English-speaking congregations.[42]

Sometimes I am left totally gobsmacked by the way some tunes come in from the cold and replace already popular ones. My main dislike, and I speak from Methodist practice, stems from the use of the tune *Hereford* instead of *Wilton* to Charles Wesley's *O Thou Who Camest From Above*. Everyone likes *Hereford* but why is this languid, although pretty, tune thought to be the perfect partner for the fiery hot and heated lines of Wesley? I see it well suited to old-fashioned tea afternoons with wafer thin sandwiches, and fancies that always draw the gasp of 'I shouldn't' but the speaker does consume. Such a sentiment is not shared by a past President of the Hymn Society who saw it as the perfecting setting for Wesley's hymn. It is the John Major of hymn tunes, of sun filled afternoons, and the sound of ball against willow, the occasionally excited cries of fielder, and dotted around the village green there are picnics and women knitting. Men

---

42   Baptists have set this famous Welsh tune to
      What A Friend We Have In Jesus.

with hats pulled down over their eyes, half slumbering, and feeling dreadfully uncomfortable even with white blazer — it's the tie and buttoned shirt at the neck that occasions redness of face. And so we choose to sing *Hereford*, and relax as we meander through power-packed verses. Wesley's hymn brims with energy and feeling, of walking into a fiery furnace or that of a steam engine and to marvel at the sheer velocity of heat that moves and drives, and so it is with the Holy Spirit, and so it is expressed more than any other place in *Wilton*. When you sing *Wilton* you are fired for duty, when you sing *Hereford* you might as well decide enough is enough, and look back to pleasant times. There are no battles to be fought, only memories to satiate.

O Little Town of Bethlehem, though I quite like singing *Forest Green* to it, it is a pity that Barnaby's *Bethlehem* has fallen into disfavour, and more so, *Christmas Carol* from Walford Davies; no British hymnbook runs with *St Louis*, the favoured tune in the United States.

Some hymn texts can be unlucky. Before *Cwm Rhondda* [43] in 1963 decided to exercise a limpet grip on to *Guide Me O Thou Great Jehovah*, these popular words of William Williams had already had found some powerful tunes, including *Caersalem*. Should Welsh religious history have any reverence from compilers then the Methodist committee should never have deleted one of the great hymns of the last great revival of 1904-05, *Come Ye Sinners* to *Bryn Calfaria*, but then *Hymns and Psalms* further snubs one and all by not including *How Vast Is The Ocean*. The fine tune does find a place in *Hymns and Psalms* where it is set to the words *Lord, Enthroned in Heavenly Splendour* as it was in the *English Hymnal* of 1906. It might be asked what is wrong in setting it as it was first intended, and remained in

43   I do possess an early copy of *Cwm Rhondda*,
      priced one and half pence, (The Red Dragon
      Press, Cardiff, early twentieth-century song
      sheet. Finally appeared in the *Methodist Hymn
      Book*, Methodist Publishing House, 1933). It
      first surfaced in leaflet form at the Baptist
      Singing Festival at Pontyprtidd, 1905.

popularity in Wales to Gwaed dy Groes sy'n Codi I Fyny. The English and Welsh could follow on from each other as is the method deployed for *Guide Me O Thou Great Jehovah* in *Rejoice and Sing* (345).

It is mystery to me why some church hymn books have more verses than others, or the words have been altered. Compilers seem unable to resist the temptation to meddle. Best examples must be:

- H.E. Fosdick: *God of Grace and God of Glory*
- Isaac Watts: *When I Survey The Wondrous Cross*
- Charles Wesley: *O For A Thousand Tongues To Sing*
- and *Lamb Of God, Whose Dying Love*

How is this for a tasty mix:

> The present verse 2 is a combination of the first quatrains of the original verses 2 and 3. Omitted are the second halves of each verse.[44]

One of the oddest verse deletion scenarios is surely *Great Is Our Redeeming Lord* by Charles Wesley where the *Companion* book (438) actually prints the omitted verses and calls them 'extremely forceful and dramatic'! For any spotter of the favourite words of Charles Wesley, this hymn has all his loved words when it comes to celebrating the power of redeeming love, phrases such as 'power, and truth, and grace' and then into 'faithful love', 'saving power' and 'pardoning love'. As a piece of writing it is an excellent example of how a Psalm (in this case Psalm 48) can be taken and given a Christian colouring, and it stands as a great example to many a modern 'praise' style writer who often runs to the book of Psalms, but in modern verse has nothing to touch the Anglican Charles Wesley.

Henry Sloane Coffin is one of many eminent writers of books for ministers, choirmasters, students of divinity, and of sacred music, office bearers in the Church, and others

44   John Ellerton, *Shine Thou Upon Us, Lord, Hymns and Psalms*, (Methodist Publishing House, 1988), p.330. 44

who lead worship. He is far from alone on pondering the odd affair of missing verses from one hymnbook to another. He wonders why for instance this verse is often deleted from texts of *O Come All Ye Faithful*:

> Child for us sinners,
> Poor and in a manger,
> Fain we would embrace Thee, with awe and love;
> Who would not love Thee
> Loving us so dearly

For him it is as lovely a stanza as any in the entire hymn and he cannot see why editors omit it.[45] Coffin might also have instanced the loss of a Wesley verse in his well-known *Love Divine*: originally it had four verses but the verse was already omitted in his brother's collection of 1780.

> Breathe, O breathe, thy loving Spirit
> Into every troubled breast,
> Let us all in thee inherit
> Let us find that second rest;
> Take away our power of sinning,
> Alpha and Omega be,
> End of faith, as its beginning,
> Set our hearts at liberty.

The Christmas hymn *Hark the Herald Angels Sing* was originally written as ten four line verses, of which at most six are now used. Wesley's first line was 'Hark, how all the welkin rings/Glory, to the King of Kings.' Welkin is a reference to the sky or heaven, even clouds. Within this context the hymnologist will record the omission of some verses in particular collections.

The Methodist Hymns and Psalms does not give the complete text to Christina Rossetti's *In The Bleak Mid-Winter*, perhaps it was felt that gatherings would be unhappy singing the third line 'A breastful of milk.' Of course sometimes the actual writer has second thoughts: Isaac Watts in his very well known hymn *When I Survey The*

---

45   Henry Sloane Coffin, *The Public Worship of God*,
      (Independent Press, 1950), p.107. Originally
      published USA.

Wondrous Cross originally wrote for the second line 'Where the young Prince of Glory died' – a fascinating and tantalising line, but in the second edition of his *Hymns and Spiritual Songs,* he substituted '*On which the Prince of Glory Died*' and this more metrically pleasing line has remained. The Wesley classic *O For A Thousand Tongues To Sing* originally had 18 verses and began 'Glory to God, and Praise and Love.'

Occasionally the word change is slight, but enough to throw a congregation that is well versed in their denomination's previous rendering. If you hear an older congregation with a smattering of more recent attendees you notice word clashes. So some may sing 'Good Christian Men Rejoice' while others with noses in their books might sing 'Good Christians All Rejoice.' And in another Wesley hymn, 'Jesu, lover of my soul' now becomes 'Jesus' – nit picking maybe, but the result can be an initial confusion. And do I invite people to sing *O God Our Help in Ages Past* or *Our God* ...?

Some cleaning up is required where the word's original, and often proper, meaning has been hijacked, or time has added a different nuance. The word 'gay' can no longer be left, even if once it meant light-hearted and free. So also the word 'intercourse'. I doubt the wisdom of one Anglican hymnbook for leaving the lines in the hymn *Fill Thou My Life*:

> and having intercourse with my beloved
> on hearth and open space.

I remember a school assembly when this was sung, and many of the boys broke out in spontaneous laughter, although unfortunately the Headmaster failed to respond in similar manner, and saw it as an attack upon his cast iron control.

The words 'anger' and 'angry' have also undergone change; we do not find it particularly meaningful these days to sing John Keble's:

> When God of old came down from heaven
> In power and wrath He came

For 'wrath' is not a word we choose in the 21st century, even if the second verse has:

> But when He came the second time,
> He came in power and love.

With all this in mind, I find his fourth verse slightly amusing:

> And as on Israel's awe-struck ear
> The voice exceeding loud,
> The trump that angels quake to hear,
> Thrilled from the deep, dark cloud.

Henry Sloane Coffin also makes us aware that some of the earliest hymns arose as answers to heretical hymns. This was certainly so in reference to the doctrinal upheavals of the third and fourth centuries where the heretics attempted to promulgate their views via verse. Sloane also suggests to us that at best the poetical and symbolic are attempts to put into language that which passes understanding and is unspeakable:

> We should not sing hymns critically, weighing every word. We take our part in the fellowship of Christ's people in their glowing adoration of Him for whom all human thought and speech are admittedly inadequate. We have to speak to Him in symbols and metaphors, and those hallowed by long usage carry with them emotional overtones that newly minted expressions lack. We are also obliged to adopt words acceptable and familiar to the mass of our fellow believers if we would share their common worship.[46]

Some songs are short on biblical reference. It is not simply that at Christmas some church halls will ring with the sound of *Rudolph, the Red Nosed Reindeer*, but congregations will tenderly sing *Away In A Manger*, or at very least increase the emotional weight by having it sung by children. Yet there is nothing more than a romantic imagination at work to speak of Jesus being born among animals, of cattle lowing, and the on duty oxen. Sadly, the source of this is the apocryphal gospels.

Political agendas: Ian Bradley takes the view that the carols we sing at Christmas time are not at all the orthodox hymns of joy for the nativity we might imagine. So *O Come*

46   Ibid. p.108.

All Ye Faithful is not as straightforward as it seems: he posits a thesis that it may have been a coded message to rally Jacobites. He refers to a 1990 gathering of the Catholic Family History Society in which the speaker:

> suggests that the carol, which was written in Latin two years before Bonnie Prince Charlie's rising, and not translated into English until a hundred years later, may have been a disguised Jacobite call to arms.[47]

The hymn has Roman Catholic roots yet is sung by ardent Protestants, and its tune appeared in Charles P Dudos' comic opera, *Acajou*, witnessed by Parisian music lovers in 1744.

Bradley disturbs even further by suggesting both *Angels From The Realms of Glory* and *It Came Upon The Midnight Clear* may have a political message lurking among their lines.

It can of course be argued what does it matter – or to repeat the over used cliché – 'why should the devil have all the best tunes' although the word 'best' is not usually subject to definition. The Salvation Army has achieved most notice for setting words to well-known tunes, and most of their efforts are commendable. It can also be said that we take words now as we find them. ForMethodists, it may be interesting to know that Charles Wesley's hymns were a response to his own time. J.R. Watson draws attention to Wesley's emphasis on the Incarnation as 'God and sinners reconciled' – a reminder that his hymns were written between 1738 and 1788, in answer to his own demanding personal needs and in response to the state of the Church and the world in the 18th century.[48]

I admit to a very liberal attitude to the question of where a tune comes from, even if it is good to write a new tune or

47 Ian Bradley, *The Times*, (Saturday, December 21, 1991).

48 J.R. Watson, *Pitying Tenderness and Tenderest Pity: The Hymns of Charles Wesley and the Writings of St Luke,* The A.S.Peake Memorial Lecture, (2005), printed in *The Epworth Review*, (July 2005), p.33ff.

find an existing ill-used one to fit. But even I was a little amused, in the context of 'praise' styled worship, and a 'chill out' moment, to hear *What Shall We Do With The Drunken Sailor*. I approached the young musical director, and remarked upon this. For him this was obviously new information, and not something he wanted to know. He had no idea of the origins of this tune. To him it was a tune he remembered from somewhere or the other, and he thought his own improvisation radiated a sense of the Spirit moving.

The 1985 BBC *Songs of Praise Festival* ran a competition to find some new hymns. One by John Kendall, alias the Reverend Michael Saward, was *Happy Are Those Who Acknowledge Their Need*. He set this to the 18th-century traditional drinking song *Here's To The Maiden of Sweet* (Bashful) *Fifteen*. He wanted a happy and jolly tune. Most people probably have no idea where a tune has come from, it either suits the words or not, or as a tune it sounds good.

Suspect theology can take an interesting course. At one time the favourite Victorian Epiphany Hymn of Reginald Heber, *Brightest and Best*, received dismissal because the lyric made the star the point of worship, and because its metre suggests a dance. In the end it is unlikely that much will be achieved by rampaging through popular hymns and discarding those in seeming error. It is much easier and less confrontational to simply avoid choosing them. After all the broad Christmas season is loaded with choice, and who will notice—not a sleight of hand, simply practical sense.

There are hymns in most mainstream collections penned by those who do not subscribe to Trinitarian beliefs. *It Came Upon The Midnight Clear* was written by the Unitarian American minister Edmund Hamilton Sears. The much sung *Come Down O Love Divine* may have come from unorthodox or dissenting groups within the medieval Italian church.

In *Hymns for Today's Church*, the editors draw attention to their sterling efforts at modernising language. 'Thee' and 'thou' are a perennial worry for some, and it is not always easy to see why. The language is archaic but congregations are aware. Do young people have much time for their use?

Probably not, but then they will probably not be singing them anyway. In any case many of them quite happily deal with the issue in theatres where 'thou' and 'thee' and a host of other archaic words are employed. The main issue is whether we understand what is being said.

Even more of a minefield is the use of the word 'Father': as recently as 2006 I heard a proposal that the word be deleted altogether simply because it evokes unpleasant imagery for those who have been abused, and says nothing to those who have not had a father. It is difficult to know where to stop for there is always something lurking that is not palatable to some. Do we cease to sing about children because there are many who have not been able to have offspring, or because bad childhood memories come surging back? Do we insult single people who have yearned and longed for a child?

There is also the question of sexist language. Brian Wren, one of the best contemporary writers of hymns, says no new hymn should use 'man' and 'men' and the same applies to words 'brethren' and 'sons' used in a generic sense. He takes issue with those who say it reflects New Testament language. He lists a number of translations where the 'male' orientation has been reinforced in translation. In the journal *News of Hymnody*, he comments:

> As a white middle-class English Christian, I have come to see that my society is deeply male-dominated. The questioning of sexism in language is not a frill, an 'extra', or a surface-issue. It reflects deeper stirrings, questioning social inequalities. Such matters ought to find a particularly keen interest among Christians whose Lord approached women in a radically different, dignity-perceiving, way from social conventions of his time, and who founded a church based on the unity and equality of free and slave, Jew and Gentile, female and male.[49]

> ... I am not sure that there is anywhere an assertion that male imagery is 'right' and female imagery is 'wrong'.[50]

---

49   Brian Wren, *News of Hymnody*, issue 7, (July 1983 p.5).
50   Ibid. p.7.

He reminds us that when 'man' (or variant spellings) was first used in English, it meant a human person of either gender. He instances:

> 'His mother was a Christian named Ellen, a very full-of-faith man, and extremely pious', said Aelfric in about AD 1000.[51]

Today, words like 'man', 'men', and 'mankind' suggests 'maleness' but it still leaves the question of whether it is worth tampering with the old unless it rings with a new found sense. Interestingly the compilers of *Methodist Hymns Old and New* say in their introduction:

> 'Inclusive language' is a modern concept and fits modern hymns, but we are satisfied that people understand the generic terms 'man' and 'mankind' and are prepared to sing them in older hymns.[52]

The publication of the new *Lutheran Hymnbook* in the USA in 2006 (it follows previous editions of 1921, 1941, 1982) has also been assailed by some, with voices asking what is wrong with the old Victorian language? But then the same critics do not walk around speaking the Victorian language. Others accuse the compilers of being inconsistent. In the final analysis, it is a question of balancing the expectations of visitors and seekers with the habits of faithful attendees.

There are some deep and abiding 'mysteries' in the world of hymnology which have engaged scholars for many an hour. There can be considerable debate about the association of a particular hymn with what might seem a most important moment in someone's life. Nothing comes more complex than deciding what was the conversion hymn of John Wesley.

To this, the answer seems simple. It's there for all to see in the words in the 1933 *Methodist Hymnbook*. After all who should know but the compilers of the once venerated volume, that *Where Shall My Wandering Soul Begin?* is 'The Wesleys' Conversion Hymn.' However, unfortunately

---

51   Ibid. p.4.
52   Foreword, *Methodist Hymns Old and New*,
       (Kevin Mayhew Ltd, Stowmarket), 2001.

---

there is good reason to doubt such a statement. No one seems to doubt that Charles wrote a hymn immediately after his brother's conversion experience, and both would sing it but what exactly did they sing? Early Methodist sources submit the possibility of the lyric *And Can It Be*, while a third possibility is *Granted is the Saviour's Prayer*. In a sense the whole thing is odd, John kept copious journals, and Charles was much given to words, yet there is no explicit statement that can lead anyone to dogmatically identify with certainty which of the three. From time to time the Wesley Historical Society proceedings give space to the arguments for which title we can reasonably be assured is the right one. It would appear that *Where Shall My Wandering Soul* wins, but with doubt. I cannot remember hearing it sung, outside of my own production *Charles Wesley 1707*, and when it comes to the tune, there again the hymnologist has a minor field day. We sang it to *Crucifixion*, the first tune set to *Hymns and Psalms*, which was also the tune set to *And Can It Be* in Wesley's *A Collection of Tunes Set To Music As They Are Commonly Sung at the Foundry* (1742). The 1933 Methodist publication set it to Roger's *Old 23rd*, and said it might be sung to *Crucifixion*, which was placed rather unceremoniously in a section of Additional Tunes. *Hymns and Psalms* changes the situation and makes *Crucifixion* the first tune, provides Henry Carey's *Surrey* as an alternative, and snubs the *Old 23rd* by leaving it out of the hymnbook altogether.

Wesley loved the word 'bowels' and so did constipated Martin Luther lacking his roughage, and Wesley like Watts was much given to the word 'worm'. As well as describing our spiritual state as the lowest of the low, in Wesley's hymn, *Father, Son and Holy Ghost* verse two has:

> Vilest of the sinful race
> Lo! I answer to Thy call

while a verse later:

> If so poor a worm as I

Humorists have always found good fare in hymns. After all for a wedding day there should be sung *Come O Thou Traveller Unknown*, or *Dear Lord and Father of Mankind* with its second line of 'Forgive our foolish ways' and without intending irreverence there is the hymn which has the first two lines:

> When shall thy love constrain,
> And force me to thy breast

While words written before 1906 have an uncanny ring in the light of how people regard current politicians, as in the hymn *O God, who Holdest in Thy Hand*, there are the lines:

> And teach us how to choose,
> Good men and wise
> The heat of party strife abate,
> To guide the State
> The evil to refuse.

Hymnologist and writer Chris Idle tells of an Epiphany service in the East End Mission of the Methodist Church in Stepney, London, in which the congregation sang the printed words:

> All the bells are peeling,

And there must be many a tale of such typographical errors. It can occur in any field, as I well remember when H R Rookmaaker's *Modern Art and the Death of A Culture* was printed in one of my past books as *Modern Art and the Death of a Vulture*. Equally so there is the 'mysterious', when there is no typographical reason lurking in the wings, to explain why in another of my texts, a chapter was headed 'Jesus in Japan'. Fortunately, it was only at the proof stage.

In innocence no doubt, the compilers of the *American Armed Forces Hymnal* present their men and women with *O Saving Victim* (351).

> O saving Victim, opening wide
> The gate of heaven to man below,
> Our foes press on from every side
> Thine aid supply, Thy strength bestows.

It may or may not, I suppose, give comfort as the shells land. On the other hand George W.Bush or any leader could feel uncomfortable in singing number 392, as the ratings come in from the various polls to test popularity, and where G.K. Chesterton's hymn begins:

> O God of earth and altar,
> Bow down and hear our cry;
> Our earthly rulers falter,
> Our people drift and die

One thing is sure, nothing is static, even if at times the Church seems to have eternity in view when it comes to actually making a decision, sometimes it is imperceptible, occasionally there is much noise! Still there is nothing more pleasing than to find a nugget of hymn gold. Occasionally, and joyfully, I discover something old that is strangely beautiful, and should never have been pushed aside, whether in words or tune, and I want everyone to know about it! That is I suppose a little bit of hot love. One such is the tune *Sarah*, and Charles Wesley's *And Am I Born To Die*. Perhaps the words need editing, maybe only the verse beginning 'Thou Art The Way' can be sung in the 21st century, but if not for congregational use, it makes a wondrous solo, and I used it in my play *Charles Wesley 1707*.

Last, but not least, in the world of hymn compilation there are all kinds of practicalities when it comes to issuing a hymnbook. Hymn collections must not be too large, otherwise choir members have a huge volume to hold, since their copy will carry both lyric and tune. The heaviest collection for anyone to grasp is the words and music edition of *Methodist Hymns Old and New* that posted, as a single copy would cost in 2007 the princely sum of £7.25 and weighing in at 2.1 kilos. Failing that, as with the organist's copy of the *Methodist Hymns and Psalms*, there can be two volumes, but this is slightly irritating for organists tell me they have to remember where they have placed one or other volumes, and this becomes worse when they might have to play from some other general hymn and songbooks, such as *Mission Praise*. For those who play the small more modern electronic organs, the space for books is limited. There are hymn books of over a thousand pieces, but generally the figure seems to fall around 700 to 800, and depending on whether there is an additional section of psalms and canticles. *Rejoice and Sing*, the book used by the United Reformed Church has 668 hymns, and this is followed by 88 psalms and canticles.

I find that some hymn books are expressly published by particular churches for their flock. Church groups do like to have their own world, even if it might seem an extravagance to the outsider. Other offerings beyond the official imprimatur of a denomination are sometimes published to meet the needs of a small cluster of churches, too small to finance their own book. Others such as the often mentioned *Mission Praise* may be used across the breadth of Christendom where there is comparative agreement with the publication's aim and overall ethos. There are still collections issued for a particular purpose, such as an event that draws together over a short-ish period thousands of people, e.g. Keswick Convention, Spring Harvest, and Easter People gatherings. Here, as elsewhere, nothing stands still:

> the creative world of hymnody and Church music continues to grow and evolve. [53]

Fortunately for those interested in the background to hymns, their writers and tunesmiths, there are countless books available. Some merely tell the story behind a hymn, how the writer felt at the time, and why the eventual words came to be written. Others relate hymn text to the Bible, or go further by speaking of the text, aligning all with Scripture, and adding some personal observations. In times past it was a popular discussion topic for weekly guilds and women's meetings. Arguably the most frequently told story is the background to the once popular hymn *Rock of Ages Cleft for Me*. However it is not a dying genre, for there are books, originating mostly from America, giving background and spiritual thought of some 'praise song' and even the most simplistic lyric may well have an accompanying experience from the writer.

Most denominations, and gatherings such as the Salvation Army, issue a book behind the hymn book, and these are often excellent companions. Arguably the best of these is the *Methodist Companion to Hymns and Psalms* (MPH

53   Kenneth Trickett, 'Strengthen for Service', *The Methodist Recorder*, (19 October, 2006), p.20.53

1988), a veritable treasure trove, detailed and scholarly and a must-have possession for anyone who loves hymns.

The most revered book for hymnologists is Julian's, whose official title is *Dictionary of Hymnology*. It runs to 1,616 pages; first published in 1892, with John Julian, its compiler the Vicar of Wincobank, Sheffield. Julian engaged a number of people to contribute the text. It runs in alphabetical order in title of hymn by a writer/composer, in 9 or 10pt print and contains extraordinary detail. In an antiquarian listing, it may be offered at £100 or more. A new 21st century version is being compiled by Professor Dick Watson, ex-Professor of English at Durham University, a Methodist local preacher, and author of the highly regarded *The English Hymn*. Watson is the Editor of *An Annotated Anthology of Hymns* (Oxford University Press, 2002). The present 'worship song' is not of interest, and attention is particularly directed to the history and variety of the traditional, strophic hymn that has been found in mainstream English churches since the Reformation. In reviewing this 452-page volume, Elizabeth Cosnett comments:

> Young and/or trendy clergy and worship leaders should also dip into it to help them understand those who feel truly bereft when established classics are removed from the repertoire. We all share such a loss.[54]

However even Julian pales in the presence of *A Concordance to the Plymouth Collection of Hymns and Tunes* (1855) [55] The hymnbook was the work of Henry Ward Beecher, a Congregational minister of Brooklyn's Plymouth Church. When Beecher arrived to take charge he found little music, and such as there was, it was mostly in the hands of a paid choir. He sought to change this, and increase the singing efforts of his flock, and so he brought out his own collections, a small one in 1851 and a larger one four years later, of a no less than 1,431 hymns. It became the first

---

54   Elizabeth Cosnett, *Epworth Review*, Volume 30 Number 2, (April 2003), p.88-9.
55   Where the 1984 issue has 3,013 pages on diazo microfiche..

hymnal in American religious expression to have both words and music. *Concordance* is a staggering piece of work since it features the 144,768 important words in the hymnal, as well as texts of the 1,431 hymns! Beecher's choice as to what shall be included rests less with literary quality than their evangelical thrust, and what he termed 'power to excite religious emotions'.

Hymnology is obviously a vast subject across the Atlantic, so blatantly made clear to any doubters or uninformed, by the years of work accompanying the following:

- *Dictionaries of American Hymnology.*
- *A Bibliography of American Hymnals* (it lists 7,500 sources)
- *Dictionary of American First-line Index*[56]
- *Handbook for American Catholic Hymnals*
- *To Him Be Praise* (St Paul Publications 1982)

This last listed book contains hymns (and prayers) covering the whole of the first 1,000 years of Christianity, and almost the whole geographical area reached by it. In the preface the compiler Costante Berselli reminds us of St Augustine's words in the days following his baptism, the echo of the hymns and canticles sung during the ceremony still filling him with emotion:

'at the sound of such voices the truth sank into my soul with greatest sweetness' and 'in the tears that flowed copiously, I found great contentment.'

I confess that on occasions when I sing a hymn I block out the endless mishmash of information encircling the simple process of singing some words to a tune!

---

56   At least American Catholics can breathe a sigh
      of relief that *History of American Catholic
      Hymnals, Survey and Background,* has only 286
      pages. (Hymn Society of United States &
      Canada, 1982).

CHAPTER FOUR

Shaping and Influencing

There are hymn books, and there are hymn books. The plethora of hymn and song collections together with their date of issue, provides a wonderful insight into the prevailing faith and society pattern of particular times. This brings to mind Albert Van Den Heuvel's words, 'Tell me what you sing, and I will tell you who you are.' My shelves groan with their weight.

In the history of hymns the big publishing period was 1840-80, with the star turn *Hymns Ancient and Modern* (1861). It may not have been officially authorised in the established Church, but this collection has exercised enormous influence across the worldwide Anglican Communion and affected other hymn books beyond its own boundaries. *Hymns Ancient and Modern,* as befits collections used by the Church of England, was published privately. It served the constituency of the Church of England, taking note of the festivals and general worship liturgies of that communion. It was revised in 1904 with a number of editions under various titles since that date. It was called the country's most famous hymn book, but to some extent this description underlies another tendency to see the Christian Church as being understood simply in Anglican terms. As with virtually every collection it had its underlying purpose.

It sought to improve the tastes of churchgoing Anglicans in the directions suggested by the authors of the Oxford Movement. [57]

Certainly *Hymns Ancient and Modern* had no time for the florid 'Methodist' style, not that every Methodist today would wish to travel that path, and it is possible to go from week to week in worship and not hear this genre. It's interesting that when Methodists are urged to consider their identity, hymnology is rarely mentioned, yet in the 19th century their hymnology was a distinguishing feature. [58]

Routley describes this Methodist musical style of the mid-to-late 19th century as having ornamental melody, static bass, occasional frugalities in the tune, and repetition of words. It would seem the great man had no soft spot for Methodists and their early distinctive musical feel:

> we have less good to say of the undisciplined music of Methodism. [59]

He has even stronger words to say of this period:

> Vulgarity is not too strong a word. The folk-song of the English churches in the nineteenth century had become cheap beyond what any seventeenth century singer could have conceived. A cult of amateurism had ensured that mediocrity would be accepted: easy and cheap printing made the uncritical dissemination of music possible and a substantial bourgeois population of churchgoers created a demand for what would undisturbingly adorn their acts of worship. Hearty singing in nonconformity went with a predilection for what was easy to sing; sol-fa sight-reading settled choral taste into a strictly eighteenth-nineteenth century rut.

57   Erik Routley, *Twentieth Century Church Music*
      (Herbert Jenkins, 1964), p.197.
58   Also important was the role of the local
      preacher. Thus Methodism emphasised its oral
      nature of sermons and hymns. It also
      encouraged reading.
59   Erik Routley, *The Music of Christian Hymnody*
      (Independent Press, London, 1957), p.174.

Routley is not speaking of the 'amateurish' as necessarily having come from the backwoods of the local Bethel where there is someone given to writing new words and music. He has a more distinct use for the word 'amateurish', including such names as Barnby, Sullivan, and Stainer. Here, as he says:

> are professional musicians of their time, and with considerable repute, but their church music was, as it were "amateurised" through their connection with the church. That is to say that a tradition had established itself by which, not craftsmanship or imagination, but rather conformity to a certain set of conventions and the evocation of a certain well-defined atmosphere, presented themselves as the first necessities to the composer's mind. [60]

He compares them with someone such as Parry who wrote pieces for the Church equal to those written for the concert hall. In my theatre life I sometimes have to tell an actor at audition to stop saying and doing what they assume to be religious, and simply to 'be'.

In an article for *Epworth Review*[61] Michael Austin points out the dilemma of speaking 'truth' within a church context, but where else should truth be found? The point was made further by a great friend of mine, Peter Moreton, that writers whose work is represented in Christian circles sometimes dumb down their message, or lace harsh truths with more acceptable vocabulary.

Competing for attention and space in any Anglican history of hymns is the *English Hymnal*. The first edition of *EH* appeared in 1906. Compared with *Hymns Ancient and Modern* it carried more early psalm melodies, with 63 German tunes compared with just four in the other book. *EH* gave little attention to Victorian writers. The various editions have been noted for their musical input, particularly the inclusion of 19th-century Welsh tunes, and 16th and 17th century French Diocesan melodies.

60   Ibid. p.18.
61   Volume 25, Number 2, (April 1998).

A revised *EH* appeared in 1933 and saw no change in the tunes suggested, but did include 100 new compositions, and it was followed by *English Praise*. *The English Hymnal Service Book* was also published at a similar time. The 1986 edition of *EH* included almost two-thirds of the original 656 entries.

In the excellent book *Strengthen for Service*,[62] Julian Onderdonk contributes the chapter 'Folk Songs' in the *English Hymnal*. He makes this arresting comment relevant to the context of this chapter

> The increased demand for new hymns and hymn tunes (during the Victorian period) coupled with the emergence of a Romantic aesthetic stressing individual expression above all else, meant that 'originality' became the sine qua non of hymn tune production, while the kind of 'arranging' that had characterized the older adaptation of melodies fell into disrepute. The result was a huge increase in the writing of wholly original hymns and hymn tunes that significantly altered the way congregational church music had traditionally been produced.[63]

In my opinion, the crowning glory of *EH* rests in its, and Ralph Vaughan Williams' interest in, adapting many English traditional melodies. There are 63 tunes adapted by the great man mostly from English and Welsh sources. Ralph Vaughan Williams was not free from criticism. There were those who felt the folk tune evoked secularity in the 'holy' place. Even in the 1970s the negative comments remained, and while some tunes were acceptable, others were ill matched to the solemnity of the Prayer Book services.

Hence Ralph Vaughan Williams was not so much 'breaking new ground' as renewing past practices. However, Onderdonk would remind us of one important difference between Ralph Vaughan Williams' editorial

62   Alan Luff, *100 Years of the English Hymnal*,
      (Canterbury Press, London, 1906-2006).
63   Julian Onderdonk, *Folk Songs in the English
      Hymnal*. Ibid. pp.191-2.

methods and the way in which folk and secular tunes had traditionally been converted into hymns. Ralph Vaughan Williams set out to discover the obscure rather than using popular melodies which might prove an 'instant' hit with church outsiders, while leaving some church members gasping with horror. I applaud Onderdonk's statement:

> Is not folk song the bond of union where all our musical tastes can meet? We are too apt to divide our music into popular and classical, the highbrow and the lowbrow. One day perhaps we shall find an ideal music that will be neither popular nor classical, highbrow or lowbrow, but an art in which we all can take part.[64]

One church hymnbook committee of recent times, spoke of the need for material to have the possibility of 80 years of life. I am still trying to get into the mind set of those who can imagine such a time span considering the rapid pace of the modern world. Even Bach thought weekly, and Charles Wesley by the day!

Hymn compilers maintain that it is difficult to achieve an acceptable mix of material when they envisage their book being used for several decades to come. The writer of the preface to *100 Hymns for Today* (one of the supplements to *Hymns Ancient and Modern*, 1969) explained:

> We have tried to steer a middle course between restatements of the traditional and ephemeral or 'pop' productions ... or to include those written in an idiom likely to be so short-lived that any book containing them will be dated within months of publication.

The preface does make an interesting comment: new words have been difficult to find, the metre and rhythm of an older age are no longer employed by modern poets. The new hymns at the time included Sydney Carter's:

- *When I Needed A Neighbour*
- *Lord of the Dance*
- *Every Star Shall Sing A Carol*

The earliest born lyricists are:

64   Ibid. p.212.

- Fred Kaan and J.K. Gregory (born 1929)
- David Edge (1932)
- Edward Burns (1938)
- Brian Wren (1936)

These men were in their thirties, representing the younger end of the church membership. Interestingly Wren is still spoken of as one of the younger hymn writers, nearly 40 years later. However even in the late 1960s a hymn book such as *Hymns for Today* could contain these lines:

> O sing a song of Nazareth,
> of sunny days of joy,
> O sing of fragrant flowers' breath
> and of the sinless boy. (80)

However the book did manage to bring to the attention of many Anglicans some of the treasury that had been sung by other Christian communities. It also said of itself:

> This book does not assume, as older hymn books did, a society more agricultural than industrial, untroubled by questions of race relations and human rights. Nor does it presuppose a church untouched by the fierce conflicts of the century.

Wonderful stuff, if only the contents matched up to those sentiments. If only any book took them on board! The golden age of endless hymn and song publications has long gone. This has coincided with a decreased churchgoing population, with the practical disappearance of evangelistic campaigns, for many of the publications were designed for those missions. To a degree it also has coincided with the demise of the importance of the written word in people's lives. There was a time when worshippers retired home from church, and after being satiated with the Sunday roast, those who managed to stay awake in front of the roaring log fire would take in an afternoon's reading from volumes such as:

- *Christian Treasury*
- *Sunday at Home*
- *The Church Age*
- *The Quiver*
- *The Sunday Companion*

- *Christian Herald*

I remember reading from these publications before tea with relatives in the 1950s.

Certainly there is a major difference in how people spend their leisure time. Once Church and Chapel dominated the life of the community, especially in small towns and villages. Something of this can be glimpsed in the musical provision of the Methodist Church. There were specialist collections for children, those at public school, for evangelistic campaigns, midweek meetings. The Methodists, said by some to be born in song, issued *The Missionary Hymnal* (1894) with words and tunes suitable for use at great popular:

- Missionary gatherings
- Missionary Services
- Women's Meetings
- Watchers' Band and Christian Endeavour Society Meetings
- Children's Festivals
- Missionary Ship Demonstrations
- Communion, Consecration and Farewell Services

In times past some mainstream churches published collections of hymns and melodies suitable for use in 'popular' services, in itself a very odd though tantalizing concept viewed from today's perspective. The thought was that something lively would attract people, perhaps inadvertently suggesting that the usual Sunday offering was stuffy, or was there an assumption that spiritual growth meant moving from the easy to the difficult, or travelling from liveliness to boredom? 'Popular' services I suppose been replaced these days by 'Shoppers' Services' although the emphasis there lies not with singing more lusty styled tunes but with the time factor, as possible attendees are told the service will not exceed 30 minutes, and in some cases 15. In many places they prove popular. As yet I am not aware of a Shopper's Hymnal. However faced with the possibility of long check out queues they could well prepare themselves by singing:

> May I run the race before me,
> Strong and brave to face the foe[65]

Or in anticipation of the store opening, perhaps:

> If it bring unknown distress,
> Good is all that Thou canst bless;
> Only, while its hours begin,
> Pray we, keep them clear of sin.[66]

The latter line could refer to importing foods from overseas when home grown sources could be used, to save on pollution, while for the person who insists on either shopping by whatever aisle takes the fancy, or goes against the general flow as wished by the supermarket, there could well be sung:

> Lo from the north they come,
> From east and west and south[67]

Again, as seems to be the wont in this style of presentation, the musicologists must issue their warning note, or at least excuse the fact that they have been involved in such a down-market affair. For, as is evident from the plethora of books for 'general' gatherings, it was felt that the hymnbook for Sunday worship was not for use during the various weekday meetings. I do recall it was almost a 'sin' to take books from the Chapel to the schoolroom, and there were separate cupboards for the Sunday book. There was also something 'forbidden' about the Chapel. It was as though it were a body lying in rest, not to be disturbed save for the worship day, or when there was a special event. It was always very cold and unwelcoming.

There was once a surfeit of books for each and every occasion. As a result, my shelves creak from the weight of around 400 different hymn books. I own only a fraction of the total published, although I possibly possess most of the mainstream collections issued. From time to time, I exercise a steely self discipline to resist buying yet another edition.

---

65   From *May The Mind of Christ my Saviour*
66   From *At Thy feet, O Christ, We Lay*
67   From *Hills of the North, Rejoice*

There is an ever-growing 'praise' library of new hymns and songs being published, many of which can also be heard on record or disc issued by companies such as Kingsway and Integrity. Much of this is also published in sheet music form; I have mainly desisted from starting another collection!

However beyond general changes in 'religious' life and observance, it is becoming an expensive proposition to publish a bulky hymnbook. New song copyrights can be costly, and even Christian concerns exhibit a desire for money that would make any true capitalist explode with praise. There is always the niggling thought that a new edition will carry 80 per cent of the previous, although the musical settings and harmonies may be altered. That is a dilemma for all churches. Much of their material overlaps, but they seem unable to find a common mind that would give us a *Christian Hymnbook for all Churches*, albeit augmented from other sources with their distinctive corner, unless CHB was a hefty affair of 2,000 hymns! Sufficient weight to capsize the frail. There is considerable disagreement across the Christian spectrum on verse and tune. Fairly recent collections previously issued in several volumes, when combined, were costing between £29 and £40 pounds in the summer of 2006 for the music and words edition.

I still visit antiquarian bookshops in the hope of finding something unexpected. It's a thrilling chase for the unusual, and I take a careful look to see not just what might be found on shelves, but what may be propping up a table. There was the occasion in Llandudno when I found the 'sought after' volume two of Mrs Booth Tucker's history of the Booths, doing precisely that! I replaced it with a less worthy tome! Just occasionally, I am driven to make a further purchase. Foraging in a bookshop in Holmfirth I came across the 18th century *Houldsworth's Cheetham's Psalmody* that has an engaging title notice 'To the Reverend the Vicar and Clergy of the Parish of Halifax. This Selection of Sacred Music, is by permission, Most Respectfully Inscribed.' The first edition was issued in 1718, with an eventual 12 editions, with an enlarged edition in the early part of the 19th century, and subsequently followed by the edition that I found, so no huge monetary find.

This book followed a common practice of the time in possessing a long introduction explaining the grounds of the music with the aim of persuading people that there is a correct way to sing the psalm-tunes. Sometimes, doggerel came to the fore to make the point:

> Therefore unless
> Notes, Tunes, and Rests
> Are perfect learn'd by Heart,
> None ever can
> With Pleasure scan
> True Tune in Music's Art [68]

Before its music, there is an introduction to the art of singing, even down to the different sorts of notes and their proportions. It is stressed that to acquire a good and firm tone of voice, the mouth should be opened about a quarter of an inch, and to be avoided as much possible, closing the teeth, or the tongue touching them. So too a distortion of the countenance must be avoided, as well as singing through the nose, or too much in the head, as the tone ought to come freely from the chest. The greatest nicety should be observed, that is to have the voice perfectly in tune with the teacher's, or with some well-tuned instrument. This is followed by advice on breath, especially that it shall be taken without noise, and only at proper intervals. As for words there should be distinct articulation, and words should be read over several times before singing. Finally, pronunciation should follow the most correct and approved method.

Within its pages the score consists of the Tenor and Alto written in the Treble Clef; an octave above their real pitch; and the Treble or Air, with the harmony for keyed instruments, is placed next to the Bass, for the convenience of the performer.

Methodists would be familiar with the preface of a hymn book laying down what is and what is not acceptable. Their estimable John Wesley whose hymn collections

68   James T Lightwood, *Hymn-Tunes and Their Story* (Charles H Kelly, 1905), p.109.

formed the first basis for what Methodists sing had very strict ideas as to how a hymnbook should be compiled and how singing should proceed.

John Wesley writes:[69]

> It is not so large as to be either cumbersome, or expensive: and it is large enough to contain such a variety of hymns as will not soon be worn threadbare. It is large enough to contain all the important truths of our most holy religion, whether speculative or practical; yea, to illustrate them all, and to prove them both by Scripture and reason: and this is done by regular order. The hymns are not carelessly jumbled together, but carefully arranged under proper heads, according to the experience of real Christians. So that this book is, in effect, a little body of experimental and practical divinity.

As for singing the great man asked his people to sing with the spirit and with understanding, and he would say in wondrous fashion without hesitation:

> not in the miserable, scandalous doggerel of Hopkins and Sternhold, but in psalms and hymns which are both sense and poetry, such as would sooner dispose a critic to turn Christian than a Christian to turn critic. What they sing is therefore a proper continuation of the spiritual and reasonable service; being selected for that end, not by a poor humdrum wretch who can scarce read what he drones out with such an air of importance, but by one who knows what he is about, and how to connect the preceding with the following part of the service. Nor does he take just 'two staves', but more or less, as may be best raise the soul to God; especially when sung in well-composed and well-adapted tunes, not by a handful of unawakened striplings, but by a whole serious congregation; and these not lolling at ease, or in the indecent posture of sitting, drawling out one word after another, but all standing before God, and praising Him lustily and with good courage.[70]

69   John Wesley, *Collection of Hymns for the use of the People called Methodists,* (Wesleyan Conference Office, 1877).
70   John Wesley, *Letters,* (Standard edition), 111.226f.

Wesley had seven rules for singing: sing them exactly as printed, sing all of them, sing lustily, modestly, sing in tune, above all sing spiritually, with an eye to God in every word.

Wesley's collection consisted of 525 hymns, all of which bar ten were written by members of the Wesley family, the overwhelming number written by Charles. The preface to the 1904 *Methodist Hymnbook* asks,

> For in what other publication of the kind have you so distinct and full an account of Scriptural Christianity? Such a declaration of the heights and depths of religion, speculative and practical? so strong cautious against the most plausible errors, particularly those that are now most prevalent? and so clear directions for making your calling, and election sure: for perfecting holiness in the fear of God?

Dr Martineau quoted famously in Henry Bett's book that:

> it was after the Scriptures, the grandest instrument of popular religious culture that Christendom has ever produced.[71]

Those who have set aside the words of Charles Wesley would argue that his language is that of the King James Bible—archaic. J.R. Watson, the eminent hymnologist, in delivering the 2005 Peake lecture, says that in the hymns of Charles Wesley there is a powerful element of felt experience and human understanding, his awareness of imperfect humankind. For others, while most of his hymns will never be sung or heard outside of special occasions, they will serve as the place of devotion. Few other writers lead the Christian beyond the first romance and love affair with Christ, and in that particular area the neglect of his verse is a cause for sadness. For the most part contemporary Christian groups pay little heed to what Wesley wrote. Some would see this as grossly criminal.

> Charles Wesley filtered high culture through to ordinary people by way of Scripture. His mind was stored with all the best in the literature of the English, Latin and Greek

71   Erik Routley, *The Musical Wesleys*, (Herbert Jenkins Ltd.), p.32. Henry Bett, *The Hymns of Methodism*, (Epworth Press, Norwich, 1945), p.3.

languages. By associating this culture with Scripture, he produced the amazing spate of lyrics by which his people were taught. But the small fraction of his work that most Christians now sing largely hides from them the fact that their author was primarily a teacher, and that his hymns were a body of divinity designated to illuminate not only Scripture but the prayer book itself.[72]

Charles Wesley's obsession was with the greatest things, and consequently he became indifferent to historical setting, cosmic backgrounds, times of day and seasons of the years. He was frankly neglectful of any serious attempt to insert the gospel into natural religion, which leads Manning to observe:

concern with all these things is no doubt needed in each generation; but the more appropriately and fully the work is done for a particular generation the more dated and transient it is.[73]

How would Methodists feel if they were assailed next Sunday with the worship and music of their Founder? I fancy they would go elsewhere. The Methodist John Swarbrick sets the scene as to what would be found:

So what would be sung by those early Methodists? Broadly speaking, the metrical psalmody used unofficially in Anglican parish churches and derived from the Swiss Reformation; and Moravian-style hymnody with its roots in Lutheranism. Add to that the enormous, almost overpowering, influence of Handel on eighteenth-century English music, and we have the main ingredients.[74]

In somewhat different form and ethos, towards the end of 2005 I discovered a fairly rare copy of *A Collection of Hymns for Camp Meetings, Meeting, Revivals, &c. for the use of Primitive Methodists*, dated 1832. It is a little treasure. In the

72   Bernard Lord Manning, *The Hymns of Wesley and Watts*, (Epworth Press, Norwich, 1988), p.46.
73   Ibid. p.47.
74   John Swarbrick, *Jesus The Soul of Musick Is, Music and the Methodists* (Methodist Sacramental Fellowship, Cornwall, 2003), p.4.

introduction by Hugh Bourne, one of the instigators of the Primitive Methodist Movement, there is argument to justify the open-air meeting. Bourne would take us back to the Garden of Eden, and point out that Noah, Job, Abraham, Isaac, and Jacob celebrated worship in the open presence of heaven. So also did the Children of Israel at Mount Sinai, and it was established by the hand of Moses. Even more than this, Bourne reminds the reader that in the Promised Land, the ten thousands of Israel regularly celebrated the worship of God in the open air. All this was a long way from the first meeting in England bearing the simple title 'A Camp Meeting' with the date stamp of May 31, 1907. It took place at Mow, a large mountain running between Staffordshire and Cheshire. 2007 saw centennial anniversary meetings and services, with lusty hymns permeating these gatherings. My copy has 154 hymns, and as with many of the early Methodist worship books it contains only lyrics. Sometimes an existing tune is suggested, at other moments the metre, and in the latter a gathering is asked to find their own tune. The first lyric well and truly sets the scene:

> Christ he sits on Zion's hill,
> He receiveth poor sinners still;
> Will you serve this blessed King,
> Come, enlist, and with me sing:
> I his soldier sure shall be,
> Happy in eternity.

Apart from anything else, it tells clearly where the theological nuances lay, and what kind of gospel was preached at the time. Much emphasis was placed upon sin and redemption and with life-expectancy being non too high in the nineteenth century, there is stress on the short nature of life.

> The grace is nearer the cradle seen,
> How swift the moments pass between!
> And whisper as they fly[75]

—or—

> Oh ye young, ye gay, ye proud
> You must die and wear the shroud,
> Time will rob you of your bloom,
> Death will drag you to the tomb
> Then you'll cry and want to be,
> Happy in eternity. (117)

—or—

> When on my dying bed I lie,
> Lord give me strength to shout and cry[76]

The Wesleys laid much emphasis upon the 'shout' and especially at death's door, as was the case when their mother Susanna passed over.

Number 26 in this shortish volume becomes even more heated on the subject of death, the afterlife, and more so the fate of those who fail to repent:

> See millions of poor wretched creatures,
> Compell'd by justice to appear:
> Deep horror's painted in their features,
> And colours them with dark despair.
> Dire their cries and lamentation,
> But no relief for them be found;
> The Judge pronounces condemnation,
> And seven thunders echo round,
> Down to the lake of burning fire,
> And never more my face to see:
> You're doomed to bear my dreadful ire,
> And blow the flames eternally.

There was a strong belief in the existence of Satan, and the continuing battle. Songs with defiant shouts to the evil one are very much present, but into the scenario comes the

---

75   *A Collection of Hymns,* (Primitive Methodist
      Connexion, 1832), No. 18.
76   Ibid. No. 20.

reason for the Christian's hope—it is in the great Redeemer. To this there is also added a great sense of journeying, from earth with its pains to a land that is fairer than day.

> Let Satan rage and boast no more,
> Nor think his reign is long;
> Tho' saints are feeble, weak, and poor,
> Their great Redeemer's strong.
>
> *(31)*

– and –

> Tho' the world revile and mock,
> We are built upon the rock;
> And while thus we dwell secure,
> Christ will make our goings sure.
> Let us then with faith go on,
> Till our heavenly race is run;
> Though the world and Satan frown,
> We shall soon obtain a crown.
> We shall soon with Jesus be
> Happy in eternity

The hymn that fascinates me most is number 51:

> Is there anybody here like weeping Mary?
> Call to my Lord Jesus, and he'll draw nigh
> O glory, glory, halleluia
> Glory be to God who rules on high.
>
> 2 Is there anybody here like sinking Peter?
> 3 Is there anybody here like blind Bartimeus?
> 4 Is there anybody here like faithless Thomas?
> 5 Is there anybody here that wants salvation?

The Camp Meeting was not a British creation. It can be traced back into the early part of American revival and gospel history, revolving around the movement of early settlers westward as they moved beyond the influence of the established churches. Camp Meetings would last several days. Families would roll up in their wagons with the women sleeping inside and the men underneath. Hymns were simple and direct sometimes with only two lines changing from stanza to stanza. Often the leader would leave the chorus to the gathering, and with a heightened fervour they would sing whatever chorus seemed apt, and it might be sung, or others might follow. The great hymn of the Movement, and of the Primitive Methodists, was *Hark the Gospel News is Sounding* with its invitation to all to receive the Lord Jesus. It was the theology that possessed power, to offer new life, new blessing and an everlasting future. It was welcomed especially by those who felt worthless. However, they felt affirmed, but they had need, whereas the problem for those that have, whether in money or brain power, is not to fall in love with their self-sufficiency.

The Camp Meetings, the cries of salvation from the Primitive Methodists is there in many hymn and songbooks and clearly shows there have been powerful times in Christian history when a prevailing theological nuance has taken centre stage to the diminishment of other cherished stances.

To many, conservative evangelicalism at its best is the faith that is found in classic hymns.

> Diligent preaching, an incredible organisational energy, and learned theology have gone into the creation of modern evangelicalism. But nothing so profoundly defined the faith of evangelicalism as its hymnody; what evangelicals have been is what we have sung. Perhaps because it is so obviously a creature of the Bible's salvic themes, the hymnody of evangelicalism defined a religion that was clearer, purer, better balanced, and more sharply focussed than much evangelical practice. [77]

The writer, Mark A Noll, the Professor of Christian Thought and Professor of History at Wheaton College, USA, adds:

> The classic hymns—their overriding message and the single offence upon which they insist is compacted into the four words that best summarise their message: Jesus Christ saves sinners... it is evangelical to insist that humans are redeemed by God's grace rather than by the achievement of their own

[77]   Mark A.Noll, *Christianity Today*, (July 12, 1999).

> perfection; it is evangelical to claim that the righteousness on which we rely is a forensic gift rather than in personal possession.[78]

In my youth, there were still many preachers who laid stress on atonement, and the need to be saved. Yet it is rare now to hear the great 'evangelical' hymns of one's youth. By this I mean a hymn such as *Great God of Wonders* that might have owed much to a powerful tune such as *Sovereignty*, but for many the words spoke clearly of the prevailing theology of the time:

> Great God of wonders! All thy ways
> Display thy attributes divine
> But countless acts of pardoning grace
> Beyond thine other wonders shine
> Who is a pardoning God like three
> Or who has grace so rich and free

> (*Hymns and Psalms* 38)

That hymn is instanced from the current Methodist hymnary, but missing from it is another of the great atonement hymns, *I Hear Thy Welcome Voice*.

> I hear Thy welcome voice
> That calls me Lord to These
> For cleansing in the precious blood
> That flowed on Calvary
> I am coming, Lord!
> Coming now to Thee
> Wash me, cleanse me, in the blood
> That flowed on Calvary.

> (*Golden Bells* 240)

Once churches rang with the sound of:

> Full salvation! Full salvation!
> Lo, the fountain opened wide
> Streams through every land and nation
> From the Saviour's wounded side,

---

78   Ibid. No page number

Full salvation!
Streams an endless crimson tide.

(*Hymns of Faith* 337)

– or –

I hear the words of love,
I gaze upon the blood,
I see the mighty Sacrifice,
And I have peace with God

(*Hymns of Faith* 342)

Hymns of Faith, 1964, from which the last two references are taken, was based on the 1890 and 1926 editions of *Golden Bells*, both emanating from the Scripture Union. It also contains one of the great past hymns from Philip Doddridge that is rarely heard, *Grace! 'Tis A Charming Sound* that bears great similarity with John Newton's still much sung *Amazing Grace*, and is also marked for its lusty singing to the tune *Cranbrook*.

The most odd feature is the classic evangelical theology, as instanced by the American professor, pours out from the hymns of Charles Wesley, but these days Methodists seem to value Wesley more for his devotional verses than those that speak the language of the blood. Wesley's hymns continually speak about sin and the sacrifice made on the Cross, and the redeeming power of the blood. Emotion is always present, but always carefully controlled. That could be a reason why most of his hymns have been ignored in selections of hymns focussing on the Cross in more lively books than those of the mainstream churches. His aim was to teach doctrine, and with his brother his hymns were part of their overall educational campaign. However, modern minds without a historical and literary perspective can easily walk away from some of Wesley's deepest insights on the Cross. D.W. Bebbington would bring to their notice the line:

Impassive He suffers immortal He dies

and sees it as profundity that is mingled with paradox. [79]

The 'blood' still features widely in the songbook used in Salvation Army worship, and in independent evangelical circles where the charismatic emphasis is lacking, but I speak mainly of the mainstream sector. It is certainly part of the present American country music religious territory. The hymns and songs from the country gospel in the United States repeat ad nauseam the 'old gospel' as some would call it, the preaching of sin, judgement, salvation, and heaven. American country gospel is the extreme edge. Sometimes the language is laced with imagery from the book of Revelation, without taking on board the political realities of that great biblical book. At other times it is more in keeping with an ideal existence in which everyone seems to live in harmony with neighbour, and be comfortably off, where there is no need left unsatisfied, 'if you want it, God gives it!'

> Sometime you'll find me touring that city
> where the Son of God is the Light,
> You'll find me there on the streets,
> so pretty, made of gold so pure, so bright; [80]

And this is sung without qualms among a nation that consumes much of the world's resources in this life, and wishes to protect them for its own use and affluence.

You can search in vain through many American gospel collections for a verse such as this:

> Feel for the parents who've lost their child
> Feel for the women whom men have defiled

79   D.W Bebbington, Evangelicalism in Modern Britain—A History from the 1730s to the 1980s, (Unwin Hyman Ltd., London, 1989), p.68.
80   A. Harold Lane, *Touring That City*, The American Country Hymnbook, (Canaanland Music, 1972), p.142.

> Feel for the baby for whom there's no breast,
> And feel for the weary who find no rest[81]

Although in fairness its imagery would make many mainstream hymn committees quake, especially if comprised mostly of men.

Hymnology is fascinating both for a religious and social understanding of particular times, and if there have been major outbursts of Atonement preaching, to take out the swords and laid clearly down, then also I find some marked contrasts. I find hymns between 1830 and 1860 reflecting the sense of achievement that was found in American society, where there was a sense of involvement in building the Kingdom of God in this world. Man was seen as capable of positive achievement, of moral progress. American society was producing hymns that the seasoned English churchgoer will recognise well—*City of God How Broad & Far*, *Eternal Ruler of the Ceaseless Round* and the jaunty much sung *Mine Eyes Have Seen the Glory of the Coming of the Lord* but on singing has probably little awareness of their rightful context. Hymns such as these pushed aside the predominant thinking of man totally corrupt, sinful, and desperately in need of divine grace.

In the late 19th and early 20th century there came the hymns of brotherhood and expectation that human endeavour with some support from the Almighty would rid the world of its ills, and there would be no more war, while in other quarters, and still one of the few hymns sung, could be heard:

> O Perfect Redemption, the purchase of blood!
> To every believer the promise of God;
> The vilest offender who truly believes,
> That moment from Jesus a pardon receives.[82]

Into this context falls *The Labour and Church Hymn and Tune Book*, first published in 1893, revised in 1912. For me, its

---

81   John Bell, Graham Maule, *Love From Below*,
      Wild Goose Songs Volume 3, (Iona Community),
      1988.
82   *Mission Praise*, (Bibles/Liturgical Music), p.248.

---

presence was unknown, until I saw its dour binding on a bookshelf, only noticed because I was in one of those moods when I will go through every book on the shelf. Opposite its preface can be found:

> Socialist and Labour Church Union—The Union exists to give expression to the religion and general principles of Socialism. It is not theological, and each individual's personal convictions upon such matters being respected.

No personal conviction could encompass the name Jesus: God, whoever, yes, although many who were influential within the Movement were Christians. Unitarians would have been quite at home. The tunes were very much from the general Christian collections, and some of the titles can be found in mainstream hymn collections between 1890 and 1920 where the general expression is one that believes better times are ahead, if only …

> These things shall be! A loftier race
> Than e'er the world has known shall rise
> With freedom in their souls,
> And light of a scene in their eyes
> [* the 1904 Methodist Hymnbook prefers 'knowledge']
>
> Nation with nation, land with land
> unarmed shall live as comrades free;
> In every heart and brain shall throb
> the pulse of one fraternity.

Another familiar song to Christians is the inclusion of *Work, for the Night is Coming,* a favourite to many from *Sacred Songs and Solos.* With its tune from General Gordon, there is *Honour To All.*

> Honour to all who are aiming
> The welfare of others to serve,
> Still by their actions proclaiming
> They never from duty will swerve
> Honour to noble devotion
> Surrendering comfort for toil,
> Seeking with earnest emotion
> The strongholds of evil to spoil. (88)

Some Americans use the term 'ethical culture', and so we can find a verse such as:

We are builders of that city;
All our joys and all our groans
Help to raise its shining ramparts;
All our lives are building stones,
Whether humble or exalted.
All are called to task divine;
All must aid alike to carry
Forward one sublime design.[83]

It would be foolish to insist this verse is 'the' verse to represent the term coined but it does point to the centrality of this kind of religious expression. It is one that respects particular human values, endorses freedom, and sees Jesus not as the Christ, but rather as a fine thinker who has positively benefited humankind by his overall message of brotherhood, and love of neighbour. It is though impossible in this relatively short volume to cover more than a few areas, for in just American hymn terms alone one could spend much time examining the input of Unitarians, Universalists, Shakers, and the differing nuances of the major churches, including Presbyterians. I single them out simply because of reading the book *Holy Fairs-Scottish Communions and American Revivals in the Early Modern Period*.[84] The editors do throw up the interesting observation that Americans sang folk hymns throughout the 19th century without being very aware of the fact, although truer of the South, whereas those in the North, where folk hymnody was first apparent, did not entirely close the door. More recently, especially since the 1950s the recorded disc has had considerable impact, as indeed explorations of American traditional folk catalogues by known music names such Bob Dylan and Joan Baez. Many of the songs on early Baez albums are spirituals and hymns, whilst Jean Ritchie once stunned me by singing so powerfully the old American hymn *What Wondrous Love Is This*.

83   In Janer, Hughes, Sprague Smith (eds),
       American Hymns Old and New, (NY: Columbia
       Press, 1980), p.535.
84   Leigh Eric Schmidt, (Princeton University
       Press, 1989).

Whatever the input of particular theological and religious understanding, all traditional hymn books set out a framework, rather than working from A to Z in titles, sometimes there is added considerable notes on themes and scriptural passages that are said to underlie the hymn.

The *Methodist Hymns and Psalms* set out with *The Eternal Father, The Eternal Word* and *The Eternal Spirit,* all of which fall under the umbrella of God's Nature—God's Being and Majesty.

This meant for Methodists an end to the tradition of Charles Wesley's *O For A Thousand Tongues* opening their song catalogue. In view of the decision to start in the way that has just been described it was no surprise that the book opened with *All People That On Earth Do Dwell.* It proceeds into categories such as God's World (a very limited one) and God's People.

Should one go back to the *Methodist Hymnbook 1904* it is to find that the overall initial cover is *The Glory of God* with the immediate subtitle of *Adoration and Worship,* allowing it of course to print first the aforementioned Charles Wesley hymn. Again something of a religious social history can be gathered from hymn section titles, and thus in that 1904 book there are the following sections in the stated order:

- Invitations and Warnings
- Death
- Judgement
- The Future State
- Time, Death and Eternity
- Hymns for Children and Young People

Congregational Praise, 1951, focuses first on God, then Jesus Christ, then the Holy Spirit with a finale for that section, The Trinity. As befitting a time when I was at school, as I described earlier, there is a considerable section on Social and National. *The Church Hymnary* of 1973 reserves its largest section for The Word of God: His Mighty Acts. Long ago there would be a section for Backsliders? But were they there to hear their admonition sung? One assumes it gave a greater sense of rightness to those who were the 'regulars' and occupied faithfully their paid pew. Dr Pete Ward sees the use of hymns in general mainstream worship as:

> a kind of glue joining the different parts of the worship together[85]

He sees the prayers and sermon, and other elements of worship as the filling, and the hymns are the bread. Therefore, within this kind of setting it is right that hymn books have a doctrinal structure. However, in charismatic worship hymns and songs are central, and presumably from that they can be given in A to Z form in such a book as *Mission Praise*, which has the advantage that it is easier to find titles if they are arranged in alphabetical format.

I confess after reading through countless hymn collections, and accompanying literature, I am left in some appreciation for what was provided at the particular time, but on other accounts I am left cold. Even if I take the 1950s and the following decade as a starting point, and so *Congregational Praise*, I am left with the feeling that the big bad world out there is almost pushed aside, and on to all things is imposed a religious framework. While *Congregational Praise* avoided the kind of material that would adorn the Billy Graham songbooks of the time,[86] it hardly listens to the songs and music that were being put out by Tin Pan Alley and beyond. By the mid to late 1960s all hell was let loose in popular culture but you would not know it from *Congregational Praise* or the 1973 *Church Hymnary*. This situation did not usually change in books of the 1980s. There were only a few attempts to provide the rhythm and feel of the age, and to find words that were written since the Second World War! In general hymnody, until the present time, it is hard to find hymns that suggest 'revolution' could be on the agenda. It is equally hard to find capitalism as seen as one of the biggest evils hoisted on humankind. Few hymns deal with the wide divisions in

---

85   P.Ward, *Selling Worship*, (Paternoster, 2005) p.198.

86   Although it does include *Great God of Wonders* but not to the tune *Sovereignty*.

society between haves and have nots, or that wealth should be redistributed, or that Christians should be actively seeking to redress areas of exploitation and injustice, or that corruption is endemic and wrong, or that racism is another evil.

In a slightly different context Colin Buchanan [87] told the readers of the *English Church Music Journal* for 1976 that:

> From our standpoint, the Liturgical Commission of the late 1950s looks very much like a don's dining club. They had obviously met and discussed interesting parts of patristic history, and had interesting dreams about what the Church of England's liturgy would one day look like. But the actual possibility of bringing in new liturgy in the near future was obviously one which was not well focussed by them. That was inevitable. Three hundred years of an unchanging liturgy had left Anglicans with a deep sense of 'as things always had been, so they always would be.' [88]

Common to all Christian traditions, and the hymns they sing, there is sadly a pronounced deficiency when it comes to placing material under a contemporary and social categorization. Apart from the racial and gender disparity this absence worries me most. My journeying convinces me that it speaks of a Church which, at least in worship terms is totally lopsided. Hymns of the church may talk the language of creation, the natural world, and they may speak of individual conversion, growing in grace and knowing fellowship. However, when it comes to 'doing' we have a plethora of material that for most part lacks a cutting edge, although in the 'exceptions' you can find a hymn such as *God In His Love For Us Lent Us This Planet*, with lines such as:

87 At the time Vice-Principal of the Anglican based St John's College, Nottingham.
88 Colin Buchanan, *English Church Music* Journal, (The Royal School of Church Music), p.5.

> Long have we wasted what others have need of,
> Poisoned the fountain of life at its source.[89]

Whatever the hymn or songbook, there is a lack of modern images and references, even if the hymnbook dates from the last 20 to 30 years.

Quite extraordinarily, in the Methodist 1983 *Hymns and Psalms, God of Concrete, God of Steel* was excluded. This was one of several fine hymns by Richard Jones that failed to make it from the supplement of the previous Methodist hymnbook. Jones in his powerful hymn mentions atoms, cable, motorway, satellite, worlds of speed, science, map and graph, design and art. Together with the title's two words, and a last verse that clearly speaks the gospel, this hymn employs pretty good contemporary text, set to a useful tune *New Horizons* from Francis Westbrook. Writing in the *Methodist Church Music Society Bulletin* Michael Dawney recalls how it was praised for its stark modernity by Professor Hutchings of Durham. In 1981 at the Oxford Hymn Society conference, a Baptist minister, the Revd Eric Sharpe, referred to its magnificent words, and commented that none of the many tunes set to it had caught on:

> The real, urban imagery appeals to me and so Dawney contributed the tune *Metropolis*. [90]

Hymn book collections are rarely in empathy with the harsh demanding truth that God 'takes flesh in Christ' in a world that might have pretty flowers, rolling seas and picturesque mountains, but also the law of the jungle rules, corruption is endemic, and the worship of money considered the highest laudable goal. Generally that is not the way hymn committees think—not because the various members are deficient either in musical awareness or overall brainpower! It is a question of where you start. At the same time it must be said that unreality in hymn singing usually occurs when

---

89   F. Pratt Green, *343 Hymns and Psalms*,
        (Methodist Publishing House, Peterborough,
        1983).
90   The Revd Eric Sharpe, MCMS, Bulletin, No. 36,
        (July 1985), p.6.

some emotion is expressed that very few present are likely to experience. Alan Dunstan instances:

> Saviour, when in dust to thee
> Low bow the adoring knee;
> When repentant, to the skies
> Scarce we lift our weeping eyes.

This is 'unreal' for two reasons:

> First, it suggests that we are acceptable to God, in Father Harry Williams' phrase, 'only by eating the maximum amount of dust possible'. Secondly, it is unlikely that 'anyone' in the congregation is 'weeping' for his 'sins'. There are those who argue indeed that we should do so; but if we cannot and do not, surely this sort of thing is inappropriate in public worship.[91]

In other words, as with traditional folk songs, someone needs to tell the congregation what they are going to sing, and why. What it means is that we sing it 300 years later in a world so vastly different, even if human beings can be subject to emotions and actions recognisable in any age and time, although the latter may well be the link. Or, as my friend Roy Jones would ask, 'Has it made them interpret the world in a way that has left them immobilised, trapped in ineffectuality?' If so, then, horror, and I have the feeling he is right.

Praise songs are no different when it comes to spotting the lack of modern imagery and reference. And let's face it, a great deal of praise material is simply old-fashioned. In the journal *Christianity + Renewal*, August 2003, Nick Page has some pretty harsh things to say about the praise song catalogue of material. In observing lyrics, he sees many new writers writing words 'that just sound like the Bible' in what he terms 'a kind of ye olde Scriptural English.' He adds for good measure, 'The result is songs that sound like the Authorised Version of the Bible as rewritten by J.R.R. Tolkein.' Doubtless this is because biblical images are safer.

91   Alan Dunstan, *These are the Hymns*, (SPCK, Poole, 1973), p.26-7.

His other pertinent remark rests in what he terms the under-use of modern images. His analysis is pretty devastating. In *Songs of Fellowship* with 640 items, he finds three songs using modern images, while Spring Harvest manages four among 250 and in *Soul Survivor & Update*, there are seven from a content of 300.

Page has another worry, what he calls 'nonsense verse' people singing 'Ba bap bup bup bah' to take one line, of one song, that engagingly has 'copyright' stamped after it. Page is aware that his views will find a cold shoulder in some circles, and he will be criticised for being a musical Victor Meldrew. However he feels this needs to be said. Peter Ward's two books *The Liquid Church* and *Selling Worship* also offer trenchant analyses of the 'praise song', and the overall impact of this genre.

Page could have added that much 'praise' writing is of a poor quality, and it is offensive that some people can claim copyright for a lyric that reads something like:

> I thank Him
> thank Him, thank Him
> I thank Him
> thank Him, thank Him.

Some of its practitioners claim 'divine guidance' and approval.[92] This same point is taken up in an amusing, though slightly disconcerting narrative in the book *Christian Culture*, where the writer meets a songwriter called Susan. Susan objects to criticisms of both her singing and writing, and simply says:

> The Holy Spirit gave me that song. It is not mine to change. He entrusted it to me.[93]

She finds agreement on that from the writer, although not in the sense she wants:

92   This is something I regularly experience when receiving independently made demo records.
93   Matthew Paul Turner, *The Christian Culture* (Relevant Books, USA, 2004), p.77.

> Well, I agreed with her there. I wouldn't have felt comfortable claiming that song as mine, either.[94]

The upshot was our writer losing patience and telling her that if the Holy Spirit indeed wrote the song then something nasty had happened to it in transmission.

Kendrick has expressed his desire to get his doctrine right:

> Ask people to quote scripture and they'll usually quote the version that was put to music. If the theology is dodgy, that's what they get into their heads. I believe that, alongside with our simple worship choruses, we need some songs that have got some meat in them. I find those the least easy to write.[95]

There are other voices within the praise world, working in specialist fields that exercise some doubt over the plethora of praise songs written in the first person.

> In some circles, worship has become even more egocentric with the focus of the song diverted away from God onto the believer... some people on some days find egocentric worship songs empowering. I know I do. They provide a means to express devotion in personal and intimate ways. Yet, the same songs can also be quite disempowering at times. Participants unable to proclaim total devotion are left feeling emotionally distant from God. It is not that they are unable or unwilling to worship God; they just can't use such bold language. Youth work and ministry does not measure young people's worship by the songs they sing. Youth workers and ministers help young people to express themselves in meaningful and accessible ways. If this means using less emphatic language then so be it.[96]

A major figure in the praise world, Chris Bowater, in an interview for the now sadly defunct magazine *Cross Rhythms*, revised his earlier comments about the low quality of praise music, and worship personality cults. He

---

94   Ibid. p.77.
95   Graham Kendrick, *Easy Songs are Hardest*,
       interview with Mike Fearon, *Church Times*,
       January 1990, p.22.
96   Danny Brierley, *Joined Up* (Lifestyle/Oasis,
       2003), p.174-5.

---

speaks of the danger of worship becoming me-centred, my-centred.

> We are here for the Lord, being here for my feelings is a by-product, it isn't the reason for my existence ... the cult issue of worship will always exist ... I think the whole ministry thing is very seductive ... the biggest dilemma in a church or in a celebration meeting is to try and avoid spectator worship ...[97]

However, there are a number of interesting writers emerging from the praise orientated gatherings, including Matt Redman, Chris Bowater *et al.*[98] Exciting music has stemmed both from Vineyard and Hillsong communities.

My trip down memory lane cheers me a little, for among the lack lustre on display, the expected and conventional, there have been unexpected moments of discovery, even of humour!

97   Chris Bowater, *Windows on Worship*, Cross Rhythms, Issue 50, April/May 1999, p.45.
98   Stuart Townend, Dave Bilbrough, Noel Richards, Sammy Horner, Tanya Riches, Darlene Zschech, Dave Fellingham and Ian White.

CHAPTER FIVE

Hymn Disorder

It may not hit the headlines, even in religious papers, let alone the 'story seeking' tabloids, but there is a war 'out there' in Church and Chapel land. It revolves around how and what shall be sung. What tunes should be used? Or is it rather a question of what are we allowed to sing, and which tunes are deemed suitable? Whatever the case, there are angry people who feel things are not quite right. Certainly this is not a new phenomenon.

In 1927 Oxford University Press issued a general hymn collection with a preface from the Right Hon. D. Lloyd George. The eminent politician's thoughts began with:

> There is evidently a growing dissatisfaction with the choice of hymns for Divine Service. The number and variety of our Hymnals bear witness to the need of an accepted standard: this need is accentuated by a diversity of use and practice that has already passed the bounds of a reasonable freedom.[99]

However, even though in his advisory capacity (as to what is described as the 'problems of Welsh hymnody') the Revd H. Elvet Lewis managed to squeeze a number of powerful Welsh tunes into its content, it was very much Anglican in tenor. It had little time for the hymns and songs of the people, or at least little favour toward the more boisterous and less pleasing to the classical ear:

99   The Right Hon. D. Lloyd George, *Hymns of Western Europe*, (Oxford University Press, 1927), Preface.

> It is a matter of common experience that this vital portion of our service has been marred by the intrusion of verses and melodies which in point of purity, of dignity, of reverence, fall short of the ideal which worship should rightly demand.[100]

Lloyd George went on to express satisfaction that 'the standard, which all would admit to be desirable, can in practice be realized.' It meant that with one exception no tune by a living composer was included, and the bulk of material was said to come from the chief accepted treasuries of Western Europe. For the most part that meant either British, French or German sources. I am aware that some hymns are so precious that their proposed omission from a new collection can arouse sentiments that have little to do with Christian charity. Hymns invariably do have a personal attachment, and a certain one may have been sung at someone's wedding, relation's funeral, commemorative occasion, even down to 'mum's favourite and she always sang it when getting ready for church.' These hymns can acquire something approaching 'divine' status for the individual concerned, and must be defended at all costs. In a more general fashion it is usually the exclusion of what some fondly called 'the old-fashioned' hymns that gives rise to red-hot anger. But the word 'old' is of course used very loosely. The discussion is not about 13th-century text, or even the Wesley years of the 18th century. It is predominantly about songs that came out of the latter part of the 19th century.

Hymn book compilers do face resentment out there in 'pew land' — when the committee for the eventual Methodist *Hymns and Psalms* issued a list of proposed inclusions in *The Methodist Recorder*. All hell was let loose in the letter columns of that weekly paper. It seemed that every member had a view. It was the same when the Welsh speaking Wesleyans and Calvinists of Wales came together with the production of a common Welsh language hymn book in mind. The well-documented proceedings toward this project notes:

100   Ibid.

> Credaf na chondeminwyd cymaint erioed ar un Ilyfr arall cyn
> eiweled ag a wnaed ar y casgliad hwn o emynau (I do not think
> any other book was so condemned before it was seen as this
> collection of hymns).[101]

There is anger directed at hymn book compilers who change words and verse structures of a loved hymn, delete the popular tune, and even worse, they leave out the title altogether.[102]

Canon David Winter, at the time Head of BBC Radio's Religious Broadcasting, told the Hymn Society Conference at Coventry in 1985, in his talk, Hymns in Broadcasting, that the 'wrong' hymn tune can jam BBC switchboards for a considerable time. David Bridge, a fine and perceptive British religious newspaper columnist, tells me that any 'ill' mention of a particular hymn sends a flurry of readers into indignant activity, and subsequently his mailbox bulges with their ripostes. Some of these people believe there is no place for texts that make contemporary reference, assuming of course you can find hymn texts that reflect a global, city and urban, technological, multinational, multiracial world. They would see hymnology free from social and political allusions.

Unfortunately, there is no doubt that skulduggery of the highest order has emanated from some hymn committees. In fits of absentmindedness the compilers have reduced and altered the verse structure of many an old hymn. Having done this, like magicians and the favoured hat trick, they produce a new tune. Naturally this process has a triple whammy effect, for by changing verse structure they can delete the dreaded chorus, forget the 'old' and often ranting tune that has so often in their view led to lusty 'uncontrolled' singing. Their contact with the Almighty has led them to believe there are only certain ways and

---

101 R.Pritchard, Eurgrawn 119 (Swyddfa yr
      Eurgrawn, Wales, 1928) p.33.
102 Andrew Pratt's book, O For A Thousand Tongues
      (Epworth 2004) provides a wonderfully
      detailed story of the compilation of Methodist
      Hymns and Psalms (1933).

emotions in which religious faith and fervour shall be expressed. Subtle and clever, for when possible content is printed in advance only a title is given, not what might happen to the verse, the refrain, the tune. And they complain when the verbal battalions line up protesting.

To God Be The Glory retains popularity. It has a four-line verse and refrain, in 11.11.11.11 form. In *One Voice*, in the *Church Hymnary*, the refrain is binned, and so it is sung as a four-line verse, and the somewhat insipid tune *St Denio* is printed. In the third edition of the *Church Hymnary* (1933) *I Need Thee Every Hour* is retained, but the familiar tune by Lowell Mason, much loved by male voice choirs let alone many congregations, is not printed. Which, let's face it, was plain stupid and elitist. However, CH4 restores the old tune!

The popular *God Be With You Till We Meet Again* is found in most hymnodies. The great grouse is the omission in some mainstream collections of the Sankey tune. Instead the pleasant tune *Randolph* is usually substituted, and admittedly it suits well the words. That said, the so-called 'old' version is still sung in many places, and perhaps Tomer's tune is rejected because it appals some 'naice' people with its unbridled heartiness. Whatever the feelings of some hymn committees it should be offered as a choice, it seems downright petty to tell people they ought not to be singing the words to a tune they love.

I Hear Thy Welcome Voice, much loved by male voice choirs, and quartets enacts the same process. The familiar tune of Robert Lowry is removed by some worthy misguided editors. Methodist *Hymns and Psalms* (1983) doesn't even include it, in itself suggesting that some people do not have their ears to the ground. In the *Anglican Hymn*, published in 1965, the much liked tune to *My Faith Looks Up To Thee* is deleted, and even more amazingly the popular tune *Converse* to *What A Friend We Have In Jesus* finds no place. At very least in deference to so many people's preference, and popularity with trad jazz bands, the compilers might have made it the second tune, or found the usual escape when a committee wishes to assert its own believed superior taste by placing a tune in a section at the end of the book either under Alternative Tunes or Other

Tunes. *Converse* also finds no favour with the Australian *With One Voice,* and here the two tunes are *Sicilian Mariners* and *Blaenwern,* the latter more associated across the board these days with Charles Wesley's *Love Divine All Loves Excelling.* These days it would be hard for someone not to play *Cwm Rhondda* to *Guide Me O Thou Great Jehovah,* but perhaps it is only a fear of a backlash that prevents too many organists from trying to wean the congregation away. Certainly some musicians dislike the tune and they would equate *Cwm Rhondda* with exuberance of the wrong kind, and speak of tub-thumping at the end of the tune *Diadem* to *All Hail the Power of Jesus* or the elongations of some Methodist tunes in distressed tones. 'Sometimes', says David Appleby:

> the songs have been forged in the heat of the battle for the souls of men. [103]

To a degree organists and accompanists are caught in 'no man's land' for where there is more than one popular tune to a much sung hymn there is inevitable dissension. Wesley's *Jesus Lover Of My Soul* has two equally competing tunes, *Hollingside* or *Aberystwyth.* For many the latter wins, partly because of the mounting phrases in the second half of the tune, with the final 'doff of the cap' to the words in its sombre close. In *Is That The Right Tune?* Brian Spinney says there is a fallacy in his title, in that there is no such thing as the 'right' tune for a hymn. He says editors have to bear in mind the ecumenical situation, and editors and their committees see what hymns and tunes are used across the various churches. However, it is difficult to find the 'right' tune that may suit such a gathering. It can occasion much dismay in the ecumenical situation when familiar words are announced and then a relatively unknown tune is played. Spinney focuses on 40 hymns, and from his listing only the tune *Dix* to *As With Gladness Men Of Old,* and *Angels Song* by Gibbons and set to *Forth In Thy Name O Lord I Go* would appear to be the standard offering among the

103   David P. Appleby, *History of Church Music,*
      (Moody Press, Chicago, 1966), p.145.

nine mainstream denominations he chooses for his interesting exercise. The most likely candidates to cause irritation would be:

- *Breathe On Me, Breath of God*
- *There's A Wideness in God's Mercy*
- *O For A Thousand Tongues to Sing*
- *Love Divine*
- *In Christ There is No East or West*
- *God Is Love; Let Heaven Adore*

However when someone in the pew is annoyed no amount of explanation of this nature suffices. It would seem that in many instances tune compilers of the various churches go their own way.

Few people in pew land can belong to a hymnbook selection committee, but from one description I have read the putting together of the book *Cantate Domino* was a galling process. This is a publication emanating from the World Student Christian Federation.[104] By this time it had passed into the hands of the World Council of Churches. When the first meeting was held to discuss the new content, it was the beginning of another outbreak of church disease, usually excused by saying it is democracy, working parties, and researchers, and lots of reports back!

Eight drafts of the book were assembled. Eventually, as Church affairs go, something has to happen even if the matter is referred back for further consultation, there was a book with 202 pieces, 72 of them in English, with French and German the other two predominant languages, and it mirrored many cultures, styles and languages. It seems everyone was on board, even Roman Catholics and Orthodox. Of particular interest was the addition of 40 liturgical pieces, of which two Coptic pieces were seen as possibly the oldest Church music in present use. Outside of

---

104   With a history as far back as 1924, revised in
       1930, given a third edition in 1951, and was
       seen in further need of revision.

international affairs, and perhaps Churches in an international city such as Geneva, it was hard to see it enjoying a general church use, but obviously it was a fascinating if topsy-turvy path to fruition.

It would be wrong to say that it is simply a question of 'them and us' meaning cold and distant hymn compilers and church attendees at war, for even within the 'pew' ranks there is disagreement among its own. Rarely (sadly) though is it about 'doctrine' — more often it is simply about style. For some, the relief is not having to sing the 'old' hymns, for others the feeling similar to that of emigrants venturing to Canada, that they are part of something 'new' and relevant, they have chosen to be part of the future. For some contemporary Christians the stand of many older worshippers express no more than a desire to live in the religious faith of the past, some of which has now been discarded. They belong to the new times, often this means the nebulous. However even in 1970 the much respected hymnologist Lionel Dakers when posing the question of 'why are many church choirs depleted today?' would bravely say that the archaic images, together with the language, genuinely causes embarrassment to many young people. He sees the uncommitted outsider viewing the Church as thoroughly alien and living out a shaky existence in an unreal atmosphere. He also speaks of church services being dreary and stereotyped.[105]

There is little evidence to say anyone has particularly listened to Daker's analysis. I find his pronouncement spot on.

Dakers is not advocating the Sankey genre to answer the dilemma posed. However, he has to face the fact that there are hundreds of religious tunes that can kill worship stone dead, even if some might see them as objects of beauty, possibly only to be sung by those who know how to sing. Some hymns may have the most marvellous poetic

---

105   Lionel Dakers, *Church Music At the Crossroads*,
       (Marshall, Morgan & Scott, London, 1970),
       p.98ff.

language, and theological allusions, but, if not understood are they but little better than the doggerel of the Sankey genre that at least may make sense? Older Christians retaliate by saying much of the new material is of a pop nature, not really suited to congregational singing. They do not want guitars, drums and an amplification system that blares away and rocks the pews. A hearty helping of this attitude finds its way into one of the most contentious issues for mainstream churches in the singing, and accompanying, of what is loosely called 'praise'. A little about this has occupied an earlier chapter, and will be considered again in my eventual summary, but here it falls into a different context. This has become in mainstream churches an issue that has divided congregations, and in many cases it has led to the dissatisfied removing themselves from familiar worship abodes to new pastures, and more often than not to the setting up of independent churches. Sarah Boseley reported in *The Guardian* that traditionalists considered the new hymns carrying 'unspeakably dreadful tunes redolent of the outdated dance hall, and appalling—even blasphemous—lyrics.' And to think Thomas Aquinas once wrote:

> A hymn is the praise of God with song. And a song is the exultation of the mind dwelling on eternal things bursting forth into voice.[106]

All of this is confusing territory, with much criss-crossing of the various elements involved. I have no qualms with anyone deciding to root out what they do not like if it is their own book, but when it is supposedly representative of the whole Church, then what right have they to deny something to many people? I can feel boots hitting the cobblestones, as the great march of protest gets underway, to the bemusement of the great mass of the unchurched who are more interested in what might be marked down in price at the nearest House of Fraser. *Rejoice and Sing*[107] as used by United Reformed Churches virtually makes extinct the

106   *The Times*, (December 30 2004), p.17.
107   (Oxford University Press, 1991).

so-called 'old hymns' from Victorian times with just three inclusions, whereas the *Church Hymnary* of the Presbyterians did include lyrics that would be associated with *Sacred Songs and Solos*. *Songs of Praise*, first published in 1936, has just two hymns of this nature. But let no one doubt that these 'old' hymns retain popular appeal. At least, that is my experience of gathering the most popular for hymn sing evenings from a wide cross-section of people. It is again confirmed by the selection of hymns in BBC's *Songs of Praise* (1997), although it must be added that there is a considerable diversity in this volume. There are Victorian chorus hymns, and among these:

- *Blessed Assurance*
- *Will Your Anchor Hold*
- *To God Be The Glory*

Also included is contemporary praise material, texts and tunes from *Taizé* and *Iona* and items from world music from outside Europe and North America, and what the preface terms items which had not previously been thought of as hymns or songs for public worship. [108]

The best illustration of this is *When You Walk Through A Storm*, a song popularised by Gerry and the Pacemakers in the Autumn of 1963, sung fervently by supporters of Liverpool F.C. and universally adopted by others. The actual derivation is of course Oscar Hammerstein II. The BBC's *Songs of Praise* volume is arguably the best guide listing of what the general Christian worshipper wants.

One of the merrier absurdities in Church life concerns people with deeply held prejudices who blissfully and happily sing material whose source in another context they reject. It's all rather like the Anglican attendee of a performance of John Wesley who said she had come to find out more about this Methodist, oblivious to the fact that both John and Charles were, if you like, sons of her Church. And I remember when once I took Morning Prayer in a

108   BBC1—*Songs of Praise*, (Oxford University Press, 1997), preface vii.

Methodist Church I was told in no uncertain terms at the door as a lady took her leave that John Wesley must be turning in his grave after such a service. So it is that those who have little time for the wobbles of Unitarians will happily sing *It Came Upon the Midnight Clear*, and some of my past 'Protestant right or wrong' acquaintances seem unaware that when they sing *O Come All Ye Faithful*, its source is the Roman Catholic Church.

Doubtless hymn committees would put up a stern defence against their critics, even if we go back to the first half of the 20th century. The introduction to the *Congregational Hymnary*—it replaced *The Congregational Church Hymnal* of 1887—tells us that it was the result of six years of labour, that it was compiled because each generation requires, or at least demands, its own hymn book. In deference to a widely expressed desire, the Council of the Congregational Union went ahead.

However the dissatisfied may rejoice that new publishing methods mean general hymn book compilers are fast losing out to modern technology. Christian gatherings can decide to follow their own whims and fancies, and are no longer tied to the choice made by their denominational hymnologists. They can decide what their area or church understands by 'what the soul sings'. Christian gatherings, hopefully aware of copyright, can issue their own worship volumes. Some church collections that I have seen of less than 80 selections cannot in any way equal the more varied and catholic taste of a large denominational collection. More often, the choice rests with the most known and sung from *Songs of Fellowship* or *Mission Praise*. Therefore, the gatherings sing their favourites, which is hardly a recipe of a wide and varied Christian experience.

Cotton picks up an important sideline, should hymn books be jettisoned in favour of screen projection? Many churches are still 'out' on that issue. It does deny the worshipper the opportunity of looking ahead (from observing hymn numbers on the hymn board) before hymns/songs are sung, or reflecting later. Perhaps, as at Chapel Street, Penzance, the best solution is to use both methods. One marked loss by utilising the projector rests in not displaying the musical score.

My research finds that the anger is not confined to the 'pews'. Eminent musicians take to arms. They have their own axe to grind against those who compile and edit the material that we sing. They speak of sexual innuendo running riot in the hymns. We must hearken to their lead. However, not all their efforts find praise from fellow musicians. Some hymnologists can rail against their own kith and kin. Let us take *The Baptist Church Hymnal*, Psalms and Hymns Trust (1933 UK) to someone such as Douglas Webster.[109] In his very readable and worthy book this collection is disappointing. He writes:

> one could hardly regard the book as a product of this century
> .... it seems to be a repository of all that is weakest in
> Nonconformist hymnody ... one is conscious that no musician
> of eminence was responsible for the musical editing ....

In fairly recent times enter Donald Webster[110] and Simon Lindley. In *The Guardian*, Mr Webster felt the position of music in churches was more divisive than women priests. He believed there was a disastrous mix of sacred and secular and it had led to profanity. He instanced such lyrics as 'Here I am wholly available'; 'Let me have my way with You' and 'Jesus, Come Closer To Me Now.' It would be interesting though to know what he thinks of 17th-century German hymns—take one familiar example, *Jesu, Priceless Treasure*. The hymn was modelled on a German love song that began 'Flora, meine Freude, meiner Seelenweide.' *Julian's Dictionary of Hymnology* sees the hymn expressing 'the longing for the inward and mystical union of Christ with the soul.' The Methodist *Companion to Hymns and Psalms* says many feel it is unsuited for public worship, but

---

109 *Our Hymn Tunes*, (The Saint Andrew Press,
     Scotland, 1930).
110 Webster's accreditations speak impressively,
     fellow of the Royal College of Organists, author
     of *The Hymn Explosion and its Aftermath*.

---

also says that it can be a moving experience when sung by a solo voice. Webster calls it all near blasphemy.

Simon Lindley traces the decline back to the 1950s to the productions of folk masses by Geoffrey Beaumont. He cites with distaste the tune Patrick Appleford wrote for *Living Lord* that echoes in its title the pop hit of the time *Livin' Doll* from Cliff Richard. He describes some hymns as 'tired 1920s idioms of Blackpool's north pier'. His other pet dislikes include use of the tune *O Waly, Waly* to the hymn *An Upper Room Did Our Lord Prepare* because the original setting of the music is to a folk song that advocates secular, selfish love, something quite distinct from 'our Lord's sacrifice on the cross,' which he sees as the supreme example of selfless love.

In rivetting language, Lindley told *The Guardian:*

> it is sexually explicit. It is about love growing cold as you get older, and not being able to get an erection any more.

Should this be so, then obviously it would be a weight upon the shoulders of many men in church congregations. He is also quoted as having no objection to the theology of the hymn *We Have But A King Who Rides A Donkey* but objects to the tune of *What Shall We Do With the Drunken Sailor* being set to it. It would seem that he is not against some of the better revivalist hymns:

> As I am on the extreme end of Anglo-Catholicism, in hymns I have much more in common with the ultra-Evangelical.

So, he gives a thumbs-up to *Blessed Assurance* and *What a Friend we have in Jesus* — it must have gained him many new friends! And will continue to do so.

The article at its end brings into the fray Geoff Weaver, then director of studies at the Royal School of Church Music. Weaver's main objection focussed around too many hymns bearing colonial references.

Some hymns will invariably disappear without protest, occasionally they are rediscovered. For all that, there is a lack of real evaluation in the present time, and especially so when we are speaking of the praise movement, where the output is phenomenal. At times it would seem that anyone who claims to be in receipt of the Spirit can push their wares.

This pales against the fact that in times past even the mighty Isaac Watts or Charles Wesley were subject to rejection notices. After all, even Wesley's best published source, the British *Methodist Hymnbook* does not include over 6,000 of his lyrics. At the same time in more revivalist circles much of the enormous output of Francis Jane Alstyne, otherwise known as Fanny J. Crosby (although some sources say she had 214 other names), is not included in such collections as *Golden Bells*, *Grace*, and *Sacred Songs and Solos*.

Such of course was the output of Wesley and Mrs Crosby that each could fill at least six volumes of a hymnbook compilation that resembled for instance the *Congregational Hymnary* of 1916 with its 1,002 items. But in common with many, they could be accused of repetition or failing their own set standards. Others fell by the wayside, their thoughts and expressions found wanting with the passage of time. Erik Routley says:

> When Wesley crashes, he crashes rather less attractively than Watts. Watts has the imagination that brings great doctrines into juxtaposition and lets them explode against one another. Wesley is a sounder and safer theologian and craftsman.

Watts, as we well know, could rise to the heights. At a moment's notice he could slip on a banana skin and there is always something solemnly and arrestingly remarkable about a puritan slipping on a banana skin.

Routley instances a verse of Watts:

> He said, 'Let the wide heav'n be spread'
> And heav'n was stretched abroad
>
> 'Abram, I'll be thy God', he said
> And he was Abram's God[111]

An important question remains for those who would wish to see the hymn retain pride of place. Why do the various churches not spend more time in aiding and creating the process of producing new and lively words and tunes? To do so of course might mean producing a generally flexible

111   Erik Routley, *Music Sacred and Profane*
        (Independent Press, London, 1957).

hymn book to which at yearly or two yearly intervals new material could be added. In the United States people are given time and place to develop and write new works. The extremely talented British writer Brian Wren is one of those favoured.

Few churches have hymn writers in residence, and I do not know any British church that pays someone to spend time relating theology to situation. Obviously some British churches have their own known writers, but I am not aware that the Church of England maintains Timothy Dudley Smith, or at one time the Methodists, the late Fred Pratt Green, or the United Reformed, although of course their hymns are widely and deservedly sung across the Christian boundaries. Certainly it seems to me that mainstream churches should support such a course of action if they are serious in their deliberations and attempt to appeal to the 21st-century, but one suspects that they are content to let things happen.

It is interesting to ponder why certain texts and music become untouchable, accorded almost 'divine' status. They must never be altered or tampered with, and shall only be sung in a certain style. Equally so there are those previously alluded to who feel that anything 'modern' set to familiar words is not right. It is perhaps ignorance that leads people to make such assertions. I instance the Revd G R Woodward of the *Cowley Carol Book*:

> If there be any persons who dislike the old practice of pressing secular tunes into the service of the Church let them consider that, provided these tunes be of a suitable, devotional, and ecclesiastical style, there is no solid ground for their objection. How much poorer German Hymnody would have been, what a loss to the 'Church throughout the world',
>
> had our musical forefathers acted otherwise! As it was, they adopted and adapted many secular melodies.[112]

112   G.R.Woodward, *Songs of Syon*, (Schott & Co., London, 1910), Ch.3.

CHAPTER SIX

The Troublesome Hymn Duo
— Moody and Sankey

It was a Sunday morning at Islington Central, London. The congregation was small—well, it grew as we progressed. At one point there were ten or so, including two visitors from Rochdale. Before the third hymn the congregation numbered 15, and was 21 by the time an agitated soul appeared during the last hymn. There was no pianist, and no organist. A brother struck up the tunes, sometimes we wavered, at other moments displayed a strength befitting a greater number. There was one exceptional moment. That was in the singing in Methodist *Hymns and Psalms-Blessed Assurance, Jesus is mine.*

I had already solicited a warmth and blessing for choosing this hymn from the Senior Steward, for of others there was less enthusiasm. When it was sung, it seemed to be a personal telling, people's eyes fixed ahead for many knew the words and needed no book, there was a clarity, but also an inner strength. It was an odd experience that is hard to describe, almost like hearing a chant, and in the back row a sister swaying, eyes closed, a radiance of face, a smile, a conviction.

This was Moody and Sankey territory, but it seems almost spurious to talk of the song belonging anywhere, other than with those people. It rode across all the words I had been reading from musical experts with sometimes too much to say. I was being taken, almost dragged into life wombs, to hear a story, their story, their walk with the Lord. If only sometimes musical critics and compilers listened to the so—called ordinary people, and stood with them, and heard their simple but heart-felt cries. No, they didn't tell me, but somehow you knew, this black congregation had been on a journey, and they had come through, and would continue to walk all over the Devil.

The service fell in the middle of putting together this book. I was well aware that writing about the Moody and Sankey song era raises so many general issues about hymns and songs, but oh dear, thank you compilers of the *English Hymnal* for foisting upon one and all the snobbishness that often pervades the English upper classes, and supposed intelligentsia; it was done in such a delightful way. What else would one expect? I was using the guillotine in my print shop, and had much to do. A young man and his gal came into the shop, and made for the guillotine area when they spied me toiling away. Surveying me, the young man barked a fruity 'carry on'- it's the same kind of attitude that permeates the reaction of many to the music often termed Sankey.

The little material that was included in *EH* from the Moody and Sankey era falls under the title 'Not suitable for general use.' And who would want respectable and responsible people singing 'how marvellous' or 'how wonderful' about their faith or swinging in the manner of the drunken and unkempt to Gabriels' persistent refrain of *Send the Light* or building up a head of steam as they bounce along to *More About Jesus Would I Know*.

The other respectable book *Hymns Ancient and Modern* allowed people to sing *Rescue the Perishing*. It would be sung at mission services when it might be hoped that the publicans, alcoholics, drunkards, thieves and robbers and those of dubious virtue might be present but if not then an upright righteous community can sing the words and full well know who are the 'perishing'! To include such a song in conventional Sunday worship would not be worship: modest and seemly. They dropped the song in their 1950 edition.

C.S. Phillips,[113] speaking of Mission Hymns, simply asks:

> How far is this taste to be yielded to? It cannot be denied that
> to simple and uneducated minds such hymns make a great
> appeal ... the crude language and metaphors and floridly
> vulgar tunes of many early Methodist hymns, the sentimental
> catchiness of 'Moody and Sankey', the adaptation to pious
> words of popular tunes of the moment by the Salvation Army [114]
> ...

Mr Phillips views most in the pew as Philistines, and
concludes that is something unlikely to change:

> In religion as in other matters he likes to express himself in
> ways that seem rather crude to a cultivated taste. We must
> take him as we find him ... we must not refuse him a measure
> of what he likes nor bolster up our refusal by pretending that
> such hymns make him 'less of man', when he is often more of a
> man than his better educated critics ... the reader may
> remember the poignant scene in a modern novel where a
> number of miners entombed in a pit sing 'Hold The Fort', and
> the author's comment: 'Each and all realised that there are
> worse ways of going to one's death than singing a battle song
> by Moody and Sankey.'[115]

That writer's hope of musical streets paved with gold here
rests in the thought that given time most, if not all, of these
hymns will have bitten the dust, as he suggests in the late
thirties:

> The inferior specimens among the "Georgian" hymns now
> being produced are likely to be just as much a nuisance to the
> musical reformers of fifty years hence as the bad "Victorian"
> hymns are to those of today.[116]

---

113   Mr Phillips was Chaplain of the College of St.
      Nicholas, Chislehurst, formerly fellow and
      lecturer of Selwyn College, Cambridge.
114   C.S. Phillips, *Hymnody Past and Present* (SPCK,
      Poole, 1937), p.251.
115   Ibid. p.254.
116   Ibid. p.2.

Elsewhere, Dr Routley speaks of the revivalist hymn and tune as the refuge of the dispossessed, speaking of the vast numbers who knew dejection and homelessness:

> The Moody and Sankey output was placed in the context of the music hall. The words have almost the same nostalgia and yearning for heaven that is to be heard in Negro spirituals; it is only a step from *Swing Low Sweet Chariot* to *Safe in the Arms of Jesus*.

He continues:

> for what Tipperary did for soldiers who were involved in nameless and unimagined horrors in the France of 1916, *Safe in the Arms of Jesus* and *There Were Ninety and Nine* did for the industrialised peasantry of England and America.[117]

For this famous commentator it was the very beauty and serenity of English and American hymnody in the nineteenth century that

> produced by reaction the rantings of the salvationist songs; and the ranters have accomplished little more than did the poets.[118]

The one song to gain qualified praise from Routley was *There Were Ninety and Nine*, and slightly surprisingly it found its way into the 1933 *Methodist Hymn Book* but was deleted for the edition fifty years later. Hardly unexpected, since I cannot recall anyone ever choosing it for worship, although it made a good song for a soloist, as it did for Mr Sankey with his baritone voice. However, I have it on good authority that this hymn retains popularity in Scotland, perhaps because its words were written by a good Scottish woman.

On that, I cannot comment. However in sheer practical terms all this has to be set against the simple fact that certainly then, and even now, the very preciseness of English hymnody made little sense to the vast majority of people, and much was simply unintelligible. Mr Phillips suggests it is the tune that attracts the ordinary man:

---

117   Erik Routley, *Hymns and Human Life* (John Murray Publishers, London, 1952), p.238.
118   Ibid. p.240.

> The bulk of the people we have to cater for judges much more by the tune than by the words.... in the same way when a congregation sings a hymn in church with gusto it is the tune that bears them along. Many of them have only a vague idea as to what their favourite hymn is about.[119]

I would rather give people more credit, but who can deny some people sing without understanding when they are often driven in that direction by words that cannot just be read, sung and understood, there and then. Equally Mr Phillips and those of his persuasion must ask why there are so many tunes set to hymns that are themselves pedantic and uninteresting.

He does indeed question the lyrics of hymns from times past, and is not particularly favourable to Charles Wesley:

> Written to serve an immediate need they served it with acceptance; but the religious atmosphere they reflect is different from that of our day, and they have lost the power to stir men's hearts.[120]

In adopting a somewhat negative attitude toward Mr Phillips and in this instance Erik Routley, I am not then pushing for an unqualified 'yes' to Moody and Sankey material. Apart from anything else, *Sacred Songs and Solos*, whatever its musical and word evaluation, doesn't offer anywhere near a sufficient diet for regular Christian worship. American writer James Sallee says they come with two special characteristics:

> A subjective text (expressions of personal spiritual experiences) and a tune that was either of folk origin or composed in the folk idiom.[121]

The vast majority of songs in *Sacred Songs and Solos* are intended for those dreaded mission meetings envisaged by the *Ancient and Modern* hymnbook compilers, and thus have the intent of persuading people to make a public

119   Ibid. C.S Phillips p.252.
120   Ibid. C.S. Phillips p.258.
121   James Sallee, *A History of Evangelistic Hymnody*
       (Baker Book House, North America, 1978),
       p.43.

confession of faith. These were popular songs that would reach people with the personal message of salvation, and in Sankey's time they were led by a choir of several hundred. That said, this is insignificant when set against the statistic of a Rodeheaver choir that often numbered several thousand, for the singing of many of the same song catalogue. There were differences, for the Rodeheaver songs had a self-confident air to them, and were of marching triumphant nature. Others had a personal warmth.

Moody and Sankey always drew large crowds:

> 5,000 each night in Brooklyn and at their next meeting in Philadelphia, 13,000. The crowds included people from every walk of life, drunkards, cultured atheists, prominent citizens, church members: young and old, musical and nonmusical.[122]

However in the song catalogue associated with Moody and Sankey there are some songs that do work at some depth, employing reasonable liturgical and poetic symbolism. In the ensuing years we see a wider range of users for the selection found in *Sacred Songs and Solos*. Some used the book like any denominational hymnbook was used-central to worship, and in the context of a nonconformist free-ranging structure.

Henry F.Foote comments:

> The Gospel songs represent the nineteenth-century phase of that search for an utterance 'more to popular liking' than the staid hymnody of the churches. [123]

Sankey material can be sung easily by the untrained. That in itself is anathema to many who ask what right such people have to make music within the holy of holies. There is an odd perversion 'out there' that feels uneasy if there is something the untrained can cope with. It is as if some Masonic secrecy is the province of those who believe they are not so much guarding the crown jewels as a few hundred hymns that long ago should have been set aside.

122   James Sydnor, *The Hymn and Congregational Singing* (John Knox, 1960), p.66.
123   Louis F.Benson, *The English Hymns* (George H Duran & Co, London, 1915), p.483.123

In his introduction, Lyman Abbot writes that:

> Music has become the expression of the spiritual life for
> thousands who before were without voice in public worship,
> and as suppressed feeling easily dies, were often without any
> share in the public worship.[124]

There had already been several great awakenings in the
United States where music has always been important. In
early times it was the singing of hymns by Isaac Watts, and
many of his lyrics also made considerable impact in the
black community for example. The Second Great
Awakening saw even more hymn singing activity, this time
with the hymns of Charles Wesley well to the fore. By the
early mid-19th century, evangelicalism (to evolve into
Fundamentalism of one variation or another) became more
than a religious phenomenon-it had eaten its way into the
larger American culture itself. By the 1880s, the songs
popularised through Moody and Sankey campaigns
reigned supreme, although there were some groups who
remained unmoved. When people thought of gospel
hymns they thought Moody and Sankey!

Along with or emanating from their revivalist spirit in
America were countless other publications which spoke the
evangelical viewpoint, 'grace for all'. There were many who
preferred the Calvinist ideas about the wrath of God, the
conviction of sin, and the sinner as 'filthy rags' without
marrying it to ideas of faith and forgiveness. But some
joined the two together producing a powerful cocktail seen
in Moody's sermons and songs featured at his meetings.

The years 1881 to 1889 in America saw 38 publications,
and many of these were by writers whose contributions fill
the pages of *Sacred Songs and Solos*.[125] Whether it be Moody

---

124 The *Plymouth Hymnal* (Outlook Co, New York,
 1894).
125 (Morgan & Scott, London, 1877). These
 included *Precious Hymns: For Times of Refreshing
 and Revival*, and the book was was edited by
 John Sweeney and William J Kirkpatrick, who

or someone else, there was great emphasis on reaching children lest they should die without faith.

Whatever one thinks about the Moody-Sankey world, their large scale meetings of 10,000 or more people, together with huge choirs, must have been deeply moving, albeit emotional moments. They stemmed from the conviction that it was essential that all shall be saved who are called. There was a deep sense that hell awaited the unredeemed sinner.

Their work spawned future ministries such as Charles Alexander and R A Torrey, and then Homer Rodeheaver who gained fame as the song leader for Billy Sunday. The latter held their meetings in specially built temporary buildings where the floor was covered in sawdust. From this the term 'hitting the sawdust trail' became descriptive of walking down the aisle in response to the call that one should give oneself over to Jesus.

The multitude of Sankey-style music books beyond the basic 1,200 pieces, is itself witness to the fact that many found something to their taste, and within their realm of accomplishment. The nearest to that today, albeit in a different style, is the enterprising work of Roger Jones. Jones writes music that is fairly easily performed, and countless churches have played one of his growing library of works. It has occasioned considerable satisfaction, and from those I have interviewed, it seems that Jones offers people the chance to do something well in a genre previously closed to them.

As for Moody and Sankey, from the vantage point of the 1950s Routley believed these songs should not be sung without asking the question of whether they are the best instruments for achieving the same purpose as was originally their intent – namely engaging the non-Christian. (Although the evangelists did attract a veritable entourage of divines on to their platform, and Moody was commended

also combined for *On Joyful Wing: A Book of Praise and Solos.*

by many respected teachers and theologians, including Disdale Young.) He points out that the American duo directed their mission toward those whom the Anglican or Dissenting churches failed to reach:

> On the one hand, the line of division between those who approved and those who abhorred this music was drawn as cleanly as was the social line between the class that used it and the class that did not. One the other hand, wherever the 'established' church (and the orthodox Dissenting churches) felt that they must make an effort to join in the work that the Salvation Army alone was doing with consistent faithfulness, they felt that the music they must use ought to be modelled on the 'Sankey' pattern.[126]

If there had been no Moody and Sankey, where are the words that, in direct fashion, may make sense to many people? What is more apparent is that some of the intelligentsia of the hymn world merely feed themselves at their own table, regardless of the tastes of others.

Dr Routley lays down what he considers to be good music:

> It is not music that is morally uplifting-for there is no such thing. It is music which can catch and hold the attention of a cultivated musician. It may have all the qualities that enable it to catch and hold the attention of the uncultivated-attractive melody, rhythm, harmony, ease in singing, and effectiveness in performance. It need not frown at anybody. It need not be taciturn. But goodness that is musical is that which the musician can recognise. It cannot be anything else ...[127]

This is not a call for deliberate half-baked theology; merely a shout for composers and writers who can communicate beyond their own loved and respected territory. It is a call for imaginative and clear theologians to do their job and address the masses. Any would-be lyricist should study the economy of style and language employed by tabloid journalists. I soon learnt at journalism school that life is more than *The Times* and *Guardian* or *Telegraph*. There is skill

126   Erik Routley, *Twentieth Century Church Music*,
       (Herbert Jenkins, London, 1964), p.198.
127   Ibid. p.206.

in writing for, editing and subbing papers such as *The Sun* and *Mirror*.

All of these know the economy of language.

However what the question does not address is the simple fact that the songs themselves can be reinterpreted, and given a different musical emphasis. This is certainly true in the way some black gospel singers find a new statement in their reading of a hymn such as *Blessed Assurance*. To hear someone such as the gospel singer Marion Williams sing the Fanny J Crosby composition is a wondrous journey.

The blues and soul singers have made their own exploration of these songs, and with adaptation have made them their own. It is a mistake to say these songs shall only be sung by those with Christian commitment. Many who sing them may not subscribe to their theological nuances but what they do express often rests in the manner and spirit of the lyric. I would point to my own theatre production *Feel The Spirit-Moody and Sankey*, a pastiche on that time, for some intelligent musical reworkings from the Musical Director of that show, Peter Bye, that breathed new life into the music.

Another person who saw fit to 'explore and improve' was Mr Charles Cleall, who in 1961 produced *Sixty Songs from Sankey*. He was at the time organist of the then famous St Paul's Church, Portman Square, London. While some would applaud his interest, not all would approve of the language he employed. He described the Sankey catalogue as 'nursery' songs, songs of pre-conversion, although their language is anything but. Routley is quoted saying:

> To seek milk, when we ought to be digesting stronger meat, is the mark of carnality; of self-gratification; of a determination .... like that of Peter Pan, not to grow up. [128]

Routley commenting on the efforts of Mr Cleall says:

---

128   Erik Routley, *Twentieth Century Church Music*,
(Barrie & Jenkins, 1964), p.204-5.

> Mr Cleall does rightly in giving his 'Sankeys' a heightened intellectual content - in making them worth singing by musicians, worth attending to and at the same time in admitting that they serve a transient purpose and that childish things should soon be put away.[129]

Somewhat fatuously he remarks that neither Moody and Sankey nor General Booth and his army could prevent the tragedy of secularism, and lost faith, so evident in Western civilization. Some hymn writers have achieved this, and there is something positive in saying that much of the Moody-Sankey material did for a while provide songs for everyone to whistle and sing, believers or not. He does not really address why they are so popular, for it isn't really 'on' to indirectly suggest that the great mass of people are so illiterate that all they can stomach is the Sankey style. People want to feel their hearts stirred within.

I am sure he is right in suggesting that the writers of this period did not set out to raise or improve either musical or poetic standards. I doubt if the great Charles Wesley placed this at the top of his agenda. What they did have was an ear to their period's popular, and sometimes vulgar, music, and like the early days of the Salvation Army they took the familiar, and gave it a gospel twist. It was here in Britain that the term 'singing the gospel' first gained usage, and before the arrival of Sankey it was unknown to describe someone as a 'singing evangelist'.

It was also novel that a preacher had an associate to take charge of the music. A friend of the duo, George Stebbins would write of Sankey:

> He brought the service of song in evangelistic movements to the front in so striking a manner, demonstrating its importance as an aid in enforcing the claims of the Gospel upon this world .... and establishing the custom of evangelists

129   Ibid. p.207.

going out two by two, preacher and singer, preaching the
Word in sermon and song.[130]

In my initial preaching forays as a teenager in the late 1950s,
people in Cornwall would sometimes ask if I was bringing a
singer with me, or was I singing some solos.

The texts of their collection might not touch the high level
of culture and literacy found in many early American
hymns, but does everything grind to a meaningless halt
because it fails to meet such a criterion? In any case many
supposedly intelligent people like to mix high and very low.
In my late teens I sold newspapers to those who were
catching the Scillonian ferry from Penzance to the Isles of
Scilly, and noted in September, when the more affluent
arrived free from the invading hordes in July and August,
these educated ones would buy *The Times* and slip a copy of
the *Daily Mirror* in between its pages!

It would be hard to argue against Erik Routley's musical
dissection of Sankey music - it does not possess much
sophistication, the tunes do have a general similarity and
style, and there is sometimes an extreme naivety of rhythm,
harmony and melody. The vocabulary is often a limited
series of clichés, and they demand little. But even Norman
Goldhawk doesn't deny that some of these hymns possess a
warmth which many greater hymns and tunes lack. His
major criticism rests in saying the Sankey material arouses
emotions that bypass mental effort, and this frequently
becomes an end in itself rather than a motive for action. He
acknowledges they have their part, and role, in the faith of
many people, and is willing to go along with this provided
they are not over-used, or confused with the great
evangelical hymns.

It is beyond argument that many of them over emphasize
individual salvation, but that has to be offset against other
remarks by Routley about of the sprawling lost city souls. At
one time in his life Moody was one of them, journeying from

130   George C Stebbins, *Reminiscences and Gospel
       Hymn Stories pp.206-7* (George H. Duran, New
       York, 1924).

a relatively rural area to the hardships and squalor of a city like Chicago. What he knew for himself, and would find crying out from others, was the yearning for self-affirmation, and that from the badly paid exploited workers of the time who had gone to the City expecting to find streets paved with gold. Liquor and prostitution were always near.

Writing in the early 1950s, Routley managed to add a general comment on the Moody and Sankey era, which seems to summarise much of what he feels toward the M and S fan club:

> Their home is in the rallies of the Salvation Army and in the women's and men's meetings, Pleasant Sunday afternoons, and weeknight missions of the churches.[131]

Yet he was also to write: some of us have poked fun at the trite jingles of the Sankey revival. But trapped miners have sung, *Hold the Fort*, and who knows how many people have calmed elemental fears of death with *Shall We Gather at the River?* and beaten off the growing fear of hunger and insecurity and dispossession with *Will Your Anchor Hold.*[132]

Much of the material that is found in *Sacred Songs and Solos*, the 1200 edition is characterised by its rudimentary harmonies, the use of chorus, the varied metric schemes, and the motor rhythms. The writers of *American Hymns Old and New* in their chapter 'Revival and Gospel Hymns' focus on the song *Shall We Gather At The River*, speaking of its march-like movement as especially typical:

> the device of letting the lower parts echo rhythmically a motive announced by the sopranos became a mannerism which was abused by later writers (see the chorus of *There's A Land That Is Fairer Than Day*) ... the gospel hymn developed its own manner of performance ... the best of the gospel hymns have a direct simplicity which has appealed to singers ever since the first gospel hymnals ... their enormous popularity stimulated a voluminous production of imitations which

131   Ibid. op.cit, p.241.
132   Erik Routley, *Hymns and Human Life*, (John Murray Publishers, London, 1952) p 152.

continues to the present day, especially in the Southern states.[133]

The song itself is very much part of the Moody-Sankey story. Moody had determined he would find a singer to accompany his mission work. He had heard of the singing appeal of Ira D Sankey, and during a YMCA Convention he asked Sankey to meet him on a street corner. When Sankey arrived he found a crowd of people already assembled. He was asked to stand and sing on a provided box, which he did. He was challenged by Mr Moody to obey what he knew was the will of God that this man should join him. In receiving the affirmative from the former Inland Revenue officer, the two, followed by the crowd marched off singing *Shall We Gather At The River*.

Sankey simply gathered together much of what seemed the best evangelistic hymnody of the time, occasionally working with different writers. For some of it he wrote tunes, and the occasional lyric, but overall he was a collector. In my book *Moody and Sankey-Feel The Spirit* (Jasperian Publishing, 1994) I attempted to collate the Sankey involvement. I discovered that he wrote the words and music for *Home At Last, Thy Labour Done* a hymn that is found in the 750-piece edition, but not the 1200. His *Not Far, Not Far From The Kingdom* is in the 750 and 1200. I found musical compositions numbering 99 of which seven were arrangements, the best-known being one with C.C. Converse for *Hark, Hark, My Soul*. In a sense the huge output of writers at the time resembled the New York pop scene of the 1950s and 60s where there were people employed to write melodies for the hits of tomorrow. Like most areas of life, if someone found a style that generated a hit, then before the following day's dawn there would be a plethora of new songs in that same successful idiom.

Routley embellishes some of his comments from his own despair at the popularity of the Sankey song. They did have

133   Carleton Sprague Smith, *American Hymns Old and New* (New York: Columbia University Press, 1980), p.364-6.

an appeal to the poor and less well educated but it flies against all recorded evidence to say that the Moody campaign meetings in Britain were attended by only those of what might be called the 'lower strata' of society. His meetings were fashionable, and attracted crowds in excess of 10,000 at the nightly gatherings throughout Britain. The hearers were drawn not only from those who would be described as dejected and homeless but also from the whole spectrum of Victorian society. His platform was often filled with some of the then mighty divines.

Ira Sankey in his autobiography writes of the occasion when the hymn *Almost Persuaded* was sung in the Agricultural Hall, London, 1874, the refrain of which goes:

> *Almost persuaded now to believe;*
> *Almost persuaded Christ to receive.*

The Right Hon. W.E. Gladstone was present. At the close of the meeting Mr Moody asked the congregation to bow their heads, while Mr Sankey sang this song by P.P. Bliss. Sankey says the stillness of death prevailed throughout the audience of over 15,000, as souls were making their decisions for Christ. It seems Mr Gladstone stayed put.

Sankey says in his book he was persuaded by writers from beyond the American constituency, and he had a taste for the songs of Charles Wesley with *Behold The Man* one of his most favoured (the title given to Wesley's *Arise, My Soul, Arise*). Of his own catalogue, and in naming his favourite hymns, he chose his music written for *Beneath the Cross of Jesus* by Elizabeth Clephane.

Less well known, but always attracting much interest from its inclusion in my William and Catherine Booth musical (it was sung at Catherine's funeral) is his rather fetching music to Sarah Doudney's, *Sleep On, Beloved*. It's the kind of song I would imagine being performed by an eclectic folk-ish band of yesteryear, *The Incredible String Band*. Sankey also favoured the music hall inspired song *Where Is My Wandering Boy Tonight* with words and music by Robert Lowry. He says the singing of this song brought back many wandering boys (in his time many boys either had no real home or left their homes). Of Lowry, Sankey writes:

> Dr Lowry will continue to preach the Gospel in his hymns long after his sermons have been forgotten. Many of his hymns were written after the Sunday evening service when his mind refused to rest.[134]

When I bring to mind the songs of Lowry that have survived, I think of *I Hear Thy Welcome Voice, I Need Thee Every Hour*, and for Sankey followers, *Shall We Gather at the River*. The first two are often sung by Cornish and Welsh male voice choirs-something of which I doubt hymn compilers have the slightest awareness.

The most interesting source of hymns from this 19th-century period is Ian Bradley's *Hymns* for Penguin Books in 1989. Bradley takes the reader through the best-known hymns in the English language. Bradley has 69 hymns from the 19th century, and among them Moody-Sankey associated titles such as the already mentioned *Blessed Assurance*, and others such as *Will Your Anchor Hold, What A Friend We Have In Jesus*. He also lists *Shall We Gather at the River*, and admits this is a matter of personal preference, adding, 'I find this Gospel song one of the best and most moving of its kind.'[135]

His choice of *Ho, My Comrades* was equally if not more surprising. He instances the hymn writer and poet John Greenleaf Whittier's stated distaste for its vulgarity. To Bradley, it is the supreme example of its genre, 'with all the faults as well as the strengths to be found in the gospel songs of 19th century America'. Bradley finds it uplifting and stirring:

> At a time when many inferior modern choruses are heard increasingly frequently in churches, it seems a pity that such tired and proven old favourites are not also being given an airing. No one would claim it is great poetry or great music, but it has a genuine simplicity.

134   Ira Sankey, *My Life and Sacred Songs* (Hodder & Stoughton/Morgan & Scott, 1906) p.287.
135   Ian Bradley, *Hymns* (Penguin, London, 1989) p.358

Britain provided the actual birthplace of the first collections. It was during the mission to Newcastle that the need became paramount. Until this moment, in the early 1870s the duo had made much use of the book *Hallowed Songs* from Philip Phillips. Initially Sankey thought he might republish the Phillips collection with a few additions, but he was turned down by the publisher.

The need became so pressing that Moody arranged with the British publishing house Marshall, Morgan and Scott to pay for a pamphlet of 16 songs. It would be called *Sacred Songs and Solos*. It sold at 6p a copy. It was used at services alongside the 'Phillip' volume. New songs were added, a words-only edition was published and the first advertisement for the new volume appeared in *The Christian* of September 18, 1873. It proved an embarrassing success, it sold so well, and detractors of the two Americans soon shouted aloud that it was all a money making racket.

Meanwhile in America, P.P. Bliss had brought out *Gospel Songs*, with the majority of its content self-penned.

Moody thought he might find success by working with Bliss, and so published *Gospel Hymns and Sacred Songs*. There were six gradually expanding editions, as new songs kept appearing. Eventually this led to the first edition of *Sacred Songs and Solos* containing 441 songs. The next edition had 750, and soon there was the 888 edition, until the 1200 became the last of this ever-growing catalogue of Christian songs. The latter far more than the others resembled a conventional style hymnbook, and if it had a revivalist air there was nonetheless place for historic hymns.

The hymns of Bliss were striking and dramatic. They were destined for popularity, and of his work the most used today across the wide Christian spectrum is arguably *Man of Sorrows, What A Name!* Mr Hugh Branwell, organist at Chapel Street Methodist, Penzance, a strong Wesleyan, during his 30 year reign, would never allow a chorus hymn to be played. But every Good Friday, there would be featured this Bliss hymn-it was the one Bliss hymn that had music to arouse interest.

The various editions seemed to have their own appeal with the 441 collection suggesting Moody and Sankey's desire to reach Scottish followers by including a number of *Psalms and Paraphrases*. One thing was sure, and it lay in the frequent use of an American tune, rather than one that may be enjoined by Christians elsewhere. Sankey worked with a number of writers beyond Bliss, to include the prolific George C. Stebbins and Charles H. Gabriel. The most famous 1200 collection seems to have been an attempt to gain general acceptance.

It is only now in Britain with the prolific output of what is often termed praise music that we are seeing a new avalanche of material. Much of this, as with the missions of the evangelists named, also stems from events, such as Stoneleigh, Keswick and Spring Harvest. There are now distinct record labels issuing month-by-month new songs, and some of these arise out of worship bands. This avalanche has also produced such books as those often mentioned in this text, *Songs of Fellowship* and *Mission Praise*.

The Moody and Sankey material, and the songs emanating from the Alexander crusades of the early 20th century were songs of the time, the music hall in particular; they were heard on the streets and in public houses. Of course it is the case that in those days there were not the endless radio stations, I-Pods, stereo systems producing music at the touch of a switch. In other words religious material of any kind had an advantage over modern times, it was in a receptive marketplace. Argument will continue as to the use of material from *Sacred Songs and Solos*, and similar books, pre-eminently the two that have already received reference, namely *Golden Bells*, and *Alexander's Hymns No.3*.

Peter O.Hughes, a British Methodist minister, speaks of fresh interest in this genre:

> The recent rediscovery of Moody and Sankey has been an interesting theological exercise, but I am not sure that we would want to reinstate too much of their material into worship as a regular feature. Research into the melodies sung

by Wesley's converts might be a more interesting and wholesome exercise.[136]

However, even within the Sankey camp there is choice being made, and much of the 1200 is not sung.

Few people these days wish to sing:

> Oh, the dear ones in glory
> How they beckon me to come (969 *I Shall Know Him*).

The greater bulk of songs of this nature fall under the umbrella of Aspirations after Heaven, Heaven Anticipated, The Redeemed in Heaven, and Death and Resurrection, which in *Sacred Songs and Solos* can take us from 907 to 1046, an extraordinary plethora of hymns, and in the mere number there is commentary as to where much Christian teaching and biblical emphasis lay in the 19th century. It might even be said that we have foolishly lost the sense of heaven and eternity, and in general terms prefer the search for everlasting youth.

And beyond these obvious classifications there are many other hymns that speak of the ultimate rest, some found in the section 'Comfort In Sorrow.' One instance is *On The Mountain's Top* (734) with its third verse:

> Enemies no more shall trouble,
> All thy wrongs shall be redressed;
> For thy shame thou shalt have double,
> All thy Maker's favour blessed:
> All thy conflicts
> End in everlasting rest.

It might be asked where the two for one idea comes from!

These hymns associated with the gospel period and beyond (many of the songs were featured in the Billy Graham campaigns) appear less in British-Australian-New Zealand denominational collections. For a much higher use, you can turn to *Golden Bells*, *Redemption Hymnal* and the various editions of the

---

136   Peter Hughes, *Music in Methodism, Theology Reflects on the Arts*, (Epworth Review, Volume 22, No.3, September 1995) p.17.

Salvation Army Songbook, but every now and then an unexpected source brings a song from Sacred Songs and Solos back into prominence as for example when the popular Irish singer Enya recorded My Life Flow On In Endless Song. The song also appears in Common Ground, a publication of the 21st century. My own research of mainline hymn books suggests an inclusion of material far beyond the few titles that Routley uses in Hymns and Human Life. The Baptist Hymnbook of 1998 includes 45 titles (and I am not including traditional hymns found in Sacred Songs and Solos, as for instance All People That On Earth Do Dwell). Hymns of Faith published by Scripture Union in 1964 has 40 and the 1973 Church Hymnary of the more solid Presbyterian included 17. Hymns for Today's Church, 1982, has seven, and Mission Praise 1983, 21. Alexander's from the early part of the 20th century has 103, so Routley may have a point - they are sung far less. The 1933 Methodist book includes 45 and its successor Hymns and Psalms has only 15, again using statistics to make his point.

The songs from Sacred Songs and Solos will lose their power to hold as they are deleted from these current collections. A few will remain in the general consciousness. Mission Praise has brought the attention of many to the existence of this kind of material. Some good songs will be lost, and inevitably those who compile new works for singing may be unfamiliar with the contents of a songbook that has exercised such influence. As with most things, there will always be 'outposts' where the genre is found, most noticeably in Cornwall, South Wales and the West Midlands. However, the majority of church-going people have only a smattering of awareness of its existence. It is largely confined to those areas of the country to which I have already alluded, and largely to those over 70. Should this rather simple analysis possess some truth, it cannot be denied that the age of most of its supporters leaves doubt for its continuance as a musical form. This state of affairs will be welcomed by some, but if so, they should also take on board the simple fact that much of their own world is passing into neglect.

Chapter 8 takes me into gospel, blues, jazz and folk, where I do at some points drift from hymns, but it also leads me into a different worship and 'meeting' territory that isn't dictated by a choice of hymns, or by a poor pianist or organist. It offers the distinct and welcome possibility where people can forget about singing hymns from a book or screen, and simply savour the richness of another's experience of faith with some possibilities of singing along! This will come through DVD or CD, where the demand is for a good sound system.

CHAPTER SEVEN

Hymns for Children and
Young People
(or perhaps not)

Nothing taxes some Christians more than how they can engage with the young. Within the realm of hymnody there is much that is counter productive. Until fairly recently, hymn/songbooks, whether for general church use with a children's section, or those aimed solely at the young, have exhibited an overriding obsession with making young people enjoy what adults consider to be good. Songs and hymns were nothing more than a disguised teaching arena, paying little heed to the natural maturation of a child, and devoid of youth cultural reference.

John Wesley in his preface to his *Hymnbook for Children* (1790) said there were two ways of speaking to children, the one 'to let ourselves down to them, the other to lift them up to us'.

John's prolific lyric writing brother Charles published in 1763 *Hymns for Children* which included: *Gentle Jesus, Meek and Mild*. A somewhat less than astonishing book of the previous year *Short Hymns and Scriptural Passages* had an almost unbelievable 2,030 new compositions.

The great hymnist Isaac Watts could both let children sing the message, and then in another hymn, offer a good flogging:

> Christ is your own Master,
> He is good and true,
> And his little children
> Must be holy too *(Alexander 589)*

> There is a dreadful hell,
> And everlasting pains;
> There sinners must with devils dwell
> In darkness, fire, and chains, (*Divine Songs,* 1715)

Watts[137] would have children reproving themselves:

> But children you should never let
> Such angry passions rise;
> Your little hands were never made
> To tear each other's eyes.

In a modern context Watts would be suggesting to some teenagers that gun culture is not a good way to live your life. Julian's massive *Dictionary of Hymnology* reminds us that special hymns for children in public worship (whatever the style of their content) were virtually absent until the 18th century. Upon the establishment of Sunday Schools the need for special books became apparent. One of the earliest sources that I have found is most engaging: I find no parallel amongst British denominational hymn books to rival *The Sabbath School Bell* (1859). This was America's first popular Sunday School book. There is a preoccupation with the death of children, and this would have been a taxing subject for anyone young considering the statistics for premature death at this time. Even so it seems amazing that children would sing such words as:

> Little Willie's gone to Heaven: Praise the Lord!
> All his sins have been forgiven: Praise the Lord!

This comes with a truly delightful chorus:

> Joyful let your voices rise
> Do not come with tearful eyes,
> Willie's dwelling in the skies,
> Willie's gone to Heaven!

Girls had something more garish:

> Little Ella's an angel in the skies
> Sing, merrily sing

137   In his *Divine & Moral Songs for the Use of
      Children* (Religious Tract Society, London,
      1715).

> Come brother and sister, cease your sighs,
> Sing merrily sing
> Let the chorus joyful ring!
> Ella's an angel in the skies.
> Sing merrily sing.

On the other hand there is William Cowper's:

> We feel for your unhappy state
> (May you regard it too)
> And would a while ourselves forget,
> To pour our prayer for you.[138]

My journey through numerous collections of hymns and songs for children induces nausea. Most hymns and songs for children, and most markedly for 13-17-year olds are hopelessly tasteless. So many are condescending and patronising. I do not detect church members or teachers rising up in protest against the drivel that still adorns books for the young.

My overall feeling may sound over dramatic, but whatever view is held, few doubt there has always been a problem when it comes to providing material for young people.

Norman Goldhawk, prominent for many years in Methodist music circles, and once a university lecturer in Church History, writes of this being the subject of debate for over fifty years:

> Children's sections, which appeared in most denominational hymnals, are now generally out of favour. Many no longer like the wistful style of hymn writing, with its endearing epithets, which they contained. It is claimed that most of the hymns assume a background of a heavenly realm 'above the bright blue sky', which is misleading and unnatural to children. Others are not so sure, agreeing with C.S. Lewis that 'the huge dome of the sky is of all things sensuously perceived most like infinity, and that when God made space and worlds that move

---

138   *Olney Hymns 11*, (John Newton & William
Cooper, London, 1779), xi, v.4.

in space, and clothed the world with air, and gave us eyes and imagination, he knew what the sky would mean to us'.[139]

The Methodist *Hymns and Psalms* removed the children's section in their 1983 collection, and scattered about the book can be found children's favourites like *Tell Me The Stories of Jesus* and *Children of Jerusalem*. The same process is enacted in *The English Hymnal* (1986). In the 1906 publication there can be found a list of hymns deemed suitable for children. *Church Hymnary: Third Edition* (1988) also follows the same process.

Times of course change, and the world of children of today bears no resemblance to that of the 1950s. Prevailing social mores and behavioural patterns are drastically different. At one time you could serve up the 'dear little children' innocence, or at least impose a discipline in which hymns would be sung whether any young person liked them or not. It would be the case of endure rather than enjoy such lines as:

> Make us bright as silver;
> Make us good as gold;
> Warm as the summer roses
> Let our hearts unfold. (*Songs of Praise* 354, v.5)

– and –

> 0 once in a while
> We obey with a smile
> And are ever so modest and prudent,
> But it's not very long
> Before something is wrong,
> And somebody's done what he shouldn't

To make the point even more children sing in the next verse of how the animals are so good, even the flowers, and if they are, why not boys and girls?

> In meadows and wood
> The cattle are good

139   Norman Goldhawk, *On Hymns and hymn books*, (The Epworth Press, Norwich, 1979), Ibid. p.116. The Lewis reference comes from *Miracles* (The Centenary Press, 1947), p.189.

And the rabbits are thinking no evil;
The anemones white
Are refined and polite
And all the primroses are civil.

In the third verse the heavenly schoolmaster looks down, not with threats or cane, but with the magic remedy to make all boys and girls welcome to every adult who passes their way, a 'pride and joy' no doubt to their mothers:

O Saviour, look down
When we sulk or we frown
And smooth into kindness our quarrel;
Till our heart is as light
As a little bird's flight
And our life is as free as a squirrel![140]

Erik Routley instances these words in his book *Hymns and Human Life*, and the chapter on 'Youth and Hymns', and says it is perhaps the only example in all of the literature of a hymn that intentionally uses humour. On that, he could have fooled me! It is funny, if not tragic, and I cannot conceive that the compilers of *The Church and Schools Hymnal* imagined that school assemblies would roll with genuine laughter at being asked to sing it. Certainly, if my experience is anything to go by, humour is rarely present at a school assembly, or at least, not intentionally so from the headmaster's viewpoint. There was at one time a hit *007* from Desmond Dekker, and some school wag arranged the hymn board with those numbers, duly announced by a serious minded Head, and to be greeted with much merriment, of which and for which he saw no reason. Conversely, children could be made mild and obedient by letting them feel a little moral superiority as to who has right on their side:

Have you seen our badges new?
Pure white ribbons!
Don't you want to wear one too?

---

140   *The Church and Schools Hymnal*, 277
(SPCK/Seeley Service & Co./The National
Society, date unknown).

> Pure white ribbons!
> They are emblems of a band
> That is working hand in hand,
> And for temperance they stand,
> Pure white ribbons![141]

Music historian Norman Goldhawk says:

> The general principle between this and kindred books [he is referring to *With Cheerful Voice: Hymns for Children* A&C Black, 1969] is that the subjects of the hymns and songs should be firmly within the actual experience of the children themselves, which means, of course, what adults imagine that experience to be.[142]

He might have instanced:

> I love to think, though I am young
> My Saviour was a child;
> That Jesus walked this earth along
> With feet all undefiled.

711 Congregational Hymnary.

As Norman Goldhawk mentioned, most denominational hymn books have a 'children's section' containing hymns which could have been listed under different sections. *Congregational Hymnary's* section 'For Children and Young People' ran from number 707 to 756, with seven other suggestions. The composition of the selection committee carries its own story, ten clergymen, one lay person and a male chair. Not a woman in sight. Its successor *Congregational Praise* (1951) ran its children's section on a slightly lower input, with hymns encompassing a stretch from numbers 683 to 705, with a later index to the general hymns with suggestions for hymns within the experience of young people. This time its committee ran to six male clergy, four laymen and one woman, with a male chair and

---

141   Rodeheaver, *Songs for Service*, USA, (19th
       century/early 20th.) Children's Section, No. 189.

142   Norman Goldhawk *On Hymns and hymn books*,
       (The Epworth Press, Norwich, 1979).

---

editorial secretary; both clergy. It is salutary to note that of the 23 hymns, 17 mention animals or nature, none refer to the city, flats, shops, buses, trains, sport, clothes, even sea and ships, and so forth. Doubtless the country chapel child would feel fairly relaxed; hardly so the city child.

Wesley's words at the outset of this chapter are instanced in the Preface to *The Church and Schools Hymnal,* an undated book, but in small type format it mentions a cost of sixpence, in larger it is 1s 6d and in cloth with white edges it would set the purchaser back by 8s 6d. I learn later the date is 1926; the year of the General Strike. The introduction makes a bold claim for the editors:

> They have attempted to compile a book of which words will be quite suitable on children's lips, pandering neither to precocity nor to unreality. Many hymns for children have hitherto been self-centred or sentimental, or full of unreality.[143]

So, you can see, my strictures of a few moments ago were seen a long time before I arrived! Did they really believe children might sing:

> Come to this happy land,
> Come, come away!
> Why will ye doubting stand?
> Why still delay?
> O we shall happy be,
> When, from sin and sorrow free,
> Lord, we shall live with Thee,
> Blest, blest for aye! (205)

Naturally it has elements that run with a time when sixpence bought something, and child mortality in poorer households could easily be 50-60 per cent of live births. So, of course, lyrics express the general church desire to reach the un-Christian:

> Trumpet of God, sound high,
> Till the hearts of the heathen shake (119)

– or –

---

143   *The Church and Schools Hymnal* (SPCK/Seeley
       Service & Co/The National Society).

> Little lips Thou hast made
> 'Neath the far-off temple's shade
> Give to gods of wood and stone
> Praise that should be all Thine own. (118 v2)

There is an intriguing song maybe intended for children attending boarding school or those occupying stately homes, *The Martyr First*:

> A noble army, men and boys,
> The matron and the maid,
> Around the Saviour's throne rejoice,
> In robes of light arrayed. (79)

Even heaven it seems has its upstairs and downstairs!

Interestingly, and commendably, the committee was keen to secure a good melody, bold and simple; for, as they said, seldom would they be sung in four-part harmony, 'more's the pity'. The pitch was kept within a moderate compass. With due gravity, a nod and a wink, the introduction stressed that 'a few tunes of lesser worth have been admitted,' but lest they be seen as snobbish they would add how difficult it was to draw a 'hard and fast line between those which are worthy, and those which are not'.

While British Methodists at the beginning of the 1980s argued about inclusion of the National Anthem, here, in 1926, the year of the General Strike and social unrest, the national song is firmly placed in their hymnbook's content, at number 124 of a 338 selection. There is *And Did Those Feet In Ancient Time*, and most interestingly *England, Arise! The Long, Long Night Is Over* with its last verse beginning:

> Forth then, ye heroes, patriots and lovers!
> Comrades of danger, poverty, and scorn!

... and also containing a line or two that might have been used when referring to the England football team on the eve of their World Cup adventure.

> Giants refreshed in joy's new rising morn

to end with:

> and the day is here.

But then it wasn't, unless it was seen as the day of judgement on over-paid football players. There are 12 hymns in the National section. Number 261 is an interesting hymn, in so far as it espouses one brand of baptismal teaching:

> I was made a Christian
> When my name was given,
> One of God's dear children,
> And an heir of heaven,
> In the name of Christian
> I will glory now,
> Ever more remember
> My baptismal vows

In the past major public schools issued their own hymnbook for use in weekday worship. There was also a general Public School hymnbook. The Methodist Church with its own educational establishments issued several hymn books for young people. These appear largely similar to their mainstream church parent, but soothingly free from hymns on death, well disposed to lyrics stressing public service and a rightful giving to the community. One of Methodism's past greats, Rupert E. Davies, sees it this way:

> We must have a different hymnbook for children and for adults; in the former we may not limit our hymns to those which express the actual experience of those who sing them, for one of the purposes of the book (*The School Hymnbook of the Methodist Church*) is to lead children to a deeper and higher experience, but equally we may not include in it hymns which are so far beyond a child's range that the words become meaningless jargon.[144]

Fair enough - the sentiments, yet somewhat unsatisfactory. This growth of spiritual perception will only gain lasting worth if it is rooted in the world in which the child lives. Mr Davies later says that the compilers of the *School Book* set out to present the best hymns of the best, which if I may add seems not a million miles from many a general hymnbook:

> ... meaning by the past the whole period from the beginning of Christianity until the middle of the nineteenth century, with

---

144   Rupert E. Davies, *Making Melody, Introducing the School Hymnbook of the Methodist Church* (Methodist Youth Department, 1950), p.26.

special emphasis on the great period of English hymn-writing during the Methodist Revival. We have added to these the hymns written since then which either possess the elements of greatness or for other reasons are inspiring, moving, or truly devotional. [145]

There is little in the material, erudite as it may be, in *Making Melody*, that conveys any sense of what it was to be young. You might well say the late 1940s and early 1950s still saw youth waiting to be fed scraps at the tables of more knowledgeable adults. Of course I am judging it from the perspective of half a century later. There is an overriding impression that too many writers were writing their thoughts and mini-sermons to instruct. It is not easy to imagine people singing:

> When the mothers who had brought them
> Heard men say:
> 'Tis no place for little children;
> Go away!'
> They were sorry; but their sorrow
> Soon was gone;
> For He raised His hands and blessed them
> Every one. (594)

It beggars belief that someone would think hearty noisy boys would sing without embarrassment:

> God make my life a little flower
> That giveth joy to all,
> Content to bloom in native bower,
> Although the place be small. (305)

Next to that hymn is another epic:

> Oh, what can little lips do
> To please the king of heaven (306)

And who in their right mind can ask young boys and girls to sing Francis Xavier's:

> My God, I love Thee, not because
> I hope for heaven thereby

---

145   Ibid. p.27.

> Nor yet because who love Thee not
> Are lost eternally (146)

At least I applaud the section that commences on page 31 entitled 'Traditional Melodies and Folk Songs' with tunes from Switzerland, France, Germany, India, and the wealth of English traditional airs, tunes collected by folk's legendary Cecil Sharp, Irish airs and folk-songs, Scottish airs, Welsh airs, and even three tunes from the Isle of Man, to ensure that the Manx Fisherman's Evening Hymn is not the sole representative. Should this collection be by the bedside of certain current Western leaders they must sing 321 nightly:

> Great nations still enchained
> Whose freedom must be gained;
> Great causes to be won
> Through daring deeds well done

Naturally there is a desire among some to ensure young people 'get' the message. Just in case they do not hear it, they can sing it, assuming of course they even notice what it is they sing. One instance is Michael Baughen's *All Scriptures Are Given By The Breath of God*:

> All Scriptures are given by the breath of God,
> Are inspired of God
> Are the Word of the Lord!
> All Scriptures are given by the breath of God,
> And glorify His Name! (*Youth Praise* 87)

Those, and many others, fuel my ever increasing despair that many of the songs help people to run away from what they see as a half-baked sentimental faith, where Jesus is seen as simply kind and good. It's also interesting to get a feel for the time from the general headings used. Sometimes a seemingly odd entry, e.g. *Were You There When they Crucified my Lord?* appears under World Missions.

Trawling through this book there is nothing to suggest that its compilers related religion to life other than in its National section. There is a hymn that refers to 'dusty city streets', and a few hymns with anger (such as *When Wilt Thou Save The People*) but these are exceptions to what is basically a book little different from any adult hymnbook. The real world is absent. On a more positive note it does, for the most part, avoid the trite. But would anyone know by reading through its contents that at the time of writing there was considerable turbulence in the world, let alone strife and unrest in Britain?

However *Making Melody* can be set against a remarkable book of its time, *The Youth Sing Book*, edited by Sid G.Hedges, and published in 1953. It has two sections: hymns, and general songs. I feel myself instinctively reaching for the poisoned pen; to me such division is a complete negation of what the Incarnation is about. However, this was the early 1950s and it was a fairly brave move to even put both within the same book cover. The intent of the book lies in providing material that might be sung at religious and general events. Mr Hedges describes things as follows:

> There are many occasions in adolescent life when singing fits in: the rollicking informality of singing songs when flippant fun songs come most easily; the quieter time with songs that go much deeper, and those still more potent hours when great hymns take hold. All such needs could be met in part from many sources in many books. What seemed lacking was a single book to cover it all. [146]

Hedges displays a considerable acumen in including material in other languages than English, and so almost from the start we can sing the great hymn of the centuries *All People That On Earth Do Dwell* in French or English. His listing of 'help' aids in the book's compiling is in itself a minor social commentary on the times, and makes a pertinent commentary if one was to compare the 1950s and the present day. The text instances:

> National Association of Boys' Clubs, National Association of Girls' Clubs and Mixed Clubs, National Federation of Young Farmers' Clubs, National Sunday School Union and Christian Youth Service, Co-operative Youth Movement, Youth Hostels Association, Methodist Association of Youth Clubs. [147]

146   Sid Hedges, *The Youth Sing Book*, (Pilgrim, 1953), p.4.
147   Ibid. p.4.

Socially too, it was still a period when adults scrambled for the youth allegiance by providing endless places and events for their interest, and not surprisingly the Hedges collection has some emphasis upon living a clean life, respect for authority, and a willingness to serve Queen and country. There is also the desire for young people to experience some pride at belonging to Sunday School. Hedges contributes his own hymn:

> We all unite to hail
> Our Sunday School;
> 'gainst time it does prevail,
> Our Sunday School.
> Striving with steadfast aim,
> Bearing their Master's name,
> Great souls have built its fame
> Our Sunday school.

He gives everything a wider context in his second and last verse:

> We in turn will serve
> Our Sunday School;
> From sloth and ease preserve
> Our Sunday School;

and then the wider brief:

> Our town's most happy throng,
> It's work shall be our song.[148]

Hedges certainly casts his net wide, for in the Hymns section he includes Byrd's canon *Non Nobis, Domine* and the exquisite *Sanctus of Clement*, written sometime toward the middle of the 16th century. Surprising choices perhaps when considering the target audience but in contemporary material there is little to excite. The major plus factors come with the inclusion of a number of Negro spirituals, and indeed oddly, or perhaps planted on purpose, even in the general song section, where can be found the attractive *Jacob's Ladder*. In its Christmas section carols rather than hymns find place, and unlike virtually any of the

148   Ibid. p.166.

denominational hymn books, we have such titles as *The First Good Joy That Mary Had*, *Good King Wenceslas*, *We Three Kings*, *I Saw Three Ships*, *In That Poor Stable*, the neglected French Carol, *On This Day*, *Ding Dong Merrily On High*, *The Holly and the Ivy*, the poignant and beautiful *Coventry Carol*, *Lully Lullay*, and *Masters in this Hall*. All made for singing and celebration, unlike many traditional hymns that otherwise fill the allotted section.

A number of general publishing houses both here and in America have attempted to make inroads into the young person's market, and not always with the best of titles such as *Songs for Little People*. This American publication professed a unique plan, including songs for every day, and songs for Sunday, songs of one stanza for the 'wee' ones, and songs for the older members of the class. The verses are described as simple, childlike, and poetic. To take one song *The Alder by the River*:

> The alder by the river
> Shakes out her powdery curls,
> The willow buds in silver
> For little boys and girls.
> The little birds fly over,
> And oh, how sweet they sing!
> To tell the happy children
> That once again 'tis spring.
> Who is it brings the flowers,
> Adorning earth anew?
> 'Tis God, oh happy children,
> He makes them all for you.
> He makes them all for you.

Some of the children's hymns are distinctly odd. This is the lyric for *Our Singing March*.

> Once again with singing
> March the children's feet

> Happy voices ringing
> All in music sweet[149]

It has some point if children are singing about other children, but would they sing these lines about themselves? In this style there is nothing unusual, adults putting words into the mouths of the young, but never writing words the young might feel comfortable singing.

Quite valuable for its scarcity is *Songs for Service* with two well known names of revival and general evangelistic musical circles, Homer A. Rodeheaver and Charles H. Gabriel, responsible for contents partly aimed at the Sunday School. Much of the fare is familiar to *Golden Bells* or *Sacred Songs and Solos*, most of the material is raw and catchy, such as Gabriel's own music to *Send The Light*, but quite what is specific to those of Sunday School age is not easy to see, although there was until fairly recently a Cornish Sunday School which had pupils into their late sixties and beyond. They had attended at the same time each and every Sabbath.

The Chapel Hymnal is from an American source with the first edition published in 1931. While it looks smart and is cleanly presented, with a pleasing printing of several tunes to some hymns, rather than suggesting the accompanist might find the 'wanted' tune elsewhere, and so have two books running at the same time. It is simply a smaller version of the larger volume utilised by churches. It does contain Tennyson's *Crossing The Bar*. Almost all the hymns were written before the 20th century.

Among the British published material, one volume that catches the eye is *The Daily Service, Prayers and Hymns for Schools*, (Oxford University Press 1936). The list of hymn editors makes impressive reading for that time - Percy Dearmer, Ralph Vaughan Williams and Martin Shaw. The general editor was Canon G.W. Briggs. It was a book adopted by many educational authorities. It contains a number of horrors. It begs credulity to imagine that impressionable young people were asked to sing these

149   Carey Bonner, *Child Songs*, (The Pilgrim Press,1949).

words, from the hymn *Can You Count The Stars That Brightly Twinkle*:

> Do you know how many children
> Rise each morning blithe and gay?
> Can you count their jolly voices,
> Singing sweetly day by day?
> God hears all the happy voices,
> In their pretty songs rejoices;
> And he loves them every one.

That said the book does contain some interesting texts, some of which have been lost to general use, and undeservedly so.

Hymns for Young People, 1967, shows little sign that out there in the big bad world everything was exploding. For the most part it prints the plainer, less wordy, hymns that adults sing so meaningfully, including *Holy, Holy. Holy.* It includes just one song that owes something to folk music, namely Sydney Carter's *Lord of the Dance*. The book contains an advert for the *Gospel Song Book* with introduction from Sydney Carter, where it is claimed can be found many new songs about the men, women, and children who were friends of Christ while He walked on earth.

Youth Praise published at seven shillings and sixpence also contained for its time in the 1960s some interesting songs outside of the traditional hymn, including the spirituals, *Little David, Joshua Fit The Battle of Jericho, Lord I Want to be A Christian In My Heart, Sinner Man*, and *The Gospel Train*. Amidst those, and others of popular lore such as *Thank You* (that gave Petula Clark a hit song), there is the old-time gospel:

> How long, how long before
> You come to the Saviour (78 *Youth Praise*)

– or –

> Jesus is knocking, patiently waiting,
> Outside your heart's closed door (73 *Youth Praise*)

However the big bad world is not entirely absent. It made itself felt in the briefly mentioned earlier *New Life*, published in 1971. It was a serious attempt to take religious people out of their cloisters into the actual world where things are not always nice and palatable. In *The Times Educational Supplement* (December 10, 1976) it was seen capturing the ferment of prayer, praise and protest movements. It was intended to be utilised by schools at the morning assembly, and there was a recognition of electronic communication and the advent of pop culture. As a side effect, it presented some religious education teachers with a question or two about what it was they should be about, and whether life at the chalk face was more than bouncing off antiquated materials being published by conventional publishing houses.

So it was that you could find hymns and songs dealing with poverty, capitalism, humankind's love of war, inequality of opportunity in Britain especially for those disadvantaged by gender, disability, and race, which have been suggested as arising from a consumer-dominated society and economy.

There were, perhaps for the first time, in explicit terms in such a book, expressions of doubt, conflict, even blasphemy of seeming to question traditional truths. Not unexpected, therefore, were the voices raised in anger at the publication of such a book. However, few rant and rail against old-fashioned obscurity. This is what the Church often asks its people to sing, including young people who more than most are weighing up their life options. And you want to shout 'WHY?!'

New Life raised cries of alarm from readers of some national newspapers who worried about what the youth of this country might be singing, and especially that they might be indoctrinated by leftish claptrap! There were the traditional songs for young people to sing, *Come, Thou Long-Expected Jesus, For The Beauty of the Earth*, the wondrous *Of The Father's Love Begotten*, and surprisingly the mystifying *Immortal, Invisible*, and oddly even *Hills of the North Rejoice*, with its lines:

> Lands of the East, Awake,
> Soon shall your sons be free

But any intelligent school kids would know that something contrary to Western systems had arrived. However, it wasn't this that worried some. The fury was reserved for lines such as this:

> Twenty fags, a jar of ale,
> A quid each way on 'Monkey' (42)

– or –

> Across the hills black clouds are sweeping,
> Carry poison far and wide,
> And the grass has blackened underfoot (124)

– or more horror with –

> We choose the road of peace and prayer
> Countless pilgrims trod,
> So that Hindu, Moslem, Christian, Jew,
> We can all worship one God (121)

– or –

> In the slog, slog, slog of the factory
> Did you really see people there,
> Or was it some half-human shadows
> From whom there was no need to care (108)

A year later, although doubtless undergoing preparation almost simultaneously with *New Life* came *In Every Corner Sing*. Its brief lay in providing material for the school assembly. Although far too much traditional language remains, it not only includes the folk style of Sydney Carter but music and words by Pete Seeger, popular at the time. Also some Negro spirituals that never die, and Donald Swann's, *We Ask That We Live* and *We Labour In Peace*. Some of Carter's fascinating work can be located in *Songs of Sydney Carter—In The Present Tense,* and other publications by Galliard.

Certainly to my taste is *Hymnal for Contemporary Christians*, compiled by Norman Johnson and Don Wyrtzen, and published by *Singspiration Music*. This American derived book visits and revives old historic folk melodies of many lands, through spirituals and contemporary gospel songs to 'composed folk'. Published sometime in the 1970s it has a relaxed air, of songs chosen for gospel purpose, but free from the religious baggage that afflicts many books where you feel the compilers are looking over their shoulders lest the powers that be deem a choice politically incorrect.

A more recent book for young people with a due sense of where we are living and what kind of world it is can be found in *The Complete Come and Praise*, compiled by Geoffrey Marshall-Taylor. It brought together the two books published in 1988 and 1998. It has 149 typical, lyrical and festive songs, and the content was originally selected for listeners of BBC School Radio's popular assembly programme *Together*. Bravely it only contains a small number of hymns that might be found in current mainstream books.

In 1993 Stainer and Bell in conjunction with the Methodist Church Division of Education and Youth published *Story Song* with a rather mundane un-adventurous cover that could lead someone to suppose there was no good stuff within its pages. Songs have scripture reference and more appealingly there are songs about many positive Christian figures down the ages, to include George Fox, Elizabeth Fry, Josephine Butler and Martin Luther King Jnr. However as is often stated in useful footnotes the songs often need a careful introduction, although there is no such note to the first two lines of *My Name Was Jacob*:

> I wrestled with a man on the slopes of the hillside,
> The danger of reprisal, held me guiltily at bay[150]

Fine, if the story is known, although even then it might fetch some ribaldry from young people. Like many books for the young it has a degree of heaviness in the lyrics, and while some of the lines read well, they are not always so forthcoming if thought in terms of group singing. Some are best sung by a soloist who in more folk traditional style would either teach the gathering the words as a whole, or suggest some of the lines might be sung by them, although it is more effective if the song has a refrain. So picking one

---

150   *My Name was Jacob, Story Song*, (Stainer and
       Bell, London, 1993,) no. 65, p.77.

song at random in the book, *Who Better Than Mary?*, there is the opening verse lyric:

> Saint Mary, the Virgin said 'Yes!' to the angel,
> Consenting to bear the Messiah of God

Which after that, and all other seven verses, leaves a refrain:

> Who better than Mary his mother can say:
> 'This is my body; this is my blood'?[151]

In 1998 the praise song market zapped once more into action with *Let's Praise*, sub-titled *The Worship Songbook for a New Generation*, compiled under the invitation of the Baptist World Alliance. It did include five songs from Jacques Berthier that take us into the Taizé territory, 45 Graham Kendrick compositions, several Jewish melodies, a West Indian melody, but overall in its general ethos it could have been any praise collection. Particularly lacking is a sense of young Christians taking on the world in God's name, aware of the problems and issues that face humankind, the struggles and depths of the human condition. The nearest calling point is the three Procession songs from *Make Way*, but these lack specifics, unlikely to challenge anyone, for example:

> The Lord Is Marching On
> The Lord is marching in splendour,
> in awesome and majesty he rides,
> for truth and humility and justice;
> his mighty arms fills the skies

I am not asking that each and every hymn and song has to have a social and prophetic edge, although it would be good to find some among praise style groups among the mainstream churches. I am asking for a faith offered, celebrated among the people.

Among numerous other publications in praise territory, there has been *Songs of Fellowship for Kids* in 1992, and eight years later, *The Big Spring Harvest Kids Praise*. The latter comprises 120 songs compiled using *Spring Harvest Kids*

151   Ibid. No 73.

Praise and *Little Kids Praise* during the preceding 12 years. I wonder how many kids would understand *If Jesus Is Divine* and the invitation in the song to bear 'fruit in the Kingdom of God'. So would they understand the word 'divine?' and what would they say is 'The Kingdom of God'. I ask whether young kids can really sing lines such as:

> I adore you, there's nothing I would rather do than simply
> adore you; I want to live my whole life through simply
> adoring you.[152]

What do they make of:

> I'm gonna walk by faith, not by sight -
> I'm gonna walk by faith, not by sight[153]

– or –

> So let's call together all the saints, their voices proclaim
> That the Father, Son and Spirit will forever be the same,
> And the day will come when every knee shall bow at Jesus' name.
> Almighty God is here. [154]

– or –

> Jesus is greater than the greatest heroes,
> Jesus is closer than the closest friends,
> He came from heaven and he died to save[155]

All of these songs and lyrics offer difficult existential, theological, and biblical reflections that would even exercise many adults, let alone the under-11s. Much better is something like *Some People Laugh:*

> Some people laugh
> some people sing

---

152   May My Praise Be Sung, no. 82
153   Ibid. No.64
154   Ibid. No.30
155   Ibid. No.70

some people clap
and so they bring their worship
to the King of kings.
What do you do?
what do you do?[156]

Sammy Horner then says that some people dance, bring a word, march and raise their hands, some are quiet but understand: at least pictures are being painted, something that is often missing from the general output of praise writers (the place of allusion, simile and metaphor is almost foreign territory). There is somewhere for the imagination to go, there is place for the child to speak of times he has laughed, sung and clapped his hands, for someone to show pictures of people in good times and moments, to suggest that the people of God do all these things.

Beyond official hymn and songbooks there was in the late 1950s and early 1960s a trend to adapt current pop tunes to hymns. Occasionally it worked, but it still meant sometimes carrying the burden of words written in another time, and from a different religious culture. Erik Routley was much involved in this process in terms of some of the music that was part of the 1963 Student Christian Movement Conference in Bristol. He may have been willing then to see a popular tune such as *Telstar* (number one hit in 1962 for *The Tornados*) adorning worship. It was set to words written by Congress members. I was at the Congress and we sang *The Strife is o'er* to a hit tune of the time, *Wonderful Land* (recorded by *The Shadows*). Mr Routley said it was an unusually evocative "pop" tune. But this doesn't seem to have lasted, for by the end of the decade the great man of church music was much pre-occupied with the pervading influence of pop and dismissed it, 'as not so much a musical form as a gesture.'[157]

This at a time when the rock element of pop was at its most creative with the likes of *Dylan*, *Beatles*, *Who*, *Love*, *Neil*

156   Ibid. Sammy Horner, No.93
157   Erik Routley, *Words, Music and the Church*,
        (Herbert Jenkins, London, 1969), p.120.

Young, Pink Floyd etc. He continued by recalling a statement made in 1965 by the pop singer Adam Faith when interviewed by the Archbishop of York during a television programme:

> One of the inept things that Adam Faith said was that the church was at fault in its hymns, because the lyrics were incomprehensible. My point is that a great many popular songs are rooted in a mythology that people no longer understand, but that this doesn't stop them singing them.[158]

Perhaps not, but that is not the point, for you expect to be in the land of the real and meaningful if you are singing about eternal things, and Faith's point was not answered.

Routley had more to say:

> Perhaps we might add that nearly all the products of composers who have sought to integrate pop idioms with the needs of church music arouse the principal complaint that musically they are exceedingly dull.[159]

Routley was not enamoured of the pop hymn tunes of the Twentieth-Century Church Light Music Group, and expressed reservations about some of the material delivered by Malcolm Williamson. However, while in worship usefulness certain adjuncts of the pop style were seen as self-evidently incongruous, he did have a liking for the guitar - naturally not amplified! Much more in overall favour was folk music but:

> The fact that atheist anarchists and Communism are prominent among the folk singers makes the church understandably cautious about their techniques.[160]

However, he did advocate folk as the one musical form out of the current culture of which he was prepared to say:

> If public worship as we know it cannot accommodate this, then we ought to consider altering public worship so that it can.[161]

158 Ibid. p.121.
159 Ibid. p.121-2.
160 Ibid p.124.
161 Ibid p.125.

These days in terms of young people, and popular music of whatever genre, and there are so many forms, the place of hymns and songs falls into a much wider context,the remit of which is outside of my own set brief. It is asking whether there can be such a thing as youth congregations or youth churches? If so, then what shall or shall not be sung, or played, or danced, and like anything even the question hinges on definition. A discussion of this question is contributed by Russ Oliver in too short a chapter in the book *Fast Moving Currents in Youth Culture* published by Lynx Communications. This book brought together the results of a massive nationwide survey of 13,000 teenagers on the issues affecting them. Within its pages 27 Christian youth leaders examined what this meant for youth ministry in the 1990s. Oddly the place of general song, let alone hymns, is not considered in the book, notwithstanding that music, and its various sub-cultures is one of the most formative influences among young people. The book does however contain chapters dealing with Church and youth work, and even the process of learning.

Postscript

When it comes to looking at hymns with the younger element in mind, especially those in their early to mid-teens in the 21st century, it is almost 'a search in vain' through hymn collections to find reference to anything belonging to a young person's world. There are few songs reflecting the 'growing up' process, the sense of 'adventure and imagination', the joys and fears in trying new things, of games and dressing-ups, of sport, the world of electronic offerings, of parents or none, and so one can continue.

Jim Wallis told students at Virginia Theological Seminary:

> We like to think our ideas are shaped by the ideas we have, the books we have read, and the classes we have taken. In reality our perspective is most shaped by what we see when we get out of bed in the morning. What we touch and taste and feel, what we know is close to us, or where we have decided to

place ourselves. Touching the pain of others is the key to understanding.[162]

The huge and massive negative in terms of maturation of a young person has rested in creating a faith world that does not impinge upon basic experience. The world of the children's hymnbook is not the world they see, hear and know. It would be an interesting hymnbook that set out to place material under 'life' headings, such as Joy, Laughter, Anger, Sex, Pain, Suffering, Being and Doing, Knowing Achievement and Failure, Space, Running, Vulnerability, Fear of Commitment, Signs of The Other, and so forth. In the meantime many of the hymns and songs sung by young people serve no more purpose than persuading them that the Faith has little to do with their lives in the 21st century. It is nothing short of criminal.

162   Jim Wallis Zabriskie Lectures 1992, *Virginia Theological Seminary Journal*, December 1992 p21

CHAPTER EIGHT

Singing A New Song When It Matters

Now the adventure takes me into areas where my pulse races, mostly black musical areas. This can be hymn singing with a difference. At the same time there is a strong American South white gospel tradition that often gets overlooked, until someone hears old Elvis Presley recordings, and realises that the King of rock'n'roll was a church-going boy who loved to sing songs such as *Peace in The Valley* and *It Is No Secret,* both admirable in tune for his rich voice. This is territory with so many nuances that it is impossible to summarise briefly, and I merely instance some lines found on the sleeve notes to the album of the New York-London show, *Black Nativity*:

> The field of Christian Church music is a very wide one encompassing a variety of expressive forms, from the old Gregorian chants to Lutheran chorales and the simple hymns that are sung in churches and chapels. There are however within the bounds of sacred music, completely independent musical forms: the spirituals and gospel songs of the American Negro. This music is a flexible, quite self-contained expressive medium. The spirituals and gospel songs frequently take the form of a spirited antiphon between the preacher and the congregation. The music is strongly rhythmical, the mood deeply and fervently devotional. [161]

161 *Black Nativity*, sleeve notes to production, (DJM 22056), original cast album, Stateside SL 10026.

As I write I can hear on record the Revd. I. D. Beck leading the congregation of the Mount Olivet Regular Baptist Church, Kentucky. He's just given a testimony of a little under seven minutes. The gathering is singing *When Jesus Christ Was Here On Earth*, a ballad-like movement out of the life of Jesus. The style is known as lining-out, and so it proceeds:

LEADER AND CONGREGATION:	When Jesus Christ was here on earth
LEADER:	They said he was a spy
LEADER AND CONGREGATION:	They said he was a spy
LEADER:	He healed the sick and raised the dead
LEADER AND CONGREGATION:	He healed the sick and raised the dead
LEADER:	Go thou and prophesy
LEADER AND CONGREGATION:	Go thou and prophesy

The text makes it obvious, 'lining' is a teaching method, a way of learning, long before the big screen that now adorns many Christian worship centres. The preacher sings the first line, and the congregation follows, and so it continues. To some it is more than a way of learning, or a way that derives from the lack of money to buy songbooks, and sometimes serves those with reading difficulty. Essentially it is a style, a practice that exists because it is seen as the 'way' to meet in fellowship and offer praises. There is no reason why the practice should not be part of any gathering.

There is also one other important element, that in this worship there are no musical instruments. Here is one of the oldest forms of song style in American communities centred on the church, but it struggles to survive. As far as I know something close to its heart in Christian circles continues in

Both are only likely to be found in second hand shops that specialise in soul, R&B, and Gospel.

the old Presbyterian congregations in Calvinist Scotland, and the Pennsylvanian Dutch Amish. In the latter a line can take a minute or more to sing, being so heavily ornamented syllable by syllable with slides, melisma (a group of notes sung to one syllable of text), and grace notes.

Historian Alan Lomax, the supreme authority on American folk music, comments:

> The complexity of the text, the rhythmic freedom, and the variation of ornament from singer to singer in this lined-out style create striking and often rich heterophony. In a world survey of song styles I have found the style is most frequent in the ritual music of the Mediterranean, the Middle East and Orient. [164]

The service would have started in the morning, with the church clean and neat, simple and direct:

> Old Regular Baptists shake hands a lot. Most church members will shake hands with everyone else. Up one aisle and down the next we go to enjoy a precious handshake and a warm embrace as we experience the love of God flowing from breast to breast. [165]

Often while the handshaking proceeded, people would sing. Several songs are sung in succession, perhaps another as someone is moved to begin it. Silence endures only long enough for someone to start another. It ceases when the minister steps into the pulpit.

The previous illustration was pretty simple, but the great use of Watts and Wesley while teaching doctrine through hymns cannot have been the easiest, but Watts, and those in his spirit, has always touched the gospel community, black or white. However, a pitfall awaits the unknowing, for an easy error is to assume that when the title Dr Watts is used in black gospel music it refers solely to

164   Alan Lomax, album sleeve notes, the *Gospel Ship - Baptist Hymns & White Spirituals from the Southern Mountains*. (New World Records, NW 29. Library of Congress 1977).
165   Elwood Vornett, Moderator, Indian Bottom Association, Old Regular Baptists, Southeastern Kentucky.

the great British hymnist. It is of course a mark of considerable respect that his name should be taken but in gospel, particularly that of the black tradition, the hymns of Watts, Wesley, William Cowper, Lowell Mason and John Newton are generically known and sung as Dr Watts! Tony Heilbutt's *The Gospel Sound - Good News and Bad Times* makes 26 references to Dr Watts.

Mahalia Jackson says here:

> Man, I was down South. You should hear those choirs in South Carolina and Georgia. They sing those hymns, and tears run from my eyes. I just want to jump up and shout. Looks like I find myself when I hear them. We lose something up North, ain't no need fooling ourselves. But when I hear those folk, I sort of get refilled, get what I had when I was a child.[166]

Mahalia said repeatedly when she sang such songs as *Amazing Grace* and *The Day Is Past and Gone:*

> Dr Watts? Now you're talking about the POWER. These songs, hmmmm, they come out of conviction and suffering. The worst voices can get through singing them, cause they're telling their experiences.[167]

The comparative demise of simple unaffected singing has similarities with the effect that organ-gallery bands had on unaccompanied music and singing of the 19th century. There was a time in the American South when choirs, organs and musical directors arrived, and the folksy Baptist and Methodist were threatened. It was music being made by some, while the congregation passively listened. It led to folk departing, and the birth of song-heavy sects of the Holiness movement. My adventure in hymn digging reveals that until the early to mid 1950s even the piano and harmonium were rarely heard in the 'folk' churches. Elsewhere though, without the big choirs and conductors, there may have been a guitar and the banjo. At one time some described the fiddle and banjo as instruments of the Devil.

166   Tony Heilbutt, *The Gospel Sound* (Anchor
         Books, Random House, 1975).
167   Ibid. p.59.

Reticence is not so obvious elsewhere for in the black-store churches, there are string groups, drums, trumpets, trombones, and as historian Alan Lomax has put it:

> Almost any combo may turn up anywhere in the now populous Holiness and Sanctified churches. Along with the instruments have come the tunes and sounds of secular music, including ragtime, jazz, blues, swing, and rock, all permitted according to the preference of the congregation.[168]

It was certainly so at the first Pentecostal church in Azusa Street, where no one stuck their noses in books, they just sang.

Thus far, I've basically mentioned white gospel, and even with that in mind I wish to say, sing a new tune when it matters. Nowhere is it more obviously practised and recorded than in the history of the Afro-American community, and especially its world of black gospel music and hymns. Here are riches galore. Here at very least you are not asked to take on board a people's tradition, rather to understand, share. At this point I write of traditional 'gospel' rather than forms and styles of recent years that have to some extent merged with the mood of popular music. Obviously, since the 1950s various black artists, Ray Charles being a great example, have utilised the dynamics of gospel song, and many of these artists have come from an early church background. As Craig Werner points out the producers and musicians who turned gospel into Chicago soul and Motown never forgot that the best gospel records always sound 'live' because they encapsulate energy unleashed by the call and response mode:

> The calls and responses of the Curtis Mayfield and the Impressions came straight from the churches of Chicago's south Side; *Smokey Robinson and the Miracles* re-created the dialogue between Claude Jeter and the Swan Silvertones. And

168   Ibid.

those sounds had their origins in the slave songs and coded spirituals created in the centuries-old struggle for freedom.[169]

But all of this was foreign to me until one Sunday evening, when I must have been around 14 years of age. Such a blessed evening and moment! For some reason the family radio was tuned to the Home Service. The actual BBC programme's title I cannot remember, but I've never forgotten the fact that I was bowled over by a mighty wind as St Paul Church Choir of Los Angeles, all 150 of them, thundered forth with the choir's radio theme from KFWB radio, *I'm So Glad (Jesus Lifted Me)* and then the slow burner of a song *God be with You*.

It was a mixed choir, a group creating great rhythmic surges of harmony. The pastor and choir leader the Revd. John L. Branham said the majority of the letter writers to the St Paul's were not churchgoers at all, but somehow they responded to the music. I did not merely hunt down the record that was played on air, but I began to delve into the world of black gospel hymn singing. It was most certainly a place where my soul wanted to sing, and be at ease, not that it stopped me exploring and singing hymns from the Methodist or Congregational hymnals of the time. However, I had found a new world, and I loved it. I could not fathom why this material was not found in the hymn books I knew, but then I was a mere impressionable teenager.

As I write this book, I thumb through to the index of the Heilbutt text referred to earlier in this chapter, and find mention of this choir

> In 1948, the St Paul's Church Choir, directed by Professor J. Earl Hines (and featuring the wonderful Sallie Martin), overwhelmed the market with *God Be With You*, ushered in a series of choir records only distantly related to the 'shouting preacher' discs of Prophet Michaux and Reverend Gates.

---

169   Craig Werner, *A Change is Gonna Come*
(Canongate, Edinburgh, 2000).

Within a five-year period gospel produced several smash hits.[170]

There is of course, often intertwined with 'gospel' - the spiritual, and 'the blues'. The spirituals were anonymous folk songs, whereas gospel and hymns have an affinity in that both are written songs. Langston Hughes says that spirituals can be made into gospel songs by adding that little extra. That said, if it does not seem too confusing, Negro gospel singing is folk singing, for as Langston Hughes says 'in the pure state it never follows arrangements or pat notations'.

Much has been written within the black community as to whether blues are good or evil. Blues singer Willie Thomas didn't see the blues as being contradictory to the nature of God, and John Lee Hooker believed "when the spirituals was born it was born on the blues side". For some blues singers their eventual life progression led to the Church.[171] In the case of those named to go from blues to gospel was a coming home, so they sang a new tune when it mattered personally, but many never threw off the past.

The book *Protest and Praise - Sacred Music of Black Religion* reminds us of how the prodigal who returned in black religious tradition was:

> not only expected to tell the story, but to authenticate his conversion by telling the story within a story.[172]

Spencer tells of former blues musician Gatemouth Moore, who made the journey from a known Chicago nightclub singer to preacher, and whose story within a story was simply:

---

170 Ibid. p.270.
171 So it was for the Revd. Robert Wilkins, or Revd Rubin Lacy, or Revd. Jack Harp, or Revd. Nehemiah "Skip" Jones or the better known, Revd. Gary Davis
172 John M. Spencer, *Protest & Praise, Sacred Music of Black Religion*, (Minneapolis, Fortress Press 1990), p.24.

He stood on stage to sing....as he opened his mouth - silence!
Again, he storied, he went on to the stage - nothing! a third
time - this time to his own surprise there issued from his lips a
church song.[173]

Moore confessed 'I was converted in a night-club'.

And when it comes to deciding what your soul sings,
then was it giving up the cigarette that was central to the
story of the Revd Harp, or the 'voice' he heard? On
occasions when he stood in the porch for his regular smokes
he heard a voice telling him that he had smoked his last. It
took him, and his wife, to services and prayer meetings until
he was 'saved'. Other than the unusual occurrence of
believing he saw the Holy Ghost descending from a
Christmas tree, he was born again eventually of the Spirit.
For him though the blues were pushed aside. He said 'If I'm
saved and sanctified and sing the blues, I'm not clean'.
However, C. Eric Lincoln — professor of Religion and
Culture at Duke University, would accept that the spiritual,
the ring shout, the 'blues', the freedom songs, are all a
response to the divine initiative.

For many some of the great tunes and words of Thomas
A.Dorsey make labels almost pointless as he, more than
others, plays the narrow line between blues and sacred
music. For all time he will be remembered for the song I later
reference, *Precious Lord*.

The saga of blues and gospel or blues versus gospel is a
subject in itself, but it is well documented that blues singers
were uncertain as to whether blues was good or evil. Rev
Rubin Lacy is quoted in an interview:

> Sometimes the best Christian in the world has the blues
> quicker than a sinner does, 'cause the average sinner ain't got
> nothing to worry about .... But a Christian is obliged to certain
> things and obligated not to do certain things. That sometimes

173   Ibid. p.129.

causes a Christian to take the blues. What is the blues. What is the blues, then? It's a worried mind.[174]

Revd Lacey recalled that Blind Lemon Jefferson said 'no' to an invitation to gig on a Sunday, and informed that he would never do so whatever the money.

Lacey said:

> I need a fellow offer him $20 to play him one song one morning ... shook his head ... he says I couldn't play it if you gave me $200. I need the money but I couldn't play it. My mother always taught me not to play on a Sunday for nobody.[175]

There are countless stories of similar mould to be told, but not here. This is not a book about 'gospel' music, or blues, merely a chapter on a musical life-giving form that has heavily etched itself into my soul, and helped me believe. In any case there are already many erudite volumes, but a few brief descriptions of this genre that would seem useful if I am to follow through 'gospel' in terms of what the soul sings, how and when.

The great gospel singer Mahalia Jackson said, 'We Baptists sang sweet',[176] and religious ecstasy was paramount over polished phrasing or perfect pitch.

It could be, as Craig Werner observes in church time when:

> the sanctified church could erupt with a collective energy that transformed centuries of bitter hardship into moments of pure connection-with self, community, and the soiled presence of the Lord.[177]

174   Revd Rubin Lacy in an interview with David Evans, *Blues Unlimited*, no.43 (May 1967, p. 13-14).
175   David Evans, *Blues Unlimited* (no.42, March-April, 1967), p.3.
176   The sleeve notes on her original vinyl album, Mahalia Jackson, Philips BBL 7289, (Newport 1958).
177   *A Change Is Gonna Come* (Craig Werner Canongate, Edinburgh, 2002), p.5.

James H.Cone says the function of the song is to sing the truth as it is lived by the people. Truth, he says is also disclosed in the movement of the language and the passion created when a song is sung to the right pitch with tonal quality.

> Truth is found in shout, hum, and moan as these expressions move the people closer to the source of their being. The moan, the shout, and the rhythmic bodily responses to prayer, song, and sermon are artistic projections of the pain and joy experienced in the struggle of freedom. It is the ability of black people to express the tragic side of social existence but also their refusal to be imprisoned by its limitations. [178]

Fr. Norman O'Connor, writing of Gospel music, says:

> But through the history of revival meetings, house parties, the church choirs, and the singing of the blues, the test of the hymn and the gospel song is not what the music and words bring, but what the artist gives this small creation. [179]

> That said, those reared in discipline and containment of synagogue, or chant, of the discipline accorded to a choir, might well be taken aback by the looseness and almost chaotic formlessness of the gospel-singing form .... the form doesn't demand concern about notes and accents. These are handled as you want them to be at the time you sing. [180]

Let alone those who prefer the tidy form of Matins and Evensong!

Rhythm is paramount in the gospel song, and like the melody it can take back seat, and also of course everything is dependent on the singer. Sometimes a word, a line, a phrase becomes grabbed and imbued with fervour, and as Langston Hughes puts it, 'an isolated word becomes an affirmation of divinity'. And what eventually happens depends on how the Spirit moves, and who can resist the

178 *God of the Oppressed,* James H.Cone, (SPCK, Orbis Books, 1997), p.22.
179 Fr. Norman O'Connor, album sleevenotes, Mahalia Jackson, (Newport 1958, Philips BBL, 7289).
180 Ibid.

mounting rhythms that stir both spirit and body. Langston Hughes blithely remarks:

> On the wings of song, the singers get carried away, and there is then no telling what may happen in their singing, for something is happening in their souls.[181]

So, someone might say, 'the lyrics are often banal' - perhaps 'but they talk about the things that matter to poor people' is the repost from Tony Heilbutt, one of America's foremost writers on gospel and black culture. And can we confuse 'banal' with 'simple' and can we then wrongly assume 'simple' in this context means 'of low intelligence' rather than easily understood, plain and uncomplicated?

I loved reading how Mahalia Jackson described herself and fellow musical travellers in terms of 'it's how we carry ourselves' and Dr Heilbutt remarks:

> once you get to know them, you learn that gospel singers are experts in all the ugliest sides of American life. But they always stand tall and walk upright. 'We're Marching to Zion' on a 'Highway to Heaven', which takes all the best of them, those who don't sell out, through hell.[182]

On that August day when Martin Luther King spoke to thousands at the Lincoln Memorial in Washington DC, Mahalia Jackson sang *I've been 'Buked and I've Been Scorned* to remind the marchers of their real journey. Yet it was years before, in 1939, that another powerful black singer Marian Anderson had also adorned the Lincoln Memorial steps. Not allowed to sing at Washington's largest auditorium, Constitution Hall, owned by the Daughters of the American Revolution and at the time still running a segregated ship, she chose to let thousands hear a voice, and share a message. As Werner remarks, her singing of *My*

---

181 Langston Hughes, *Come in the Room*,
     sleevenotes to the album by Clara Ward and
     her singers (Fontana TFL 6016).
182 Anthony Heilbutt, *The Gospel Sound*,
     Introduction (Limelight Edition, USA).

Country'Tis Of Thee was a challenge to white America to 'live up to its betrayed ideals.'[183]

Mahalia was on the artist list at the Newport, USA, Jazz Festival in 1958, and the record of her contribution to the event stands out as one of the most moving, stomach hitting performances I have ever heard. There is the DVD of the whole event that gives treasured visual moments of a momentous free flowing occasion. None more powerfully in the whole history of visual recording is to be heard, and seen, than her singing of *the Lord's Prayer* to Malotte's 1910 setting. Such is the expressive nature of her face and body, such is the passion and sheer vocal brilliance. That artist was blessed with astonishing presence, for as Fr Norman O'Connor has remarked, she can kneel, close her hands, lift her head, assume any gesture, and whatever the audience does, she dominates, and speaks, loves and claims hearts.

It was at the Festival on July 6th, when Willis Conover, long associated with the American Forces Network, and with jazz music, simply said 'Ladies and gentlemen, it is Sunday morning, and time for the world's greatest gospel singer'. The crowd had stayed through pouring rain (little wonder on the transcript there is laughter when Mahalia said she was going to sing *Didn't It Rain*) and indeed as she began there was a fresh downpour, but not even the elements can stop the wonder of genius, or the Spirit's power. On that evening at Newport that woman broke through communicatory forms that have their own distance, and brought Jesus so much closer, in the greatest prayer ever written. Mahalia herself spoke of a close correlation between her style and the pulpit, stressing the way both reacted to their peoples' moan. She is quoted as saying:

> It is the basic way that I sing today, from hearing the way the preacher would sort of sing in a-I mean, would preach in a cry,

183   Craig Werner *A Change Is Gonna Come: Music -
       Race and Soul of America* (New York, Plume,
       2006).

a moan, would shout sort, like in a chant way—a groaning sound that would penetrate my heart.[184]

Mahalia benefited greatly from her piano player Mildred Falls who read the mind and spirit of the audience, let alone that of the artist. She urged Mahalia toward the mountaintop, letting her know, in good times and bad, that she isn't alone.

To sort out and name events with a musical bias, and which have a black consciousness is in itself a dangerous thing, for by so doing it can suggest that it is in essence something that occurs every now and then. To be sure there are its highs, but it always has to be remembered that music was central to the black person's fight for their God-given right. As Cordell Reagon of the Southern Christian Leadership Conference says bluntly:

> Without these songs you know we wouldn't be anywhere. We'd still be down on Charley's plantation, chopping cotton for 30 cents day.[185]

It wasn't a daily church-going Sunday affair, but for one prolific writer in the black community Gerald Massey, it was simply that Sunday was designated the heaven of the 'weary pilgrim'. It is a mistake to assume that the majority of songs were concerned with redemption, and the salvation of the individual soul. The field secretary of the SCL, Phyllis Martin, suggests what the soul sang was determined each and every minute by circumstance, and much of this came by way of extreme hard labour, poor working conditions, bad wages, and tyrannical employers:

> The fear down here is tremendous. I don't know whether I'd be shot at, or stoned, or what. But when the singing started, I forgot all that. I felt good within myself.[186]

Cone translates this into the experience of his mother. Her favourite song was *This Little Light of Mine*. It's a song popular in the sing-a-longs of many groups, whatever class or colour, or even faith. It's also a favourite within some

184 Ibid. p.14.
185 Ibid. p.9.
186 Ibid. p.12.

sections of the Christian community in so-called 'free' services. The lyric is basic, the tune undemanding and easy for singing by those who would not describe themselves as singers. But heard and sung within a proper context it assumes a different quality. It takes on its rightful clothing and expression when sung with the due degree of jaunty defiance, and against the backcloth of 'six days of wheeling and dealing with white people' and the question of 'whether life was worth living'. The song, in common with others was part of the process where the slave and burdened black person made it plain that in ultimate terms the white slave owner owns nobody's soul.

Says Cone:

> I only knew that when my mother sang her favourite song *This Little Light of Mine*, she was affirming much more than what was apparent in the lines ..... The 'Light' was what illumined her existence, an alternative view of life, different from the current estimations of her being in the world. It was her attempt to make a statement about her life, and to say to the world that she is who she is because and only because of the presence of God in her world.[187]

An extraordinary version of *This Little Light of Mine* is found on the much heralded album by Mavis Staples - *We'll Never Turn Back,* issued in 2007.

How I wish I'd been there that memorable day when Dr King extemporised and recalled words from previous sermons as he dreamt aloud his dream, and Mahalia sang with the angels. But I was at the Constitution Hall, the home of the Daughters of the American Revolution, in Washington DC, when the walls had come tumbling down, and black faces raced through hitherto virtually always 'white man's' land. The vast space echoed in 1968 to James Brown, and Aretha Franklin, and when Peter, Paul and Mary came into town singing their hit: Dylan's song, *Blowin In The Wind*. Change was afoot in race relations.

It was the year when Aretha's home town Detroit declared an 'Aretha Franklin Day' and being just a few

187   Ibid. p.12-13.

yards away from the stage was to be in the presence of greatness, and to catch a little of her vision of possibility for black people. She would sing soul, and then suddenly gospel, as if we were in church, to remind us of our real roots, black and white.

To what degree early memories in her life affected her soul is open to conjecture, but speaking of the fact that her mama deserted the family when she was six, and who died four years later, she did say 'the whole family wanted for love'. Her father ministered on the fringes of the Detroit city's East Side ghetto, 'To the pimp, and the hustler, the numbers man and the dope man'.

She tells why she became a singer. It happened at the funeral of one of her aunts, at which Clara Ward sang an old Thomas Dorsey song, *Peace in the Valley*. Such was the spiritual electricity thudding through her that she shouted herself into a trance, and hurled her hat to the ground. Aretha says it was the moment when she knew she wanted to become a singer. When she sang, it was, as British gospel writer Viv Broughton has remarked:

> church feel matched to R&B, and the Baptist preacher's daughter became the undisputed Queen of Soul. [188]

In the year after I came back from the States, in 1970, she appeared on a David Frost British TV show, and the abiding memory of that is her suddenly playing the piano and singing *Precious Lord* and then shouting to camera 'I'm strong in my religion. I wish other people knew Him like I do'. It led to her deciding she should make a gospel album, in 1972 with James Cleveland and his Southern California Community Choir.

The double record album bore the title of *Amazing Grace*, and her version of the famous song lasted almost eleven minutes. Not long after, Mahalia died, and if the wondrous Ms Jackson had sung over the body of Martin Luther King,

188   Viv Broughton, Black Gospel: *An Illustrated History of the Gospel Sound* (Blandford Press 1984), p.99.

it was now Aretha's turn to do the same over that of Mahalia with *Precious Lord.*

On one unforgettable Sunday, I would be at the church of St Stephen of the Incarnation. On the Saturday the streets in that part of Washington DC had rung to the shouts of disturbance. There were fires, lots of them, and shops and houses burning, but these were belongings of black people, not whites. Sunday was quiet and Sunday was church, only on that day, the Church couldn't let the walls of a building bind and imprison. The Church took to the streets, some kind of wagon affair giving height to preacher, if not choir. Familiar hymns took on a new light. Words really mattered. We were singing them in situation and they had to matter. No time here for traditional hymns slunk in the vagaries of the past.

There was no Aretha, but there was another. Her name was Roberta Flack. She would often sing at this remarkable multi-racial church that was given to 'event' and so if we read of *Jesus the Bread of Life* we would already have been down in the kitchen making and smelling real bread.

At this Church people of different race and religion came together, smiled at each other, someone danced ballet, corks from sparkling burgundy hit the ceiling, and Roberta would sing *I Told Jesus.* One prominent bandleader of the time, American, Les McCann, I noted down, without actually recording the source, said 'her voice touched, tapped, trapped and kicked every emotion I've ever known. I laughed, cried and screamed for more.

And more came — and more — and more — and more!'

My own note from then speaks of her as a singer who takes you where the action is ... where agony, brutality, despair threaten to overcome. Doubtless I had that memorable Sunday in mind, but for her it was reality known and lived, for she grew up among the dirt of a Washington ghetto. Her first two albums are marked by songs with lyrics from various people with cries for justice, for man to learn something about love, to bring the positive into confusion, to wrench the good out of an already violent situation.

The music and song of that Church hit home because it was invariably sung amidst the social and political realities of that time. I recall someone remarking how you could preach a sermon, even Dr King, but what radio station would pay much attention. On the other hand make a record, and someone out there would play it four times in an hour, and it might carry social commentary, albeit sometimes 'coded or masked', as some in the black community would say for those in the know, while others would just hear it as a record, and not get the message. As the great gospel singer Mavis Staples said: 'sometime, some place, King and others could preach it, and they [the family group simply called the Staples] would sing it.'

In these events there was a sense of 'kairos' — of what St Paul would describe as the new time, of the event, the coming of Jesus, to illumine the darkness of soul and world. Those there on that Sunday could sing with realism, with the voice of anger and protest, and still stretching out the hand of Christian love for those who would grasp, and turn away from bad and find good. As Leroy Jones puts it in succinct fashion:

> It was Sterling Brown, the great Afro American poet and my English teacher at Howard University, who first hipped A.B. Spellman and me to the fact that music 'was' our history.[189]

He would also write:

> The music was the score, the actually expressed creative orchestrations, reflection of Afro American life ... as orchestrated, vocalised, hummed, chanted, blown, beaten, scatted, corollary confirmation of the history ... explaining the history as the history was explaining the music, and that both were expressions of and reflection of the people.[190]

As I was soaking in something of the American black struggle, and seeing faith dressed in its vibrant and exciting clothing of music, in Britain on April 20, 1969, Mr Enoch

189 Leroy Jones, *Blues People Negro Music in White Americas* (Perennial Press, 2002), intro viii.
190 Ibid. ix

Powell made his widely reported speech warning members of parliament against passing the Race Relations Bill. As David Etukudo Udo remarks:

> The irony was that Enoch Powell was one of the British Government ministers who in the mid 1950s encouraged and welcomed the recruitment of black people from the Caribbean and other former colonies to come to live and work in Britain.[189]

How right he was, and it was interesting recalling those words when thinking of the late 1960s, and describing what I experienced and saw in the United States. That memorable experience I knew in black culture and music was also matched to a degree, but so differently, on the other side of America, at Berkeley, at the People's Church on Parker Street, and in the Cecil Williams ministry at Glide Memorial, arguably one the most innovative multi-racial churches in the planet's Christian community. Parker Street's gathering was predominantly white. It met in a nondescript room, with a few chairs, couple of tables, and cushions. There was a set time to the service, but people came and went, and sometimes they brought their animals.

The weekly service had no real recognisable form, the pastor, Dick Yorke, would tell the Jesus story in ordinary language without affectation. Someone would sing a topical song. The church's manifesto would be read, prayer asked, a litany to the great and suffering of Faith read, and we would sing songs such as *Kum Ba Yah, Down By The Riverside, All My Trials*, and *They'll Know We Are Christians By Our Love*, many of which can be found in several volumes issued by the Lutheran Church, and entitled *Hymns for Now*. Hardly a gospel shout time, but in its laid-back style still moving, even if without the more overt exuberance of worship at Glide Memorial, San Francisco. At Glide, as elsewhere, a song invariably goes with a testimony, or a song has been written because at that moment the soul has to sing what the Spirit has so led.

189 David Etukudo Udo *King of Love and Justice*
(African Caribbean Education Resource, UK).

These have been brief impressionistic notes, and I am fully aware that these have been surface reactions, for I am doubtless, realised or not, part of a Western culture. I like to think I am free from some its restraints, but I may be deluding myself!

I bow to some words I read from Leroy Jones:

> It was, and is inconceivable in African culture to make a separation between music, dancing, song, the artefact, and a man's life or his worship of his gods. Expression issued from life, and 'was' beauty. But in the West, the 'triumph of the economic mind over the imaginative', as Brooks Adams said, made this dreadful split between life and art. Hence, a music that is an 'art' music is distinguished from something someone would whistle while tilling a field.[192]

Some of this came back to me many years later, when taking a Racial Justice Sunday service in Britain, 2005, in a London Methodist Church in Kilburn. The songs we sang did include, yes, *We Shall Overcome* and *Freedom* and I was amazed to find I was tapping into something unexpected from a mostly black gathering, mostly African but some Caribbean.

I thought these songs might be forgotten. They belong in some way to the Civil Rights Movement but *We Shall Overcome* was not a new song, even if we thought it was as we stood arms together in those late 1960s days. Few, I guess, would have known that the 'anthem' of the civil rights movement is a mix of text from C.A. Tindley's gospel hymn *I'll Overcome Someday* and a tune of an old Baptist hymn *I'll Be Alright*. Songs such as this were always subject to extra verses as the situation demanded, whether from an individual or out of a group experience.

It was a little of what I mentioned earlier, and refer to again, it tapped into people consciousness, history flashed before them, perhaps to lurking somewhat undefined in their own movement.

192   Leroy Jones, *Blues People: Negro Music in White America* (Perennial Press, Oregon, 2002).

I found warmth and passion springing from that congregation, the words were being owned in a way that the general hymns were not. Suddenly we had words that evoked memories, hurts and disappointment, perhaps to a sense of movement and achievement. It illustrated well that the blues speaks for the individual, gospel for the community. But there was no foot stomping, shouting and fainting; hand clapping yes. And there were no drums or percussion, let alone pots and pans, but then this was no sanctified Pentecostal church. Suddenly in a moment they had made my service and sermon theirs, without anyone making such a claim. You just felt the Blessing was theirs and there. And I was privileged in some small way to be part of this collective experience.

In London's West End, I was to attend the James Baldwin play *The Amen Corner*, and to see on different occasions with different casts versions the Christmas gospel styled *Black Nativity*. This musical tells simply, and beautifully, the birth of Jesus as told in the New Testament with references to Messiah expectations, as found in the Jewish Scriptures. It was written by the distinguished American poet and playwright Langston Hughes. Hughes in the late 1920s was a prominent figure in the Harlem Renaissance, a literary and artistic movement that brought to the fore other extremely talented black writers. He went on to write plays and numerous volumes of poetry, and edit two monumental anthologies, *Book of Negro Folklore* and *Poetry of the Negro*. Later again he assumed academic posts at Atlanta University and The University of Chicago.

Black Nativity was sub-titled 'A Gospel song-play'. Musically it drew on Negro Christmas spirituals and gospel songs. Many of the songs featured, and others expressive of Christian understanding, can be easily sung by a congregation, whatever its form. American hymn books, particularly those of Baptist, Methodist and Independent traditions, do carry numerous gospel songs and hymns for congregational singing, while there are general published volumes specifically devoted to this genre. My most prized possession is *American Negro Songs* that contains 230 folk songs and spirituals, religious and secular. It was brought together by Dr John Work, who is associated with the celebrated Fisk Jubilee Singers. This choir first presented to the world the Negro song in their tours of America and Britain between 1871 and 1878.

Mr White decided on a style of singing the spiritual that eliminated every element detracting from the pure emotion of the song. Harmony was diatonic and limited very largely to the primary triads and the dominant seventh. Dialect was not stressed but was used only where it was vital to the spirit of the song. Finish, precision, and sincerity were demanded by this leader. While the programme featured the spirituals, variety was given it by the use of numbers of classical standard. Mr White strove for an art presentation, not a caricature of atmosphere.[193]

On hearing these songs and hymns, Mr Colin Brown, Ewing Lecturer on Music, Glasgow University, found their performance to possess a richness and purity of tone, both in harmony and melody.

At the same time even the history, derivation and use has been tarnished by the long drawn-out battle between the two supposed camps—church and world and woe betide anyone from the first who sings in the second. Ridiculous as it may seem, even the glorious Christmas Song, *Wasn't That A Mighty Day*, majestic in melodic line and words, found itself beyond the pale because some secular artists deigned to sing it, and so in the eyes of some devalued its spiritual pull.

While I do not think there is anywhere in either current British Baptist or Methodist hymnals words that ask a congregation to sing and at the same time dismiss the other, it was not so in early Negro hymn lore. Dr Work points out that being a Methodist was sufficient reason for a Baptist to disdain friendship. He instances:

> There's a camp meeting in the wilderness
> I know it's among the Methodes'.

---

193   John W. Work, *American Negro Songs*
       (Minneola, New York: Dover Publications,
       p.115).

> My father says it is bes'
> To live and die a Methodes.

The Baptists asked their folk to sing:

> I'm Baptis' bred and Baptis' bo'n,
> And when I'm dead there's a Baptis' gone.

The Baptists presumed triumph over the Methodes came in another hymn:

> 'Twas at the River Jordan
> Baptism was begun
> John baptized a multitude
> But he sprinkled nary a-one.

However Dr Work says in what might have been sympathy or late Christian love, there was another eventual verse:

> The Baptists they go by water
> The Methodists they go by lan'
> But when they get to heaven
> They'll shake each other's Han' [194]

There are countless albums featuring both the old and traditional Negro hymn, as well as much more contemporary Christian music that often features powering gospel choirs of some number. These albums can provide a 'heard' commentary into material that might be used in general worship. Both the major chains HMV and Virgin (now taken over by Zavvi) carry a goodly selection of material, and many of the albums that feature old-time gospel hymns are low priced and containing 30 or more songs. Many of the early songs kept company with early pop songs, in being fairly short in length, often below three minutes. Some of the modern style can be caught in a number of major British cities where there are independent churches with congregations of several thousand, and huge choirs.

The best known British choir singing gospel hymns and songs is The London Community Gospel Choir. For the *British Methodist Recorder* I interviewed its leader and

---

194   Ibid. p.23-4.

mentor Basil Meade to gain a sense of where gospel is today, and its place within current worship.

You watch the *Des O'Connor Show*, tune into GMTV, follow the long running *Top Of The Pops*, make a date to hear the yearly *Royal Variety Show*, or hear records made by contemporary record artists such as Tina Turner, George Michael, Sting, Sir Paul McCartney and Diana Ross, and somewhere either to the forefront or simply in backing the overall sound there is a choir—perhaps the London Community Gospel Choir.

Do not forget they have headlined shows in their own name, and have just issued their eighth album. They have also participated in the soundtrack recording of Walt Disney's big box-office film, *The Lion King*, performed for Nelson Mandela during his memorable visit to London in 1996, and perhaps less spectacular but media worthy, sung at Spice Girl Mel B's wedding in 1998.

High flying gospel choirs are ten-a-penny across the Atlantic, whereas in Britain there are relatively few that can operate on a media basis, and the only one with real stature is the LCGC. Call them adaptable and flexible, revel in their dynamic sounds with the richest of harmonies, groove along to their traditional and soulful arrangements, fusing up-tempo gospel, swing, R&B, but never forget this choir is a 'faith' choir, and its purpose rests in spreading the gospel in a myriad of ways.

But anyone who attempts to pitch their tent and sell their wares in the big, bad world is never going to escape the snarls and spite of Christians who should know better.

Choir founder and mentor Basil Meade told me of constant battles to persuade people 'that it is right to sing outside the church'.

You wonder how people can carp when confronted with 60 exuberant happy young people singing their hearts out for the Lord, but then again:

> I think many in the community have come with what I call the old way of life, and find it difficult to take on board new life influences and attitudes. There are so many ways to communicate and share the Gospel, and because you work in the wide world it doesn't mean you accept some of the

life-style that can be encountered. The Church has often closed
its doors on young people. We don't take anyone in this choir.
I find it difficult to take anyone without a faith but having a faith
doesn't mean choir entry. We have our vocal standards.

Meade, an ordained pastor, as well as possessing extensive
music credentials, tells me, 'There is regular worship,
prayer and bible study for choir members'. Some of those
who regularly gather have found churches unresponsive to
where they believe they have been called:

I do exercise a ministry beyond the demands of the choir. I am
always available. Sometimes we are on the road for weeks and
choir members do have their needs and wants, and
insecurities. I think it is so important worship is at the centre,
that we remember we are called not merely to make music and
sing, but to keep the life, the spirit of His teachings.

As with many who have a barrage of criticism coming their
way, and the constant seeming demand 'to prove'
something, Meade (in his interviews with me) finds it all an
uncalled interference with his mission to bring the good
news into every home:

This is tiring work, sometimes I do get physically weary,
emotionally tired, mentally asleep, but you go on because you
know that true to you is a call. I say, why limit God, why
worship in one style, why function between imposed walls
with a board outside saying this is so-and-so church. I do
believe something unique has been created with this choir.

Meade is in no doubt that popularity for the choir does run
with an unqualified belief that 'He has blessed this group.
The Holy Spirit is at work. Real music is when God blesses'.

No chapter of this length can in any way be more than a
surface impression, but if I wish to say one thing, it is
essentially how I have been fed by the black community. It is
a tragic loss that within the predominantly white Churches
and their hymn collections you might conclude there are no
black written hymns, no black hymn experiences, no black
hymns of social protest, no black hymns of adoration, of
faith, love and humility, none of those Bible stories, almost
as it were giving an oral version of the Bible: no black
anything.

And is the praise movement free from this accusation? Of course not. It is essentially almost completely a white movement singing white compositions and running with white culture, but in the name of a God who is not white, who may be black, who may be of no colour. Yet this is not to say that within black religious culture there is always innovation. Harold Courlander in his much admired book *Negro Folk Music* U.S.A. writes:

> Listening to Negro religious songs as they are sung in the South, one cannot fail to be impressed with an element that is best described as conservatism. In any community, there may be a large repertoire of religious songs on which to draw. Selections are made according to circumstances—that is, songs appropriate to an occasion are sung. Despite an effect of spontaneity, innovation is not a daily phenomenon.[195]

AD 604 saw the first St Paul's Cathedral in London established on the top of a low hill that would overlook the Thames. These days the Thames is not for seeing, it's hidden behind buildings and their owners who have wanted the sight. The services in September 2006 reflected on the story of jazz music and some of its most inventive practitioners in the light of Christian faith.

It featured songs sung by Peter Moreton, and I had better say he is a good friend of mine, but he is very good, so I am being objective, rather than being cosy. One song was his own composition, but otherwise we heard *Drunken Hearted Man* from Robert Johnson, John Lee Hooker's *No Shoes*, Ella Fitzgerald associated *Five O'Clock Whistle*, and one of the best songs around in 20th-century composition, *Nobody Knows You When You're Down and Out*, known to many for its rendition by Bessie Smith, who nearly 70 years back was killed a few miles from Clarksdale, Mississippi. The song has the immortal lines:

> If I ever get my hands on a dollar again,
> I'm gonna hold on to it till the eagle grin

195   Harold Courlander, *Negro Folk Music* (New York, Dover Publications, 1992, USA), p.36.

In 1987 in the New York *Newsday*, the journalist Murray Kempton marked the half-century since her death and so wrote:

> I had to say that Sarah Vaughan is the greatest jazz singer I have ever heard. 'What about Bessie Smith?' a bystander enquired. I could only answer that I had concluded that there could never have been a Bessie Smith; the moulds where they stamp out human beings are just too small for stuff of those proportions.[194]

On that September evening in the most illustrious setting, the gathering had little to sing, save a response to some prayers, and almost the finale to the evening with the spiritual *Were You There When They Crucified My Lord?* The proceedings were linked by the Cathedral's Precentor, Lucy Winkett, who set a balance and tone that ran with the music and general order. She gave a potted history of the blues, and there were some prayers and meditations. The gathering was in the 300/400 mark, and there was a noticeable presence of young people. By the end of September the numbers had grown even more, enough to cause the two mentioned, and perhaps others, to consider where they might go next.

Just down the road at St Anne and St Agnes, a Lutheran Church, on the month's third Sunday there was Jazz Vespers. The guest was the amazing L.D. Fraser from New York. Fraser marries the various styles. He comes with a seeming effortless ease, his piano playing is authoritative, the voice not always strong, but compelling. He is also someone who gets his audience to join with him on many songs. These jazz worship affairs have a history stretching back 20 years or more, sparsely attended. At St Anne's I have heard *Body and Soul* played during the offering, but I cannot say that my mind floated to some desirable person. It was a music and lyric which within the time and place spoke more of giving ourselves to His service in an act of dedication that comes with the blessing of an offering.

194   Robert Gottlieb, *Reading Jazz*, (Bloomsbury, London, 1997), p.629ff.

This brings me into the world of jazz, a musical style that is not always welcomed in some Christian quarters. It hasn't deterred Kirk Byron Jones who has written a persuasive and powerful book *The Jazz of Preaching—How to Preach with Great Freedom and Joy* (Nashville, Abingdon, 2004) where the author produces a compelling vision for a time that calls for 'creating a way out of the way'. His book is about life. It is about preaching, and the two are inextricably intertwined. He finds in jazz, improvisation, creativity, being open to the Spirit, and not being confined by preconceived ideas as to what music is, and is not. In a sense to walk the jazz musician's way is a process that should also be the preacher's.

According to Elwyn Wienandt writing first in 1957:

> Only in the past few years has any attempt been made consciously to introduce jazz style into places of worship in the form of either functional or supplementary music. These intrusions into the hitherto relatively serene precincts of the church have caused a furore out of proportion to their numerical occurrences.[195]

I assume he means 'white' churches. What he says might well make sense today, some 60 years later. Jazz is still relatively new and 'untried' as an expressive form to celebrate Faith within, in the white community. As far as I am aware there is only one church in the whole of Britain offering regular worship with a jazz infusion, and that only on a monthly basis. That is the forementioned St Anne's Lutheran Church, Gresham Street, London. From time to time elsewhere there are notices and reports of gatherings of jazz-worship occasions, and more often than not in a traditional jazz form that ideally of course feeds off many of the early gospel hymns and spirituals from the black community in America.

---

195   Elwyn A. Wienandt, contributory chapter, (ed.)
      Finley Eversole, *Jazz as a Christian Expression,*
      Christian Faith and the Contemporary Arts,
      (Abingdon Press, 1957-62), p.171.

Such times usually feature *Just A Closer Walk with Thee* and *What A Friend We Have In Jesus* to the tune *Converse*. In the more West Indian areas of London there has been a revival of the tradition of having a jazz band play ahead of the funeral cortege. The worship at St Anne's does have a liturgical base yet exudes a spontaneous air. There is also a creative feel to the proceedings that partly stems from involving an ad hoc choir comprised of anyone who is willing to arrive several hours previous, and be taken through expectations by a talented director musician. From time to time some prominent American jazz musicians with a Christian experience drop by. It can be a time for mighty praise.

However perhaps another voice with a different tune comes from a lecture delivered at the Incorporated Association of Organists' Congress in Newcastle, 1974, from Arthur Wills. Wills recalls attending a memorial service for Duke Ellington held at London's St Martin-in-the Fields. Excerpts were broadcast on radio and television, and one of these gave rise to what he termed a 'somewhat plaintive' letter to the *Daily Telegraph* from a lady who said: 'People used to go to church to glorify God, now it seems they go to glorify themselves'. Wills felt she was expecting from an Anglican service an Anglican noise, or as he put it with perhaps tongue-in-cheek:

> The cool voices of boys or student girls induced to sound as much like boys as possible and a repertoire from Tallis to Ralph Vaughan Williams or Walton.[198]

Shortly after this, the lecturer, hardly one assumes one of those wild people alluded to a few paragraphs back, goes on to say that sounds immediately posit associations, and who would disagree. However his ensuing thoughts set up an 'either/or' in terms of agreement or disagreement:

198   Arthur Wills, lecture reproduced as chapter in
        English Church Music, (The Royal School of
        Church Music, 1976) p.39ff.

> Ellington's music easily suggests the secular rather
> forcibly-the sultry world of the nightclub—sex, drink,
> gambling and all the ideas commonly associated with sin.[199]

Perhaps for a moment the lecturer had a nagging thought that he might be travelling into stormy weather, and so adds:

> But—we have to remember here that Ellington always
> thought of himself as a religious composer and increasingly so
> as he grew older [author's note: it was a view not taken into
> the heart of many jazz critics and writers who often pass and
> gloss over his spiritual adventures]. It is quite clear that his
> sound was an expression of himself and his feelings about God
> and other people and that there was no distinction between a
> secular and a sacred sound. In fact Ellington's work can only
> be usefully divided into two categories—the good and the less
> good and I suggest that this should be our only criterion also.[200]

The latter remark does suggest the lecturer has a wider opinion than merely seeing Ellington or any other jazz musician in somewhat negative, and to my mind ridiculous terms. He does say at the very end of his interesting lecture that he wished to see contemporary music working equally in sacred and secular fields. His great desire is to see an exciting rebirth of Church music, that rebirth placing 'it in the forefront of contemporary art'. He looks back to the time when the Renaissance masters such as Monteverdi and Bach worked in the church but were also 'masters at the very front of secular music'.

On that note, I would play the same tune.

Of course in the Renaissance masters' society the role of Church and the life of people were very much intertwined. This is not the case today. What is engaging for some is that people who, relatively speaking, are outside the Church are creating music to express Christian and general religious themes. Jazz has always contributed. Pop music has given the most, and folk the virtually unrecognised voice in a media age in capturing spiritual dreams and hopes.

199   Ibid. p.42.
200   Ibid. p.41.

It is professed by some that religious music has always been created by the religious, or at least true religious music would come under this description. However, as I have suggested in another chapter, many well-known hymns, especially tunes, have not come from tidy reverent cloisters.

Wienandt throws some engaging words of Archibald T. Davidson into the ring:

> If it is true, as I believe it to be, that the partition of music into categories such as dance music, church music, school music, and yet others is justified not by anything intrinsic in the music itself, but because these names connect themselves with music through suggestion, association, or the circumstances surrounding performance, or through the employment of music jointly with language in some form, then it may be said that church music is only music set off by a manufactured title from the remainder of the art, possessed of no special capacities or limitations, and subject to the same laws and the same analytical process, both technical and psychological, as all the rest of music.[201]

Wienandt then tosses his hat into the ring, and I am in agreement with what he says:

> Nevertheless, we speak of church music as if it were a separate musical style with ethical qualities, capable of arousing ideas and attitudes that other music cannot encompass. Actually there has never been a time in Christian history when a musical style used in the church was not also current in secular life, or at the very least, was not closely related to existing secular styles and devices. Although Plainsong would appear to represent an exception to that pattern, we have evidence, even in our limited knowledge of artistic life outside the church in the early Middle Ages, that a parallel musical style served secular activity as well.[202]

I return to Ellington for a special memory of Jazz and Church or Jazz and Faith. It was one of those times when we

---

201 Archibald T. Davidson, quoted in Wienandt,
   Church Music: Illusion and Reality,
   (Cambridge/Harvard University Press, 1952),
   p.5.
202 Ibid. p.173.

didn't sing hymns as such. We heard them in a different way. The setting is Coventry Cathedral. The musicians are welcomed. They are the renowned Duke Ellington and his band of musicians, called on that night by the Bishop an 'orchestra' which makes it all sound a little more refined for those who suffer indigestion at such an event taking place.

The renowned jazz critic, Max Jones, is there among nearly 2,000 people. So too recording and broadcasting is ATV television. Jones notes Ellington walking to his piano, blue suited and urbane, to begin his first performance in a British Cathedral. This was Ellington's *New World A'Comin'* given full and rhapsodic keyboard treatment, a rare work from the 1940s, revamped, set to sail once more. There was the piece *Come Sunday*, a music and song with a long history stretching back to the 1930s, and used in *My People*, a 1963 revue that drew together many aspects of the Emancipation Proclamation. There was *Come Easter*, a new piece apparently receiving its first airing. Among the jazz musicians and singers to excite and stir, were artists such as Jimmy Hamilton, Paul Gonsalves, Harry Carney, soloist George Webb, Lawrence Brown, Cat Anderson and the extraordinarily talented Johnny Hodges.

The British input came from Cliff Adams and choir. There is the dramatic moment when the words 'In the beginning God' were heard and the musical interpretation stunned the imagination. The sound filled the nave which is 80 foot wide and 80 foot high, and more than three times that in length. Even if it wasn't perfect sound, it was compensated for by the uniqueness of the occasion. For Jones it was a case of:

> For the normally brought-up jazz admirer it was a remarkable occasion the new Cathedral is an impressive building, though not in a way which subdues the spirit—and just to see the Ellington band set up on the Chancel steps, in front of the high

Altar and Graham Sutherland's Great Tapestry, was a memorable experience.[203]

Ellington would play the same programme at St Paul's, London, and it would feature a phenomenal dance routine that embellished and adorned some of the music. It was a moment when this art form could be taken within itself, and was allowed to express the moving of the Spirit, the wind that blows where it will and no one hears the sound until it comes. His third and final concert was in Westminster Abbey on United Nations Day, October 24, 1977, just six months before his death. It was attended by the Prime Minister of the day, Edward Heath, and by royalty's jazz fan, Princess Margaret. On vocals was Alice Babs, who had been given the song with a rhetorical question in *Is God a Three-Letter Word for Love?* Other numbers included *Ain't Nobody Nowhere Nothin' Without God, Every Man Prays in His Own Language,* with the final selection, *The Majesty of God.*

In 2006 Ellington's religious suite would return, the great man now with the mighty jazz band of the heavens, and fronted on this occasion in its magnificent earthly venue in London's St Paul's by Stan Tracey, another legendary figure from the jazz world.

Religion and faith was hardly a new subject for the man they call The Duke. His specifically religious jazz pieces can take us back to the 1935 film *Symphony in Black: A Rhapsody of Negro Life* where he featured music entitled *Hymn of Sorrow* that was penned around the death of a young child. And although Max Jones was to hear *Come Sunday* in the 1960s, the data bank can say that it first appeared in Ellington's very first appearance at America's legendary Carnegie Hall, as part of *Black, Brown and Beige.* Mahalia Jackson would later record the song with the Duke. An article in *The Christian Century* instanced cultural critic Jeremy Begbie comparing the piece

203   Max Jones, from *Melody Maker*, reprinted in the journal *Crisis*, (p.2, undated, probably mid-1960s.)

with the works of Messiaen and Ronault in its power to portray human experience in the light of fall and resurrection.[204]

Ellington would also play at the Cathedral Church of St John the Divine in New York, and musically roar away throughout the States. I'm not too sure how some particularly right wing evangelical American Christians would see the Ellington religious suites—there is no message of salvation by blood or cross, and God is certainly present, but Jesus sparingly so, although from his early background Ellington was surely familiar with at least the cries of black theology.

Yet as Janna T. Steed recalls so well:

Things have happened in such a way as to prove religion to me ... it makes you feel that if you are God's son, you are strong and don't have to worry.[205]

Janna Tull Steed believed that Ellington relied on that sense of divine destiny throughout his life. For him it was the 'source of his remarkable resiliency and adaptability'. Steed, an American writer, sometime research fellow at Yale's Institute of Sacred Music, Worship and the Arts, and a minister of the United Methodist Church, writes of how Ellington once said: 'All my music comes directly from the book of life', and she adds:

In the *Sacred Concerts* he gathered up huge slices of life—secular and sacred, trivial and profound, earthly and ethereal-and expressed them in his eclectic musical language.

Ellington always denied he played the piano. He said he just dreams, and it's about the dream that the piano sounds, interprets, and articulates:

Bono's comment sticks in my mind and head - 'how to praise God and be honest' that's it really, and apart from direct musical appreciation it is a reason for admiring Ellington's enormous catalogue of work, but that said, 'honesty' is not an

204   Janna T. Steed, *Nothin' Without God*,the
       Christian Century magazine, (October 12, US,
       1954), p.925.
205   Ibid. p.925.

excuse for sloppy theology, or for vagueness, and the Duke is not free from those criticisms.

In a programme some years ago for Radio 4 that drew together jazz and worship, I took the listener through many areas of jazz, to countless artists from time immemorial who have explored this area, for it is quite untrue that it has suddenly happened. The script lies somewhere, but I may have mentioned *The Sermon or The Preacher* from Jimmy Smith on Verve, a seven-minute bluesy affair that opens with a fetching guitar solo from Kenny Burrell, or the album Baptist Beat that includes Rev Moses, sub-titled *Pulse from the Pulpit*, and Hank Mobley's, *A Baptist Beat*, sub-titled *Gospel A Go Go*, or the quasi-religious *I Believe* from Courtney Pine's album *Journey To The Urge Within*, a number which he describes: 'To have faith in our destiny we must believe in tomorrow'. The album also has a delightful 1:27 brief outing, *Sunday Song*, in which Pine says he captures the 'spirit of the 7th day and all the peace it brings'. Pine recorded most of the tracks including the latter in July 1986; he might change his ideas on the seventh day as seen in the noise and bustle of the 21st-century Sunday. *Old Time Religion on Message to our Folks* from Art Ensemble of Chicago, and Donald Byrd's *I'm Trying To Get Home* are two other records. The latter includes Brother Isaac (it fuses memories of religious music, and memories of his family), Pearly Gates, Noah and the title cut. On the sleeve notes of the album, exploring the title track's title, Byrd remarks:

> That expression is used quite often in church, but I didn't think of it as a title for a number until one night in Philadelphia, while on the street, I began to conceive this song. A drunk stopped me, asked for a cigarette, and I gave him one. Then he said to me, 'I'm Tryin' To Get Home'. It hit me instantly that what he had just said had the same rhythm as the song's basic motif. And I also remembered the use of the same phrase in church. [206]

206   Donald Byrd, sleeve notes, *I'm Tryin' To Get Home* (Blue Note BST84188).*208*

New and Old Gospel has among others Jackie McLean on alto sax, and Ornette Coleman on trumpet, with one of the two tracks on the second side of particular interest, *Old Gospel*. Ornette Coleman in his sleeve notes says it has an old-time church feeling - the type of rhythm that people responded to in the South:

> And not only in church. This is the kind of religious belief you can see in the streets. These are the sounds of people happy they've just had a blessing .... *Old Gospel* is not about being good or bad. It's about being.[207]

Many will feel at home with the other track *Strange As It Seems*, not overtly 'religious' but capturing the spirit and manner of Jesus, seen by Ornette akin to a love affair with someone who does not walk the same philosophical road but whom you know loves you all the same.

The album's final sleeve note thought takes us further into how we might worship the Almighty, how we might discover fresh treasures. Nat Hentoff, possibly the most distinguished jazz critic of all time, writes:

> The album as a whole reminded me of what Ornette has told columnist Ralph Gleason: 'Why I like music is that it's like walking down the street naked'. Part of the unnecessary clothes that get in the way of music, Ornette has always felt, are the labels that are put on the different ways, different people feel and express the music inside of them. Jackie McLean agrees. 'I don't want to hear any more', he says, 'about bebop or hard bop or this and that category. Titles hang things up. The music is just good or bad'. To which Ornette adds: 'There's no bad music, only bad musicians'.[208]

Hentoff's notes conclude with Ornette's observation that what is happening is what always happens with the best of music—it 'gets the present to exist'.

---

207   Ornette Coleman *New & Old Gospel*. (Blue Note BST4262).
208   Nat Hentoff's observation on Ornette Coleman's remarks.

One of the finest more recent recordings that marry jazz infusions with faith is the superb album *Lift Every Voice* from Charles Lloyd (ECM 1832/3t) that includes nearly five minutes of a wondrous working around the tune for *Amazing Grace*, other spiritual tracks in the more obvious sense of title and theme include *Go Down Moses, Deep River* and *Prayer, The Crossing*.

My Radio 4 programme on jazz and faith did definitely major on John Coltrane's *A Love Supreme*, and such is its influence, its power, its glory, that there is a beautiful book with a fine narrative, bearing that title and sub-titled The Creation of John Coltrane's Classic Album. Since the book runs to almost 260 pages, it is hardly likely to be well covered by any writer who has a general brief like mine, where I am alluding to a number of jazz writers and practitioners who explore in spiritual depth. Coltrane is not everyone's cup of tea, and even the album with its persistent title line is not easy listening, unless versed in his style of jazz, although the artist was helped in the 'getting to know all about it' stakes by a recording made by John McLaughlin and Santana, on their *Love Devotion Surrender* album. Santana is quoted in Ashley Kahn's *A Love Supreme* as saying that he dreams big, and he would love to record *A Love Supreme* with African drummers, Brazilian musicians, a bevy of top jazz players, with the consequence that when people hear it they'll be dancing in the aisles, laughing and crying at the same time like they have the Holy Spirit in them.[209]

The piece has a four-part journey of faith: 'Acknowledgement', 'Resolution', 'Pursuance', and 'Psalm'. When it comes to this record you can talk over why an unusual key choice is made at the outset, as some have; or ask whether or not there is dubbing over vocal on the title line. Were the horns too close to the mike, and talk of a four-note bass line, of equalization but Ravi Coltrane speaks

209   Ashley Kahn, *A Love Supreme, The Creation of John Coltrane's Classic Album*, (Granta Books, 2002), p.204.

what many of us feel with respect to this extraordinary piece that it's not just a tune or record, or an idle offering, or with a purpose that's aimed at being hip or cool—it simply speaks the sacred. 2006 saw a Coltrane compilation of recordings for Impulse, *The Impulse Story*, with *A Love Supreme* (Pt 1), *Greensleeves*, and the extraordinary *The Father And The Son And the Holy Ghost* (00236), that in common with *Dear Lord* and *Welcome* take us into his mid 1960s love of hymn language titles.

Coltrane, born in North Carolina, on September 23 1926, died from liver cancer a few weeks short of his 41st birthday, yet even now his music is ever being discovered. He has exercised enormous influence on all who play the tenor saxophone. As Richard Cook has said those who speak of him exude a reverent glow:

> ... that he could be so quiet, selfless, and respectful of others when simultaneously possessed by talents so gargantuan that they almost shook him apart—well, it sounds extraordinary, it sounds ridiculous. And yet it seems, insofar as any retrospective can be, to represent the truth. Coltrane's spiritual search—an endless one, its goals ever greater, its demands ever deeper—entailed personal impositions that only the most dedicated of men could make .... he sounded that way because he was that way.[210]

Cook later writes of Coltrane's quest for a literally divine beauty and his anguish at spiritual poverty.

Some of his followers named a church in his honour. In San Francisco there is St John's Orthodox Church, a storefront establishment where you can hear his music during the Sunday service, but its actual location has moved several times. Clive Davis, describing this place, describes how his image is displayed:

> His image (is) displayed alongside Christ and the Virgin Mary.

As the church's saxophone-playing Bishop Franzo King once observed:

---

210   Richard Cook, *Tribute To A Jazz Giant*, (New Musical Express, December 25, 1982), p.60.

> When somebody asks me, 'When did John Coltrane become a saint?' I say, 'When we demoted him from God'.[211]

By the time of his death, Coltrane, a reformed heroin addict, is reported to be arriving at a style more akin to speaking in tongues. Davis sees his early death as contributory to his saintly status. Coltrane had his opposites, for he could run a gamut of emotion from bombastic and torturous note bending and yet duet with Duke Ellington on *In A Sentimental Mood*.

With so little space for jazz in British worship it is difficult to find someone who would speak positively of jazz from the standpoint of a preacher. One who can is Anthony Reddie, a Research Fellow and Consultant in Black Theological Studies for the Queen's Foundation. For him, growing up in Bradford, and attempting not to be swallowed up in white culture, a jazz hermeneutic has been a way of reconnecting to his black roots:

> Just as a jazz musician has to respond to the unique context of every performance, bringing new knowledge to life, in a split second of a moment, so too must the preacher ....[212]

Yet, not unexpectedly there is literature that would push jazz out through the door, either quietly and gently or with robust distaste. The voices that rail would speak of it destroying the dignity and majesty of true worship. It is also the voice that sees no place for the new, as though there has been certain music that is and is for all time the only acceptable. At the same time there must be acceptance that the 'new' must always cause conflict with the 'old' and no music of itself is capable of meeting all needs, and no music can ever claim to be the only way in which we sense the presence of God, whether in church or permeating all things. I have not argued as to whether jazz meets this and that criteria, I have tried to suggest by inference that it

211 Clive David, *Melody Maker*, (January 4, 1998, p.10).
212 Anthony Reddie, chapter in Geoffrey Stevenson, (ed.) *An Interactive Odyssey, Pulpit Journeys*, (Darton. Longman & Todd, 2006), p.161.

speaks to the soul. I am conscious as well of the concluding words of Elwyn Wienandt in his contributing chapter to the book *Christian Faith and the Contemporary Arts:*

> Whatever style of music is to be presented, it must be done with the understanding that communication needs to be achieved between composer and listener. Music is not, as the old saw would have it, a universal language. Any form of communication must be equally clear to both the communicator and the audience. Jazz is no more universally understood than is Arabic or Hindustani; our current church music is likewise incomprehensible to a majority of the world's people.[213]

As Wienandt also says, whatever the style of music:

> Handel or Palestrina, or the idiom of the hymnbook or the jazz combo, it is on its capacity to lend spiritual strength and vigour that it must be judged, and not in its strange newness.[214]

This is the world where people are asked to listen and appreciate, to feel stimulated, to receive someone's offering, to feel that it is good to be alive, and to celebrate God's presence among us! Moments that are suggestive not definitive. Some of the music named may be hummed, even at times sung along to, as might be the repetitive title line of John Coltrane's masterpiece.

I agree with Erik Routley as he writes:

> Those who try to shrug this off as an affectation or form of deceit, and to dismiss jazz as something trivial, have been sufficiently exposed and convicted of false arrogance by many serious writers.[215]

The more participatory jazz form comes with 'Trad' jazz. Many traditional hymns suit this mode, with the best known *What A Friend We Have in Jesus* to the tune *Converse*. There is nothing to prevent the inclusion of traditional

---

213   Elwyn A.Wienandt in Finley Eversole (ed.),
       Christian Faith and the Contemporary Arts,
       (Abingdon, 1957), p.178.
214   Ibid. p.178.
215   Erik Routley, *Twentieth Century Church Music*
       (Herbert Jenkins, London), 1964 p.1.

songs arranged in a trad jazz format to be part of any hymnbook, and this is so in a number of American hymn collections that also contain jazz and blues pieces outside of the more obvious 'trad' input. Trad's familiar sing-a-long songs are *Just a Closer Walk with Thee, Steal Away to Jesus, Down by the Riverside* and *Give me that Old, Time Religion*. This basically takes us to the style and manner emanating from New Orleans Gospel that has grabbed many:

> 'New Orleans Gospel' is not only an example of profane religious North American cross-breeding but, of greater importance, it is a deliberately anachronistic encounter between the New Orleans repertory and contemporary Gospel singing. 'New Orleans Gospel' boosts such natural energy that, amazingly enough, we discover a new musical genre.[216]

A good record to hear and to gain some sense of the genre and its religious associations can come from hearing *Jazz Funeral In New Orleans* from George Lewis (Tradition TCD1049) which contains various standards, including *When the Saints* and *Down by the Riverside*:

> How to sift through the muddle of choices that is your life and turn it into a prayer? I don't know how but I was listening to someone who did.[217]

216   Tory Robinson with the Vintage Jazzmen, New Orleans Gospel Live, Sleevenote, (Fremeaux & Associates FA 455).
217   Ibid. p.212.

CHAPTER NINE

Reflections - Despair and Hope

More recently it has been the *Mission Praise* collection that has found a wide Christian audience, even if it is lacking in some ways. It must have been startling, worrying and pleasing to the various understandings in the British Church of England that in the Report of the Archbishops' Commission on Church Music,[218] a survey found 36 per cent of churches used both *Mission Praise* and *Junior Praise*, compared with 28 per cent for the traditional Anglican book, *Hymns Ancient and Modern*. Conservative parishes reported higher percentages than catholic ones, each having of course their own theological axe to grind. Brian Castle,[219] writing in the bi-monthly journal *Theology* comments:

> The main features of the book include a large number of hymns addressed exclusively to Jesus, a high proportion using the first person singular, a low view of humanity and the world, a strong theology of glory, and a marked sectarian tendency. This combination results in a heavy emphasis on a personal (at the expense of a corporate) relationship with God the Son that is expressed in terms of emotion: 'Jesus, how lovely You are/You are so gentle, so pure and kind'.[220]

218 *In Tune with Heaven* (Hodder and Stoughton, London, 1992).
219 Then Vicar of North Petherton and Northmoor Green in Somerset.
220 Brian Castle, *Hymns - More than Songs of Praise*, (*Theology* magazine, March/April 1992), p.201ff.

At the time of writing, I have two Methodist Church services in my diary for the next fortnight. Twenty years ago, I would have been asked to choose hymns from the official hymnbook for that church, *Hymns and Psalms*. In this instance the first church uses the *BBC Songs of Praise* hymnbook, but I am told it does have a few *Hymns and Psalms* lying around. The other church said they use *Songs of Fellowship,* but if I wished, it being a smaller evening service, they could rustle up some *Hymns and Psalms*. This unscientific analysis gives room for thought and reflection. Within that simple illustration it is clear that there is little chance of a definitive answer to that plaintive cry of Albert van den Heuvel's 'Tell me what you sing, and I'll tell you who you are'. Methodists are uncertain. It seems the same elsewhere. It is the Independent and House Church sector that exhibits confidence. Their 'new' music, much of it derived from American sources, has entered the bloodstream of all Christian churches, and within the evangelical sphere it has bounced off earlier foundations that focussed on the CSSM chorus book, later the songbook *Youth Praise*, and then *Songs of Fellowship*, which I have referred to in another context. The momentum is considerable, and seemingly relentless, with new songs arriving by the day. These songs can arrive with a commercial market driven sell to almost drown whatever else may be thrown up by those who offer word and song for what might still be called 'these crisis days'.

When it comes to music with a popular appeal, the mainstream Churches appear dated and insignificant, and one correspondent writing to the *Methodist Recorder* asks why the Methodist Faith and Worship committee continues to focus on hymn music. The writer poses the disturbing question:

> Does anyone know of a church that still focuses their musical 'offering' on traditional hymns and is experiencing significant growth. I want to visit it.[221]

221   John Foster, *The Methodist Recorder*, (January 20, 2005), p.6.

The independent church 'music' input has a dimension beyond a piece of music with words that appear on a music page or on the screen of an overhead projector. It has been driven by running with, and copying, much that would be recognised in the commercial world, on how to market and sell a product. Indeed many of those whose names can grace the story of popular Christian expression since the late 1960s have come from a 'selling' background. Within the musical output there is no distinctive Christian edge, for it is secular land that dominates style and performance, with only the presumed faith of the artist to bring some difference. It can be argued that whereas in the Reformation and Plainsong times church music was in the vanguard, now it seems we are inferior followers, and that 'praise' music is the stepchild of rock and its sub-categories. In more recent time there is little doubt that it can offer a standard of musicianship, writing and recording that is un-recognizeable from the days of the 1970s when three chord wonders were prevalent, and musicianship was a bad second to a desire to evangelise.

An organisation such as Spring Harvest invariably issues a new bulky songbook for its annual event, and wishes to eat into the life of fellowships afterward. The new material is given promotional push by an album and tape, and at the event itself the 'new' songs will be prominently featured.

Arguably the best-known songwriter from outside the denominations, Graham Kendrick, for once British, was speedily able to make known his compositions. Kendrick formed his own company *Make Way*; he began to issue worship albums, and books, and at times these would be linked to marches and large worship gatherings, some in public places. Hence some of his songs have an appropriate driving rhythm for the thudding of feet along the highways and byways. It all added up to this quiet likeable person exercising enormous influence. Kendrick's songs are now sung anywhere and everywhere.

For a Church with many forms of worship there is also the question of how many praise hymns are useful, in terms of a prolific writer there is always the dilemma of how many of their items shall be included. This is the quandary with Graham Kendrick. The ignored compilers of the terribly non-U *Methodist Hymns Old And New* (meaning their efforts were not authorised) use his rather good, but not that well known, *Beauty for Brokenness* among 29 compositions! The generally contemporary *Common Ground* gives him five entries: *Meekness and Majesty, O Lord, The Clouds Are Gathering, Restore, O Lord* inevitably *Shine Jesus Shine* and last his other rave fave *The Servant King.*[222]

It's far from easy on talking with this modern hymn writer to note what he thinks about either himself or his work, although he cannot have been delighted to read himself described thus by the television critic of the *London Evening Standard*:

> The loathsome evangelist Graham Kendrick. His nauseating songs always bring two verses of Scripture to my mind: Matthew ch 27:5 ('And he went and hanged himself"); and Luke, ch 10:37 ('Go and do likewise').[223]

Kendrick's universally known hymn anthem is *Shine, Jesus, Shine*. Ian Cotton says it has 'honeydew tones' and reflecting on the lines:

> Shine, Jesus, shine
> Fill this land with the Father's glory.
> Flow, river, flow,

---

222   Here perhaps the compilers were playing a little to the gallery (why include *Shine, Jesus, Shine*), or *The Servant King*, in terms of the collection's more radical approach in selection, and ignoring traditional favourites, although their place in the content may encourage a wider group of buyers! I would love to know why *Beauty for Brokenness* is not included. Yes, there are many Kendrick popular numbers, but there is in this hymn a Christian social and radical depth sadly lacking in the overall praise collections. His early rec ord albums are worth exploring for songs with a social dimension.

223   Victor Lewis Smith, *Evening Standard*, (April 4, 2005), p.29 .

> Flood the nations with grace
> And mercy

He comments:

There were chirpy thirty year olds in Fair Isle sweater and common-sense slacks, moody eighteen year olds with dangly hair, and crosses in their ears, florid fifty year olds, fluffy OAPS, all smiled amiably on as, come the hymns, a line of Salvation Army officers in the middle of the hall broke into a twist. One of the things about dancing as you sing is that hymn books can be a bit cumbersome, hence the Charismatic tradition of projecting hymns onto a screen in front of the congregation, the better to act out those experimental motions. Far preferable, this, to old-style, hedged-in, hymn-book in hand Gutenberg because Touch is not limited to the tame injunction 'ok turn to the person next to you and give the Sign of Peace.'[224]

Cotton notices the charismatic style of running three or four hymns together:

One after another, seamlessly, into a kind of emotional ski run uninterrupted by any sermonising or rationality. That Thursday evening we had just such a troika on the trot, two jolly hymns, one moody, until we arrived, duly mellowed, at the one of the few traditional hymns charismatics still sing, *When I Survey the Wondrous Cross.*[225]

Cotton's observations, as much as that of the acerbic Victor Lewis Smith, will hardly be respected by the support club. However, the kind of underpinning he has for his ministry is far beyond that offered to some of mainstream's best living new writers - such as those briefly mentioned earlier - Brian Wren, Fred Kaan, Timothy Dudley Smith. They are left to make their own way. It would be too much for mainstream churches to offer funding so that their work can be better known. It stands as an example of the lack of imagination and a reading of the current situation among the denominations who are either dragged down by financial or bureaucratic empires, or as with the Anglican

---

224   Ian Cotton *The Hallelujah Revolution*, (Little,
      Brown & Company, USA, 1995), p.26.
225   Ibid. p.27.

church worldwide use their energy on issues such as acceptance or not of those with a gay orientation or as British Methodists tediously debate whether 'Bishops' can be adopted within their structures. The only hope for the writers I have named in mainstream areas is occasionally to find their material making the pages of a new hymnal. However these publications have lessened. The Scottish songwriter John Bell takes his songs to Church conferences, and runs workshops where the interested can learn new songs that have in the main a 'folkish' air and often something of Bell's Scottish heritage. It is another example of the general malaise and total misreading by the mainstream denominations. While many in the more traditional fold, whatever their theological emphasis, plough on, and usually in fields long past their life span, and deride the modern songs, they are at the same time clueless to stem their own haemorrhaging. What seems indisputable rests in the new churches having brought into their fold new disciples, but many of their members have come across from mainstream circles. Mainstream Churches have been overtaken by the sheer brashness and commercialism stemming from the independent church sector, in itself largely springing from the unease of some younger Christians at the dullness and lack of evangelistic fervour from the main denominations:

> To a degree mainstream churches have been both caught in a timewarp; it might be said that death is today's unmentionable, even in Christian circles. It was inevitable that something had to give. Much of their worship had fallen into idle acceptance of the familiar. Didacticism ruled. Nobody denies there were provocations that justified the protest—declining attendances at Sunday services made the problem obvious ... it was particularly the young who objected that the church was dull and stiff, lacking in a lively sense of community.[226]

226   B.A. Gerrish, Foreword to Ernest Marvin,
       Shaping Up, Reforming Reformed Worship,
       (United Reformed Church, London, 2005), p.iii.

However, stability remains in many areas of British Christian life. It was well expressed in the top 20 hymns voted by viewers in 2005 to the long running and highly successful *Songs of Praise*. This was virtually free of anything that has been written in the last 20 years, and was heavily weighted toward the traditional, and expected. The BBC list was given in no particular order, and contained such hymns as:

- *I Vow To Thee my Country*
- *Praise My Soul*
- *Abide with Me*
- *The Day Thou Gavest*
- *What A Friend We Have In Jesus*
- *Jerusalem*
- *Dear Lord and Father of Mankind*

Ernest Marvin, a minister in the United Reformed Church, and still applauded in some circles for his masterpiece in 1959 when with Ewan Hooper he created *A Man Dies*, writes in his book *Shaping Up* of the style of worship known in some quarters as 'the Hymn Sandwich':

> This is the term that, on the one hand, can be used to typify those acts of public worship which are devoid of shape and movement, a mishmash of prayers, readings, preachings (the 'fillings') loosely bound together by a number of unrelated hymns/songs (the 'bread') ... sadly not uncommon today.[227]

Marvin relates the story of David, who only came occasionally to church:

> 'David!', I ventured to say one Sunday morning during coffee hour. 'I notice you never sing the hymns: why not?' 'I only sing when I'm happy and I'm never happy in church.' There was no quick answer to that, but what should worship have done for David?[228]

At least there are those who have attempted to bring hymnology into their own time. One fruitful period

227   Ibid. p.67.
228   Ibid. p.ix.

---

coincided with various hymn publications of the 1970s. Much credit must go to the quite amazing Bernard Braley of Galliard and its parent company, Stainer and Bell. Bernard ran worship gatherings throughout Britain and naturally displayed his published material. We sang new songs and read experimental liturgical forms. People were often perplexed by their earthly and radical nature. Few were not challenged.

Braley had one simple trick up his sleeve. He would ask those attending to write down their hobbies and special interests. He would then analyse the information and inform the church that within its membership there were seven poets, eight decorators, four painters, three songwriters, two graphic artists, four who loved playing with lay-outs, seventeen people who loved singing, three experts on opera, five on folk, nine with a considerable record collection, twenty cooks, three playwrights, eight actors, ten flower arrangers and gardeners, twenty-four into costume, thirty interested in make-up, and so it continued.

Then would come Braley's 'rabbit out of the hat moment'; he would say this church is brimming with talent, but how much of it is used, or how many have thought they could bring their skills and knowledge into the living arena we call a Church, let alone seeing all in the wider community usefulness. It often produced some emotional moments; there is nothing like discovering you are wanted in a place that is supposed to affirm you.

Hence as is surely plain, the aspect of Braley that particularly impressed was his constant desire to take on board Incarnation theology, the simple but hard process of letting Faith be found in what we do and are. Not everyone was happy with his direction, but in the main those who voiced objection, and even distaste, were those who could not bring themselves to feel that normal everyday things could be endowed with spiritual seasoning, or that God might be found amidst the pots and pans.

In many of his liturgies which appeared in his publication *Lornehurst Bulletin* his allusions were so matter of fact they seemed ridiculous, but that spoke more of other people's theology than his, for after all the tea-room meet and chat is often where many of us are at peace with Maker and universe. Is not God's 'grace' inclusive of working and eating, the strolling in the hillside, by the seashore, the embrace and understanding of the hand that holds and helps the sick to rise?

Braley's work was not confined to the 1970s, he continued as an activist into the 21st century publishing resources, laying down his markers in more substantial form by authorising a number of what were seen as 'risky' hymn and song publications, not least *Reflecting Praise* (1993) with *Women in Theology*, that contained new writing exploring female images of God. *Partners in Praise* issued jointly with the Methodist Youth Department (1979) was considered by some Methodists, not to mention others, to contain material that could only be described as irreverent. After all it's much more lively to sing *All Things Bright and Beautiful* than to launch into some words by Basil E. Bridge:

> The cat hunts the bird and the lion the deer;
> The rose has its thorn, and the heart has its fear,
> We cannot say why—yet the Father is near.

It was a book where virtually every hymn and song had a contemporary reference. It should in fairness be said that there was a considerable and varied bunch who were given the title of Joint Music Editors. However the selection was very much what he would want, and the preface and guide to its use was very much Braley's.

> Avoid only using those hymns you like best. Others with different tastes will be worshipping too. We only grow by using that which does not immediately appeal.

With the Scottish St Andrew's Press, he published *Songs for the Seventies, A Collection of Contemporary Hymns* in 1972. Its tenor was well set in words by Ian Fraser, with verse two reading:

> Christ, holding
> Atoms in one
> Loom of light and power
> To weave creation's life
> Man moulding
> Rocket, gun

> Turns creation sour
> Plots dissolving strife

There is a fascinating hymn by Richard G. Jones on the Adam and Eve story with a third verse reading:

> Thirst after pow'r is this sin of my shame,
> Pride's ruthless thrust after status and fame,
> Turning and stealing and cowering from thee.
> Lord, forgive Adam,
> For Adam is me.

One of his larger and more ambitious publications was *The Rope of Love—Around The Earth in Song*, written, composed and arranged by the then extremely popular Donald Swann. At intervals with Alan Luff he published *Hymns and Congregational Songs*, smallish booklets with new and interesting material, drawing on a very wide Christian constituency.

Arguably Braley's most notorious book is *New Life*. John Bailey, an extremely gifted writer, teacher, educationalist and folk singer, was appointed editor.[229]

Braley also edited a series of four hefty, somewhat expensive books called *Blueprint*, another Galliard publication.

Braley also published one of the few big selling Christian songbooks of the late 1960s, the hugely popular *Faith Folk & Clarity*. This was one of a trilogy, *Faith, Folk and Clarity/Nativity/Festivity* edited by Peter Smith. Smith had marvellous foresight in reading the times, and the book had enormous sales. Less successful in sales terms, but not in content, was his edited *Jesus Folk* (1974).

These songs reflect the response of many people from a wide variety of backgrounds, traditions and nationalities. They look at the life, teaching and influence of Jesus, and

---

229 Bailey was then working for the Christian Education Movement, and would soon become the advisor for humanities and religious education in Lincolnshire. Notes on this text can be found in some detail in the chapter dealing with books for young people.

meditate upon His significance for us today. Braley, a Methodist, has never received from that Church the honour that is his due, and indeed his funeral was marked by the relative absence of Church officialdom. It wasn't as though he came across as some dangerous radical bomber of all things safe in Faith. He was fairly quiet and gentle, of unbridled enthusiasm, and someone who was out to 'change' things, and that is never the safest of choices in the Christian Church. He could be perceived as being difficult.

Braley was not the only one trying to drive the Christian community into the present time, but he had his publishing arm to put his aims and desires into effect reasonably quickly. Others included Brian Frost, one of the main instigators of a group which organised in London one huge ecumenical outbreak of different worship and practices in many Churches in the early 1970s. For a while London became an exciting place of church diversity and practice, some Churches and Christian groups admitted into their pristine sanctuaries forms of worship, and hymn-song material that had never hitherto darkened their doors. For a while it seemed reality was here, and possibly here to stay. We could be Christians for today. I had caught more than a glimpse of this some years previously in the United States. If I hadn't found myself a student on both coasts of America in 1968 and 1969 I might have settled for two different worlds, the old beloved sacred and secular. Against the backcloth of student unrest, especially at Berkeley, of an awareness over there of the impact of the ill-judged war in Vietnam, the broader life or death dilemmas in the world, it was a case of celebrate the good, but more often than not weeping for the follies of humankind. It was from the perspective of what was happening that we prayed, here many new songs were born, some coming out of the folk revival. Hardly surprising, traditional hymns never got a look in.

Braley was not the only one pioneering new forms of worship allied to music and the arts in general, but arguably he was the most persuasive, and acting from the beneficial base of being able to publish and disseminate. Also prominent in this period was a group of talented musicians and writers called *Reflection* with Michael Lehr and Mike Jakins very much spearheading its work. Their publication *Sounds of Salvation* still stands a good guide to faith expressed in contemporary manner. Speaking of how they might use hymns, the publication states:

> The modern supplements and hymn collections are something of a disappointment. Few of the hymns successfully conquer the problems of imagery that date traditional hymns. To some extent, the concept of salvation itself is not easily expressed in modern hymnody.[230]

To answer that question 'Tell me what you sing, and I'll tell you who you are,' I am even more conscious that I have not defined or attempted an analysis of 'worship' other than in passing, for its very concept will largely determine what shall or shall not be sung. But here again we can wander into other important fields, such as church architecture, church lighting, colour, even down to the person who will lead, the musical accompanist, not to mention the door stewards, and whether coffee afterward is served in a plastic container, to be accompanied by a soggy biscuit.

The general Church offers flowers, sometimes the only relief from its otherwise harsh and boring interior. It doesn't zero in on how people feel, and what they see when they enter the portals, and how all of us are simply affected by where we are. Usually the organist or accompanist will be playing chords at random, and doing nothing more than using up time before the service starts. Should the light be dim, and the organist and pianist be slow, we will sing softly, and even the most passionate of cries from someone such as Isaac Watts or Wesley in their hymns will be treated with lack lustre vocal projection. Perhaps this subject belongs to another book. It may be insufficient but I quote:

> Worship to be maximally effective must provide not only a symbolic reordering of experience but an element of consummation and fulfilment. The experience of worship should produce an influx of life and power, a feeling of wholeness, of the grace of God, of being still at the centre of a turning wheel. If this happens there may occur a shift in the

230   *Sounds of Salvation*, (1974), p.3.

definition of the boundary of the self, as with Blake, an identification with everything that lives, but at any rate a transformation of motivation, commitment, and value that may galvanize not only individuals but the collectivity of worshippers. If worship does not 'work' it may not be because it is 'irrelevant.'[231]

At the outset, such a task as this is beset by a major difficulty, for the Church is typically multi-generational rather than mono-generational. Worship has to make sense to all the age ranges. The person who preaches has to reach across the generations.[232] The music chosen somehow has to make sense to a musically diverse gathering. Unlike the modern radio station the Christian Church cannot tailor its output on demographic lines, although in recent times there are Churches with two or three worship services of a different nature taking place at one and the same time somewhere within its building. Whatever the case, in recent times, within many a denomination, music has been a major divisive influence, with battles raging in some quarters between 'praise song' and 'traditional' often causing congregational splits. Some of the latter are fiercely outspoken against either speaking in tongues or giving undue prominence to Paul's words on speaking in tongues, as opposed to the place of other gifts of the Spirit.

The Revd Professor B.A.Gerrish, John Nuveen Professor Emeritus, The University of Chicago Divinity School speaks of 'Worship Wars'; in one corner readying for the fight we have the 'traditional' in the other the 'contemporary'.

Alwyn Marriage, past editor of the one-time quarterly journal *Christian*, simply says:

> The gulf between cathedral evensong and 'happy clappy choruses still looks as wide as that between hell and

231   Myron B. Bloy, *Multi-Media Worship*, (The Seabury Press, New York, 1969), p.55.
232   For a lengthy and absorbing read on this latter point I can only point you for starters to *God and the Generations: Youth, Age and the Church Today*. (Paternoster Press, London, 2002).

Abraham's bosom...elitism is partly responsible, with those who enjoy the classical tradition believing they have better taste than those who favour more popular forms, and chorus enthusiasts feeling spiritually superior to those left cold or embarrassed by them. But this elitism is in turn fed by insecurity, as people find they are not free to respond honestly to what they hear for fear of being thought 'square' or 'uncultured'.[233]

Sometimes a kind of peace reigns with a degree of unease, usually where the minister and leaders have stressed tolerance and understanding in the Christian family. This is not too difficult if it is simply a matter of mixing styles, and so in my case, when taking mainstream worship as opposed to house and independent fellowships, I may choose two or three traditional hymns, and a few from the 'praise song' catalogue. In this worship format one song may be used before something else, and like a hymn, often used to embroider what has come before or that which follows. The 'song' replaces the hymn, but this is not the way of Pentecostal gatherings, for at root they have a totally different concept of worship.

Some charismatics say you meet God as you sing, although it might be said this is hardly something new, as Billy Bray, the King's Son from Cornwall would testify. Yet if a song leads people to God it has to say something about God, otherwise the worshipper has nothing but the Word itself, unless it is presumed the worshipper sings big religious words having already been led by a preacher to understand what they mean.

Whether traditional or praise, speaking as someone who often has to select ten hymns for two Sunday services, I find it very frustrating. I see Scripture as being totally relevant to the issues of today. This is not my problem. My problem rests in finding hymn words for an age that is so drastically different from most of the mainstream hymnbook writers. To take a concrete example: I am preaching on Racial Justice

---

233   Alwyn Marriage ed., *Christian*, (93/3 Summer issue), p.1.

Sunday, so where are the hymns in *Hymns and Psalms,* and probably most other hymn books, written by black writers? Where are the sentiments in faith of those who have known the struggle of being black? Where are the songs that talk that language, or in their terminology might refer to particular shaping events not only in the African Negro struggle in the States, but in South Africa or Bradford? In terms of black culture in America a recent publication has much to interest. In his introduction to the American *New Baptist Hymnal* (2005) the publisher Dr Theophilus B. Boyd III, says there was a twofold purpose: first, to enhance all aspects of worship; second, to preserve the church's great religious heritage and music for generations to come. Unlike many a preface, this publisher speaks of offering features that will add 'enjoyment.' The other interesting mention in the *New Baptist Hymnal* relates to 'heritage' and in terms of the book's content I feel the publisher is alluding to something more than the Baptist story. He is alluding to the words and tunes that have helped shape the Christian cause in the United States, particularly the Baptist tradition, and again from looking through its listing I am conscious that it takes account of both white and black communities. In both the *Baptist Hymnal* and the 1989 *The United Methodist Hymnal*, there is inclusion of traditional blues and gospel, and so it includes standards like *Nobody Knows the Trouble I See, Precious Lord, Take My Hand, I Want Jesus to Walk with Me* and *Steal Away to Jesus.*

Such songs as these are very much for Christian brothers and sisters across the Atlantic. However, this is to overlook one important point, namely that the music of the States has exercised enormous influence in Britain and elsewhere, and that many have adopted, taken and sung these songs. They are sung by known soul, R & B, folk and gospel artists. They are universally known, and there is no reason why some of these should not be included in a hymn and song collection for people to sing. Certainly as it stands, they belong to the 'outs' of what the soul may sing in British churches, outside of the relatively few churches, such as St Anne's Lutheran, London, with its monthly evening jazz service. There is a longer deliberation on this at a later stage.

I have admittedly focussed in various areas of this book on Methodism; I have done so in the sense that I see it as being broadly representative of non-Anglican traditions in worship structure. However within the sacred portals of the established church in Britain, the faltering giant otherwise known as the Church of England, there can now be found an enormous variety of worship forms, not least the popularity of free forms of worship that have made the set forms hard to maintain. It is music that is the driving force behind this, allied to a crucially significant change within society where the informal has replaced much of what was formal, and is seen to be important because it was of this nature.

Whatever the tradition and emphasis, Albert van den Heuvel is surely right when he says the Christian community must find the kairos of the time, of our history, and that is something that escapes the 'praise world' let alone the traditional fold. Heuvel throws forward Bonhoeffer who said, during the time of Hitler that the only person who is allowed to sing the Gregorian chant is he who cries out for the Jews. What now for the Palestinians? Heuvel adds that in Bonhoeffer's harsh statement the unbreakable link between involvement and liturgy is given for all time. One can only sing in church, when one is really connected with the dynamic principle of history.

Yes! Yes! I shout. The prophets of Old Testament times would be out there blowing their trumpets in support, so would Paul and Peter, as their texts focus on living Christ in the world.

Michael Marshall calls music in church the 'bicycle of the liturgy' (that is a rather good term) although it does depend on how well it is ridden, and sometimes by whom! It also makes one wonder whether 'punctures' are part of the bicycle imagery! Marshall is confident that the clergy will be expert riders:

> Sensitive ministers of religion will acquaint themselves with many dozens of hymn books that are now available. They will probably have a whole shelf in the study given over to nothing other than hymns, psalms and spiritual songs in various settings and with various tunes. From their detailed knowledge of a rich supermarket of varying musical opportunities, they will, in consultation with the readers, musicians and the leaders of

worship, with greatest care style the liturgy for a particular Sunday or a particular event in a particular place.[234]

To take Bonhoeffer's words on board, and perhaps in the setting slightly over-described by Bishop Marshall, would at very least introduce a severe setting and context before any worship and hymn committee involved with a Sunday service. How many of them would ever place before themselves the lectionary or chosen readings, the preacher's theme if different, and do so in the context of the day's or week's newspapers? Or sit in front of the main television news, to take into account what is happening of any consequence in that community, and then proceed as a group to plan worship? One thing is for sure - there would be change!

So, let's assume there is a new hymnbook in the process of being compiled, and dare we think it might encompass a fairly broad Christian spectrum: what should we be looking for?

A church thinking of compiling a new general book would hear what the world is singing in popular culture, and this is a subject so broad that I do not feel justified to explore it here. It will form much of a second adventure into pop and contemporary music with a spiritual edge, although in the music worship gatherings stemming from charismatic quarters, a band such as Delirious can play rock as good as many. Delirious can also produce some moving new songs of faith that have an 'anthem' quality that enables audiences to sing with them. Contemporary worship gatherings, sometimes stretched over a weekend or at a Festival, draw thousands of young people, but how far this can be reconciled with some basic Christian community understanding remains to be seen.

Lionel Adey takes time at the end of his book on hymns to see how the different ages, from 1700 to 1920, have dealt in their hymnal with various subjects. He chooses:

234   Michael Marshall, *Free to Worship*, (Marshall Pickering, London, 1992), p.118.

God, Pastoral Care, Nature, Love, Light, Blood, Water, Nature, Existence and Childhood[235]

and it proves an interesting concept.

I would take on board some of his suggestions, were I to ask of contemporary writers to find songs on the varieties of life experience, of coping with modern technology, communicatory systems, even down to the joys and pleasures that come from living in a society that is full of adventure and experiment that would stun those who wrote hymns before the Second World War. I want a global and multi-racial feel. I want hymnal texts that acknowledge the city and urban sprawls, of ecology and the greening effect. I want hymns that speak of the wonder of architecture, the huge arena of clothing and fashion with its skills and design, of those who deal in colour and design for interiors. There must be texts that mention bleakness and lost-ness, the modern sense of being crushed by multi-national concerns, of the nasty teeth that can be capitalism, of sprawling masses, of the arts, of sport.

In other words I am pleading for relevancy, the reality of knowing God present, of the impact of the Incarnation upon all aspects of life in its myriad forms. I would particularly press this home to the general charismatic world, for most of the writers I name do not have particular allegiance to that aspect of the Christian world.

It means a hymn committee will call in with expectation to Iona, the inspirational thoughts of Kathy Galloway, and the terrific work of people like John Bell and Graham Maule. (The hymnbook of the United Reformed Church was published in 1991, and included compositions such as *The Love of God Comes Close* and *Before The World Began,* and the *BBC Songs of Praise* in 1997 has nine compositions from Bell-Maule). It will converse with the most adventurous set going, and that is the Church of Scotland. The new book could pay some attention to the much neglected Welsh speaking tradition both lyrically and

235   Lionel Adey, *Hymns and the Christian Myth,*
        (University of British Columbia Press, Canada,
        1986), p.199.

musically, to Gaelic contributions, and to see more from June Tillman, Brian Wren, Albert Bayly, Alan Gaunt, Fred Kaan, and Timothy Dudley Smith. Kaan in particular has written some sharp lines, to include:

> ... the plight of the hungry
> while harvests are left on the field
> for orchards neglected and wasting
> for produce from markets withheld

He has also translated material, with *The Love Of God Is Broad* (*Rejoice and Sing* (108) reminding us of the neglect of contemporary European and Scandinavian material. Most hymn books do contain numerous German texts of 16th and 17th-century vintage, fine and still singable, including two neglected Christmas pieces, *All My Heart This Night Rejoices* and *From Heaven Above To Earth I Come*. Like many a hymn, the actual physical context is important, and the latter makes for a wondrous processional hymn, set against the glow of candles and the dress of those both officiating and singing.

In Methodist circles there is Martin Eggleton, Andrew Pratt, Brian Hoare, and Peter Sharrocks. Mr Pratt excepted, all were born before the end of the Second World War. Fred Pratt Green has left behind many splendid hymns. Philip Carter, who among many things co-ordinates the Methodist Organ Advisory Service, tells of the time when Erik Routley made the statement:

> Charles Wesley was such a great hymn writer that Methodists seem to have been almost totally inhibited from writing hymns. Charles Wesley's mantle has floated through space for 200 years looking for worthy shoulders on which to alight, and only now in the late twentieth century has it found its true resting place on the shoulders of Fred Pratt Green.[236]

Philip Carter wrote to me:

> I told Fred about this and with his usual modesty he said 'I do wish that man would shut up!'[237]

236 Philip Carter, recounted in a letter to Jasper.
237 Ibid.

A new general hymn and songbook will notice Taizé, and some fine hymns coming out of many Asian churches, and the world church in general. However neither the 'praise' world or the conventional have cottoned on to the fact that the Christian Church, like our society, is made up of diverse groups, and as I have said elsewhere, major elements are missing, whether it be Afro-American, African and Asian. There are also songs of faith from Taiwan, Bangladesh, Thailand, Latin America, and beyond, to the other great Christian traditions of the East. When it comes to gospel, blues and soul, the committee needs to know there is more to life than *Go tell it on the Mountain*, or *He's Got The Whole World In His Hands* which are seemingly the only two gospel-spiritual-blues known to many British hymn compilers.

Obviously some people need a crash course, and quickly so, for in some multi-racial areas, and anywhere come to that, the sole served ingredient comes almost entirely from white culture and understanding. There is no sense that black theology exists, nor of its riches. Is there an incipient racism that assumes white culture possesses the main entry into theological truth, that it has the hymns for all, and who is to say that the commercial bandwagon of mainly American companies does not wish to take all before them, especially with their almost fetishistic desire to slap their 'copyright' on all that musically moves.

There is a perpetual dilemma for the younger churches in the emerging nations not to be swallowed up by the West, and a sense of this comes across in Howard S. Olson's preface to *Set Free—A Collection of African Hymns:*

> These African hymns come out from an unwritten, oral tradition. In one sense one feels that the music is done an injustice when it is notated. Yet we are fortunate to have a notational system in which this music may be brought to Western cultures and thereby enrich worship outside Africa …. some years ago I urged musicians in the west, for the sake of cultural integrity, to resist giving harmonic arrangements to these songs. Culture is never static, and has changed since my

original observation. Now worshippers in African congregations often sing hymns in part.[236]

It is more forcibly expressed in a publication from the Lutheran World Federation:

> In the last century missionaries delivered the Gospel via cultural structures and methods in retrospect blatantly imperialistic. That same kind of imperialism is at work again. This time its results are more insidious since current electronic gadgets enable the projection of Western musical will across time zones to any place in the world ... Luther's basic insight about music, nature, and creation can and must be taken up anew in our midst. Care for the micromusics of this world should lead us to resist profit-motivated plundering of earth's wondrous sounds, to tell the real story of MTV, and, above all, to nurture local musics without and within the church.[237]

Maggie Hamilton, in 1993 a project worker for Counterpoint, then a new project sponsored by Christian Aid to encourage third world music, giving reaction to its *Sing Freedom* publication, wrote in the journal *Christian:*

> These may be songs that help us to recognize our spiritual poverty and lead us towards humility. And they may be songs which push open our narrow, cramped horizons to give a glimpse of the cosmic god, far more loving than we, who draws all creation together into that unfathomable well-spring of love where at least we shall find our true liberation from the fear that paralyses us.[238]

Free and flowing in observation with an important question at its end comes comment from the source of some paragraphs back:

> When Martin Luther, following Augustine's lead, boldly asserted that music was part of the creation, he was probably

236   Howard S.Olsen, *Set Free*, (Augsburg Fortress, Minneapolis, 1993).
237   Mark P. Bangert, *Worship and Culture in Dialogue*, (Lutheran World Federation, Dept. for Theology & Studies, 1994), p.184-187.
238   Maggie Hamilton, (*Sing, Christian*, Summer 1993), p.7.

not thinking of 'bhajans' from India, for instance, but his theology welcomes that new song too … as younger churches explore their own musics, and older churches re-examine assumptions about liturgy and music in a world musically complex, is it possible to lift up some common dynamics which can serve all Christians seeking to channel the music impulse in worship?[241]

Sally Morganthaler addresses her remarks to Christians who play the 'pretence' game, in which there is pretence that "all is well," when it is not, and in terms of worship songs that means finding a genre of new millennial worship:

Songs that don't gloss over the doubts, the cynicism or our own humanity? Songs that refuse to minimize pain, but rather lend a voice to it? If we refuse this challenge, I fear that even our Gen-X evangelicalism will become uninhabitable by real people.[242]

Her scriptural warrant is interesting, the book of Psalms - yet this is the book from which many worship songs derive their life, sadly praise writers pick and choose with astonishing ease to suit their religious framework.

An American publication *Confronting Contemporary Christian Music*, speaking from a fundamentalist background, offers the thought that:

It is rare to now hear songs from Christian composers that are hitting the target … let us not be afraid to write with power and conviction rather than to write songs which are safe to be sung in any church … magnificence for Christ in both music and preaching is spiritual passivism unless there is accompanying biblical militancy …[243]

I have largely mentioned male hymn writers. Within all the areas mentioned, an adventure into the world of hymns and

241   Ibid. Bangert, op. Cit, p.185.
242   Matt Redman, *Inside Out Worship: Insights for Passionate & Purposeful Worship*, (Regal Books, New Zealand, 2005), p.47.
243   Dr. H. T. Spence, *Confronting Contemporary Christian Music*, (Companion Press, 1997), p.155.

songs soon impresses upon me the overwhelming presence of 'male' writers. It has to be asked why few if any women join the ranks of the ever-growing list of contemporary contributors.

In *Half Hours with the Methodist Hymnbook*, a commentary on the 1904 publication, Mary Champness, gives notes on 41 women hymn writers. She takes us through such names as Mrs Alexander, Anna Letitia Waring, Frances Ridley Havergal, Anne Griffiths, Anne Steel and Annie Marston. There is reference to Mrs E.R. Pitman's *Lady Hymn Writers*, and where it is written:

> God's singers have come from all walks of life, as well as from all branches of the Church militant. Some have worn queenly crowns, others have toiled for a daily living; some have been nursed in the lap of wealth among the aristocracy, others have filled very humble positions in life; some have rejoiced in health and vigour, others have been lifelong invalids; some have adhered to orthodox and fashionable church systems, others have clung to unorthodox faiths, and to the chilling shadows of dissent. Yet in one and all we can trace the family likeness.[244]

Erik Routley devotes a chapter to women hymn writers, which some might say was very good of him, but that 'women' should be given a chapter clearly shows that there has been a limited female input (outside of the prolific blind Fanny J.Crosby) or is it interest from compilers? Routley admits much verse once came:

> Now it happens that women have made a contribution to hymnody parallel to that which they have made to English letters[245]

But from his vantage point of 1952 he is saying they are no longer writing acceptable hymns. But as in theology, and other fields over the last hundred years, where the woman's voice is absent, it also speaks of extraordinary

---

244   Mrs E.R Pitman, *Lady Hymn Writers*, (T. Nelson
       & Son, London, 1892), p.19.
245   Erik Routley, *Hymns and Human Life*, John
       Murray, London, 1950), p.203.

---

loss. Lavinia Byrne in edited her book *The Hidden Voice-Christian Women and Social Change* is willing to travel with Routley, and to ask why women were so prominent in hymn writing from the late 18th and 19th centuries? One reason advanced rests with the fact that hymn writing was the area in which a woman could express herself in a painfully male dominated world. Within hymnody she could be radical and outspoken. She also draws attention to the close relationship of the feel of women's preaching with their hymn writing:

> Lucy Bennett asked people what they thought; she hunted out the core nature of their belief and rounded on them with all the ferocity of a John the Baptist. [246]

Lavinia cites Lucy Bennett's nine verse composition *For an Open Meeting*. The hymn's second verse posesses a Trinitarian formula of some interest:

> What think ye? that He will not do?
> As He hath ever done?
> Our First, our Last, our Centre too,
> Blessed Father, Spirit, Son. [247]

Valentine Cunningham in *The Guardian, Saturday Review* would tell us that Victorian women gave the Anglican church its greatest hits, although I am not too sure why the Anglican church, not famed then for singing hymns, should receive particular attention. To those names already mentioned, the writer adds Anna Letitia Waring (*In Heavenly Love Abiding*), Charlotte Elliott (*Just As I Am*), Sarah Flower Adams (a radical Unitarian who wrote *Nearer My God to Thee*, often said to be the hymn sung as the *Titanic* sank, and based on Gen 28:10-22, where the text handles the causes rather than its consequences), and the Manchester poet Catherine Winkworth.

246 Lavinia Byrne, *The Hidden Voice - Christian Women and Social Change*, (SPCK, London, 1995), p.28.
247 Ibid. p.28.

Cunningham does raise an interesting aspect of women hymn writers, namely the life background from which some of them wrote:

> These writers understood domesticity, child rearing, sickness, bereavement. As daughters and wives of the vicar devoted to parish visiting, they met the population's female troubles first-hand. Charlotte Elliott edited *The Invalid's Hymnbook*...these women often wrote their hymns on a sickbed. Frances Ridley Havergal suffered horribly from erysipelas—nervous inflammation of the face. Fanny Crosby was blinded at six weeks. The insistent 'I' of their verses is clearly the *manifestation of Victorian female selfhood marginalised, disenfranchised, propertyless* ...[248]

The Guardian writer makes us aware of the sometime highly sexual nature of women's writing. There is the virginal Ms. Havergal picturing herself as the penitent prostitute Mary as she writes the hymn *Take My Life and Let It Be*, and I imagine there must be few worshippers in singing these hymns who are aware of her point! The hymn Take My Life usually falls under the category of a 'consecration' hymn and was much sung in my younger days as part of an altar call.

> Take my love;
> my Lord, I pour
> At thy feet its treasure store
> Take myself, and I will be
> Ever, only all for Thee.

She also mentions Anne Brontë, the impoverished governess who would have us sing:

> In my Redeemer's name
> I give myself to Thee
> And all unworthy as I am
> My God will welcome me

And in this adventure I am brought up stark by the use of 'blood' by women writers. The place of 'blood' is always present in Scripture, and in many revivalist hymns, and for

---

248   Valentine Cunningham, *The Guardian*,
       (Saturday Review, March 30, 2002), p.5.

me in a superb singing of the old hymn *What Can Wash Away My Sins* (Nothing But the Blood of Jesus) by Tom Waits, the contemporary songwriter and vocalist. Yet I confess, I have not been conscious of what Valentine Cunningham writes as:

> When these writers think about the blood of Christ it's with a complicity the male hymn-writers can never share. For these poets bleed too, because they menstruate, which makes them taboo and in their own way outsiders, like the dying Jesus. "Lord, whence are the blood-drops all the way / That mark out the mountain's track?"[249]

Catherine Winkworth, as with many of her time (1829-78) sought 'heaven' as soon as it might be granted her. In her translation *Jerusalem, Thou City Fair* (taken from *Laudamus,* a hymnal for the Assembly of the Lutheran World Federation), she would have us sing:

> And when within that lovely Paradise
> at last I safely dwell
> from out my soul what songs of bliss shall rise!
> what joy my lips shall tell!
> while holy saints are singing hosannas o'er and o'er
> pure alleluias ringing
> around me ever more (83)

Another verse contains these lines:

> How many times I longed for thee of old
> ere God had set me free
> from yon dark life of sadness
> yon world that counts for naught

This triggers the feeling that few contemporary hymns touch the hearts and minds of those who find it hard to cope with life, or those with particular handicaps; and it is perhaps here a reason why at one time the Sankey period hymns touched the lives of people who longed for peace of mind and body.

249   Ibid. p.5.

The question 'where are the women writers now?' is not merely the cry of the disquieted single man, it should be asked within the religious community. There are loads of women book writers and preachers, yet I count only 15 women contributors in the 1998 publication *Common Ground*. Interestingly in terms of prayer and liturgy there are a number of wonderful woman writers. In the ungraciously named praise world the name of Betty Pulkingham comes to the fore, especially for her arrangements to such songs as *O What A Gift, What a Wonderful Gift!, Make Me A Channel of Your Peace, God's Spirit Is In My Heart* and *I Am The Bread of Life*. In the Methodist *Hymns and Psalms*, on a rough count, there are 37 women writers in a hymnbook of 823 titles, leaving an astonishing 786 from the male domain!

Has our whole concept of understanding the ministry of Jesus been bludgeoned by male interference and claims of rightness? That is of course in other circles hardly a new thought, but I have not seen it expressed in the area of hymnody and song, and it is one of the underlying submissions of this writer that we are more affected by what we sing than hear. Certainly outside of the input of the non-clerical and officiants in worship, congregational singing (not forgetting any litanies and verbal responses to prayers and consecrations) is the only active contribution of the ordinary people who make up the congregation.

There is also a 'drum' ministry. The founder of 'Psalm Drummers' Terl Bryant gives this form of expression a pretty big base when saying:

> Let's be abandoned to complete obedience and discover the groove of eternity. God's heartbeat[250]

Bryant speaks to the drum exponent:

> Can you see how your drumming can carry and express the words of your heart? It can carry God's word that dwells in you, and through the sounds and rhythms you make, it can

---

250   Terl Bryant, sleeve of *A Heart to Drum*,
         (Survivor, 2006).252

speak of the things of God ... if you play from the heart and purpose to bring forth a language of rhythmic words, you will be a significant voice for the Lord.[251]

Wonderful tastes of this work can be heard on *Psalm Drummers* (SURCD0980). Unfortunately this is yet another aspect of the new worship end of the Christian experience unlikely to confront a committee pondering over the nature of praise material. Nor are they likely to be concerned with worship where hymn and song singing is in reality mixed into the dance encounter, and where it might be asked how can a DJ lead people to God? So cometh mixing decks, dance and divine worship. Yet music should not be binding us to prejudices, it should be a freeing experience.

A hymn and song committee would need to tackle the pre-eminence of the tune in contemporary worship of a 'praise' nature. In 'praise' it is the tune that carries the day even more, since there is a worship band often driven by electric guitars and drums. Mentioning a 'contemporary music band' leads one into wondering whether a new hymnbook committee will print music for contemporary styled bands with a disposition toward rock.

I want to see more Christian gatherings where there are weekly 'new' songs and tunes that have a present connotation, and where they are discarded almost as quickly as they come (is that terrible? Ask Bach!) They will always have Scripture, faith and tradition in the writer's mind. They will come from those who have ears to hear and eyes to see what is happening in the drama of a fallen world. It might be said that this is precisely what some House Churches do, but do many of the songs meet the strictures I have given? An earlier analysis in this book suggests not. As for the music, it is more likely to be in a folk style, but I would not rule out any kind of music so long as it does not become the province of a few.

With all my wish for the new and untried, to be kept and discarded, I think there is still room to bring in some favourites that have never found their way into mainstream

251   Ibid. p.128.

books of the 20th century, with perhaps some lyric tweaking, deleting and adding, and so such hymns as *Who Can Cheer The Heart Like Jesus, When Peace Like A River* and *The Old Rugged Cross*. They still speak to many hearts, and not just the elderly who grew up with them, and retain an affection. I can but say that many of my theatre casts adore them. I would aim to bring in loved tunes to some hymns, such as Bradbury's famed tune to *Just As I Am* (it depends how you sing it). And lurking deep in my consciousness, when it comes to music, and Methodism, is *The Centenary Tune Book*, of 1892, joyously given to me by the late William Leary, that has some noisy but exuberant folk-styled tunes to the words of Charles Wesley. The men at the Penwith hostelry, *The White Hart*, Ludgvan, would love these.

Let's also think of a hymn and worship book. Present hymn books contain hymns for worship and the hymns are intended to be sung. No, I am thinking of a hymn committee that will think of hymns and dance, hymns and drama, hymns and lighting, hymns and mime, hymns for processional activity, hymns for darkness, hymns for light, hymns and songs for protest occasions, and so forth. This would be a huge piece of work but surely one that would bring a new vision and sense of life.

On a practical level, and so far away from the large bands and singers that characterise the large praise gatherings of such ministries as Hillsong, one of the biggest dilemmas in current 'praise' manifestation rests with finding the right keyboard player. Some years ago I ran a 'praise' styled service with a more radical edge, in so far as we had various liturgies from the worldwide Christian spectrum, and there was a variety of speakers covering a wide theological stance. We did find songs that went beyond what was found in *SOF*, although we made considerable use of its content. We had a lovely young pianist with a folksy-jazz edge, a degree of relaxation that evoked the right mood, but she found employment elsewhere, and somehow it all fell apart.

Recently I gathered together a special praise gathering at Chapel Street Methodist Church, Penzance, and it made sense apparently to people for whom such an occasion is not normally their thing. That evening benefited from another almost mandatory item of praise worship, namely having an exceptional lead singer called Anne Gray. Praise music often needs someone to vocally lead, and if it is not possible to find such a person, and there is no sensitive person on keyboards, I am not too sure whether things should go ahead.

I have in different chapters alluded to the nonsense hymns that exist, and there are so many, and I can only in a final reflection repeat strongly that the continuation and inclusion of such material can only be a good reason why young people leave the Christian Church. The hymns sung in schools, where morning assembly with a Christian ethos continues, is often akin to a criminal act, possibly worse, if you are taking on board that we are speaking of the very life essence of people, and a desire to make apparent the sacred.

I am sure hymn committees are comprised of worthy and caring people, so perhaps they dare not speak out, and so continue to publish the usual accepted trivial rubbish, unless they are quite simply not up to the job?

To those who say they are lost, hardly captured by the traditional, and not always able to embrace the new as represented in the praise movement, in common with the writers of the book *Multi-Media Worship*, my thesis is that there are so many genres, we just need to listen to them, feel and ultimately know. We need forms that cannot be swallowed, which are open to revolutionary direction, and demand completion by the gathering themselves. I admit we cannot always run with the unpredictable, we do need assurance and safety at times, we do need to take on board areas that we repeat, and feel, and know. Yet we need always the sense of the God who is forever moving us on if we are willing to be led by His Spirit. I avoid answering what kind of hymn and song, other than to say 'all' within whatever framework is apt. At times you may fall in love or drop out of love with certain kinds of church and religious music. So be it.

Isn't that what we do with other forms of music?

I grew up amidst great 'revival' hymn singing-singing that was strong, even hearty, passionate, and God-centred. I have never lost those memories. In reading *Voices from the Welsh Revival* by the late and great Brynmor P. Jones, I revisit those memories. There will always be that revival gene ready to birth. His book was my main joy in writing two productions about the Welsh revival of 1904-06, revivals marked by great bursts of song.

> Some most strange joy took possession at the meetings. The only way I can describe it is this, as if a great shower was coming down the valley, I have seen it often, and you can hear the noise of it in the wind, and then by and by a few big drops come, the forerunner of the deluge. Exactly like that it came. And then we were lost to everything, and forgot about this world. We were no longer conscious of the time or of drawing the meeting to a close. However about half past three in the morning, it came to a close of its own volition, like putting one hand in the other, and we all got up and went home. And out in the road I could hear companies of people going down to Abedare singing, groups of folk in the early morning singing away with all their might. I went to bed but could hardly sleep, and when I did I was laughing in my sleep; I got up in the morning full of joy.[252]

As it says in Welsh:

> Canu'r dydd a chanu'r nos—sing all day and sing all night!

or as another fine hymn proclaims:

> Christ is alive! Let Christians sing.[253]

---

252   Annie Davies, speech in my play *Diolch Iddo!*
       (Page number unknown, play unpublished).
253   Brian Wren (Stainer & Bell, 1969).

Postscript

My journeying suggests these practical deliberations may prove useful

1. Let a group dig into the background of some traditional hymns, discover its whys and wherefores, theologically or socially, about the writer and the circumstances of its composition, and then decide if you can sing that faith and know it true now...beware of making yourselves arbiter of all things written and sung!

2. Take time yourself, or get a group of people together, to explore the vast hymn and song worlds out there from so many different Christian communions.

3. Take a mainstream hymnbook and really explore it, note its glories, but also its deficiencies. Again, note what you feel can be sung with meaning today, and ask whether sometimes an older form of English is not always at fault, that sometimes we want everything served in the way that makes us comfortable. Here, as in 4, write down what makes you feel distant from the hymn, and share those thoughts with another.

4. Do the same as 3 with a 'praise' selection.

5. Find a hymn that seems to have a good lyric, but which in the source you use does not have an appealing tune. Look up all relevant metres and see if there is something better...or write something!

6. Take the theme of a particular Sunday, and within the group look for songs of that sentiment within general culture, and discuss how that song might be useful. Do the same with popular tunes, and music for instance from a jazz genre.

7. Take what is happening in the world, find a relevant speaking Scripture passage, and then feel what kind of sound and mood would fit well with the subject.

8. Learn the art of the segue, whether as worship leader or someone who chooses hymns and tunes, segue meaning running two or more items back to back without a break but which blend or gradually on the second or third and be leading the worshipper into another musical worship field.

9. In what you are choosing, outside of something on disc or video/DVD, see which form of accompaniment is best, or which forms might at some point blend together or takeover from the other.

10. See which hymns and songs are more informal and may be best sung seated, or can be sung in-part, or lend to a spoken interjection between verses.

11. Learn to hear and listen to others and make the effort to appreciate what it is they are offering, assuming they are not going through the motions of whatever it is they bring.

12. Rule nothing out, go with any form, but know why, so if you want to play the all-time number one song by Bob Dylan, *Like A Rolling Stone,* then do so but have a reason for so doing, and ask how it fits into what else is around. Here, as with any other played source be aware of the equipment and the sound projection. It is not a good reason merely because you like it.

13. When choosing or having chosen, see if the hymn or song can be sung with a visual accompaniment or even a smell. Are there any dance or percussion possibilities, or painting, tapestry...mime and clown...spatial or temporal shaping...do not let the pew become someone's cell, not to be disturbed.

14. You must decide if what you have gathered together musically is for general worship, or will take place at a different time and even place, for all who will come. Remember music is only part of a service,

unless otherwise specified, e.g. Prayer, Scripture and Paul Simon.

15. Beware of rambling and unconnected observations, you really have to work at things, hard and long, and if you feel exhausted at the end then that sounds great! It takes a great deal of preparation to be spontaneous after possibly the first time of so being!

16. Beware of running rough-shod over others, learn about their sensitivities and preferences, take on board a musical genre you dislike, and ask why it is meaningful to some people.

17. Hear, perhaps on record, a variety of religious music, jot down your feelings, note where you had surprise, note places that spoke to you, and you felt lost. Try hearing the record again!

18. Place in front of you the words of a disc jockey who in his attempt to find a title for some Christian pop music went with 'I found Jesus and lost my talent'. Should that puzzle you, you are beyond help!

19. Ponder this thought of the then Bishop designate of Salisbury, given in *The Independent* in 1993:
'God invites each of us to make his music: the liturgy lays before us the rehearsal of that divine love. Are you ready to play your part'.

20. One for you to write.

Frederick Buechner writes in his book *Listen to Your Life:*

> Whenever you find tears in your eyes, especially unexpected tears, it is well to pay close attention.[254]

Thanks for getting to this part of my journey. I hope you are travelling too.

254   Frederick Buechner, *Listen to Your Life*, (Harper Collins, 1992), p.237.

Sermon

Sorry, you can't just muscle in on this verse, and start from there. I would very much like to run with the words 'a song of praise' and say little about the other contributions that might be made, but I cannot. I cannot isolate 'a song of praise' until I have considered the underlying thoughts behind the verse as a whole, that means focussing on the last sentence 'let everything be for edification', for whether you speak of a song of praise, a lesson, a revelation, a tongue or interpretation, it has to be said that all are governed by what Paul means by edification. To reach that point in our thinking and consideration we must read this important verse in the context of the majestic preceding chapter. It must also be seen in the light of the ensuing chapter. Rather like a sandwich, it falls apart unless there is top and bottom.

I will start with the first, it provides the base, the bottom, if you want to run for a moment with the sandwich analogy. Some term it a hymn of love, a hymn in praise of Jesus. I agree with this. Yet I believe that the passage has been hijacked. It has been lifted out of its context, and given far greater power. So what is this travesty?

I am saying that Corinthians 1:13 has been anaesthetised by some people. It has been stripped of its firepower. Corinthians 1:13 has been described as beautiful, and rightly so. It can find its way into poetry anthologies. It is read at weddings where it serves to beautify the occasion of two people deciding to take each other for better or for worse. It is not a 'filler' or an 'addendum'.

In its right context Corinthians 1:13 is far from soothing and pleasant. Paul is telling a lousy set of bitching church people that it is about time they stopped worshipping themselves, following their own agendas, and instead stopped and looked at the wondrous nature of the love exemplified by the life, teaching and death of Jesus. In this hymn you can substitute 'Christ' for the word 'love', you can alter the tenses, and there you have a majestic picture of our Lord's life. Note too that Paul doesn't argue with the Corinthian Church. He doesn't take sides. He simply points them to something higher, much higher than the Gospel they once received, a Gospel given in Grace, one which they said they would follow. That was a commitment where they said Jesus is Lord, and not themselves. Of course Paul has other words to say on leadership, one reference is Romans 12: vs. 6 & 8.

To the second: Corinthians 1:14 should also be seen in context of the following chapter. Here Paul is speaking of informed faith, sound faith. It is against this that all shall be said and done in worship. It is not a question of doing what seems fanciful, alluring, or palatable, more about being fit for purpose in the light of the demands of the very Gospel by which all are asked to live. I will read some of those sentiments into what I say, and trust I have already started the process.

With both these settings and their Pauline teaching in mind we can turn now to the actual verse. Do not despair that I have taken so long to get here. Some of you may have read sermons by, or heard the preaching and ministry of Dr Martyn Lloyd Jones, who for many years was found Sunday by Sunday at Westminster Chapel. He was a biblical expositor and brilliant at it. He might say he was running a series on, for the sake of argument, 1: Corinthians, and he would take three or four weeks on just one verse. So, you can see I have been rather quick to reach the chosen text! I feel a little like the magician who suddenly produces a rabbit out of the hat!

So, this word 'edification' that is so important: coming at the end of the verse the word edification is the 'sting in the tail' of what otherwise is seemingly a verse devoid of controversy.

Let's spell out a little more about the word. Edification means simply 'building up'. It is about creating growth; here it is willed for the believer who should be chasing after spiritual maturity. It should eat into the very heart of good worship. So what's going on? Recall what has been said about the chapters either side. We have the supreme Christian virtue, which is love. In Colossians 3:4 it is called the bond of perfection. Put simply, apart from love, the other virtues cannot really hold together. Love is not defined by Paul, he merely describes the virtue. We have Paul attempting to establish some kind of order in a Church troubled by disagreement, some of whose leaders claim for themselves the power and might that belongs only to the Lord God Almighty. Paul says that at base level the Christian Church must find itself in its worship, and without true worship the Church dies. Such worship is only made possible through the Holy Spirit. It's where our lives fall into shape. The God to whom we address our songs (and all else) is known to us in Jesus.

Everything mentioned in this verse stands or falls in the light of those teachings. They stand or fall by their ability to make people more aware of God, more conscious of their spiritual roots. This verse gives flower to the meaning of Jesus for all times and in all places. It means any old thing will not do. In terms of edification those who lead or plan worship must be about integrity and truthfulness, that is integrity and truth before God. They must judge all that they do in that light, and not be tempted take short-cuts in a futile effort to find popularity. Neither must they be tempted to indulge in modern parlance. The bad scenario is one that speaks of an endless stream of people with some kind of Christian conviction, who tour various Christian groups, and claim to be "this and that", but in each instance they stay only for a short time. They are seeking to attract an audience by superficially satisfying an emotional need, rather than seeking deeper more meaningful edification. The last thing they want is a challenge; that entails sacrifice.

They would rather avoid having to actually "do" something!

You could argue that this is symptomatic of the modern age; we expect constant entertainment. The new is being greeted almost before the old has been heard and absorbed. Sometimes people are searching for a feel, an assurance, a 'sense of well-being'. These feelings may well be conveyed by songs lacking a specific Christian content, even though these songs are sung in a purportedly 'praise' orientated church. Did not Jesus say that not everyone who says "Lord, Lord" speaks in honesty?

Perhaps Paul also understood the not particularly pleasing truth that the Church is one of the few places where you can sing, play, and read badly, without complaint from your audience. Oh, yes, and preach badly too! I might as well go the whole hog, do anything badly!

That aside this text is a simple description of worship as experienced by the first Christians; it gave rise to considerable debate and eventual division. Indeed arguments still rage, with some people claiming the pre-eminence of one form over another. I believe from this context and other allusions made by the Apostle that he had on his mind those who claim 'tongues' or 'interpretations' but who do so on spurious grounds. They like to be heard, they want to impress others as to their spiritual state, they want to feel the exhilaration of the moment and presume that God has favoured them. They are not engaging in edification processes. They leave people bewildered. They are about division, self-power and self-aggrandisement. It is so easy to become self-indulgent. On the other hand he is not against any of these forms if they are marked by the truth blessed by the Holy Spirit.

What then of the words 'a song of praise'—the translation by the way comes from Dr. Moffatt, once well known as a biblical translator.

However we need to bear in mind the context of these words. In this exciting letter of Paul the Apostle a song of praise yes is fine, but a song of praise for edification, it edifies us, the singers. Not just any old thing is good enough. Not someone's cobbled together words and music.

No one is built up by being brought into the presence of ill-considered and trite rubbish. Speaking of contemporary music as it is employed within the worship structure, this is not the place for 'trying-out' new music. One cannot assume that the gathering will happily push aside all that is traditional and familiar in favour of the new so long as the congregation is allowed to take part. Involvement in the service is not sufficient to guarantee the congregation's continued attendance.

I put this question to you all: who applies the test of what is trite, banal or mere indulgence?

One thing is evident as we read Paul, and the other letters, there are blocks of material glowing with the fervour of worship. There are many references to the importance of prayer, distinctive forms of expression, extensive use of Old Hebrew Scriptures. Read 1 Chronicles 16:8-36 and you will see more clearly what I mean. Paul loves to use one of the great Jewish shouts 'Blessed be (or is) he!' and for Paul the one-time Pharisee, dramatically changed by a profound experience on the Damascus road - the reference has become Jesus - see for instance Romans 1:25, 2 Corinthians 11:31. In prayer, in naming Jesus as the Chosen One of God, there are songs.

It may be said that praise and worship should open the door to prayer. This is certainly the case in the context of Solomon's temple being completed. There was worship, God's presence was known, there was prayer, and answer.

In the New Testament Scriptures there are spontaneous extemporizations of praise and worship. They include the incredibly moving Benedictus, Magnificat, and the Nunc Dimittis. And many sections of the Christian community still sing those words regularly. And as we pore through the text of the New Testament so we can catch what appear to be ancient hymns. For instance read 1 Timothy 3:16, or Ephesians 5:14; they are both definitely hymnic! Scholarship here is exciting. By referring us to the dramatic story of Peter's rescue from prison in Acts 12, and especially verses 6 and 7. Then read those against Ephesians 5:14, ask yourself whether the latter is a hymn built around that event. You can breathe an air of excitement knowing you might be so near to what the first followers sang.

The Greek word used for 'songs' in this verse in Corinthians doesn't seem to point back to a Psalm from the Jewish Psalter. Rather it is more likely to be a Christian extemporization. Whatever, we are sure in saying that in primitive Christian worship there were many jubilant moments. Quite the opposite of some of the worship which has permeated some Christian churches where people seem dour, unemotional, seemingly cold and detached.

Worship in those times was largely without musical accompaniment, although some commentators suggest the use of instruments such as the zither, or harp. However it is interesting to note that in the heavenly worship envisaged in Revelation 14:2 instrumentalists are present. The word used can also refer to what were known as Homeric rhapsodists, people who use their own voices, and sing to their own accompaniment. Whatever the case, the occasion is joyful. The Holy Spirit blesses.

It is of course another thing to say that worship shall be largely built around song. We have no real idea if that was the case in the early Church, it is unlikely. Many current Christian communities certainly think this should be the case now. In some mainstream churches five hymns or songs are mandatory. For one denomination – the Methodists, who are said to have been 'born in song' – and in the more recent praise world, five may be far too small a number. Singing is rarely unaccompanied, other than for effect, there is often piano playing. Sometiemes there will be musical instruments chosen for their rock sound; even a small orchestra. However most mainstream churches base their musical content round the organ.

I surprised myself once by threatening to cease attending services if a particular organist continued to play. I am not sure whether the minister was more surprised by my saying such a thing or by the fact that someone dared bring conflict into the church. Many Christians prefer to maintain the status quo rather than instigating confrontation. My decision was not swayed by the argument that this was the best that could be found. The suggestion that no organ was preferable to a badly played instrument did not enter the argument.

On the other hand churches are governed by time-keeping. Many a vestry steward has whispered in my ear 'we normally finish by twelve!' I do recall travelling some distance in order to preach at a Methodist circuit service only to be told on arrival that I should preach for a mere seven minutes. I responded by reminding them of my forty-five pound charge. To this came the wonderful reply:

'Oh, well, we'll have twenty minutes then.'

None of these things would satisfy Paul. On the basis of chapters 13 and 15, and elsewhere, extracts which are so important for understanding our text, it is plain that edification is about ensuring things are right, at their best, in so far as this is attainable within a particular community. No one expects St Cynthia's in the Parish of Spam to possess an organist and choir to rival St Paul's, nor to have a worship band and singers who reach the standards of a Noel Richards or Matt Redman! The great leveller is in other things - so important to Paul. And not just Paul, read John 4:23-24. The edification call, the building up process, comes only from worship ringed with integrity. Should it be an offering of integrity, then even a poorly played or sung piece can assume significance. A good song will combine objective truth, scriptural truth and a personal expression to that truth.

You will have realised I have strayed from the first century into the present. It means that one mighty gap is left between first and 21st centuries! To make one mad and, as an extraordinary generalisation, through the centuries of Christian turbulence, music in particular forms has given rise both to exultation and despair.

There is no question as to the importance of music, however thanks to Latin remaining the language of worship for Roman Catholics, and the refusal of the Anglican Church to allow hymns, it took until the 17th century before the arrival of Isaac Watts, often termed 'the founding father of hymn', caused things to change. Watts did hold the Psalms in great affection, but considered them defective for Christian praise.

Not to be doubted, even within a few cursory thoughts on the history of spiritual songs, it is quite clear that Christian history broaches endless musical genres, and often each is accompanied by a group of devotees eager to persuade others that their music is for all places, let alone times in the worship of God.

There are those communities who refuse to sing believing singing was rarely present in early Christian times. During the time when the teachings of Calvin were regarded by some as sacrosanct, biblical words were seen as providing sufficient spiritual sustenance, consequently 'man-made' verses or hymns were considered inadequate.

Some would even deny there has been a change in the content form of worship. They believe what they do would be recognised by Paul, by those first believers. Some of us wish them well, and may ourselves at certain times join with them, but we bat on the premise that however important the past, the Church can never be a preservation society. Some Methodists fondly imagine that much of their 21st century worship would be recognised by John and Charles Wesley, but they fool themselves.

Should Paul have been penning his letter in this 21st century he would have been antagonised by the fact that the style and music of contemporary songs can divide a congregation. That at least was one issue he did not have to face. He did not have competing songbooks, copyrights to clear, licences to obtain and so forth. I am sure he would question the lack of 'Christ-filled' songs in some charismatic churches, and other mainstream areas where denominational hymn books have been ditched in favour of new songs and music.

At their best, and most effective, praise songs of today are about creating a mood and feel that is centring on a personal encounter with God.

In the mainstream service the hymn punctuates a prayer, reading or message, this is not quite the case in charismatic worship where a succession of hymns and songs sung are worship in itself, and this 'time of worship' may be of considerable duration.

Fortunately for all his strictures Paul is grounded in the essence of the revelation given to us. In the 16th chapter of Corinthians 16:v20b-24, he urges all to greet one another with the kiss of peace, thus the grace of the Lord Jesus will be with them; he extends his love to all. He also looks for the Second Coming. However he has no time for those in the fellowship who do not love the Lord – they should leave.

It may well be that Christians of today have to learn such a mind of Christ, for if there are moral and ethical issues dividing churches, let alone orders and status of ministry, it seems especially grievous if Christians cannot worship together because they are divided over the song of praise each might contribute. It may be practical, it may keep a sort-of church together, but there seems to be something unhealthy, at least in mainstream circles, where on a Sunday morning there is a congregation that sings the so-called modern songs, and a further service, still largely based in the world of traditional hymnology.

The lifting up of holy hands in prayer and praise cannot speak with integrity unless they can hold the hands with those who desire organ and traditional-styled hymns. Equally so, the worshipper who may have a greater grasp on history, of the ages and traditions where God has spoken with force and power, must still grasp the hands of the brother and sister who see the Spirit moving differently. How can the body of Christ be divided on a contribution of song?

Indices

Index of First Lines

NEXT WE SHALL SING

Index of Tunes

General Index

THE FEMINIST DIFFERENCE

The Feminist Difference

Literature, Psychoanalysis, Race, and Gender

Barbara Johnson

Harvard University Press • Cambridge, Massachusetts
London, England • 1998

Pages 211–212 constitute an extension of the copyright page.

Library of Congress Cataloging-in-Publication Data

Johnson, Barbara, 1947–
      The feminist difference : literature, psychoanalysis, race, and
  gender / Barbara Johnson.
          p.   cm.
      Includes bibliographical references and index.
      ISBN 0-674-29881-0 (alk. paper)
      1. Feminist literary criticism. 2. Feminism and literature.
  3. Feminist theory. I. Title.
  PN98.W64J64   1998
  809'.89287—dc21   97-45009

Acknowledgments

Many of the essays included in this volume began to take shape at the Center for Advanced Study in the Behavioral Sciences in Stanford, California, during 1989–90. I am very grateful both for the funding and for the companionship, which, despite the stimulating efforts of many of the Fellows, did not turn me into a social scientist. Indeed, the difficult articulation between rhetorical and empirical analyses continues to be a source of fascination to me.

I would like to take this opportunity to thank the following individuals, who in one way or another have contributed to the writing of this book: Ellen Bassuk, Elliot Butler-Evans, Greta Edwards-Anthony, Henry Louis Gates, Jr., Joan de Jean, Deborah Jenson, Billy Ray Johnson Gonzalez, David Kennedy, Jann Matlock, Nancy Miller, Martha Minow, Humphrey Morris, Austin Sarat, Claudia Tate, and Mary Helen Washington. Marjorie Garber has, as always, been a stimulating interlocutor throughout.

Contents

Contents

Introduction

In a series of forums and workshops entitled "Feminist Criticism Revisited," speakers at the 1995 Modern Language Association convention were asked to discuss the state of feminism in the literary academy. Some declared that feminism had lost its activist passion, some took it for granted as a well-institutionalized ground for their work, but what was most striking to me were the gestures of ambivalence displayed by many panelists toward the assignment. Was it ambivalence toward feminist criticism, or toward the notion of revisitation? Was it the invitation to nostalgia or critique, or the construction of the speakers as ghosts, speaking from beyond the grave to the present about the past, but also in some sense to the past about the present? Elaine Showalter mentioned Dr. Kevorkian and gold watches. Jane Gallop repeatedly assured us that she *had* written a paper but wouldn't read it because it was boring. Nancy Miller spoke of her twice-unpublished accounts of feminists bashing and trashing each other. Bonnie Zimmerman said that she wanted to repudiate parts of her paper after hearing the others. With great wit and seriousness, speaker after speaker revealed to a packed audience that revisiting feminist criticism was not a simple task. What could have been an occasion for celebration and self-congratulation was somehow an occasion for perplexity.

Were these gestures of displacement and self-deprecation just feminist charm? the return of female socialization? Or is there something about contemporary academic feminism that requires ambivalence?

You would certainly never think so if your source of information were anti-feminist polemicists like Katie Roiphe or Christina Hoff Sommers. While all of the panelists at those MLA sessions alluded to difficult debates and conflicts *within* feminism[1] (feminists for and against the anti-pornography ordinance, the difference-versus-equality debates, the essentialism-versus-postmodernism debates, the black feminist critiques of white feminism, the Marxist feminist critiques of bourgeois feminism, the lesbian critiques of normative heterosexuality within feminism, the international feminist critiques of first-world feminism), many of the best-selling attacks on academic feminism construct it as a unified, dogmatic monolith, unable to "tolerate dissent." How do these two things go together? Is there a *necessary* ambivalence within feminism today?

Most discussions of ambivalence treat ambivalence as a temporary, unfortunate, and remediable state of feeling. But perhaps *that* is the problem. Perhaps there is something healthy about claiming the right to ambivalence. Or at the very least, there may be something deadening about having to renounce one's ambivalence too soon, on someone else's terms. If resistance is always the sign of a counter-story, ambivalence is perhaps the state of holding on to more than one story at a time. As bell hooks put it in a conversation with Mary Childers:

We live in a culture that makes it seem as though having contradictions is bad—most of us try to represent ourselves in
ways that suggest we are without contradictions. Contradictions are perceived as chaos and not orderly, not rational,
everything doesn't follow. . . We have to be willing as women
and as feminists and as other groups of people, including as
men who enter feminist discussion, to work with those contradictions and almost to celebrate their existence because they
mean we are in a process of change and transformation.[2]

One way of understanding my title, *The Feminist Difference*,
might follow from this simultaneity of contradiction and transformation: on the one hand, feminism has already (made a difference:) this
is what the MLA forums and the anti-feminist polemics both indicate. On the other hand, that difference has opened up and brought
into view the energies of contradiction that had been hidden inside
the unsayability of what feminism has now given voice to. Once
women begin to speak, we begin to differ with each other. And
normatively male power structures have responded by integrating
genuine changes, but also, in the process, by appropriating and de-
fusing the energies of feminist critique through changes that remain
superficial and reversible. One example of this self-reconstitution of
patriarchal power away from feminists has involved the status of the
academy itself in American life: just at the moment when women
(and minorities) begin to have genuine power in the university,
American culture responds by acting as though the university itself
is of dubious value. The drain in available resources away from the

humanities (where women have more power) to the sciences (where women still have less power) has been rationalized in other ways, but it seems to me that sexual politics is central to this trend.

Thus, when institutions created without the participation of women are transformed by feminism, or when the category "women" is shown to exclude many of those it should designate, new contradictions become readable—indeed, urgent. The fact that these new contradictions can be exploited by those who seek to reverse the changes made by feminism should not prevent feminists from fully inhabiting, exploring, and facing them.

One such subject of debate involves the utility of the concept of difference itself. In my previous work *(The Critical Difference, A World of Difference),* the word "difference" was used to name two incompatible but inseparable kinds of analysis: on the one hand, the investigation of binary differences with a history of effects (male and female, prose and poetry, black and white, guilt and innocence) and, on the other, the investigation of structures of self-difference, the repression of which allowed such binary oppositions to maintain themselves (male as repressing internal femininity, poetry as cutting away prosaisms, white as not-black, innocence as self-erasure). In feminism's initial gestures of opening normatively male structures to critique, the concept of sexual difference was essential. But recent feminists have found themselves working at the limits of the usefulness of difference as a governing structure. Teresa de Lauretis, following Luce Irigaray, has argued that when women are defined as "different-from-men," there is really no difference, but only one sexual identity at stake, setting the terms of the opposition. And if women are only defined in terms of, and in relation to, men, sexual difference itself can only be viewed heterosexually.[3] This means that both conflicts and attractions *between* women are unnecessarily coded as epistemologically upsetting.

Even in a legal context where it would seem inevitable to invoke the concept of difference in order to insure fairness, the difficulties and ambivalences must be preserved as a valuable storehouse of information. As Joan Scott has written about the legal case of the Equal Employment Opportunities Commission (which claimed that women were being treated unequally) vs. Sears (which claimed that women were simply not "choosing" certain kinds of jobs because women were "different"):

> When equality and difference are paired dichotomously, they structure an impossible choice . . . Feminists cannot give up "difference"; it has been our most creative analytical tool. We cannot give up equality, at least as long as we want to speak to the principles and values of our political system. But it makes no sense for the feminist movement to let its arguments be forced into preexisting categories and its political disputes to be characterized by a dichotomy we did not invent. How then do we recognize and use notions of sex- ual difference and yet make arguments for equality? The only response is a double one: the unmasking of the power relationship constructed by posing equality as the antithesis of difference and the refusal of its consequent dichotomous construction of political choices.[4]

As Martha Minow has written about the "dilemma of difference": "I suggest that the dilemma of difference is not an accidental problem in this society. The dilemma of difference grows from the ways in which this society assigns individuals to categories and, on that basis, determines whom to include in and whom to exclude from political, social, and economic activities. Because the activities are designed, in turn, with only the included participants in mind, the excluded seem not to fit because of something in their own nature."[5] The solution, then, is not to analyze that supposed "nature," but to examine the social construction of difference itself. "This switch in the focus of attention from the 'different person' to the social and legal construction of difference challenges long-established modes of reasoning about reality and about law."[6]

The final two essays in *The Feminist Difference* discuss the writings of two landmark feminist legal theorists in their analytical, but also stylistic, bursting of the seams of the legal construction of social differences. But the book begins with what has become a classic question for feminism: the question of feminism and psychoanalysis. Jacqueline Rose, one of the most sophisticated elucidators of this question, explains the place of psychoanalysis within feminism as follows: "The question of identity—how it is constituted and maintained—is . . . the central issue through which psychoanalysis enters the political field . . . How individuals recognize themselves as male or female, the demand that they do so, seems to stand in such fundamental relation to the forms of inequality and subordination which it is feminism's objective to change."[7] Glossing this sentence from Rose, Gayatri Chakravorty Spivak "troubles" this feminist psychoanalysis with a feminist deconstruction. Where Rose, in the above sentence, moves smoothly from sexual difference as self-recognition to sexual difference as a system of inequality, Spivak highlights an incommensurability between knowledge (epistemology) and change (which Spivak here calls axiology). In other words, where psychoanalysis gives Rose a way of articulating interpretation with change, deconstruction introduces a fissure between "woman" as a concept that can never be a proper name for all women and "feminism" as a movement that must—but *cannot*—consider "woman" as an epistemological ground for action. Spivak writes:

> It is the step contained in the last part of the sentence from Rose quoted above which gives me trouble. That step covers the quick shift from epistemology/ontology to the axiological project . . . If, as Rose suggests, it is crucial to admit the division in the subject [i.e., the psychoanalytic insight that identity can never be fixed], it seems to me no less crucial to admit the irreducible difference between the subject (woman) of that epistemology, and the subject (feminist) of this axiology. Perhaps I am doing nothing more than theorizing here the division between the women's movement and feminist theory.[8]

Yet for Rose as well, psychoanalysis gives feminism the "right to an impasse": "Only the concept of a subjectivity at odds with itself gives back to women the right to an impasse at the point of sexual identity, with no nostalgia whatsoever for its possible future integration into a norm" (p. 15). Including any "norm" that might be wished for by feminism.

Psychoanalysis has indeed often been resisted on the grounds that it attempted to impose a normative master discourse upon the varieties of human signifying behavior and expression. As a theory of human desire, it posits as universal what may be the perspective of a particular place and time (Freud's Vienna and the neuroses of his middle-class patients). And as a way of containing and disciplining behaviors that may have their origins in social, sexual, and economic injustice, the institutions of psychoanalysis have been seen as instruments of social control. These issues have long been debated around questions of gender and sexuality, but sometimes as though those concepts themselves were universal and ahistorical. More recently, the value of psychoanalysis has begun to be studied in a rich variety of ways around the question of "race." This is partly a result of the revival of interest in the work of Martinican psychiatrist and anti-colonial revolutionary Frantz Fanon, and partly a continuation of conversations and critiques between black and white feminists.

In a ground-breaking and ground-clearing essay, Hortense Spillers sets out the debate about the question as follows:

A framework that would properly contextualize a confrontation between "psychoanalysis" and "race" is not imaginable without a handful of prior questions, usually left unarticulated . . . Culture theorists on either side of the question would rule out, as tradition has it, any meeting ground between race matters, on the one hand, and psychoanalytic theories, on the

other. But I want to shift ground, mindful of this caveat: little
or nothing in the intellectual history of African Americans
within the social and political context of the United States
would suggest the effectiveness of a psychoanalytic discourse,
revised or classical, in illuminating the problematic of "race"
on an intersubjective field of play, nor do we yet know how to
historicize the psychoanalytic object and objective, invade its
hereditary premises and insulations, and open its insights, subsequently, to cultural and social forms that are disjunctive to its
originary imperatives. In short, how might psychoanalytic theories speak about "race" as a self-consciously assertive reflexiv-
ity, and how might "race" expose the gaps that psychoanalytic
theories awaken?[9]

Yet as Spillers herself goes on to point out, the question of "race" is
not a mere "gap" or "exteriority" in the work of the founder of
psychoanalysis.

Sigmund Freud, the details of whose life, down to his dreams and
mistakes, make up the raw material of his science, was convinced
that his ethnicity had a hand in the invention of psychoanalysis. As
he wrote in his *Autobiographical Study:*

When, in 1873, I first joined the University, I experienced
some appreciable disappointments. Above all, I found that I
was expected to feel myself inferior and an alien because I was
a Jew. I refused absolutely to do the first of these things. I have
never been able to see why I should feel ashamed of my de-
scent, or, as people were beginning to say, of my "race." I put

up, without much regret, with my non-acceptance into the community; for it seemed to me that in spite of this exclusion an active fellow-worker could not fail to find some nook or cranny in the framework of humanity. These first impressions at the University, however, had one consequence which was afterwards to prove important; for at an early age I was made familiar with the fact of being in the Opposition and of being put under the ban of the "compact majority." The foundations were thus laid for a certain degree of independence of judgement.[10]

Psychoanalysis has sometimes been called a "Jewish science," but Freud was far from presenting himself as an orthodox (or Orthodox) member of the Jewish community. In his preface to the Hebrew translation of *Totem and Taboo,* he described himself as "an author who is ignorant of the language of Holy Writ, who is completely estranged from the religion of his fathers—as well as from every other religion—and who cannot take a share in nationalist ideals, but who has yet never repudiated his people, who feels that he is in his essential nature a Jew, and who has no desire to alter that nature." The ambiguity of Freud's sense of identity is perhaps as important as its nature.[11] Both inside and outside Austrian intellectual culture and inside and outside Judaism, it is perhaps not surprising that Freud developed a science out of what W. E. B. Du Bois called "double consciousness" or "second sight."

When Freud puts the word "race" in quotation marks, his gesture anticipates one of the breakthrough moments in African-

American criticism in the last decade: the publication of the volume *"Race," Writing, and Difference.*[12] The use of quotation marks moves the concept of "race" away from an essential or biological category and into the domain of historical and social constructedness. This expression of epistemological ungrounding does not make "race" into a "mere" fiction, but it signals its *political* status: "People were beginning to say." The word "race" is in quotation marks because it is in other people's mouths.

"Race," then, is at the heart of Freud's discovery. It is not outside but inside psychoanalysis. But this does not mean that it is part of its explicit subject matter or metalanguage. On the contrary, it may be precisely the *effort* to overcome anti-Semitism that leads Freud to seek to couch his insights in universal language. As Hortense Spillers puts it: "Freud could not 'see' his own connection to the 'race'/culture orbit, or could not theorize it, because the place of their elision marked the vantage point from which he spoke. Because it constituted his enabling postulate, it went 'without saying.' Perhaps we could argue that the 'race' matrix was the fundamental *interdiction* within the enabling discourse of founding psychoanalytic theory and practice itself" (p. 89). In other words, the resistance of "race" to psychoanalysis may have its origin in psychoanalysis's resistance to "race." But to put it in these terms is to suggest that such resistances are eminently open to psychoanalytic investigation.

A recent anthology of black and white feminist essays, *Female Subjects in Black and White,* edited by Elizabeth Abel, Barbara Christian, and Helene Moglen, is indicative of the current interest, as well as the feminist complexity, in the relations among feminism, psy-

11

choanalysis, and race. Not only does the anthology offer many different and interesting ways of understanding that nexus, but it uses psychoanalytic concepts as a way of understanding its own project. The editors' introduction to the volume describes the relation between white feminism and black feminism in consistently psychoanalytic terms: anxiety, obsession, the return of the repressed. Toni Morrison's novel *Beloved* comes to stand as a test text for both the value and the limits of a psychoanalytic perspective, but also for the question of "white feminist critics' obsession with African American women's texts"[13]—an obsession in which, clearly, I share. Ann DuCille, in an essay included in the volume called "The Occult of True Black Womanhood," expresses a complex set of ambivalences toward this "obsession." Several contributors allude to Jane Gallop's controversial formulation of her transferential relation to black feminist critics: "I realized that the set of feelings that I used to have about French men I now have about African-American women. Those are the people I feel inadequate in relation to and try to please in my writing. It strikes me that this is not just idiosyncratic."[14] It is sometimes as though psychoanalysis were being used by white feminists as a way of offering those French men *to* black feminists. But of course, for many black feminists, psychoanalysis is hardly news. Hortense Spillers herself has long been a brilliant practitioner of psychoanalytic approaches to literature. By saying that the transferential relation she describes "is not just idiosyncratic," however, Gallop makes it clear that psychoanalytic concepts can and should inform, and be informed by, an understanding of the historical, political, and academic contexts of the "feelings" that are not hers alone.

Several of the essays in *The Feminist Difference* (including one that is included in *Female Subjects in Black and White*) proceed by juxtaposing a psychoanalytic text with a text written by an African-American author. Both of the texts are meant to be read as both "literary" and "theoretical," dealing with both "psychoanalysis" and "race." Other essays are built upon other kinds of pairings. The juxtapositions are meant to enable the texts to become readable in new ways. Toni Morrison and Sigmund Freud, Nella Larsen and Heinz Kohut, John Keats and Jane Campion, Patricia Williams and René Descartes, Marceline Desbordes-Valmore and Charles Baudelaire, Charlotte Perkins Gilman and Nathaniel Hawthorne, and many others are explicitly set alongside each other along the lines of salient and complexly debated binary differences: male and female, black and white, literature and psychoanalysis. In all cases, it is the "literariness" of the texts that resists and displaces the opposition.

In the final analysis, literature is important for feminism because literature can best be understood as the place where impasses can be kept and opened for examination, where questions can be guarded and not forced into a premature validation of the available paradigms. Literature, that is, is not to be understood as a predetermined set of works but as a mode of cultural work, the work of giving-to-read those impossible contradictions that cannot yet be spoken.

Part One

LITERARY DIFFERENCES: PSYCHOANALYSIS, RACE, AND GENDER

Chapter One

Is Female to Male as Ground Is to Figure?

No women, then, if I have read correctly. With the notable exception of the mother, of course. But this makes up part of the system, for the mother is the faceless, unfigurable figure of a *figurante*. She creates a place for all the figures by losing herself in the background.

Jacques Derrida, "All Ears: Nietzsche's Otobiography"

We must be cured of it by a cure of the ground . . .
New senses in the engenderings of sense.

Wallace Stevens, "The Rock"

As a way of discussing the relations between feminism and psycho-analysis, I would like to bring together three well-known texts, each of which tells the story of a failed cure: Nathaniel Hawthorne's "The Birthmark," Charlotte Perkins Gilman's "The Yellow Wall-paper," and Sigmund Freud's "Fragment of an Analysis of a Case of Hysteria."[1] While the three cases fail in very different ways, they are alike in presenting a female patient subject to the therapeutic ambi-tions of a male doctor. In all three cases, in fact, the initiative to-ward therapy comes not from the patient herself but from a man she has in some sense discommoded—which is not to say the woman does not suffer.

The question asked by my title is a rephrasing of Sherry Ortner's famous title, "Is Female to Male as Nature Is to Culture?"[2] The terms *figure* and *ground,* which refer to a certain distribution of out-line and attention, are of course drawn from the visual arts.[3] That origin is not irrelevant here, since the question of the woman in the texts I will discuss is as much aesthetic as it is medical—indeed, the texts reveal a profound complicity between aesthetics and medicine.

For a preliminary description of the figure-ground relationship, I turn to a quotation from Douglas Hofstadter's *Gödel, Escher, Bach,* which I inflect in terms of psychoanalysis and sexual difference:

When a figure or "positive space" [call this "the male child" or simply "the child" or "Oedipus"] is drawn inside a frame [call this frame "psychoanalytic theory"], an unavoidable consequence is that its complementary shape—also called the "ground," or "background," or "negative space" [call this the "girl" or the "other"]—has also been drawn. In most drawings, however, this figure-ground relationship plays little role. The artist is much less interested in the ground than in the figure. But sometimes an artist will take an interest in the ground as well.

Let us now officially distinguish between two kinds of figures: *cursively drawable* ones, and *recursive* ones . . . A *cursively drawable* figure is one whose ground is merely an accidental by-product of the drawing act. [Later, Hofstadter refers to this as a "recognizable form whose negative space is not any recognizable form."] A *recursive* figure is one whose ground can be seen as a figure in its own right . . . The "re" in "recursive" represents the fact that both foreground *and* background are cursively drawable—the figure is "twice-cursive." Each figure-

[handwritten marginalia: figure and ground from art]

ground boundary in a recursive figure is a double-edged sword.[4]

The dream of psychoanalysis is of course to represent sexual difference as a recursive figure, a figure in which both figure and ground, male and female, are recognizable, complementary forms. This dream articulates itself through the geometry of castration in Freud, in which the penis is the figure, or positive space, and the vagina the ground, or negative space. But there are limits to how recursive Freud wishes this figure to be: he wants to stop short of something analogous to M. C. Escher's drawing hands, with male and female each drawing the other. Indeed, the expression "double-edged sword" occurs in the form of a "knife that cuts both ways," which Freud, in a footnote to his essay "Female Sexuality," uses to dismiss the undecidability of his own psychoanalytic authority when the drawing of the male-female relationship threatens to become truly recursive. Having just discussed the difficulties experienced by the woman in accepting "the fact of her castration," Freud notes:

> It is to be anticipated that male analysts with feminist sympathies, and our woman analysts also, will disagree with what I have said here. They will hardly fail to object that such notions have their origins in the man's "masculinity complex," and are meant to justify theoretically his innate propensity to disparage and suppress women. But this sort of psychoanalytic argument reminds us here, as it so often does, of Dostoevsky's famous "knife that cuts both ways." The opponents of those who reason thus will for their part think it quite comprehensible that

members of the female sex should refuse to accept a notion that appears to gainsay their eagerly coveted equality with men. The use of analysis as a weapon of controversy obviously leads to no decision.[5]

In a footnote to Joel Fineman's response to Neil Hertz's discussion of male hysteria, which is where I first came across Freud's footnote, an additional note is cited: "The editor [of the *Standard Edition*] notes that 'The actual simile used by Freud and in the Russian original is "a stick with two ends."'"[6] Out of this regression of footnotes, the basic question is clear: is the figure of sexual difference in psychoanalytic theory cursive or recursive?

The literary equivalent of the visual image of woman as ground has been richly evoked by Susan Gubar in the form of the blank page, the raw material on which the pen–penis of male creativity inscribes its figures, the negative space surrounding what is presented as truly interesting.[7] When woman does appear as a figure in a text, notes Gubar, she is generally mute, passive, or inert, an idealized object of male desire.

The Isak Dinesen story from which Gubar takes the title of her essay offers one displacement of this figure-ground relationship. The story describes a gallery of fine white sheets hung up in a convent to display the blood stains produced on the wedding nights of royal brides. One of these sheets is blank. Gubar sees both the blood and the blank as figures for female writing—females as the subjects of writing, not merely as its objects. Both figure and ground become figure here, but the blank sheet is more recursive than the stained because it proclaims both ground and figure to be open to interpretation, whereas the stained sheets are produced with the proclamation, "We declare her to have been a virgin."

With these considerations in mind, I will now pursue the conjunction between the aesthetics of the figure-ground relationship and the therapeutics of the male-female relationship by juxtaposing "The Birthmark" and "The Yellow Wallpaper." In the Hawthorne story, a passionate scientist, Aylmer, attempts to remove a crimson birthmark from the white cheek of his wife Georgiana, in order "that the world might possess one living specimen of ideal loveliness without the semblance of a flaw" (205). He succeeds in removing the mark, but, in the process, kills Georgiana. In the Gilman story, a woman is confined by her husband, a doctor, to a country house for a rest cure. She begins to focus obsessively on the ugliness of the wallpaper until, in the end, she seems to have become a part of it. The superficial symmetry between the two stories is obvious and suggestive. In both, the therapeutic is underwritten by a strong aesthetic investment. In the male writer's story, the birthmark is an *overinvested figure* inscribed on a page that should be blank. In the female writer's story, the wallpaper is an overinvested *ground.* In the first, the figure *on* the woman-ground is erased; in the second, the woman-figure merges *into* the ground. In both cases, the woman escapes the control of the therapist.

To what extent can these stories be read as allegories of psychoanalysis? At first sight, they seem to be examples not of a talking cure but of a silencing cure. Yet if we take as a subtext the third failed treatment of a female patient, Freud's case of Dora, we find that Dora, too, has recourse to silence, not only in breaking off treatment but in ceasing her denial: "And Dora disputed the fact no longer" (125). In all three stories, it is the male observer who identifies something about the woman as symptom and who determines the nature of the treatment: Aylmer calls Georgiana's birthmark a defect, John calls Gilman's narrator "slightly hysterical," and Dora's father hands his daughter over to Freud, hoping that she will adjust to *his* version of reality. She adjusts neither to his nor to Freud's.

Let us look, then, at the shifting relations between ground and figure in Hawthorne and Gilman, beginning with Hawthorne's first description of Georgiana's mark:

In the center of Georgiana's left cheek there was a singular mark, deeply interwoven, as it were, with the texture and substance of her face. In the usual state of her complexion—a healthy though delicate bloom—the mark wore a tint of deeper crimson, which imperfectly defined its shape amid the surrounding rosiness. When she blushed, it gradually became more indistinct, and finally vanished amid the triumphant rush of blood that bathed the whole cheek with its brilliant glow. But if any shifting motion caused her to turn pale, there was the mark again, a crimson stain upon the snow, in what Aylmer sometimes deemed an almost fearful distinctness. Its shape bore not a little similarity to the human hand, though of the smallest pygmy size. Georgiana's lovers were wont to say that some fairy at her birth hour had laid her tiny hand upon the infant's cheek, and left this impress there in token of the magic endowments that were to give her such sway over all hearts. Many a desperate swain would have risked life for the privilege of pressing his lips to the mysterious hand. It must not be concealed, however, that the impression wrought by this fairy sign manual varied exceedingly, according to the difference of temperament in the beholders. (204–205)

The mark on Georgiana's cheek is a mark of intersubjectivity: it is interpreted differently by different beholders, and it interprets *them* in response. This "fairy sign manual" is what Lacan might call "a signifier that represents a subject for another signifier." It is the *relation* between figure and ground that shifts in response to another, but the ground is what responds while the figure remains constant. It is perhaps this point of autonomy that does not *simply* reflect (the woman as *"pas toute"*) which makes the mark so irritating to Aylmer. If the cheek is ground and the birthmark figure (figure of being born a woman as well as being of woman born), then what Aylmer wishes to do in erasing the mark is to erase the difference— to erase sexual difference—by reducing woman to "all," to ground, to blankness.[8] And he does succeed in consigning this woman to the ground.

In Gilman's "Yellow Wallpaper," the female narrator has been confined for treatment by her physician husband, a man of science like Aylmer, a man who "scoffs openly at any talk of things not to be felt and seen and put down in figures." As has often been noted, the first use of the word "paper" refers to the paper (called the "dead paper") on which the protagonist is writing her journal (which at first coincides with the story we are reading), even though her husband has forbidden her to write.[9] It is clear, therefore, that the paper that comes alive on the walls is related to the dead paper on which the narrator is forbidden to write. The following passages demonstrate the gradual animation of the paper through a shift in the figure–ground relationship. At first, the design is unified:

> I never saw a worse paper in my life. One of those sprawling, flamboyant patterns committing every artistic sin. (5)

A figure begins to take shape *in the ground:*

> This wallpaper has a kind of sub-pattern in a different shade, a particularly irritating one, for you can only see it in certain lights, and not clearly then.
>
> But in the places where it isn't faded and where the sun is just so—I can see a strange, provoking, formless sort of figure that seems to skulk about behind that silly and conspicuous front design. (8)

The figure in the ground begins to look like a woman:

> Behind that outside pattern the dim shapes get clearer every day.
>
> It is always the same shape, only very numerous.
>
> And it is like a woman stooping down and creeping about behind that pattern. (11)

The ground begins to rebel against the dominant figure:

> The faint figure behind seemed to shake the pattern, just as if she wanted to get out. (11)
>
> I lay there for hours trying to decide whether that front pattern and the back pattern really did move together or separately. (12)

Suddenly, we are not sure which side of the paper the narrator is on:

> By daylight she is subdued, quiet. I fancy it is the pattern that keeps her so still. It is so puzzling.
>
> It keeps me quiet by the hour. (13)

Finally, the crossing is complete:

> I don't like to look out of the windows even—there are so many of those creeping women, and they creep so fast.
>
> I wonder if they all came out of the wallpaper as I did?
>
> I don't want to go outside.
>
> For outside you have to creep on the ground. (18)

If at first it seems that the woman projected into the paper is trying to move from ground to figure, by the end of the story the narrator has moved *herself* past the outside, upper figure into a ground that cannot be located in real space. To escape figuration in the patriarchal conception of the real (the upper pattern), she has relocated elsewhere. But this alternative real can be figured only as madness.

The cursively drawable figure becomes recursive with a vengeance, turning the narrative itself into a double-edged sword. In the end we don't know which side of the paper she is on, and hence, we no longer quite know where to locate *ourselves*. Hawthorne's story, too, became recursive—"twice told"—with even more cata-strophic results. The moment the figure/ground distinction is erased, it self-destructs. Hawthorne's story can be read as a story of "failed idealism" only by readers who cannot see its recursiveness.[10]

Freud's attempt to draw the geometry of castration into a narra-tive of female development offers a similar set of complexities. Freud knows where the story starts (the mother) and where the story "must" end (Freud's "must"). While the boy child gets to keep both the original object (the mother) and the original mode (active) of his desire, the girl child must turn from the mother to the father and become passive. While castration for the boy is a threat, for the girl it is a "fact." The narrative of how the woman converts "the fact of her castration" into something desirable is a real chal-lenge, even for a storyteller as gifted as Freud. The "little creature without a penis" faces a daunting set of choices:

There is another, far more specific motive for the turning away from the mother, arising out of the effect of the castra-tion-complex on the little creature without a penis. Some time or other the little girl makes the discovery of her organic inferiority, of course earlier and more easily if she has brothers or other boy companions. We have already noted the three paths which diverge from this point: (a) that which leads to the suspension of the whole sexual life, (b) that which leads to the defiant over-emphasis of her own masculinity, and (c) the first steps towards definitive femininity. (FS 200–201)

The turning-away from the mother is a most important step in the little girl's development: it is more than a mere change of object. We have already described what takes place and what a number of motives are alleged for it; we must now add that we observe, hand in hand with it, a marked diminution in the active and an augmentation of the passive sexual impulses . . . The transition to the father-object is accomplished with the assistance of the passive tendencies so far as these have escaped overthrow. (FS 207–208)

What the Hawthorne and Gilman stories show is the *cost* of adopting the third choice, the choice of "definitive femininity." These stories are stories of an education in passivity: Georgiana is an excellent student; Gilman's narrator flunks. It is her teacher who lies motionless on the floor at the end of the story.

Yet both stories are narratives of the woman's growing complicity in her own destruction. Georgiana learns suicide as masochistic self-effacement, while Gilman's narrator learns madness as masochistic self-assertion. How does the complicity work? The stories point to a number of answers.

In both cases, the husband seems to have organized the world around his love for his wife and his concern for her problem. Aylmer stakes his scientific pride on success at removing the birthmark; John rents a house in the country and organizes family life around his wife's illness. This concern makes it impossible for the woman to protest, since she cannot do so without seeming un-grateful or at least without losing her centrality in her husband's world. Both Georgiana and Gilman's narrator are prisoners of an idealization. The cost of their attaining a valued status in the world is to become an object in someone else's reality and, hence, to have, in fact, *no* status in the world. If woman's value is only assured by the place assigned to her by patriarchy, then the alternatives can only be u-topian. The symptom that both Aylmer and John are try-ing to remove is the mark of femininity itself as both more and less than what is required of women by patriarchal structures. Feminin-ity, in other words, is by nature a "normal ill."[11]

Both the "mark" and the "paper" can be seen as figures for women's writing. Georgiana's "bloody hand," a kind of *écriture féminine* that is both corporal and cheeky, throbs to its own rhythms in response to the world until she is taught to feel so ashamed of it that she is ready to die rather than live with her horrible deformity. Gilman's narrator, too, learns to renounce her writing: "I did write for a while in spite of them; but it *does* exhaust me a good deal—having to be so sly about it, or else meet with heavy opposition" (4). Both women, in other words, internalize the rejection of their writerly self.

What this internalization indicates is that the repression of writ-ing is related to a repression of ambivalence. The woman is not al-lowed to have mixed feelings, to be "composite" or "interwoven." She must renounce everything about which she has negative feel-ings, even when those feelings are internalized from the opinions of

28

women can't be composite.
self-difference requires repression...
herself

others. Ultimately, the thing about which she feels ambivalent, and which she renounces, is herself.

In Freud, too, the "composite" nature of the woman is what is not allowed to stand. Frustrated in what Luce Irigaray has called the "dream of symmetry,"[12] Freud discovers not that woman *is* the second sex, but that she *has* a second sex:

> It will help our exposition if, as we go along, we compare the course of female development with that of the male.
>
> First of all, there can be no doubt that the bisexual disposition which we maintain to be characteristic of human beings manifests itself much more plainly in the female than in the male. The latter has only one principal sexual zone—only one sexual organ—whereas the former has two: the vagina, the true female organ, and the clitoris, which is analogous to the male organ . . . The sexual life of the woman is regularly split up into two phases, the first of which is of a masculine character, whilst only the second is specifically feminine. Thus in female development there is a process of transition from the one phase to the other, to which there is nothing analogous in males. A further complication arises from the fact that the clitoris, with its masculine character, continues to function in later female sexual life in a very variable manner, which we certainly do not as yet fully understand. (FS 197)

The irritation Freud feels at this excess organ comes out in his triumphant revelation of Dora's supposed secret: her masturbation.

When I set myself the task of bringing to light what human beings keep hidden within them . . . by observing what they say and what they show, I thought the task was a harder one than it really is. He that has eyes to see and ears to hear may convince himself that no mortal can keep a secret. If his lips are silent, he chatters with his finger-tips; betrayal oozes out of him at every pore . . .

The reproaches against her father for having made her ill, together with the self-reproach underlying them, the leucor-rhoea, the playing with the reticule, the bed-wetting after her sixth year, the secret which she would not allow the physicians to tear from her—the circumstantial evidence of her having masturbated in childhood seems to me complete and without a flaw. (*Dora* 96–97)

In this notoriously fragmented and incomplete case history, Freud's pleasure at an interpretation that is "complete and without a flaw" is striking. Also striking is the parallel between Freud's scientific ju-bilation and the triumph anticipated by Aylmer as he prepares to render his wife perfect, "without the semblance of a flaw." Indeed, that throbbing birthmark, that hand already upon Georgiana's body, that "little mark," as Georgiana describes it, "which I cover with the tips of two small fingers," may perhaps be read as the dis-placement upward precisely of that troublingly excessive female organ. Precedent for such a displacement can be found in the con-tinuation of the passage I have just quoted from *Dora*:

In the present case I had begun to suspect the masturbation when she had told me of her cousin's gastric pains . . . and had then identified herself with her by complaining for days to-gether of similar painful sensations. It is well known that gas-tric pains occur especially often in those who masturbate. Ac-cording to a personal communication made to me by W. Fliess, it is precisely gastralgias of this character which can be interpreted by an application of cocaine to the "gastric spot" discovered by him in the nose, and which can be cured by the cauterization of the same spot. (97)

It is hard not to see the scientific energies deployed by Aylmer, Freud, and Fliess in the face of this wandering spot as a sign of patri-archal befuddlement at the multiformity of female sexuality. "The Birthmark," indeed, can be read as a story of fatal clitoridectomy.

This is not to substitute a cliterocentric universe for a phallocen-tric one, but rather to take the clitoris, as Gayatri Spivak and Naomi Schor have both suggested, as a synecdoche for the possibility that the world could be articulated differently, that resistance is always the sign of a counterstory, that the "knife that cuts both ways" does so not because the stories are symmetrical but because they are not, because each of them is differently situated, serves different ends, and accounts for different things.[13] There is no guarantee that the figures in a *truly* recursive figure would fit together at all.

Freud's story of female sexuality, like Hawthorne's, is a story of renunciation required by the needs of symmetry: "In women the development of sexuality is complicated by the task of *renouncing* that genital zone which was originally the principal one, namely, the clitoris, in favor of a new zone—the vagina" (FS 194). But as Freud's own repeated analysis shows, this renunciation is never any

31

more "complete and without a flaw" than another renunciation Freud considers equally necessary: "We have, after all, long since *given up* any expectation of a neat parallelism between male and female sexual development" (FS 195; emphasis mine). What is at stake in the relationship between psychoanalysis and feminism can indeed be summed up in the relationship between renunciation *for* symmetry and renunciation *of* symmetry.

Having now reached a point of closure in my argument, I would like to end by examining how closure is marked in each of the three texts I have been discussing. I find such a gesture most emphatically inscribed in "The Birthmark." Early in the text, we are promised a "deeply impressive moral." Hawthorne does not fail to deliver what bears all the stylistic marks of an authoritative conclusion. Yet in attempting to capitalize morally upon the failed hubris of science, the narrator actually repeats the error he has just documented. The plea for interwovenness and incompleteness is couched in a language that attempts to achieve the same type of objective mastery its message is designed to demystify.

As the last crimson tint of the birthmark—that sole token of human imperfection—faded from her cheek, the parting breath of the now perfect woman passed into the atmosphere, and her soul, lingering a moment near her husband, took its heavenward flight. Then a hoarse, chuckling laugh was heard again! Thus ever does the gross fatality of earth exult in its invariable triumph over the immortal essence which, in this dim sphere of half development, demands the completeness of a higher state. Yet, had Aylmer reached a profounder wisdom, he need not thus have flung away the happiness which would have woven his mortal life of the selfsame texture with the celestial. The momentary circumstance was too strong for him; he failed to look beyond the shadowy scope of time, and, living once for all in eternity, to find the perfect future in the present.

What is astonishing about this passage is that it wants to have its interwovenness and deny it, too. The multiplication of contradictory categories is contained within a grammar of moral certainty. The meaning of these assertions is open to doubt; their claim-to-mean is not.

"I did not succeed in mastering the transference in good time," writes Freud at a similar point in his story. These descriptions of failure are couched in the language of *narrative* control. From whose perspective does one say "Thus ever . . ."? Georgiana is dead, Dora is still somatizing along, and Hawthorne and Freud have gone into high oratorical gear. Whatever the damage done by their finished or unfinished business, the story must have its proper ending, its concluding scientific postscript:

Years have gone by since her visit. In the meantime the girl has married, and indeed—unless all the signs mislead me—she has married the young man who came into her associations at the beginning of the analysis of the second dream. Just as the first dream represented her turning away from the man she loved to her father—that is to say, her flight from life into disease—so the second dream announced that she was about to tear herself free from her father and had been reclaimed once more by the realities of life. (144)

"The perfect future in the present," "the realities of life": each story ends by pledging its allegiance to a larger story, a larger sense of coherence, a larger set of myths. In contrast, Gilman ends with the very voice of inconclusiveness:

"I've got out at last," said I, "in spite of you and Jane. And I've pulled off most of the paper, so you can't put me back!"

Now why should that man have fainted? But he did, and right across my path by the wall, so that I had to creep over him every time! (20)

While the figure of the patriarchal story lies senseless on the floor, the escaped story creeps wildly around in circles. Gilman's ending could not be more different from Freud's or Hawthorne's. Or could it? Twenty years later, Gilman published a sequel titled "Why I Wrote 'The Yellow Wallpaper,'" which documents the therapeutic effects of the story on other women suffering from the rest cure. It concludes, "It was not intended to drive people crazy, but to save people from being driven crazy, and it worked" (20). The impulse to put the story to work therapeutically is equally irresistible to all three authors, as it has, no doubt, been to me. Feminism is structured no less therapeutically than the normalizing patriarchal therapies it is designed to combat. The suspicion arises, however, that it is precisely the therapeutic haste toward closure that works in a countertherapeutic way.

In all three cases, then, the text concludes with a coda that takes the story itself as its object. Each author stands back from the story as *its reader,* salvaging from the wreckage of its characters the therapeutic coherence of a moral. Transference here is transference onto the story itself as value-object. A quotation from Dinesen's "Blank Page" can perhaps serve to underscore this transference onto story as the moral of *our* transference onto all three tales: "Where the story-teller is loyal, eternally and unswervingly loyal to the story, there, in the end, silence will speak. Where the story has been betrayed, silence is but emptiness. But we, the faithful, when we have spoken our last word, will hear the voice of silence."[14]

Loyalty to the story does not, however, guarantee an unproblematic relation to silence. I would like to conclude by sounding a dimension of silence that has gone unheard in my remarks. Freud, Hawthorne, and Gilman all write about middle-class white men and women. The very equation of the woman's body with the blank page implies that the woman's body is white (indeed, of a whiteness no actual bodies possess). And the concept of femininity as passivity is applicable only to a certain class of women, even within the texts we have been reading. Are there, perhaps, other figures trapped in the ground of these literary carpets?

In the Gilman and Hawthorne stories, several figures are standing in the background—Mary, who cares for the children; Jennie, the housekeeper; and Aminadab, the personification of matter and physical work, placed beside the sorcerer Aylmer as Caliban is beside Prospero. This background role is often played, in white Western literature, by non-white characters. (In pointing this out, I am, of course, prolonging the colonizing gesture of *equating* race and class.) The two most-cited capsule descriptions of black characters in white American fiction, I think, are that of Topsy, who "just grew," and of Dilsey, who "endured." This is another way of denying a character the status of figure, reserving that status for the figures that are foregrounded as if it were a natural right and not an effect of the contrast, and confining the characters in the margins to the ground. Topsy has no origin; Dilsey has no end; they have no story, no history, nothing to put into figure. Anne Tyler, in her novel *Searching for Caleb,* plays upon the invisibility—the purloined-letter status—of the black characters that occupy the ground of much white American literature. In that novel, a white family searches for a son who has disappeared, and cannot trace him until someone finally thinks to ask the black couple who were working for the family. They possessed the knowledge all along, but were never asked.

In short, there are many other invisible men and women trapped in the wallpaper of the Western canon or caught in the divisions of labor that neither psychoanalysis nor feminist theory has taken sufficiently into account—figures that have often remained consigned to the background of discussions of feminism and psychoanalysis. Could one of these figures be discerned through a reading of another birthmark, the birthmark imprinted on the face of Toni Morrison's Sula? Perhaps, but that would have to be the beginning of another essay.

Chapter Two

The Quicksands of the Self:
Nella Larsen and Heinz Kohut

Nella Larsen's first novel, *Quicksand,* was published in 1928, at the height of that period of black migration from the rural south to the urban north which led to an explosion in cultural and artistic creativity known as the Harlem Renaissance. The novel was immediately greeted with enthusiasm: it won second prize in literature from the Harmon Foundation, and W. E. B. Du Bois called it "the best piece of fiction that Negro America has produced since the heyday of Chesnutt."[1] Readers then and now have indeed read the novel as a dramatization of racial double consciousness,[2] in the form of the all-too-familiar topos of the tragic mulatto. Nathan Huggins, in his book *The Harlem Renaissance,* writes: "Nella Larsen came as close as any to treating human motivation with complexity and sophistication. But she could not wrestle free of the mulatto condition that the main characters in her two novels had been given. Once she made them mulatto and female the conventions of American thought—conditioned by the tragic mulatto and the light-dark heroine formulas—seemed to take the matter out of the author's hands."[3] In other words, Larsen's attempt to present the inner life of her main character was subverted by the force of a literary cliche

37

designed to rob her of any inner life by subjecting her to a tragic "condition."

The mulatto image, a staple of nineteenth-century literature both by white "plantation school" writers and by black and white abolitionist writers, is less a reflection of a social or sociological reality than it is a literary and mythic device for both articulating and concealing the racial history of this country. Critics like Barbara Christian, Hazel Carby, and Hortense Spillers have analyzed the ways in which the mulatto represents both a taboo and a synthesis, both the product of a sexual union that miscegenation laws tried to rule out of existence and an allegory for the racially divided society as a whole, both un-American and an image of America as such. In an essay entitled "Notes on an alternative model—neither/nor," Hortense Spillers writes:

Created to provide a middle ground of latitude between "black" and "white," the customary and permissible binary agencies of the national adventure, mulatto being, as a neither/ nor proposition, inscribed no historic locus, or materiality, that was other than evasive and shadowy on the national land- scape. To that extent, the mulatto/a embodied an alibi, an ex- cuse for "other/otherness" that the dominant culture could not (cannot now either) appropriate, or wish away. An accre- tion of signs that embody the "unspeakable" of the Everything that the dominant culture would forget, the mulatto/a, as term, designates a disguise, covers up, in the century of Eman- cipation and beyond, the social and political reality of the dreaded African presence. Behind the African-become-American stands the shadow, the unsubstantial "double" that the culture dreamed *in the place of* that humanity transformed into its profoundest challenge and by the impositions of policy, its deepest "un-American" activity.[4]

Nella Larsen herself suggests that her novel should be read through the grid of the mulatto figure by choosing as her epigraph a stanza from a Langston Hughes poem entitled "Cross":

> My old man died in a fine big house.
> My ma died in a shack.
> I wonder where I'm gonna die,
> Being neither white nor black?[5]

Where one might expect a both/and, we find, as Spillers and Hughes suggest, a neither/nor. Nella Larsen's project in *Quicksand* is to tell the story of the neither/nor self from within.

The question of that neither/nor of racial designation is tied, both in the epigraph and in the novel, to the question of *place:* shack or big house, North or South, Europe or America. In the Hughes poem, the father is white; the mother black. This corresponds to the historical realities of the sexual abuse of slave women by white slaveholders. Nella Larsen's protagonist's parentage, however, is reversed: her mother is a Danish immigrant and her father is a black American. This, I think, further complicates the question of race and place, both socially and geographically. The first sentence of the novel, "Helga Crane sat alone in her room," echoes not only the "in's" of the epigraph but even its very rhythm. The last clause of the opening paragraph of the novel continues that rhythm: "Helga Crane never opened her door." It is as though the novel originates within the "stanza" (which etymologically means "room") of its epigraph. The question of place thus intersects with a question of space, of personal space, of the inside/outside boundaries of the self. Helga Crane's closed door circumscribes a space filled with small luxuries: a Chinese carpet, a brass bowl, nasturtiums, oriental silk. Her room symbolizes the issue of the self as container (of value, positive or negative). And the title, *Quicksand,* extends the metaphor of space in a nightmarish direction: the self is utterly engulfed by the outside because there is nothing outside the engulfing outside to save it.

What, then, is the nature of the quicksand into which Helga Crane sinks in Nella Larsen's novel? Critics have offered various answers. Hiroko Sato writes: "The title, *Quicksand,* signifies the heroine Helga Crane's sexual desire, which was hidden beneath her beautiful and intelligent surface and came up at an unexpected moment and trapped her."[6] For Deborah McDowell, Hortense Thornton, and Cheryl Wall, on the other hand, it is not Helga's sexuality that has trapped her but rather her attempts to disavow it—her own and society's contradictory responses to it. To be respectable as a "lady" is to have no sexuality; to have sexuality is to be a jungle creature, an exotic primitive, or an oppressed wife and mother. These readings which focus on the centrality of black female sexuality are responses to earlier readings (mostly by male critics) which focused on the problems of the biracial self. As

Deborah McDowell puts it explicitly, "In focusing on the problems of the 'tragic mulatto,' readers miss the more urgent problem of female sexual identity which Larsen tried to explore" (p. xvii). And Cheryl Wall writes, "Helga's interracial parentage—her father is black and her mother white—troubles her too, but it is not the primary cause of her unease. Her real struggle is against imposed definitions of blackness and womanhood. Her 'difference' is ultimately her refusal to accept society's terms even in the face of her inability to define alternatives . . . *Passing,* like *Quicksand,* demonstrates Larsen's ability to explore the psychology of her characters. She exposes the sham that is middle-class security, especially for women whose total dependence is morally debilitating. The absence of meaningful work and community condemn them to the 'walled prison' of their own thoughts . . . As these characters deviate from the norm, they are defined—indeed too often define themselves—as Other. They thereby cede control of their lives. But, in truth, the worlds these characters inhabit offer them no possibility of autonomy or fulfillment."[7] As these quotations make clear, *Quicksand* is a complex analysis of the intersections of gender, sexuality, race, and class. It seems, therefore, somehow regressive and discordant to ask what use a "self-psychological" psychoanalytic perspective might be in understanding the novel. How can any insight be gained into all these structures by focussing on intra-psychic processes? Yet the inside/outside opposition on which such scruples are based is one that the novel constantly forces us to reexamine. It will also, I hope, force us to reexamine that opposition in the assumptions and interpretive frames of psychoanalysis.

As we have seen, critics often praise Larsen for her psychological sophistication, but then go on to interpret the novel in social, economic, and political terms. Such readings illuminate many aspects of the novel, but there are certain questions that they leave untouched. How, for example, can one account for the self-defeating or self-exhausting nature of Helga Crane's choices? At several points, Helga achieves economic autonomy—when teaching in a Southern black college or when working for an insurance company in New York—but she seems each time all too ready to flee to dependency. Economic autonomy does not provide something which economic dependency seems to promise. Then, too, Helga repeatedly reaches states of relative contentment—in Harlem, in Denmark, in Alabama—only to fall into depression again for no obvious reason. Chapter breaks often occur where psychological causation is missing. It is the *lack* of explicit precipitating cause that calls for explanation. And it is the difficulty of defining the causes of Helga's suffering that leads to irritation in many readers. Mary Helen Washington summarizes a common reaction to the novel, before going on to critique the terms of such a reaction:

Nella Larsen . . . published two novels, *Quicksand* and *Passing,* which dealt with this same problem: the marginal black woman of the middle class who is both unwilling to conform to a circumscribed existence in the black world and unable to move freely in the white world. We may perhaps think this a strange dilemma for a black woman to experience, or certainly an atypical one, for most black women then, as now, were struggling against much more naked and brutal realities and would be contemptuous of so esoteric a problem as feeling uncomfortable among black people and unable to sort out their racial identity. We might justifiably wonder, is there anything relevant, in the lives of women who arrogantly expected to live in Harlem, in the middle-class enclave of Sugar Hill, to summer at resorts like Idlewild in Michigan, to join exclusive black clubs and sororities? Weren't the interests that preoccupied Larsen in her work just the spoiled tantrums of 'little yellow dream children' grown up?[8]

The Harlem Renaissance was indeed the literary coming of age of the black middle class, but, as Hazel Carby and others have pointed out, it was as much a critique of middle class values as an espousal of them. But the description of Helga Crane's problems as "esoteric," "arrogant," and "spoiled" suggests to me a parallel with the vague, ill-defined complaints of the middle-class patients treated by Heinz Kohut under the category of "narcissistic personality disorders." I will therefore turn to the work of Kohut as a framework for understanding what Larsen understood about the psychological effects of social conflicts, and then I will take Nella Larsen as a framework for questioning the limits of Kohut's description of the phenomenon he calls narcissism. But first, a summary of the novel and of Kohut's theory of narcissism.

The novel opens with Helga Crane's resolution to leave Naxos, the stifling black school where she teaches, because rather than stimulating growth and creativity in its students, it teaches confor-

43

mity, low horizons of expectation, and imitation of middle class white values. She goes to the office of the principal, Robert Anderson, to hand in her resignation, and is momentarily tempted by his discourse of service into reconsidering, until he inadvertently insults her and she flees to Chicago, where her white uncle, her mother's brother, Peter Nilssen, lives. Hoping to enlist his support while she looks for a new job, she encounters his new white wife, who wants to have nothing to do with her husband's sister's mulatto daughter. Thrown on her own resources, Helga is rejected for a library job because she lacks "references" and for domestic work because she is too refined. Eventually she gets a job as a speech editor for a prominent "race woman," Mrs. Hayes-Rore, through whom she finds work in an insurance company in New York. In New York, Helga lives with Mrs. Hayes-Rore's elegant niece, Anne Grey, through whom she gets to know Harlem's glittering society life, and, for a time, feels quite contented. But her contentment doesn't last, and, when a check arrives from the remorseful uncle Peter, Helga sails to Denmark, where she lives with her mother's relatives the Dahls. There, she is treated as an exotic treasure, dressed and wined and dined in splendor, and courted by the famous painter Axel Olsen, who paints her portrait, propositions her sexually, and then, in the face of her non-response, asks her to marry him. Insulted by the way in which the proposal expresses his generosity and her objectification, she refuses. Homesick for Harlem, she returns to New York for the marriage of Anne Grey and Robert Anderson. Later, at a party, Anderson kisses her, and she is overwhelmed with desire. At a later meeting she intends to give herself to him, but he wants only to apologize and re-establish distance. In despair, she walks into a church, has an intense conversion experience, sleeps with the black minister, Rev. Pleasant Green, marries him, and goes south with him to his rural congregation, where she is soon buried in the physical exhaustion of bearing and caring for four children. As the novel ends, she sees nothing in her environment to value, and is pregnant with her fifth child.

Heinz Kohut is known for having developed a psychoanalytic theory of what he called "Self Psychology." This theory has been seen by Lacanians as itself an example of entrapment in the fictions of the autonomous self as generated by the mirror stage. While such a critique may be justified, I would prefer to see Kohut's work as a parallel and much richer exploration of structures of mirroring of which the mirror stage is one example.

What does Kohut mean by a self? The self, he writes, should not be confused with the ego. The self is not a subject. The self is an image, a representation. Indeed, there may exist simultaneous contradictory self-representations in the same person. "The self, then, quite analogous to the representations of objects, is a *content* of the mental apparatus but is not . . . one of the *agencies* of the mind."[9] How is the self formed? Kohut answers: through empathic mirroring. The self is the internalization of the gaze of the other, generally the mother in Kohut's account. Instead of Lacan's statuelike visual self-representation in the mirror, for which the mother serves only as a baby stand, Kohut's self-representation derives from the approval-conveying "gleam in the mother's eye." In the early stages of the formation of the self, therefore, other people are not

45

selfobjects [margin annotation]

perceived as separate, true objects, but as parts of the self, as selfobjects. The function of selfobject can continue to be played by other people throughout an individual's life, including sexual partners, and especially, for Kohut, psychoanalysts.

The psychological structures appropriate to the earliest phase in the development of the self, according to Kohut, are the grandiose exhibitionistic self ("I am perfect") and the idealized omnipotent selfobject based on the parent ("you are perfect but I am part of you"). "The need of the budding self for the joyful response of the mirroring selfobject, the need of the budding self for the omnipotent selfobject's pleased acceptance of its merger needs, are primary considerations." If the child is not appropriately mirrored, is not given the message "what you are is valuable" at this stage, then the grandiose self and the desire to merge with the idealized selfobject do not fade away but become split off and retain their archaic demands. Rather than being progressively reality-tested and integrated, they keep the unfilled hunger for validation intact as an open wound. This, I think, is what Helga refers to as "a lack somewhere." Like Helga, the patients Kohut analyzes often have considerable talent and strong aesthetic investments. And, like Helga, they have a tendency to "react to sources of narcissistic disturbance by mixtures of wholesale withdrawal and unforgiving rage" (p. 65). Periods of heightened vitality and contentment are followed by a renewed sense of depletion, often brought about either by the anxiety that arises from an uncomfortable degree of excitement or by a rebuff or merely a lack of attention from the environment. Kohut's theory is, among other things, a revaluation of the moral valence of the term "narcissism," which is based not on self-satisfaction but on hollowness. Helga's apparent selfishness is based not on an excess of self but on a lack of self.

What does the novel tell us about the origins of Helga's narcissistic deficit? What kind of early mirroring does the novel describe? Her father, a black man she refers to as a gambler and a "gay suave scoundrel," deserted her mother, a Danish immigrant, before Helga could form any definite relation to him. The mother, "sad, cold, and remote," remarried, this time to a white man who treated Helga with malicious and jealous hatred. Helga thus has no early relations with black people except the image of her father as both desirable and unreliable, and she has increasingly negative relations with the white people that are her only family. But instead of becoming enraged at their lack of empathy for her, she actually learns to empathize with their view of her as a problem *for them*. "She saw herself for an obscene sore in all their lives, at all costs to be hidden. She understood, even while she resented. It would have been easier if she had not" (p. 29). In other words, she learns to identify with the rejecting other, to desire her own disappearance. Intimacy equals rejection; the price of intimacy is to satisfy the other's desire that she disappear. To be is not to be. It is no wonder that Helga's mode is flight, and that her first spoken words in the novel are "No, forever." The culminating scene of orgasmic conversion in the church is a stark acting out of the logic of self-erasure in a merger with the omnipotent other. As the church service begins, a hymn is being sung:

> Oh, the bitter shame and sorrow
> That a time could ever be,
> When I let the Savior's pity
> Plead in vain, and proudly answered:
> All of self and none of Thee,
> All of self and none of Thee. . .

As the hymn continues, the refrain changes:

> Some of self and some of Thee,
> Some of self and some of Thee. . .

Then:

> Less of self and more of Thee,
> Less of self and more of Thee. . .

Then, at the moment Helga surrenders to the conversion, the moment the text says "she was lost—or saved," the hymn's final refrain is acted out, but not stated:

> None of self and all of Thee,
> None of self and all of Thee.

The religious conversion, the merger with the omnipotent self-object, momentarily overcomes the self's isolation but at the cost of the self's disappearance. The narcissistic plot here merges with the Oedipal plot: Helga's life, like her mother's, is drastically transformed by a moment of blind surrender.

This ecstatic disappearance is only the culmination of a series of encounters in the novel which present the narcissistic logic in other, less drastic, terms. Each time, Helga's vulnerable and defensively haughty self approaches a potential mirror and is, or perceives herself to be, mis-mirrored. I will analyze two of these moments, the opening encounter with Robert Anderson and the encounter with the Danish painter Axel Olsen.

Robert Anderson is the principal of the black school in which Helga is teaching at the start of the novel. She has become enraged at the school for its compliance with the low and self-denying expectations it has placed on its educational mission—complying with the image of blacks as hewers of wood and drawers of water, which has just been repeated to the assembled school by a white preacher. Helga has decided to leave the school immediately, and must tell Anderson her reasons. As she waits for him to receive her, she thinks about the school's disapproval of her love for bright colors and beautiful clothes. Upon entering his office, she sees "the figure of a man, at first blurred slightly in outline in that dimmer light." She feels confusion, "something very like hysteria," then a mysterious ease. She begins to explain her resignation to Dr. Anderson in an exchange that very much resembles an initial psychoanalytic session—he remains detached, prompting her to elaborate on her remarks, probing for her thoughts. She explains that she hates hypocrisy and the suppression of individuality and beauty. He then begins a discourse of wisdom, telling her that lies, hypocrisy, injustice are part of life that dedicated people put up with when the goals are so high. The text describes Helga's reactions to his words as follows:

Helga Crane was silent, feeling a mystifying yearning which sang and throbbed in her. She felt again that urge for service, not now for her people, but for this man who was talking so earnestly of his work, his plans, his hopes. An insistent need to be a part of them sprang up in her. With compunction tweaking at her heart for ever having entertained the notion of deserting him, she resolved not only to remain until June, but to return next year. (p. 20)

In this scene, then, Helga enters with a sense of her embattled grandiose self (her aesthetic difference, her individuality and creativity) but is drawn toward the appeal of the omnipotent self-object, the merger with the idealized other. That merger can only exist, however, on the basis of perfect empathy. Anderson inadvertently breaks that empathy in the very words he uses to solidify it:

"What we need is more people like you, people with a sense of values, and proportion, an appreciation of the rarer things of life. You have something to give which we badly need here in Naxos. You mustn't desert us, Miss Crane."

She nodded, silent. He had won her. She knew that she would stay. "It's an elusive something," he went on. "Perhaps I can best explain it by the use of that trite phrase, 'You're a lady.' You have dignity and breeding."

At these words turmoil rose again in Helga Crane. The intricate pattern of the rug which she had been studying escaped her. The shamed feeling which had been her penance evaporated. Only a lacerated pride remained. She took firm hold of the chair arms to still the trembling of her fingers.

"If you're speaking of family, Dr. Anderson, why, I haven't any. I was born in a Chicago slum."

The man chose his words, carefully he thought. "That doesn't at all matter, Miss Crane. Financial, economic circumstances can't destroy tendencies inherited from good stock. You yourself prove that!"

Concerned with her own angry thoughts, which scurried here and there like trapped rats, Helga missed the import of his words. Her own words, her answer, fell like drops of hail.

"The joke is on you, Dr. Anderson. My father was a gambler who deserted my mother, a white immigrant. It is even uncertain that they were married. As I said at first, I don't belong here. I shall be leaving at once. This afternoon. Good-morning." (pp. 20–21)

In his act of delivering a compliment, Anderson puts his finger on a wound. By juxtaposing the words "lady" (which at Naxos signifies the denial of sexuality) and the word "breeding" (which for Helga is the name both for forbidden sexuality and for lack of family), he shows not only that he is not omnipotent (since he does not really know anything about her) but that what he wants to value in her is something she thinks she does not and cannot possess. The mirror breaks, the pattern in the rug loses its design, Helga fragments into chaotically scattering pieces, and she departs in a narcissistic rage.

In Denmark, Helga is drawn to the symmetrically opposite kind of narcissistic satisfaction. There, it is her grandiose exhibitionism that is initially mirrored, rather than her desire to merge with the idealized other. Whereas Helga's difference and fine clothes have been met with hostility and disapproval in the United States, the Danes are fascinated. They urge her to become more exhibitionistic, more exotic, more sensuous. Yet they are at the same time cold and detached. Instead of being repressed, Helga's exhibitionism is instead being expropriated, objectified, commodified, alienated. This process comes to a head in her relation to Axel Olsen, the portrait painter. When she looks at the portrait he has painted of her, she says to herself: "It wasn't herself at all, but some disgusting sensual creature with her features. Bosh! pure artistic bosh and conceit! Nothing else." This has often been read as her refusal to acknowledge her own sexuality. But I think that, far from constituting a mirror designed to confirm her sexuality, this mirror gives her only someone else's narcissistic appropriation of it. She refuses the painter's offer of marriage out of a refusal to be owned by a white man. It is in Denmark that she first feels homesick for Negroes and identifies with, and forgives, her father for the first time. She returns to Harlem.

Several times in the novel, the potential mirror is not a person but a race, a "world." When Helga first arrives in Harlem, she feels keenly a "joy at seeming at last to belong somewhere." When she first arrives in Denmark, too, she says to herself, "This, then was where she belonged." Yet each time the surrounding mirror is incapable of sustaining the role of selfobject which she asks of it. The promise of belonging flips over into a pressure to conform. Each mirror limits even as it embraces. But instead of seeing that therefore she herself is composite, a mixture, a process rather than a product, that wholeness itself is a fiction—the problem and not the solution—she goes on believing that both she and the environment can be perfected, whole, non-self-different. For Helga, there is no middle, no compromise, no gray area—the only satisfaction must be total, pure, and therefore unreal, short-lived. She seeks to fill her narcissistic deficit with the environment, not for its own properties but in the attempt to substitute for a missing part of the self. The line between remedy and poison is a thin one—the magical self-object must inevitably oppress and disappoint. What is different about Nella Larsen's treatment of these dynamics is that she shows race itself to be a kind of selfobject from which a self can derive both positive and negative mirroring. Kohut occasionally suggests as much, as when, in a footnote, he writes: "It may be helpful to say that the grandiose self . . . has such analogues in adult experience as, e.g., national and racial pride and prejudice (everything good is 'Inside,' everything bad and evil is assigned to the 'outsider'), while the relationship to the idealized parent imago may have its parallel in the relationship (including mystical mergers) of the true believer to his God" (p. 27). As an analysis of the narcissistic roots of racism and race pride, this is quite convincing. But it fails to account for the fact that what is a narcissistic structure for the individual is also a social, economic, and political structure in the world. Racial pride and prejudice are not merely interpersonal phenomena, but institutionalized structures in history and culture. In dealing with individual patients, Kohut generally neglects or subsumes the *social* mirroring environment in favor of the dynamics of the nuclear family. The following is a fairly striking example:

> Over and over again, throughout his childhood, the patient ... had felt abruptly and traumatically disappointed in the power and efficacy of his father just when he had (re-) established him as a figure of protective strength and efficiency ... After an adventurous flight via South Africa and South America, the family had come to the United States when the patient was nine years old, and the father, who had been a prosperous businessman in Europe, was unable to repeat his earlier success in this country ... Most prominent among the patient's relevant recollections of earlier occurrences of the idealization-disappointment sequence concerning his father were those of the family's last years in Eastern Europe ... Suddenly the threat that the German armies would overrun the country interrupted their close relationship. At first the father was away a great deal, trying to make arrangements for the transfer of his business to another country. Then, when the patient was six, German armies invaded the country and the family, which was Jewish, fled. (pp. 58–60)

The minor role played in this last sentence by the fact that the family was Jewish is an indication of Kohut's overestimation of the nuclear family as the context for psychic development. What Nella Larsen does is to articulate the relation between the mirroring environment of the nuclear family and the social messages from the environment which *also* affect the construction of the self. It is as though, for Kohut, the child has no independent experience of history, no relation to the world that is not filtered through the parental imagos. Yet the social world can indeed set up an artificially inflated or deflated narcissistic climate for the child. Racial privilege would offer an unearned archaic narcissistic bonus which, when threatened, would lead to the characteristic narcissistic rages of racism just as surely as the undeserved narcissistic injury resulting from the insertion of a black child into a hostile white environment would lead to the kinds of precarious self-consolidation Larsen documents in the absence of a strong black mirroring environment.

No matter how empathic a mother or father might be, he or she cannot always offset the formative mirroring of the environment. Indeed, in Kohut, the burden of good mirroring falls, again and again, on the mother. His case histories sound like accusations against the mother whose own context or needs are not analyzed. What Nella Larsen does is to locate the failures of empathy not in the mother but in the impossible ways in which the mother finds herself inscribed in the social order. Neither for Helga's mother nor for Helga herself as mother at the end of the novel is the social order nourishing, or even viable. And the split between fathers—the absent black father and the rejecting white father—cannot be understood apart from the stereotypical overdeterminations of such a split in American society as a whole.

The therapeutic desire to effect change in the self alone amputates the energies of change from their connections with the larger social and economic world. As Hazel Carby has written of *Quicksand,*

Alienation is often represented as a state of consciousness, a frame of mind. Implied in this definition is the assumption that alienation can be eliminated or replaced by another state of consciousness, a purely individual transformation unrelated to necessary social or historical change. Helga does question the possibility that her recurrent dissatisfaction with her life could be due to her state of mind and that if she could change her attitudes she could be happy. But against this Larsen has placed an alternative reading of Helga's progress, that her alienation was not just in her head but was produced by existing forms of social relations and therefore subject to elimination only by a change in those social relations.[10]

As this quotation makes clear, Larsen herself does not ask the reader to *choose* between a psychic and a social model, but rather to see the articulations between them. To see Helga purely from the inside or purely from the outside is to miss the genius of the text. It is the inside/outside opposition itself that needs to be questioned.

In addition to questioning the inside/outside opposition as an adequate model for the relation between the self and society, Larsen's novel also provides material for a critique of the conception of the self as a locus of value. Throughout this paper, I have echoed and extended Kohut's economic vocabulary of narcissistic investments, deficits, and assets, emphasizing the ways in which Helga Crane alternates between surplus value and lack, grandiosity and worthlessness, between an image of herself as a luxury item and an image of herself as garbage. What luxury and garbage have in common is that each is a form of excess with respect to an economy of use or need. Thus, for instance, after humiliating rejections by Uncle Peter's new wife and by the library personnel, Helga spends what little money she has on a book and a tapestry purse, "which she wanted but did not need," and resolves to go without dinner, attempting to fulfill a narcissistic hunger in preference to a physical one. As long as need is ignored, however, the narcissistic imbalance cannot be rectified. This emphasis on the isolated self as a locus of value (positive or negative) risks duplicating, in the psychological realm, the structures Marx identified as "the fetishism of the commodity"—the belief that the commodity, abstracted from both labor and use, "contains" value in and of itself. Both Larsen and Kohut indeed analyze a self that is very much structured like a commodity. This returns us to the perceived middle-classness of both Larsen and Kohut: it may well be that both the concept of the self and the analytical framework through which we have been discussing it can themselves be analyzed as artifacts of class.

I would like to pursue this question indirectly by turning to a domain that lies in an intermediary position between the psychic and the social and economic. This is the domain of cultural forms. Kohut often mentions the role of aesthetic investments in consolidating a cohesive self, even in the face of early traumatic environments (an incubator baby, children from concentration camps). Larsen has often been criticized for her lack of investment in African-American cultural forms, which appear in ambivalent or degraded guises in her novels (the black church, the rural folk, the black educational establishment, the cabaret, the singers Helga sees in Denmark). But these forms also exert a powerful attraction in the novels, which is what gives them so much power to disappoint. Hearing the strains of "Swing low, sweet chariot" in Dvorak's "New World Symphony," Helga is overwhelmed with the desire to be carried home.

The final chapter in Larsen's life as a writer is instructive in this context as a bringing together of questions of culture, narcissism, and economics. After her two very successful novels, Larsen wrote a short story entitled "Sanctuary," in which a black woman harbors a fugitive from justice only to find out that the man she is protecting has killed her own son, Obadiah. The last paragraph of the story reads:

> It seemed a long time before Obadiah's mother spoke. When she did there were no tears, no reproaches; but there was a raging fury in her voice as she lashed out, "Git outen mah feather baid, Jim Hammer, an' outen mah house, an' don' nevah stop thankin' yo' Jesus he done gib you dat black face."[11]

The character and the plot were an unusual affirmation of black folk speech and racial solidarity for Larsen. But upon its publication she found herself accused of plagiarism: another writer, Sheila Kaye-Smith, had published a strikingly similar story entitled "Mrs. Adis" about white laborers in Sussex eight years earlier. Larsen responded by saying that she had heard the story from an old black patient in the hospital where she worked as a nurse, and her publisher produced several of her drafts. She was more or less exonerated. Mary Dearborn, in her book *Pocahontas's Daughters,* raises questions about the nature of ethnic authorship on the basis of this event:

Whether Larsen plagiarized from "Mrs. Adis," was influenced by or unconsciously borrowed from it is not the point . . . Rather, it is significant that Larsen's choice of material left her open for such a charge in just this way. Again, ethnic authorship seems to hinge on the ownership of stories. Does the woman who sets down a folk tale then own the tale? Are folk tales fit matter for fiction? Because Larsen set down a story told to her by another woman, is she then the author of that fiction? If Larsen had set it all down as it happened—recounting her meeting with the black patient, then the story—would "Sanctuary" be fiction?[12]

What becomes clear in this discussion is that the question of the boundaries of the self can arise in ways that transcend the purely psychic domain while still opening up the possibility of a devastating narcissistic wound. If authorship is ownership, how can folk material be one's own? When oral sources are written down, to whom do they belong? (This question could indeed be asked of the debt psychoanalytic theory owes to the oral histories of analysands.)[13] What is the property status of a common heritage? In this case, it is not even clear that the story "belongs" to the black tradition, since the other version concerns white workers. If Larsen was writing out of a sense of still precarious loyalty to a tradition and a people about whom her other works express more ambivalence, then there is an ironic parallel between the story and its publication. Like the protagonist of the story, Larsen, out of an act of racial solidarity, has harbored a fugitive who turns out to take away her own literary offspring. This is not the fault of the sanctuary, or of the fugitive, but of the laws of ownership and cultural heritage that define the self as property and literature in terms of the authorial proper name. We will never know what Nella Larsen might have written next, or what other stories her patients told her. After the exposure and shame of her aborted "Sanctuary," she travelled on a Guggenheim fellowship to Europe to write her third novel, but never published again.[14]

Nella Larsen has often been conflated with her heroines, whose narcissistic predicaments she is seen to share. In ending my discussion with her silence, I am making the same equation. But while her disappearance from the publishing world may well be a narcissistic withdrawal, I think it is important not to equate her novels with her psyche. As fully realized representations of intricate social and psychic structures, they are more like analyses than like symptoms. The Helga Crane of the novel is never in a position to write the novel *Quicksand*. As is the case for many similar writers—Baudelaire and Dostoevsky come immediately to mind—it is, after all, Nella Larsen that provides all the insight that enables readers to feel that they understand more about Nella Larsen than Nella Larsen does. Which does not mean that the insight is the cure. The literature of narcissism does not satisfy the desire for a workable program for social change, but it does offer the warning that any political program that ignores the ways in which the self can refuse to satisfy need or can seek self-cancellation in place of self-validation will not understand where certain resistances are coming from.

Chapter Three

The Re(a)d and the Black:
Richard Wright's Blueprint

It is not surprising that this novel plumbs blacker depths of human experience than American literature has yet had.

Dorothy Canfield Fisher

In the fall of 1937, Richard Wright published an essay entitled "Blueprint for Negro Writing" in *New Challenge,* a little left-wing magazine he was helping Marian Minus and Dorothy West to edit. In that essay he characterized previous Negro writing as "humble novels, poems, and plays, prim and decorous ambassadors who went a-begging to white America."[1] He urged Negro writers to abandon the posture of humility and the bourgeois path of "individual achievement," and to develop a collective voice of social consciousness, both nationalist and Marxist. "The Negro writer must realize within the area of his own personal experience those impulses which, when prefigured in terms of broad social movements, constitute the stuff of nationalism . . . It is through a Marxist conception of reality and society that the maximum degree of freedom in thought and feeling can be gained for the Negro writer" (pp. 43, 44). Negro writing, in other words, could fulfill itself only by becoming at once black and red.

Three years later, Wright published a novel that seemed to carry out this design, one that transformed the avuncular diminutions of previous Negro writing (including his own) into a larger and bolder form of assertion, changing the uncle, Tom, into a bigger Thomas. *Native Son* presents a new social archetype of American hunger, one that attempts to view the distorted strength of the black folk hero through the lens of a communist defense. Yet the merger between the red and the black is as problematic in the novel as it came to be for Richard Wright in life. What the communist lawyer, Max, cannot hear is precisely Bigger's "I am," his ascension to the status of speaking subject:

> Bigger saw Max back away from him with compressed lips. But he felt he had to make Max understand how he saw things now.
>
> "I didn't want to kill!" Bigger shouted. "But what I killed for, *I am*. It must've been pretty deep in me to make me kill! I must have felt it awful hard to murder? . . ."
>
> Max lifted his hand to touch Bigger, but did not.
>
> "No; no; no . . . Bigger, not that? . . ." Max pleaded despairingly.[2]

What is it about Bigger that cannot be re(a)d within the perspective of Ma(r)x?

Max's understanding of Bigger's two murders places them squarely within the perspective of economic determinism. As Max tells the court, Bigger kills because other channels of self-expression are closed to him: "Listen: what Bigger Thomas did early that Sunday morning in the Dalton home and what he did that Sunday night in that empty building was but a tiny aspect of what he had been doing all his life long! He was *living,* only as he knew how, and as we have forced him to live. The actions that resulted in the death of those two women were as instinctive and inevitable as breathing or blinking one's eyes. It was an act of *creation!*" (p. 366). It has often been assumed that Bigger's crimes can therefore be seen as that which, in the novel, stands in the place of *art.* Bigger is an artist with no medium to work in other than violence.

But is this actually the case? There is, in fact, within the novel it-self, another sort of "Blueprint for Negro Writing," one that com-plicates the notion of a creativity "as instinctive and inevitable as breathing or blinking one's eyes" (indeed, one that makes even breathing and blinking the eyes into signifying acts that are not merely instinctual).

For Bigger, in fact, does not merely kill. He also writes. He writes a ransom note to the father of the white woman he has inad-vertently killed. That note, and the scene of its writing, can be read in a way that exceeds its contextual function. And the reception of that text is as telling as its creation.

The scene of writing (166–167) begins with the silencing of Bessie, the black woman whose involvement with Bigger will soon prove fatal to her.

"I ain't asking you but once more to shut up!" he said, push-ing the knife out of the way so he could write.

Substituting the pencil for the knife, Bigger performs an elaborate ritual of concealment, self-protection, and disguise:

He put on the gloves and took up the pencil in a trembling hand and held it poised over the paper. He should disguise his handwriting. He changed the pencil from his right to his left hand. He would not write it; he would print it. He swallowed with dry throat.

Bigger's writing is designed to betray no trace of origin or signature. He is then faced with the question of pronoun: is his writing to be individual or collective? This is indeed the question Richard Wright has put before the Negro writer who wishes to write on the "left."

Now, what would be the best kind of note? He thought, I want you to put ten thousand . . . Naw; that would not do. Not "I." It would be better to say "we."

Instead of proceeding directly to his demand ("I want you to put ten thousand . . ."), Bigger now makes up a story for the benefit of the addressee, the white male reader, leading with what he knows to be Mr. Dalton's concern:

We got your daughter, he printed slowly in big round letters. That was better. He ought to say something to let Mr. Dalton think that Mary was still alive. He wrote: *She is safe.* Now, tell him not to go to the police. No! Say something about Mary first! He bent and wrote: *She wants to come home.*

As he continues the note, he makes a crucial textual revision:

Now, tell him not to go to the police. *Don't go to the police if you want your daughter back safe.* Naw; that ain't good. His scalp tingled with excitement; it seemed that he could feel each strand of hair upon his head. He read the line over and crossed out "safe" and wrote "alive."

What Bigger's visceral reaction demonstrates is his knowledge that his own fate is bound to the way in which his writing is linked, in the implied reader's mind, with the fate of a white woman. It is precisely Bigger's belief in the white father's inability to think his daughter safe that has led to her not being alive in the first place. Bigger implicitly feels the significance of his revision and all that needs to be revised behind it:

> For a moment he was frozen, still. There was in his stomach a slow, cold, vast rising movement, as though he held within the embrace of his bowels the swing of planets through space. He was giddy. He caught hold of himself, focused his attention to write again.

The details of the ransom drop follow. The only part of the note he pronounces "good" comes to him from another text:

> Now, about the money. How much? Yes; make it ten thousand. *Get ten thousand in 5 and 10 bills and put it in a shoe box . . .* That's good. He had read that somewhere . . . *and tomorrow night ride your car up and down Michigan Avenue from 35th Street to 40th Street.* That would make it hard for anybody to tell just where Bessie would be hiding. He wrote: *Blink your headlights some. When you see a light in a window blink three times throw the box in the snow and drive off. Do what this letter say.* Now, he

would sign it. But how? It should be signed in some way that would throw them off the trail. Oh, yes! Sign it "Red." He printed, *Red.*

Like Richard Wright himself in 1940, Bigger is compelled to sign his writing "Red." Yet the note is signed "Black" as well: *"Do what this letter say."* Hidden behind the letter's detour through communism is the unmistakable trace of its black authorship. Yet no one in the novel seems to be able to read it. In passing under the signature "Red," the text's blackness is precisely what goes un-read.

Bigger is in fact present at the scene of the letter's reception, but he remains unseen, "nobody":

The door swung in violently. Bigger started in fright. Mr. Dalton came into the kitchen, his face ashy. He stared at Peggy and Peggy, holding a dish towel in her hand, stared at him. In Mr. Dalton's hand was the letter, opened.

"What's the matter, Mr. Dalton?"

"Who . . . Where did . . . Who gave you this?"

"What?"

"This *letter.*"

"Why, nobody. I got it from the door."

"When?"

"A few minutes ago. Anything wrong?"

Mr. Dalton looked around the entire kitchen, not at anything in particular, but just round the entire stretch of four walls, his eyes wide and unseeing. (p. 177)

Like Poe's purloined letter, the identity of the author of the note remains invisible because the detectives do not know how to read what is plainly there before them. Behind the sentence *"Do what this letter say"* lies the possibility—and the invisibility—of a whole vernacular literature.

If Bigger's ransom note stands in some sense in the place of black vernacular literature, does this mean that in the writing of black men the life and death of white women is at stake? It is clear that this is the story the white fathers will listen to. Indeed, whatever the facts, it seems that this is the *only* story they will hear. This is what Bigger believes as he stands over the bed of the intoxicated Mary, watching the blind Mrs. Dalton approach. What *must not happen* is that he be caught alone in the bedroom of a white woman. He forces a pillow over Mary's face in order to prevent her from betraying his presence. Like Oedipus, it is through his efforts to *avoid* enacting the forbidden story that he inevitably enacts it. Like Oedipus, he participates in a primal scene of, and with, blindness.

The name of the forbidden story in America is "rape." In an essay entitled "How 'Bigger' Was Born," Wright describes his growing awareness of the character type he wished to portray. As for the plot, it was already scripted by American society:

Any Negro who has lived in the North or the South knows that times without number he has heard of some Negro boy being picked up on the streets and carted off to jail and charged with "rape." This thing happens so often that to my mind it had become a representative symbol of the Negro's uncertain position in America. Never for a second was I in doubt as to what kind of social reality or dramatic situation I'd put Bigger in, what kind of test-tube life I'd set up to evoke his deepest reactions. Life had made the plot over and over again, to the extent that I knew it by heart. (*Native Son,* xxviii)

As many commentators have noted, the myth of the black rapist is an inversion of historical fact—the frequent rape of black slave women by their white owners. Yet Bigger Thomas does not rape Mary Dalton; he kills her because he thinks that the only possible interpretation of his presence in her room is "rape." It is not surprising that the first edition of *Native Son* should have been preceded by an introduction written by Dorothy Canfield Fisher. It is as though the envelope of Wright's letter had to be made to say "The white woman is safe."

To the extent that the rape of Mary Dalton does not occur, the "rape" plot in *Native Son* may be read in terms of racist overdetermination. But what can be said about the fate of Bessie Mears, the black woman who *is* raped by Bigger, and whose murder is far from accidental? Is the rape and murder of a black woman somehow a correlative to the black man's quest for manhood, a figure for the defeminization Wright calls for in his blueprint for a literature that would no longer go "curtsying to show that the Negro was not inferior" (*Blueprint*, p. 37)? If the novel makes a plea for Bigger's victimization, does it implicitly excuse his treatment of the black woman? Does racism explain away the novel's apparent misogyny?

It would be easy to attack Richard Wright for placing violence, as James Baldwin puts it, in the space where sex should be.[3] It

would be easy to read *Native Son*'s depiction of the relations between black men and black women as unhealably troubled; indeed,
to read the novel as itself an act of violence against black women. I
would like to shift the ground of this interpretation slightly in order
to ask: Where, in Richard Wright, does the black woman stand
with respect to the black man's *writing?*

As we have seen, Bessie Mears is a silent (or rather, silenced)
presence in the scene in which Bigger Thomas writes. As Bigger
completes the ransom note, he lifts his eyes and sees Bessie standing
behind him. She has read the note over his shoulder and guessed
the truth. "She looked straight into his eyes and whispered, 'Bigger,
did you kill that girl?'" Bigger denies that she has interpreted his
writing correctly, but he formulates a plan to kill her to prevent her
from saying what she knows. The black woman, then, is a reader
whose reading is both accurate and threatening.

Bigger's ransom note is not the only example in Richard
Wright's work of a paradigmatic scene of writing in which what is
at stake is a nonblack woman. To this scene I would like to juxta-
pose a scene from Wright's autobiography, *Black Boy*. One of his
earliest attempts at writing, he tells us, was the story of a beautiful
Indian maiden.

> I remembered a series of volumes of Indian history I had read
> the year before. Yes, I knew what I would do; I would write a
> story about the Indians . . . But what about them? Well, an
> Indian girl . . . I wrote of an Indian maiden, beautiful and re-
> served, who sat alone upon the bank of a still stream, sur-
> rounded by eternal twilight and ancient trees, waiting . . . The

girl was keeping some vow which I could not describe and, not knowing how to develop the story, I resolved that the girl had to die. She rose slowly and walked toward the dark stream, her face stately and cold; she entered the water and walked on until the water reached her shoulders, her chin; then it covered her. Not a murmur or a gasp came from her, even in dying.[4]

Writing in the illustrious tradition of Hawthorne, Poe, Wordsworth, Lamartine, and hundreds of other white men of letters, Wright has no difficulty seeing the death of an idealized woman as a significant literary subject.[5] Not all male writers are candid enough, however, to admit that their heroine's untimely death is the result of a failure of imagination. "Not knowing how to develop the story, I resolved that the girl had to die." One wonders whether this might explain the early demise of Lucy or Annabel Lee—or even of Edna Pontellier.

But dead women are not the only women present in these scenes of writing, and in both cases the "other woman" is a black female reader whose reading cannot be mastered by the writer. As we have seen, Bessie reads Bigger's ransom note and begins to suspect that he has killed Mary Dalton. Later, his scheme thwarted, Bigger first rapes, then kills Bessie in order to prevent her from talking, in order to gain total control over a story that has been out of his control from the beginning. In the case of the Indian maiden, Wright excitedly decides to read his literary creation to a young woman who lives next door.

I interrupted her as she was washing dishes and, swearing her to secrecy, I read the composition aloud. When I finished she smiled at me oddly, her eyes baffled and astonished.

"What's that for?" she asked.

"Nothing," I said.

"But why did you write it?"

"I just wanted to."

"Where did you get the idea?"

I wagged my head, pulled down the corners of my mouth, stuffed my manuscript into my pocket and looked at her in a cocky manner that said: Oh, it's nothing at all. I write stuff like this all the time. It's easy, if you know how. But I merely said in an humble, quiet voice:

"Oh, I don't know. I just thought it up."

"What're you going to do with it?"

"Nothing."

God only knows what she thought. My environment contained nothing more alien than writing or the desire to express one's self in writing. But I never forgot the look of astonishment and bewilderment on the young woman's face when I had finished reading and glanced at her. Her inability to grasp what I had done or was trying to do somehow gratified me. Afterwards whenever I thought of her reaction I smiled happily for some unaccountable reason. (pp. 133–134)

It would be hard to imagine a scene of reading in which less was understood. It is entirely possible that the woman was indeed wondering why Wright was writing at all. It is also possible that she was wondering why he was writing about the death of a woman. It is even possible that she was wondering why *he* wasn't wondering that.

What Wright's writing demonstrates again and again is the deadly effect both of overdetermination and of underdetermination in storytelling. It is because the "rape" plot is so overdetermined that Bigger becomes a murderer. It is because there are so few available models for the plots of Indian maidens that Wright's heroine "has to die." And it is because the "rape" plot about white women or the "idealization" plot about Indian women are so overdetermined that the plot about black women remains muffled beyond recognition. When the black woman does attempt to take control of her own plot in Wright's short story, "Long Black Song," the black man dies in an apocalyptic fire. The unavailability of new plots is deadly. As Wright says of his Indian maiden composition, "I was excited; I read it over and saw that there was a yawning void in it. There was no plot, no action, nothing save atmosphere and longing and death" (p. 133).

Yet even when a black woman's story is available, there is no guarantee that it will be recognized. Upon reading Zora Neale Hurston's *Their Eyes Were Watching God,* Wright was able to see only red, not black; male, not female. "The sensory sweep of her novel," he wrote, "carries no theme, no message, no thought."[6] The black woman's story can remain invisible no matter how visible it is, like the black vernacular origin of Bigger's ransom note. No reader has a monopoly on blindness. But Wright's blindness here is far from simple.

In a surprising and fascinating passage in Wright's essay, "How 'Bigger' Was Born," we encounter the announcement of a novel that was never to reach completion: "I am launching out upon another novel, this time about the status of women in American society." The desire to tell a woman's story seems to infuse Wright's writing from the beginning. Yet however aborted the plots of his women protagonists, the figure of the black woman as *reader* in his work is fundamental. Silent, baffled, or filled with a dangerous insight, Wright consistently sees the black woman as the reader his writing must face. *Native Son,* indeed, is dedicated to Wright's own paralyzed mother.

the black woman reader and her voice

Chapter Four

"Aesthetic" and "Rapport" in
Toni Morrison's *Sula*

Toni Morrison's novels have often been read by African-American critics as presenting something beloved, lost, and familiar. Renita Weems, for instance, writes:

> Toni Morrison is one of the few authors I enjoy rereading. Having lived in the North for the last six years (against my better senses), when I read Morrison's novels I am reminded of home: the South. Although her first three books take place in the Midwest and the fourth primarily in the Caribbean— places I have never seen—there is something still very familiar, very nostalgic about the people I meet on her pages. There is something about their meddling communities which reminds me of the men and women I so desperately miss back home.[1]

Houston Baker, in an essay entitled "When Lindbergh Sleeps with Bessie Smith," describes an equally strong sense of recognition when he writes about *Sula:*

> Morrison "remembers" and enables us to know our PLACE and to be cool about our hair. For, in truth, it has often seemed in

74

black male writings of a putatively asexual Western technological world as our proper PLACE, that the dominant expressive impulse has been more toward an escape from "bad hair"
than from "bad air." Morrison's linguistic cosmetology allows
this very basic "badness" to be refigured as village value, as a
mirroring language—a springy "lying" down if you will—in
which we can find ourselves, and where especially black men
may yet make a jubilant response, saying, "We are *that!*"[2]

Baker's essay is in part a response to a groundbreaking essay by Barbara Smith in which she writes of *Sula:* "Despite the apparent heterosexuality of the female characters, I discovered in re-reading
Sula that it works as a lesbian novel not only because of the passionate friendship between Sula and Nel but because of Morrison's
consistently critical stance toward the heterosexual institutions of
male-female relationships, marriage, and the family."[3] How does
Sula—a novel that holds up a mirror to black men, displaced South-
erners, and black lesbians—manage to produce so strong a mechanism for recognition? How does Morrison manage to hold out so
strong a promise of "home"?

One way, I would submit, is by presenting home as always already lost. The novel begins: "In that place, where they tore the
nightshade and blackberry patches from their roots to make room
for the Medallion City Golf Course, there was once a neighborhood."[4] Morrison's novel conveys so strong a sense of what she calls
"rootedness" precisely by writing under the sign of uprootedness.
Yet it is not simply that there was once a *there* there and now it is

PLACE/ROOTEDNESS

gone, but that there is from the beginning something profoundly uncanny about "that place." Home is familiar precisely to the extent that, as Renita Weems puts it, it is somehow a place one has never been. By telling the story of a lost neighborhood called the Bottom which is situated at the top of the hills, Morrison establishes home as that which is always already its own other.

This, of course, is the discovery Freud made when, in his essay on "The Uncanny," he investigated the German word for "homey." Freud exclaims over the fact that the German word for "homey" extends itself to turn into its opposite—that the meaning of "heimlich" moves with a kind of inevitability from cozy, comfortable, and familiar to hidden, secret, and strange, so that one meaning of "heimlich" is identical to its opposite, "unheimlich." What Toni Morrison demonstrates in *Sula,* I think, is that that is exactly what home *is.* Morrison's perceptions about human intimacy, ambivalence, and desire intersect often with psychoanalytic paradigms and figures, but at the same time she dramatizes political and social forces that provide a larger context for what Freud generally analyzes in individuals as purely intra-psychic.

In this essay, I will look at some of the intersections between *Sula* and Freud's essay on ("The Uncanny,") but first, let me offer a quick sketch of the novel. *Sula* is divided into two parts separated by a ten year interval, and into chapters entitled by dates: 1919, 1920, 1921, 1922, 1923, 1927, and 1937, 1939, 1940, 1941, 1965. It is preceded by a prologue from the point of view of the present. The first part of the novel describes the girlhood of two friends, Sula Peace and

Nel Wright, up to the point at which Nel marries Jude Greene and Sula leaves town. When Sula returns ten years later, she is seen as evil incarnate by the townspeople because of her perceived disrespect for conventional constraints. They use her transgressiveness to define their own morality. Sula sleeps with Nel's husband, Jude, creating a rift between the two friends and provoking an unarticulated howl of grief which hovers within Nel until the very end of the novel.

Now for a catalogue of figures Freud associates with the uncanny: "Dismembered limbs, a severed head, a hand cut off at the wrist, . . . feet which dance by themselves . . . all these have something peculiarly uncanny about them, especially when, as in the last instance, they prove able to move of themselves in addition. As we already know, this kind of uncanniness springs from its association with the castration complex. To many people, the idea of being buried alive while appearing to be dead is the most uncanny thing of all. And yet psychoanalysis has taught us that this terrifying phantasy is only a transformation of another phantasy which had originally nothing terrifying about it at all, but was qualified by a certain lasciviousness—the phantasy, I mean, of intra-uterine existence."[5] In *Sula,* the echoes of this list are really quite uncanny. Sula's house is presided over by a one-legged grandmother, Eva, who has perhaps cut off her own leg to get the insurance money she needs to support her children, and yet who, later fearing that her grown son (who has returned from the war a drug addict) wants to crawl back into her womb, sets fire to him and kills him. Sula herself defies the

teasing of a group of Irish boys by cutting off the tip of her own finger. Toni Morrison both displaces and deconstructs Freud's notion
of the castration complex. On the one hand, the loss of bodily intactness is integral to survival, at least in the case of Eva. And the
novel itself is written under the sign of "something newly missing":
the body of a little boy named Chicken Little whom Sula and Nel
have inadvertently drowned in the river. On the other hand, castration is recognized as a mechanism of social control. Sula ironically
inverts familiar power relations when she answers Jude's lament
that a black man has a hard row to hoe in this world:

> "I don't know what all the fuss is about. I mean, everything in
> the world loves you. White men love you. They spend so
> much time worrying about your penis they forget their own.
> The only thing they want to do is cut off a nigger's privates.
> And if that ain't love and respect I don't know what is. And
> white women? They chase you all to every corner of the
> earth, feel for you under every bed. I knew a white woman
> wouldn't leave the house after 6 o'clock for fear one of you
> would snatch her. Now ain't that love? They think rape soon's
> they see you, and if they don't get the rape they looking for,
> they scream it anyway just so the search won't be in vain. Col
> ored women worry themselves into bad health just trying to
> hang onto your cuffs. Even little children—white and black,
> boys and girls—spend all their childhood eating their hearts
> out 'cause they think you don't love them. And if that ain't
> enough, you love yourselves. Nothing in this world loves a

black man more than another black man. You hear of solitary white men, but niggers? Can't stay away from one another a whole day. So. It looks to me like you the envy of the world." (pp. 103–104)

It could be said that what Morrison is doing is taking the Freudian concepts of envy, the penis, and castration, and recontextualizing them in the framework of American racial and sexual arrangements. It becomes impossible to speak about such terms in the abstract, universal sense in which Freud uses them once one realizes that the historical experience of some people is to be subjected to the literalization and institutionalization of the fantasies of others. Lynching dramatizes an unconscious phantasy of white men, but a historical and political reality for black men. Penis envy seems not to be confined to women at all, but to be a motive force in the repression of some men by other men. And one of the most revolutionary things Morrison does in *Sula* is to deconstruct the phallus as law, patriarchy, and cultural ground, while appreciating the penis for the trivial but exciting pleasures and fantasies it can provide for the female characters in the novel. Morrison reverses the Lacanian elevation of the phallus into the signifier of signifiers by restoring the penis to its status as an organ.

Home, then, in *Sula,* is where the phallus isn't. This may be one of the reasons for the pervasive uncanniness of the novel. But the uncanny image that sets the tone for the text as a whole involves not Sula but a young black soldier named Shadrack whose experience of the battlefield in 1917 is described as follows:

Shellfire was all around him, and though he knew that this was something called *it,* he could not muster up the proper feeling—the feeling that would accommodate *it.* He expected to be terrified or exhilarated—to feel *something* very strong. In fact, he felt only the bite of a nail in his boot . . . He ran, bayonet fixed, deep in the great sweep of men flying across this field. Wincing at the pain in his foot, he turned his head a little to the right and saw the face of the soldier near him fly off. Before he could register shock, the rest of the soldier's head disappeared under the inverted soup bowl of his helmet. But stubbornly, taking no direction from the brain, the body of the headless soldier ran on, with energy and grace, ignoring altogether the drip and slide of brain tissue down its back. (pp. 7–8)

Severed heads, feet that run by themselves, this would seem a perfect image of Freud's uncanny. But I think Morrison deepens the meaning of those images by describing a *psychic* discontinuity that precedes the severing of the head. Shadrack already experiences a lack of fit between his feelings and *it,* a dissociation of expectations, an affective split.

The dissociation of affect and event is one of Morrison's most striking literary techniques in this novel, both in her narrative voice (in which things like infanticide are not exclaimed over) and in the emotional lives of her characters. The most important example of affective discontinuity is Nel's reaction to the discovery of Jude, her husband, naked on the floor with Sula, her best friend. She tries to howl in pain but cannot do so until seventy pages later when she realizes that she mourns the loss of Sula rather than Jude. A good deal of the novel takes place in the space between the moment when the howl is called for and the moment when it occurs. Similarly, the scene of the death of Chicken Little is broken up into delayed effects throughout the novel. While the chapter headings promise chronological linearity, the text demonstrates that lived time is anything but continuous, that things don't happen when they happen, that neither intentionality nor reaction can naturalize trauma into consecutive narrative. Shadrack, described by the wonderful oxymoron of "permanently astonished," institutes the fort-da game of National Suicide Day upon his return from the war as a way of ritually trying to get a jump on unpreparedness, but he can only repeat the lack of fit between affect and event.

For me, the most intriguing figuration of the dissociation between affect and event in *Sula* occurs at the moment when Nel discovers Sula and Jude naked on the floor together. While the novel as a whole is narrated in the third person, this particular passage shifts into the first person to coincide with Nel's point of view. The passage runs as follows:

> When I opened the door they didn't even look for a minute and I thought the reason they are not looking up is because they are not doing that. So it's all right. I am just standing here . . . And I did not know how to move my feet or fix my eyes or what. I just stood there seeing it and smiling, because maybe there was some explanation, something important that

I did not know about that would have made it all right. I waited for Sula to look up at me any minute and say one of those lovely college words like *aesthetic* or *rapport,* which I never understood but which I loved because they sounded so comfortable and firm. (p. 105)

Aesthetic and *rapport?* At a time like this, when Nel is seeing her best friend naked with her husband, why in the world is *this* the thought she turns to for an image of reassurance? The desire for an explanation, for some domain of sense that escapes her, is certainly understandable, but why does Toni Morrison pick these two words? The very arbitrariness of these two floating signifiers tempts me to see them as keys to the preoccupations of the novel as a whole.

The words "aesthetic" and "rapport" are referred to as "college words"—they thus come out of a scene included in the novel as other, not represented, not "home." (Of course, they are also from the "other scene" of the novel's author and of many of its readers.) The fact that Sula has been away to college while Nel has not does not, however, play much of a role in their friendship as it is reestablished—at least not on the surface. Sula and Nel discuss college really only once, when Nel is trying to get Sula to talk about how she spent the ten years away from the Bottom:

"Tell me about it. The big city."

"Big is all it is. A big Medallion."

"No. I mean the life. The nightclubs, and parties . . ."

"I was in college, Nellie. No nightclubs on campus."

"Campus? That what they call it? Well. You wasn't in no college for—what—ten years now? And you didn't write to nobody." (p. 99)

Nel's desire for Sula's story remains unsatisfied. We never observe a conversation between Sula and Nel that remotely resembles one in which the words *aesthetic* or *rapport* would have occurred. What we learn Nel learns in this conversation is that college is a place of foreign-sounding words. But so, for Nel, was her voyage to her roots: Her grandmother's parting "'voir" and her mother's admonition that she and her daughter did *not* speak Creole.

The words "aesthetic" and "rapport," in addition to coming from what could be called "another scene"—both college and foreign—also both contain silent letters, signaling their status as writing, that is, as themselves silent letters. Silent because not oral—and in writing, the sign of the oral has conventionally been the missing letter rather than the silent letter, although the missing letter is marked by a diacritical mark like an apostrophe which is all the more obviously a sign of writing in its completely unphonetic dimension. And both "aesthetic" and "rapport," somewhat like the word "unheimlich," span a wide stretch of meaning. "Aesthetic" moves from the domain of sense experience to the domain of artistic forms, while "rapport" names connection and trust but at the same time, archaically, mesmerism—a much more uncanny form of trust.

I think that in many ways the novel is precisely about the relations between aesthetic and rapport. If aesthetics is taken as the domain of the contemplation of forms, implying detachment and distance, and rapport is taken as the dynamics of connectedness, the two words name an opposition, or at least a set of issues, that are central in *Sula*. In one of the novel's primal scenes, Nel and Sula are described playing with Chicken Little, whom Sula is swinging around in circles until he slips from her grasp, flies into the river, and drowns. At the end of the novel, Eva, Sula's grandmother, accuses Nel of having thrown the little boy into the water. Nel protests that it was Sula, but Eva responds, "You. Sula. What's the difference? You was there. You watched, didn't you? Me, I never would've watched" (p. 168). Nel mulls this over in her head: "What did old Eva mean by *you watched*. How could she help seeing it? She was right there. But Eva didn't say *see,* she said *watched*" (p. 170). Indeed, Nel has to acknowledge the unavowable memory of joy, of pleasure, that accompanied for her the spectacle of the boy slipping out of Sula's grasp. "It was there anyway, as it had always been, the old feeling and the old question. The good feeling she had had when Chicken's hands slipped."

Watching becomes even more of an issue when Hannah, Sula's mother, burns to death. Hannah's mother, Eva, leaps to try to save her. Thinking about this afterward, Eva muses:

> She remembered something else, too, and try as she might to deny it, she knew that as she lay on the ground trying to drag herself through the sweet peas and clover to get to Hannah, she had seen Sula standing on the back porch just looking. When Eva, who was never one to hide the faults of her chil-

dren, mentioned what she thought she'd seen to a few friends, they said it was natural. Sula was probably struck dumb, as anybody would be who saw her own mamma burn up. Eva said yes, but inside she disagreed and remained convinced that Sula had watched Hannah burn not because she was paralyzed but because she was interested. (p. 78)

What Eva is accusing both Nel and Sula of here is a privileging of aesthetics over rapport. Contemplating with detachment, with no move to intervene, they *watch*. "Interest" is the name of a lack of involvement. Curiously, Kant defines the domain of the aesthetic as the domain of *dis*interestedness. What is the difference between interest and disinterest? Interest and disinterestedness are like heimlich and unheimlich—almost impossible to tell apart. Interestingly (uncannily?), it is precisely under the category of the aesthetic that Freud inserts his analysis of the uncanny. The first sentence of his essay begins, "It is only rarely that a psycho-analyst feels impelled to investigate the subject of aesthetics . . ." (p. 219). It is as though what turns the home *unheimlich* cannot be fully understood without a passage through the aesthetic.

The question of aesthetics versus rapport is raised, in fact, by Toni Morrison's novel as a whole as well. I began by citing a number of African-American critics whose responses to the novel appeared to exemplify "rapport." Yet the fictional form forces the reader to contemplate a series of horrible images, painful truths, excruciating losses without being able to intervene. And what about the white reader? Is there a greater likelihood that the white reader will merely "watch"? Is this a form of racial voyeurism? What is the nature of our pleasure in contemplating trauma or racial injustice or the destruction of the "home" of the other? What would be a response that would embody rapport rather than aesthetics? Is this what Toni Morrison is challenging us to consider? Or is she merely trying to make us less innocent in our contemplation, our analysis, our "interest"?

It seems to me that the challenge Toni Morrison presents to the relations between aesthetics and politics lies precisely in the uncomfortable ways in which she makes it clear that the domain of the aesthetic is both profoundly political and impossible to make politically correct. By choosing to aestheticize a father's rape of his daughter in *The Bluest Eye,* a mother's murder of her grown son and a daughter watching her mother burn to death in *Sula,* and the scars on a slave woman's back in *Beloved,* Morrison makes the aesthetic inextricable from trauma, taboo, and violation. It is no accident that the plantation from which the infanticidal slave woman has escaped in *Beloved* is called "Sweet Home." Sethe, the former slave, muses again and again about her memory of Sweet Home as aesthetically beautiful, and about *that fact* as a deep violation. On the one hand, the realm of forms—like National Suicide Day—is seen as a first line of defense against the abyss. Sula is said to be dangerous precisely because she is an artist without an art form. On the other hand, Morrison runs—indeed courts—the risk of transforming horror into pleasure, violence into beauty, mourning into nostalgia. In *Sula* she represents—in all its moral ambiguity—the problematic fascination of such transformations. Thus she shows that it is not a matter of choosing between politics and aesthetics but of recognizing the profoundly political nature of the inescapability of the aesthetic within personal, political, and historical life.

Part Two

GENDER AND POETRY

Euphemism, Understatement, and the Passive Voice: A Genealogy of African-American Poetry

In his well-known essay of 1937, "Blueprint for Negro Writing," Richard Wright expresses an ambivalence toward his precursors that has been shared by many subsequent African-American writers. "Generally speaking," he writes:

> Negro writing in the past has been confined to humble novels, poems, and plays, prim and decorous ambassadors who went a-begging to white America. They entered the Court of American Public Opinion dressed in the knee-pants of servility, curtsying to show that the Negro was not inferior, that he was human, and that he had a life comparable to that of other people. For the most part these artistic ambassadors were received as though they were French poodles who do clever tricks.[1]

In this paper I would like to examine some of the more covert strategies of protest implicit in the writings of some of the ambassadors Wright might have had in mind: James Weldon Johnson, Countee Cullen, and, most particularly, Phillis Wheatley, whose 1773 volume was the first book of poems published by a black

American. While decorousness may in some ways have been disabling, I will try to show that these writers nevertheless set up conditions of utterance in which the French poodle could sometimes function as a Trojan horse.

In 1921, at the start of the Harlem Renaissance, James Weldon Johnson edited what he hoped would be a major anthology of African-American poetry. The collection was designed to remedy what he called a "lack of information" on the part of "the public." Nothing could be less inflammatory than the desire to supply information that is lacking. Through a carefully calculated use of the passive voice and the verb "is," an avoidance of black/white binary oppositions, and the elaboration of a seemingly syllogistic logic, Johnson attempts nothing less than to convince the world to acknowledge the greatness of the Negro people:

> There is, perhaps, a better excuse for giving an Anthology of American Negro Poetry to the public than can be offered for many of the anthologies that have recently been issued. The public, generally speaking, does not know that there are American Negro poets—to supply this lack of information is, alone, a work worthy of somebody's effort.
>
> Moreover, the matter of Negro poets and the production of literature by the colored people in this country involves more than supplying information that is lacking. It is a matter which has direct bearing on the most vital of American problems.
>
> A people may become great through many means, but there is only one measure by which its greatness is recognized

and acknowledged. The final measure of the greatness of all peoples is the amount and standard of the literature and art they have produced. The world does not know that a people is great until that people produces great literature and art. No people that has produced great literature and art has ever been looked upon by the world as distinctly inferior.

literature = power

The status of the Negro in the United States is more a question of national mental attitude toward the race than of actual conditions. And nothing will do more to change that mental attitude and raise his status than a demonstration of intellectual parity by the Negro through the production of literature and art.[2]

But it seems that that demonstration has already taken place. Indeed, it is not that the Negro needs to produce art and literature to be recognized in American culture, but that it is through Negro art that American culture is recognized at all. Johnson asserts that the Negro has already contributed to American culture the only artistic productions "the world" (that is, Europe) acknowledges as distinctively American: Uncle Remus stories, spirituals, the cakewalk, and ragtime. Again, Johnson uses the passive voice as a cover for unspecified (here, all-conquering) agency: "As for Ragtime, I go straight to the statement that it is the one artistic production by which America is known the world over. It has been all-conquering. Everywhere it is hailed as 'American music'" (p. 11). The real lack is not a "lack of information" that is about to be supplied but a "lack of acknowledgment" of artistic achievements that

un-American production of American culture

have already taken place and have not been properly credited to the Negro. Through his use of ellipsis, understatement, unspecified agency, and non-binarity, Johnson is thus attempting to bring about a change in the "national mental attitude" without explicitly acknowledging or processing blindness and dispossession. When such rhetorical strategies are used by a dominant discourse, the reason for avoiding naming the nature of the conflict is to avoid change. (But when acknowledging the conflict may mean granting it a legitimacy it does not deserve, when processing difference might seem to involve accepting the premises of racial separation and inequality, then the bootstrap operation of passivity and euphemism may well begin to set the stage for an unimpeded and newly empowered affirmation.)

Moving from music to poetry, Johnson continues to employ euphemism and the passive voice to describe the previous history of the African-American lyric. The list, he writes, begins with Phillis Wheatley. It soon becomes clear, however, that Johnson's own history, thereby, begins with ambivalence. The passive voice he uses in speaking about Wheatley expresses both an avoidance of conflict and an avoidance of change—that is, both an opposition to and an identification with dominant discourse:

> Phillis Wheatley has never been given her rightful place in American literature. By some sort of conspiracy she is kept out of most of the books, especially the text-books on literature used in the schools. Of course, she is not a *great* American poet—and in her day there were no great American poets—

but she is an important American poet. Her importance, if for no other reason, rests on the fact that, save one, she is the first in order of time of all the women poets of America. And she is among the first of all American poets to issue a volume. (p. 23)

Johnson, too, does not grant Phillis Wheatley her rightful place at the head of the list, but rather confines her to the space of his preface, the place of prehistory. She is the ancestor half acknowledged, half obscured, the (abjected) mother of African-American poetry. Johnson wishes to combat the injustice of her exclusion, yet cannot quite bring himself to place her first. Is this misogyny? Mere identification with male hegemony? Perhaps. Indeed, Wright's scorn for the curtsying ambassadors is also a resistance to the feminine as ancestor. But what Johnson holds against Wheatley is her avoidance of passionate oppositional utterance: "One looks in vain for some outburst or even some complaint against the bondage of her people, for some agonising cry about her native land . . . In the poem addressed to the Earl of Dartmouth, she speaks of freedom and makes a reference which cannot but strike the reader as rather unimpassioned" (pp. 28, 29). In other words, what Johnson holds against Wheatley is precisely the stylistic avoidance of conflict and outcry that characterizes his own writing in the preface. Could one not, for instance, characterize as "unimpassioned" Johnson's own use of words like "curious" and "strange," as in the following sentence: "It seems *strange* that the books generally give space to a mention of Urian Oakes, President of Harvard College, and to quotations from the crude and lengthy elegy which he published in

1667 . . . and yet deny a place to Phillis Wheatley" (p. 23). Johnson's use of "strange" here echoes Countee Cullen's use of "curious" in what Johnson himself calls "the two most poignant lines in American literature":

> Yet do I marvel at this curious thing—
> To make a poet black and bid him sing. (p. 231)

Johnson's sense of the poignancy of these lines may well stem from his own knowledge of all that a word like "curious" can conceal. Euphemism may be a way of avoiding conflict, but it also functions as an "X" marking a spot where later, perhaps, a poet will be able to say more. Protest may not yet be voiced, but at least the spot has been marked.

Countee Cullen himself is a master of the marked spot. In his poem "Heritage," he manages to keep the question "What is Africa to me?" in perfect suspension between a rhetorical and a real question. The question itself, like the poem's speaker, "plays a double part," as does the repeated phrase "so I lie," which carries the ambiguity the poem enacts between language and the body, between legend and unconscious desire. Africa may be only a book, says the poem, but nevertheless what is repressed can return. Another of the poem's ploys is its strategic use of the bad rhyme:

> Quaint, outlandish heathen gods
> Black men fashion out of rods,
> Clay, and brittle bits of stone,
> In a likeness like their own,

> My conversion came high-priced;
> I belong to Jesus Christ,
> Preacher of humility;
> Heathen gods are naught to me. (p. 224)

The wince produced by rhyming "Christ" with "priced" soon gives way, I think, to a recognition of its rightness, of all that is condensed behind that rhyme. The Christianization of Africans was indeed accomplished through their transformation into human commodities. Why should a conversion brought about by enslavement produce a *good* rhyme? The seemingly innocuous forcing of the rhyme euphemistically marks the barbarity of the historical process itself.

The art of forcing a rhyme between conversion and enslavement has its origins in the 1773 volume of poetry written by Phillis Wheatley. The eighteen-year-old slave girl from Boston stands as the inventor of a whole tradition of protest through excessive compliance.

Wheatley's poetry repeatedly describes several analogous processes of transformation: death, conversion, and the American struggle for independence. These are usually described in her poetry through metaphors of travel from one location or state to another. In her numerous elegies, Wheatley describes the dead as winging their way to a happier place:

> Ere yet the morn its lovely blushes spread,
> See Sewell numbered with the happy dead.
> Hail, holy man, arriv'd th'immortal shore,

Though we shall hear thy warning voice no more.
Come, let us all behold with wistful eyes
The saint ascending to his native skies.[3]

In her poem "On being brought from Africa to America," she writes:

'Twas mercy brought me from my Pagan land,
Taught my benighted soul to understand
That there's a God, that there's a Saviour too:
Once I redemption neither sought nor knew. (p. 53)

(This, as June Jordan remarks, is also a way of saying: "Once I existed on other than your terms.")[4] And finally, in her pro-revolutionary poem to the Earl of Dartmouth, she writes:

No more, America, in mournful strain
Of wrongs, and grievance unredress'd complain,
No longer shalt thou dread the iron chain,
Which wanton Tyranny with lawless hand
Had made, and with it meant t'enslave the land. (p. 83)

The mention of enslavement exposes the contradictory nature of the colonists' fight for freedom, but to make it explicit, she goes on:

Should you, my lord, while you peruse my song,
Wonder from whence my love of Freedom sprung,
Whence flow these wishes for the common good,
By feeling hearts alone best understood,
I, young in life, by seeming cruel fate
Was snatched from Afric's fancy'd happy seat:

> What pangs excruciating must molest,
> What sorrows labour in my parent's breast?
> Steel'd was that soul and by no misery mov'd
> That from a father seiz'd his babe belov'd:
> Such, such my case. And can I then but pray
> Others may never feel tyrannic sway? (p. 83)

By simply repeating the ideology of freedom, Wheatley exposes the contradiction at the heart of the American Revolution. She presents her reader with something like the schoolbook exercise: "What's wrong with this picture?" While the voyage from life to death, from Paganism to Christianity, and from English rule to American rule are all described in terms of a passage from bondage to freedom, the Middle Passage that serves as the source of her commitment to the ideology has clearly gone the other way. Under Wheatley's pen, the lessons she has learned so well self-deconstruct. That she knew exactly what she was doing is evident from a letter she wrote to the Indian minister Samson Occom, which she published a number of times in 1774, several months after she obtained her freedom:

> In every human Breast, God has implanted a Principle, which we call the Love of Freedom; it is impatient of oppression, and pants for Deliverance; and by the Leave of our modern Egyptians I will assert that the same Principle lives in us. God grant Deliverance in his own Way and Time, and get him honour upon all those whose Avarice impels them to countenance and help forward the Calamities of their fellow Creatures. This I desire not for their Hurt, but to convince them of the *strange*

[emphasis mine] <u>Absurdity of their conduct whose Words and</u> Actions are so diametrically opposite. How well the Cry for Liberty, and the reverse Disposition for the exercise of oppressive Power over others agree—I humbly think it does not require the Penetration of a Philosopher to determine. (p. 204)

No agonizing cry, perhaps, but controlled and devastating irony. By making explicit her history and her status and her right to speak, Wheatley in a sense wrote her way to freedom simply by letting the contradictions in her master's position speak for themselves.

In the preface to her volume of poems, Wheatley speaks of her own enslavement in the following terms: "As to the Disadvantages she has labored under, with Regard to Learning, nothing needs to be offered, as her Master's Letter in the following Page will sufficiently show the Difficulties in this Respect she had to encounter" (p. 46). There follows a letter from "the author's master" detailing Wheatley's prodigious accomplishments as a slave in his household. The *fact* of that letter speaks for itself. Wheatley has placed in her master's hand the boomerang of her compliance. While the Wheatleys send her book into the world as an ambassador of their own benevolence, it comes back with the response from the English readers it was meant to impress: "Why is she still a slave?" John and Susannah Wheatley, caught in the trap of their own self-image, grant Phillis her freedom upon her return from England. And Phillis Wheatley thus becomes the first in a long line of successful manipulators and demystifiers of the narcissism inherent in white liberalism.

Chapter Six

Gender and Poetry: Charles Baudelaire and Marceline Desbordes-Valmore

Dites "la femme souffre" et jamais "nous souffrons!"
Marceline Desbordes-Valmore, "A Mademoiselle A . . ."

J'ai cultivé mon hystérie avec jouissance et terreur.
Charles Baudelaire, "Hygiène"

Marceline Desbordes-Valmore (1786–1859) is one of the very few women poets who is represented in Lagarde and Michard's six-volume anthology of French literature. But she is *not* represented in Domna Stanton's anthology, *The Defiant Muse: French Feminist Poems from the Middle Ages to the Present.* Thus, in contrast to many women writers who are currently receiving critical attention, she has been neither completely excluded by traditional critics nor completely embraced by feminist critics. The present essay is an attempt to demonstrate that, whether she has been applauded or condemned, it has usually been for the wrong reasons.

Femininity has always been an orthopedic notion (*orthopedic:* from *ortho-* "straight, correct, right"; and *paideia,* "education"). Including but not restricted to normative notions of Beauty, the concept of femininity acts as a mold for shaping and controlling women's behavior. As Simone de Beauvoir points out: "As against the dispersed, contingent, and multiple existences of actual women, mythical thought opposes the Eternal Feminine, unique and changeless. If the definition provided for this concept is contradicted by the behavior of flesh-and-blood women, it is the latter who are wrong; we are told not that Femininity is a false entity, but that the women concerned are not feminine."[1] Femininity becomes, therefore, that from which women are always in danger of deviating. Unless of course femininity is judged a liability, in which case it is that into which women are always in danger of falling. The following comments by A. Alvarez cited on the dust jacket of Sylvia Plath's first volume of poetry stand as a good example of that danger: "Miss Plath neither asks excuses for her work nor offers them. She steers clear of feminine charm, deliciousness, gentility, supersensitivity, and the act of being a poetess. She simply writes good poetry. And she does so with a seriousness that demands only that she be judged equally seriously."[2] Alvarez is not the only critic for whom femininity and seriousness have been seen as mutually exclusive.

When it comes to judging women who write poetry, indeed, the orthopedism inherent in positive or negative views of femininity seems to become all the more rigid. When they are not excluding women poets altogether, the guardians of poetic taste often enforce their views by singling out one woman writer, praising her extravagantly, and using her as a pretext to denigrate the work of *other* women.

Marceline Desbordes-Valmore seems to have had an unusual knack for finding herself in the position of privileged exception.

Baudelaire offers a particularly acerbic version of the "divide and control" school of criticism in the retrospective article he wrote on the occasion of Desbordes-Valmore's death:[3]

> If ever a man desired for his wife or daughter[4] the gifts and honors of the Muse, he could not have desired them to be of a kind other than those accorded to Mme Valmore. Among the rather large population of women who have lately thrown themselves into literary activity, there are few whose works have not been, if not a source of distress for their families, or even for their lovers (for the most indecent men love decency in the beloved object), at least marred by the kind of masculine ridiculousness that, in women, takes on the proportions of monstrosity. We have known the philanthropic-woman-writer, the systematic priestess of love, the republican poetess, the poetess of the future (Saint-Simonian or Fourierist); and our eyes, in love with the beautiful, have never been able to get used to all these stuffy uglinesses, all these impious villainies (there are even poetesses of impiety), all these sacrilegious parodies of the male spirit.[5]

monstrous
femme

In an astute parenthetical turn of phrase, Baudelaire here indicates that woman's proper place is that of "beloved object"—l'objet aimé—not poetic subject. Not only are women writers "monstrous" for transgressing onto male territory; transgression itself—impiety, indecency, political and theoretical assertiveness—is here designated the exclusive property of the male spirit. And the male spirit is owed the respect due a god. Like Jahwe, it suffers no images to be made of it without sacrilege. And Baudelaire was not alone. Barbey d'Aurévilly agreed:[6]

Mme Desbordes-Valmore is not a woman of letters, being that there *are* such monsters that are now called *women of letters.* Our fathers, with their profound common sense, once called that kind of women *men of letters,* ironically confounding the two sexes in that hideous and vengeful appellation. But she, simple and too often careless [elle, la simple et trop souvent la négligée], has never played the androgynous genius. She has never posed for the *Muse.* Posed, her! What is enchanting, more than the talent shown in her verse, when there is any, is the total absence of pose.[7]

It is hard to like a woman who inspires such praise. The problem with Marceline Desbordes-Valmore is not that the misogynists excluded her, but that they applauded her. What they loved was her total avoidance of monstrosity, her willingness not to impinge on male territory in any way. The avoidance of monstrosity or masculinity, the avoidance of boundary transgression or mixture, is described as the total absence of *pose.* But this amounts to saying that Marceline Desbordes-Valmore succeeded in representing orthopedic femininity as if it were Nature itself. Baudelaire's essay, for example, continues:[8]

Mrs. Desbordes-Valmore was a woman, always a woman, and absolutely nothing but a woman: but she was to an extraordinary extent the poetic expression of all the natural beauties of woman. Whether she is singing the langorous desires of the young girl, the mournful desolation of an abandoned Ariadne, or the warm enthusiasms of maternal love, her song always preserves the delicious accent of woman; nothing borrowed, no artificial ornament, nothing but the (*eternal feminine*) as the German poet puts it. It is thus in her very sincerity that Mrs. Valmore has found her reward, that is to say a glory we think is just as secure as that of the most perfect artists. (pp. 146–147)

What is unsettling to me in this tribute is less its underlying misogyny (for which Baudelaire is justly famous: "Women are *natural;* that is, abominable", etc.) than its uncanny resemblance to a certain ideal of women's poetry that seems to have become pervasive in feminist criticism. The temptation to read poetry by women as testimony to what is specific to women ("nothing borrowed"), to observe a woman poet of the past "dance out of the looking glass of the male text into a tradition that enabled her to create her own authority"[9] is very great, and, as Jan Montefiore points out in her critique of the poetics of experience,[10] politically useful. But to the extent that any woman poet is made to stand as a *representative* woman, to the extent that poetry by a woman is seen as an unproblematic and authentic representation of her specificity *as a woman*,[11] the ideal of a women's poetry of experience comes uncomfortably close to Baudelaire's (and Barbey's) construction of Marceline Desbordes-Valmore—and indeed, of the woman poet as such—as a *sujet supposé sincère*.

Yet it was Desbordes-Valmore herself, in fact, who constructed the myth of her un-constructedness:

Adieu, Muses! la gloire est trop peu pour mon âme;
L'amour sera ma seule erreur:
Et pour la peindre en traits de flamme,
Je n'ai besoin que de mon coeur.
("Prière aux Muses")[12]

[Farewell, Muses! my soul can't feed on fame;
Love will be my only sin:
And to paint it in streaks of flame
My heart is all I need.
("Prayer to the Muses")]

In an autobiographical letter to Sainte-Beuve, Desbordes-Valmore describes what might be called the primal scene of her poetic practice:[13]

At age twenty, profound sufferings obliged me to give up singing, because my voice made me cry; but music still rolled about in my fevered head, and regular measures always arranged my ideas, without my thinking about it. I was forced to write them down in order to free myself from this feverish beat, and someone told me I had written an elegy. Mr. Alibert, who was nursing my frail health, advised me to write as a cure, since he could think of no other remedy. I tried it, without having read or learned anything at all, which caused me painful fatigue in fitting words to my thoughts.[14]

Far from grabbing the pen out of the patriarch's hands, Desbordes-Valmore goes to great lengths to depict her birth as a writer as a kind of victimization: she couldn't help it, didn't want it, didn't know what to call it, didn't think about it, and had no qualifications for it, but, since the doctor couldn't cure her any other way, she had to take his advice. Otherwise she would have gone on being a bother. Nowhere does her "I" appear as an active, knowing, or desiring subject. Never mind that, as an actress from the age of eleven, she had memorized her share of alexandrines. She knew the kind of woman her public could allow to become a poet. As Sainte-Beuve put it, "Elle a chanté comme l'oiseau chante, comme la tourterelle gémit, sans autre science que l'émotion du coeur, sans autre moyen que la note naturelle" (p. 124). [She sang as the bird sings, as the turtledove moans, knowing nothing but the emotions of the heart, with no technique but the music of nature.]

The poetics of spontaneous emotion for which Desbordes-Valmore is so often praised constituted, however, an entirely conventional tenet of Romanticism. Lamartine almost echoes Sainte-Beuve's statement when he writes:

> Je chantais, mes amis, comme l'homme respire,
> Comme l'oiseau gémit, comme le vent soupire,
> Comme l'eau murmure en coulant.[15]

> [I sang, my friends, as man breathes,
> As the bird moans, as the wind sighs,
> As water murmurs as it flows.]

The question is: why is Desbordes-Valmore's sincerity *believed?* I will return to this question in the second part of this essay.

But there is another kind of "primal scene" in Desbordes-Valmore's letter to Sainte-Beuve that deserves comment. The autobiographical material begins:[16]

My father gave birth to me in Douai, his native country (June 20, 1786). I was his last and only blond child. I was triumphally received and baptized because of the color of my hair, much adored in my mother. She was beautiful, like a virgin, and it was hoped that I would resemble her completely, but I only resembled her a little. If I have been loved, it has been for things other than great beauty. (p. 99)

While this purports to be a description of biological parentage, I think it more accurately describes Desbordes-Valmore's *poetic* parentage. Father-born ("mon père *m'a mise au monde*"), she inhabits the French poetic tradition (the paternal "native land"), within which the role prescribed for women is that of *image:* the blond, virginal "great beauty." For in the canonical tradition, of course, women are not supposed to write at all. In her autobiographical letter, Desbordes-Valmore is quite explicitly situating herself as excluded from the role the canonical tradition might have assigned to her. Yet it may be perhaps paradoxically *because* she situated herself elsewhere than as the "beloved object" of traditional love poetry that she came to personify—for Sainte-Beuve, Baudelaire, Barbey, Verlaine, Hugo, Vigny, Lamartine, and many other canonical male poets—the absolute voice of the native informant from the field of the Eternal Feminine.

Interestingly enough, however, the role of beautiful woman has not disappeared from Desbordes-Valmore's *oeuvre*. It is simply occupied by other women. The beautiful mother is an important presence throughout her work. Many of her poems possess a triangular structure—a female speaker, another woman, and a man. Often that other woman is a sister or confidante. But equally often she is a resented but admired rival. Yet it is sometimes hard to tell whether it is the admiration or the rivalry that a given poem is designed to express. "Aveu d'une femme," for example, begins:

Savez-vous pourquoi, madame,
Je refusais de vous voir:
J'aime! et je sens qu'une femme
Des femmes craint le pouvoir.
Le vôtre est tout dans vos charmes,
Qu'il faut, par force, adorer;
L'inquiétude a des larmes:
Je ne voulais pas pleurer. (vol. II, p. 381)

[Do you know why, madame,
I refused to see you:
I am in love! and I feel that a woman
Fears the power of women.
Yours is all in your charms,
Which one must, perforce, adore;
Uneasiness has tears:
I did not want to weep.]

This is as much a statement of identification with the position of desirer as it is of rivalry with the desired. To love is to fear the power of women. A scenario of loss of the beloved man seems inextricable from a scenario of desire for the other woman. But whose desire is it? What object takes up all the space of the poem's interest? The poem maintains a certain ambiguity to the end. Statements like "je vis de ce qu'il eprouve," which at first sight seem to mean "My life depends on what he feels about me," can also be read to mean, "I feel what he feels." The homoeroticism of many of Desbordes-Valmore's poems is definitely worthy of further study—not least in order to understand how it came to go unnoticed. This is not to make a biographical claim (although her life is interesting in its intense female attachments) but rather to suggest that Desbordes-Valmore's investment in poetry itself is in some sense homoerotic. A whole cycle of poems is addressed to a beautiful woman named Délie, who has introduced the poem's speaker to a man who was once Délie's lover. The speaker, having duly fallen in love with him, finds that he is still in love with Délie. Is it an accident that the rival's name should be precisely that of Maurice Scève's poetic heroine? It seems quite possible that Desbordes-Valmore is here working out her role of "other woman" with respect to the French Petrarchan tradition.

This is not to say, however, that the myths that have circulated about Desbordes-Valmore's life have not depicted her as the epitome of the heterosexual Romantic heroine. As Lagarde and Michard would have it:[17]

She conceives a burning passion for a man of letters, Henri de Latouche, a passion which will make her suffer, but which at first sustains her during her career worries and exalts her ardent soul. Echoes of that passion reverberate throughout her poetry. In 1817 she marries the actor Valmore, and leaves the theatre in 1823. Life was hard for this sensitive, passionate creature: material difficulties, suffering in love, cruel losses (four of her children died), she was spared nothing. But she found consolation in poetry.[18]

Nice fiction, of which Desbordes-Valmore is to a large extent the author, aided and abetted by various canonical overdeterminations. In reality, according to a new biography painstakingly researched by Francis Ambrière,[19] the story runs more like this: At age ten, Marceline began her theatrical career alongside her mother, Catherine, who had left her husband for another man. Financial difficulties forced Catherine and Marceline to sail to Guadeloupe, where Catherine had a rich relative. When they arrived, the relative was dead, there was a slave revolt, and Catherine soon died of yellow fever. Marceline returned to France, continued her acting career, had three lovers and two illegitimate children (who soon died), and then (in 1817) met and married Prosper Valmore. Only after that (in 1819, after the publication of her first volume of poems) did she meet Henri de Latouche, who became her lover. Four of the five children born during

Marceline's marriage died before she did. Latouche believed that Ondine, the third child, was his.

Thus, the mythology of the great love followed by the reasonable marriage (which is fundamental to almost all existing studies of her poetry) is quite far from the facts of Marceline's biography, if Ambrière is correct. Just as Lamartine wrote poems to Elvire assuring her of immortality ("tu peux, tu peux mourir!") before he ever met Julie Charles, all the poetic conventions drawn upon by Desbordes-Valmore were in place before she ever met the lover who has been credited with inspiring her unique passion. And it is no accident that literary history should have recognized only Henri de Latouche in that role: not only did her lovers have to coalesce into one great love in order for her not to appear to be a "free woman," but her visibility was reinforced by the fact that that lover was someone "we" (hommes de lettres) know. (Latouche was a poet and editor of the works of André Chénier, first published in 1819.) Marceline Desbordes-Valmore is thus, from the beginning, "other" than the woman depicted in the image, whether it be the image of the great beauty, the image of the unlettered songbird, or the image of the passionate, tragic, and virtuous poetess. Yet her very success in constructing an unthreatening poetics of sincerity,[20] which enabled her to maintain a place in the French poetic canon as a "romantique mineur" (Lagarde and Michard), has tended to render her unusable and invisible for feminism. As the first woman poet to "penetrate [sic] the 'Galerie Seghers,' "[21] she was sponsored by Jeanine Moulin, whose notoriously anti-feminist anthology *La Poésie féminine*[22] stands as the anti-type for Domna Stanton's anthology, *The Defiant Muse*. Stanton writes:

> In an extended preface that explores the existence of a poetic tradition by French women, Moulin iterates the stereotypes of femininity and the cliches of feminine writing that pervade traditional literary histories. The principal preoccupations of this poetry, she claims, are conjugal and maternal happiness, and a desire for love that is couched in passive emotionalism . . . Rejecting the need for "an aggressive feminism" at the close of her preface (p. 64), just as she denies the feminism of her investigation at the outset, Moulin welcomes the absence of "all traces of antagonism between the sexes" in contemporary women's writing, and points to the future disappearance of *la poésie féminine*. In opposition to this image of women's poetry, whose disappearance can only be welcome, the present volume affirms its feminist bias . . . This project began with the determination to exclude poems that privilege *kinder, kirche, kuchen,* extol conjugal bliss, passively bemoan seduction and abandonment, and seek escape into transcendent saintliness or the beauty of flora and fauna.[23]

Needless to say, it is Desbordes-Valmore's "femininity" that has led to her being excluded from an anthology of feminist poetry. Feminism too has its orthopedism.

Both applauded and condemned for that which, in her poetry, seems exemplarily, exclusively, and unprotestingly feminine, yet canny enough to have constructed that femininity out of a life that could have told a different story, Marceline Desbordes-Valmore offers her reader the chance to re-examine the relations between poetic convention and the construction of gender.

It is not enough to say that the lyric has always reflected the nature of the relations between the sexes in Western culture; the lyric has surely had a central role in *constructing* those relations. Although the first love poet may well have been Sappho, lyrical poems of desire in the Western tradition are often discussed as though they were always written by men to women. This gives rise to generalizations like the following: "In the great tradition of Petrarch and Shakespeare, the lover-poet is principally concerned with defining his own self through his desire either for the image of his beloved or for his own image mediated through her response to him."[24] Or the following, which identifies a consistent physiological metaphor behind descriptions of poetic creation: "This model of the pen–penis writing on the virgin page participates in a long tradition identifying the author as a male who is primary and the female as his passive creation—a secondary object lacking autonomy, endowed with often contradictory meaning but denied intentionality. Clearly this tradition excludes woman from the creation of culture, even as it reifies her as an artifact within culture."[25] Marceline Desbordes-Valmore acknowledges the power of this tradition when she begins a poem by stating, rather matter-of-factly:

> Les femmes, je le sais, ne doivent pas écrire;
> J'écris pourtant . . . (vol II, p. 506)

    [Women, I know, are not supposed to write;
    I write, though . . .]

The poet goes on, however, to minimize the transgression by making her writing redundant with respect to what is already written "in" the lover:

    Je ne tracerai rien qui ne soit dans toi-meme
    Beaucoup plus beau . . .

    [I won't trace out anything that isn't already, in you,
    Much more beautiful . . .]

Even in her less self-conscious love poems, Desbordes-Valmore seems to work out a similar rhythm of resistance and submission, initiative and self-effacement. Let us look at how it structures a fairly typical "elegy."

Son Image

Elle avait fui de mon âme offensée;
Bien loin de moi je crus l'avoir chassée:
Toute tremblante, un jour, elle arriva,
Sa douce image, et dans mon coeur rentra:
Point n'eus le temps de me mettre en colère;
Point ne savais ce qu'elle voulait faire;
Un peu trop tard mon coeur le devina.

Sans prévenir, elle dit: "Me voilà!
"Ce coeur m'attend. Par l'Amour, que j'implore,

"Comme autrefois j'y viens régner encore."
Au nom d'amour ma raison se troubla:
Je voulus fuir, et tout mon corps trembla.
Je bégayai des plaintes au perfide;
Pour me toucher[26] il prit un air timide;
Puis à mes pieds en pleurant, il tomba.
J'oubliai tout dès que l'Amour pleura.
(vol I, p. 50)

[That Image

It had fled from my offended soul;
Far, far from me I thought I had chased it;
All tremblingly, one day, it came along,
That dear image, and sank back into my heart.
No time to summon up my anger;
Didn't know what it was after;
A bit too late my heart realized.

Without warning, it said: "Here I am!
This heart awaits me. By Love, which I implore,
I come to reign over it once more."
At the name of love my mind was blurred:
I sought to flee; my whole body trembled.
I stammered, moaning against the traitor;
He acted shy, the better to touch me;
Then, weeping, he fell at my feet.
I forgot all when Love began to weep.]

The fact that all French nouns are either masculine or feminine creates a gendered drama among the figures in this poem which is obscured by the necessity of turning the image into an "it" in English. In French, the image is a "she", and remains so until she speaks. The gender of the "I" is never made grammatically clear. A number of observations come to mind here: that the object of love is feminine, as in the male lyric, so that on the grammatical level the poem conforms to the tradition even though the genders are reversed in "reality"; that the opening stanza sketches out the love relation in female-to-female terms, if "I" is to be equated with the author; or that Desbordes-Valmore is reversing the equation of femininity with passivity that is said to be traditional in the love lyric.[27] By giving "elle" the dominant role in the poem's plot, Desbordes-Valmore would seem to begin by empowering femininity.

Yet the net impression made by the poem is hardly one of empowered femininity, whatever the grammatical plot might say. The story seems, rather, one of resistance penetrated, the traditional story of a woman seduced, abandoned, and seduced again. If the "I" of the first stanza offers ineffectual resistance to a return of the offending "image," that resistance crumbles as soon as the image invokes the name of Love. The speaker takes on the properties of the "elle" ("elle avait fui"/"Je voulus fuir"; "Toute tremblante, elle arriva"/"tout mon corps trembla"). The rhyme scheme with its alternation between varied feminine endings and identical masculine endings (all the masculine rhymes are verbs in the *passé simple*) foreshadows the plot of repetition and masculine return: the *passé* is not so simple. However ambivalent the speaker is toward Love, she "forgets all" as soon as "he" falls on his knees and weeps. He triumphs through a show of submission; she loses her cool, her reason, and her memory.

It would seem, then, that far from presenting a picture of empowered femininity, the poem offers a story of female masochism. Before buying into the equation between femininity and masochism, however, let us look at a poem by Baudelaire:

Le Vampire

Toi qui, comme un coup de couteau,
Dans mon coeur plaintif es entrée;
Toi qui, forte comme un troupeau
De démons, vins, folle et parée,

De mon esprit humilié
Faire ton lit et ton domaine;
—Infâme à qui je suis lié
Comme le forçat à la chaîne,

Comme au jeu le joueur têtu,
Comme à la bouteille l'ivrogne,
Comme aux vermines la charogne,
—Maudite, maudite sois-tu!

J'ai prié le glaive rapide
De conquérir ma liberté,

Et j'ai dit au poison perfide
De secourir ma lâcheté.

Hélas! le poison et le glaive
M'ont pris en dédain et m'ont dit:
"Tu n'es pas digne qu'on t'enlève
A ton esclavage maudit,

"Imbécile!—de son empire
Si nos efforts te délivraient,
Tes baisers ressusciteraient
Le cadavre de ton vampire!"
(vol. I, pp. 33–34)

[The Vampire

You who, sharp as a knife,
Into my plaintive heart have pierced;
You who, mighty as a troop
Of demons, came, mad and showy,

To make of my humiliated mind
Your bed and your domain;
—Vile being I am tied to
Like the convict to his chain,

Like the gambler to his game,
Like the drunkard to his drink,

119

Like a putrid corpse to vermin,
—Damn you, damn you, damn!

I've prayed the rapid blade
To set me free at last,
And I've asked perfidious poison
To help me in my cowardice.

Alas! the poison and the blade
Have answered with disdain:
"You are not worth saving
From your slavery and damnation,

Imbecile!—even if we tried
To free you from its empire,
Your kisses would resuscitate
The body of your vampire!"]

In Baudelaire's anatomy of ambivalence, the part of phallic torturer is played by a female figure. The "I" is not only a victim; he, like Desbordes-Valmore's speaker, is addicted to his victimizer. If Desbordes-Valmore describes the image "entering" ("rentra" could mean both "re-entered" and "plunged") into her heart, Baudelaire describes it (the "you") explicitly as a knife thrust. If Desbordes-Valmore describes her submission to "le perfide" as a lapse of self-possession, Baudelaire describes his as enslavement. Where Desbordes-Valmore is touched, Baudelaire is vampirized. Baudelaire would seem to have raised the poetics of masochism to new heights. There is certainly no simple correlation here between femininity and passivity, masculinity and action.

The surprising thing is, there never was. A look at the Petrarchan tradition reveals that Baudelaire has not perverted a straightforward pattern, but that that pattern has never been straightforward. However true it may be to say that women are reduced to images in the Petrarchan tradition, those images are far from passive. To take only the hunting imagery suggested by Desbordes-Valmore's poem, there is little support for Mary Ellmann's contention that "The hunter is always male, the prey female."[28] This generalization appears to hold for a poem like Thomas Wyatt's "They flee from me, that sometime did me seek," (which Desbordes-Valmore's poem interestingly resembles), in that the speaker characterizes "them" as wild animals. But it is the hunter here who is passive, trying vainly to lure back his once-tame prey, which has scampered off through *his* excessive gentleness. In many poems by Petrarch, Scève, or Ronsard, the male speaker presents himself as having been wounded by the image of the desired woman:

> Era il giorno ch'al sol si scoloraro
> per la pietà del suo fattore i rai
> quando i' fui preso, et non me ne guardai
> ché i be' vostr' occhi, Donna, mi legaro.
>
> [It was the day the sun had overcast,
> In pity of his maker, his bright sheen

When I fell prey to peril unforeseen,
For your eyes, lady, caught and held me fast.][29]

Ton doux venin, grâce tienne, me fit
Idolâtrer en la divine image
Dont l'oeil crédule ignoramment meffit
Pour non prévoir à mon futur dommage.

[Your sweet poison, your grace, made me
Idolatrous of your divine image;
Credulous eyes have done me wrong
Not to have foreseen my damage.][30]

Ma Dame ayant l'arc d'Amour en son poing
Tirait à moi, pour à soi m'attirer: . . .
Tourne, dit-elle, à moi, et te dépêche.
Fuis-tu mon arc, ou puissance, qu'il ait?
Je ne fuis point, dis-je, l'arc ni la flèche
Mais l'oeil qui fait à mon coeur si grand' plaie.

[My lady, with love's bow in her fist
Shot at me, to draw me to her: . . .
Turn, she said, and hurry toward me.
Are you fleeing my arrow, or my power?
I am fleeing neither bow nor arrow, said I
But the eye that has wounded my heart so deeply.][31]

Ah! traître Amour, donne-moi paix ou trêve,
Ou choisissant un autre trait plus fort,

[handwritten: male poetic masochism]

Tranche ma vie, et m'avance la mort,
Douce est la mort d'autant plus qu'elle est brève.

[Ah! treacherous Love, give me peace or respite,
Or, taking out an arrow thicker yet,
Cut off my life, bring on my death,
Sweet is death, the sweeter being brief.][32]

The image of being the prey rather than the hunter, the penetrated rather than the penetrator, would seem to pervade the Petrarchan figuration *not* of femaleness but of maleness. The metaphors of desire in these poems contradict, rather than follow, the patterns that would flow from sexual physiology. This makes gender generalizations about figuration in the love lyric more complicated than any biologistic ideology would imply.[33] I would be tempted to claim that this is necessarily the case: if poetry were only a reinscription of dominant ideology, it would not need to exist.

Why is it, then, that Petrarch is not called a masochist, even though Louise Labé, using exactly the same conventions, is?[34] Why are there books published on Baudelaire's sadism but not on his masochism?[35] Why is male masochism the secret that it is lyric poetry's job to keep?

One answer, I think, has to do with rhetoric. When men employ the rhetoric of self-torture, it is *read* as rhetoric. When women employ it, it is confession. Men are read rhetorically; women, literally. Yet within the poetic tradition, it is the rhetorical, not the literal, that is taken seriously. Why should the literal be the opposite of the serious? What is the nature of the seriousness of non-literality?

When men have described love as an experience of fragmentation, wounding, or loss of psychic intactness and control, it has been read as an analysis of The Nature of Desire. When women have described something analogous, it has been read as an expression of What a Woman Wants. Rhetoric, in other words, is a way of shifting the domain of a poem's meaning to a higher, less referential, more abstract and theoretical level. And this is done by universalizing, that is, by denying the presence of the sexual difference out of which the poem springs.[36] Perhaps this is why the speaker in Desbordes-Valmore's poem "Son image" surrenders not to a man but to Amour, a figure for the whole rhetorical configuration of canonical love poetry. Indeed, in another poem, "Une Nuit d'hiver," Amour breaks the speaker's lyre and burns her verse, saying that only her silence and her tears are acceptable tributes to his power.

Yet the sexual difference on whose transcendence seriousness depends always threatens to return, which may be why "femininity" seems to be the privileged topic of male lyric poetry, or why the philosophical tradition has often viewed rhetoric itself as feminine. Disavowed femininity returns interestingly, in fact, in the very article by Baudelaire on Desbordes-Valmore with which we began. The article opens:[37]

> More than once hasn't a friend of yours, when you confided one of your tastes or passions to him, exclaimed: "How strange! that's in complete disagreement with all your other passions and with your doctrine"? And you answered:

"That's possible, but so be it. I like it; I like it probably precisely because of the violent contradiction my whole being finds in it."

Such is my case with respect to Mme Desbordes-Valmore. (pp. 145–146)

By beginning with the scoffing of a hypothetical friend, Baudelaire presents himself as safely in the bosom of the male homosocial literary world, from which the aesthetic of Desbordes-Valmore is as different as different can be. The distance at which she is placed by this conversation indicates that there is something transgressive or embarrassing about being caught reading her. But of course, Baudelaire has always claimed "the right to contradict oneself." He goes on, being careful to back up from every statement of admiration, and always keeping his implied male reader within reach:[38]

If the cry, the natural sighing of an elite soul, the desperate ambition of a heart, the unexpected and unreflective [irreflechi] faculties, and everything that is gratuitous and comes from God, can suffice to make a great poet, Marceline Valmore is and will always be a great poet. It is true that if you take the time to notice everything she lacks of what can be gained by work, her greatness will be singularly diminished; but at the very moment when you will feel the most irritated and disturbed by the negligence, the noise, the confusion, which you take—you, a reflective and always responsible man [vous, homme réfléchi et toujours responsable]—as a stance of laziness; a sudden, unexpected, unequalable beauty will spring up and carry you off irresistibly into the poetic yonder.

The opposition here is between male reflectiveness and female un-reflectiveness. Yet already there is a danger of being "carried off." The article continues:[39] "Never was a poet more natural; never was a poet less artificial. No one has been able to imitate this charm because it is completely original and inborn [natif]." The opposition glosses itself further as the artificial versus the natural; imitation versus originality; the acquired versus the inborn. There then follow the two paragraphs quoted at the beginning of the present essay: the paragraph outlining the monstrosity of all other women writers who "parody the male spirit" (monstrous because parody—imitation itself—is defined as a male prerogative), and the paragraph praising Desbordes-Valmore as the personification of the woman, the whole woman, and nothing but a woman.

But more information about what is being disavowed or embraced is forthcoming in the lines that follow:[40]

That torch, which she waves before our eyes to light up the mysterious hedgerows of sentiment, or which she places, to reignite them, on our most intimate memories, erotic or filial—that torch has been lit in the depths of her own heart. Victor Hugo has expressed magnificently, as in all he has expressed, the beauties and enchantments of family life; but only in the poems of the ardent Marceline can you find that warmth of the maternal nest, of which some among the sons of woman, less ungrateful than others, have kept the delicious memory.

The "homme réfléchi" has now become a son, and the eternal feminine a mother. The return to the warmth of the maternal nest is both the appeal and the danger of Desbordes-Valmore's poetry. And this can be read not only as the drama of separation/individuation from the Mother which can be seen as *the* topic of Baudelaire's poetry, but also as an indication that, for Baudelaire, Marceline Desbordes-Valmore is functioning as a *poetic* mother, a *maternal* line that has no proper place in the male homosocial literary world.

But Baudelaire's presentation of the return of disavowed femininity does not stop there. For the essay ends with the following description of his experience as a reader of Desbordes-Valmore's poetry:[41] "The walker, contemplating these stretches veiled with mourning, can feel rising to his eyes the tears of hysteria, *hysterical tears*" (in English in the original). The disavowed woman in Baudelaire's text is thus his own hysterical self.

Whether such hysteria should be taken seriously or not, Baudelaire is here enacting male privilege as the right to play femininity. Rhetoric is the domain of male self-difference reframed as universality. If masculinity establishes, explores, and interests itself as that which is constantly differing from itself, it arises out of the replacement of sexual difference by self-difference. But this does not mean that the replacement can simply be reversed: masculine privilege is enforced precisely by male femininity. How can the search for that which is different from male self-difference be sure that it is not already framed within male self-difference? The answer is far from clear, but at least it might be possible to conclude that to be differently empowered does not have to mean: to be empowered *as* different.

Chapter Seven

Muteness Envy

A slumber did my spirit seal;
I had no human fears:
She seemed a thing . . .
William Wordsworth

In one of the best known poems in the English language, John Keats proclaims the superiority of silence over poetry by addressing a Grecian urn in the following terms:

> Thou still unravished bride of quietness,
> Thou foster child of silence and slow time,
> Sylvan historian, who canst thus express
> A flowery tale more sweetly than our rhyme . . .
> Heard melodies are sweet, but those unheard
> Are sweeter . . .

The ego ideal of the poetic voice would seem, then, to reside in the muteness of things.

Why does Keats choose to write about an urn? Why not, for example, a Grecian frieze? Is an urn somehow overdetermined as an example of a thing? When Martin Heidegger had to choose something as an example of a thing in his essay "The Thing," he chose a jug. And when Wallace Stevens placed an exemplary object in Tennessee, it was a jar. What is it that might make an urn impose itself? Why does Cleanth Brooks entitle his New Critical treatise on poetry *The Well-Wrought Urn?*

Urns are containers. They can contain the ashes of the dead. They can also contain water, wine, nourishment. As containers or vehicles, they lend themselves as metaphors for form itself, or language itself, as in Francis Ponge's poem about a jug, which ends, "Couldn't everything I have just said about the jug be said equally well of *words?*" Urns can be metaphors for the relation between form and content, but also between body and soul, expression and intention. Like the most general description of a human being, they have an inside and an outside. Whether we speak of eating or of thinking, we see the human being as a thing with interiority, an outside with something happening inside. Thus, urns are not so much anthropomorphic as humans are urnomorphic. The thing, the human, the poem, and indeed language itself all become metaphors for each other through the urn.

But Keats's urn wears its contents on its *outside*. Does this have anything to do with its idealization of muteness?

Of course, Keats is not the only poet to have made muteness into a poetic ideal. Mallarmé oriented his theory of poetic language toward "le poème tu, aux blancs." And in what is perhaps the most explicit expression of the idealization of muteness as a prerogative of things, Archibald MacLeish proclaims in his "Ars Poetica":

> A poem should be palpable and mute
> As a globed fruit,

Dumb
As old medallions to the thumb,

Silent as the sleeve-worn stone
Of casement ledges where the moss has grown—

A poem should be wordless
As the flight of birds.

Yet these poems do not seem to be able to maintain the privilege of muteness to the end. No sooner does Keats convince us of the superiority of the Grecian urn's aphonia, than it speaks. "Beauty is truth, truth beauty," it says; "That is all ye know on earth and all ye need to know." MacLeish's poem, too, is unable to leave well enough alone. It concludes, "A poem should not mean/But be," a sentence which disobeys its own prescription, since, in saying what a poem *should* do, it is "meaning" rather than "being." "Ars Poetica" can be read as a more explicit version of the Grecian urn's final violation of its own apparent rules. Is muteness not really a value, then, or is it simply that language cannot, by definition, say so? Or is it that the utterance "Beauty is truth, truth beauty" *is* a form of silence? What is behind the poem's incomplete commitment to its own muteness envy?

In choosing the expression "muteness envy" to name a recurrent poetic condition, I am consciously echoing Freud's expression "penis envy," which for him marked the nature of sexual difference

131

from the woman's point of view. Since muteness envy seems to be a feature of canonical poetry written by men, could it somehow play into the question of sexual difference? Does the muteness that men envy tend to be feminine? Certainly Keats's urn is feminized, a "still unravished bride of quietness." Doubly feminized, indeed, if the container-like shape of the urn is denied as anthropomorphic and affirmed instead as gynomorphic. In an essay published in 1954, Charles Patterson offers a "comprehensive and virile interpretation" of the ode, comparing the urn's shape to "the outlines of the feminine body": "the urn is a receptacle, just as is the body of woman—the receptacle from which life springs."[1]

For Mallarmé too, the blanks and the "white page" that are the material inscription of silence are also the analogues of the female body. And numerous are the Parnassian poems addressed to silent female statues, marble Venuses and granite Sphinxes whose unresponsiveness stands as the mark of their aesthetic value, and whose whiteness underscores the normative whiteness of canonical representations of women. Baudelaire parodies this conceit by making Beauty *speak* her own unresponsiveness and gloat over the muteness of the poets' love for her, while Stevens parodies it by refusing either to feminize or to idealize his jar as it takes deadpan control over the slovenly wilderness. The parodic edge to these poems seems only to confirm the normative image of a beautiful, silent woman addressed by the idealizing rhetoric of a male poet for whom she "seems a thing." There is, of course, nothing new in saying that, in Western poetry, women are often idealized, objectified, and silent. Feminist criticism has been pointing this out for at least thirty years. But why is female muteness a repository of aesthetic value? And what does that muteness signify?

Interestingly enough, the silence of women seems to be a *sine qua non* of sexual difference for Jacques Lacan, too, in his translation of Freud's story of anatomical destiny into a story of discursive destiny:

> There is woman only as excluded by the nature of things which is the nature of words, and it has to be said that if there is one thing they themselves are complaining about enough at the moment, it is well and truly that—only they don't know what they are saying, which is all the difference between them and me.
>
> It none the less remains that if she is excluded by the nature of things, it is precisely that in being not all, she has, in relation to what the phallic function designates of *jouissance,* a supplementary *jouissance.*
>
> Note that I said *supplementary.* Had I said *complementary,* where would we be! We'd fall right back into the all.[2]

In contrast to Freud, whose geometry of castration implies a complementarity between presence (penis) and absence (vagina), Lacan theorizes feminine *jouissance* as something other than what would fit into that schema of complementarity. In sexual complementarity, everything is a function of only one of the terms: the phallus. In sexual supplementarity, woman is that which exceeds or escapes. Which does not mean that she speaks.

133

There is a *jouissance* which is proper to her, to this "her" which does not exist and which signifies nothing. There is a *jouissance* proper to her and of which she herself may know nothing, except that she experiences it—that much she does know. She knows it of course when it happens. It does not happen to all of them . . . What gives some likelihood to what I am arguing, that is, that the woman knows nothing of this *jouissance,* is that ever since we've been begging them . . . —begging them on our knees to tell us about it, well, not a word! (145–146)

In his efforts to collect reliable testimony from women about their pleasure, Lacan finally turns, astonishingly, to a statue, thus writing his own Parnassian poem: "You have only to go and look at Bernini's statue [of Saint Theresa] in Rome to understand immediately that she's coming, there is no doubt about it" (147). As Stephen Heath, Luce Irigaray, and Barbara Freeman have remarked,[3] this is a very odd way to listen to women. But it fits in perfectly with the idealization of female muteness already in place in the aesthetic tradition.

Returning now to Keats's urn, we find that the question of feminine *jouissance* (or lack of it) is very much at issue. By calling the urn a "still unravished bride," Keats implies that the urn's destiny is to become a *ravished* bride. The word "ravished" can mean either "raped" or "sent into ecstasy." Both possibilities are readable in the scenes depicted on the urn:

> What men or gods are these? What maidens loth?
> What mad pursuit? What struggle to escape?
> What pipes and timbrels? What wild ecstasy?

The privileged aesthetic moment is a freeze frame just prior to rav-ishment.[4] But how does pressing the pause button here make us sublate the scene of male sexual violence into a scene of general ec-stasy? How does the maidens' struggle to escape congeal into an aesthetic triumph?

If we turn now to one of the primal scenes of Western literature, Apollo's pursuit of the nymph Daphne and her transformation into a laurel tree, we will find that the same questions apply. Whether because of Cupid's mischief or out of her own resistance, Daphne struggles to escape the god's embrace, becoming a tree—a thing—in a last desperate attempt to avoid rape. But Apollo not only does not lose; he enters a whole new dimension of symbolization, pluck-ing off a laurel branch and using it as a sign of artistic achievement. "Instead of becoming the object of a sexual conquest," writes Peter Sacks in his book on *The English Elegy,*

Daphne is thus eventually transformed into something very much like a consolation prize—a prize that becomes *the* prize and sign of poethood. What Apollo or the poet pursues turns into a sign not only of his lost love but also of his very pur-suit—a consoling sign that carries in itself the reminder of the loss on which it has been founded . . . If there is a necessary distance between the wreath and what it signifies, that distance is the measure of Apollo's loss. Daphne's 'turning' into a tree matches Apollo's 'turning' from the object of his love to a sign of her. It is this substitutive turn or act of troping that any mourner must perform.[5]

Thus, "any mourner" must identify with Apollo, not Daphne, and the fact that Apollo does not carry out the intended rape is coded as "loss"—a loss that becomes a model for the aesthetic as such. The rapist is bought off with the aesthetic. And the aesthetic is inextricably tied to a silence in the place of rape.

As Christine Froula and Patricia Joplin have argued, that silence has been so inextricably tied to the aesthetics of the literary canon that even the most subtle and insightful of readers have, as we have just seen, tended to perpetuate it. Joplin analyzes the "elision of gender" and the "mystification of violence" in Geoffrey Hartman's celebration of the phrase "the voice of the shuttle" as a beautifully condensed trope for Philomela's tapestry (which testifies to her rape and mutilation after her tongue has been cut out).

> When Geoffrey Hartman asks of Sophocles' metaphor "the voice of the shuttle": "what gives these words the power to speak to us even without the play?", he celebrates Language and not the violated woman's emergence from silence . . . When Hartman ends his essay by noting that "There is always *something* that violates us, deprives our voice, and compels art toward an aesthetics of silence," the specific nature of the woman's double violation disappears behind the apparently genderless (but actually male) language of "us," the "I" and the "you" who agree to attest to that which violates, deprives, silences only as a mysterious, unnamed "something."[6]

Once again, an "aesthetics of silence" turns out to involve a male appropriation of female muteness as aesthetic trophy accompanied by an elision of sexual violence.

There seem, then, to be two things women are silent about: their pleasure and their violation. The work performed by the idealization of this silence is that *it helps culture not to be able to tell the difference between the two.*

What happens when women attempt to break that silence? Sometimes their speech is simply discounted, as when Lacan claims that feminists get it right about silence but don't know what they are saying, "which is all the difference between them and me." Even in the case of the Grecian urn, penalties apply. Summarizing a history of reservations critics have expressed about the wisdom of allowing the urn to speak at the end of Keats's poem (T. S. Eliot called the final lines "a serious blemish on a beautiful poem"), Cleanth Brooks notes that "Some critics have felt that the unravished bride of quietness protests too much."[7] His reference to Hamlet's mother's reading of women's guilty speech implies that, to many readers, the urn would have been better off keeping still. Overdetermined by the aesthetic tradition of women's silence, any speech at all appears as guilty speech. It is as though women were constantly subject to the Miranda warning: "You have the right to remain silent. If you waive that right anything you say can and will be used against you." No wonder Shakespeare's Miranda can only exclaim as she notes the completion of the patriarchal set, "Oh brave new world, that has such people in it!"

Two recent feminist approaches to the speech of girls corroborates these functions of silence. Carol Gilligan's study of adolescent girls' development suggests that when culture teaches girls that their sexual feelings are unseemly or irrelevant or secondary to the needs and initiatives of men, they learn to say "I don't know" about their desire.[8] (Interestingly, this is Maria Torok's interpretation of the nature of penis envy: girls who have learned to repress knowledge of their own sexuality project their sexual feelings as the unobtainable experience of the other sex.)[9] And recent work on child abuse and father-daughter incest, reinforced by Jeffrey Masson's *The Assault on Truth,* his account of Freud's abandonment of the "seduction" theory of hysteria,[10] suggests that girls learn silence not only about sexual pleasure but also about sexual abuse.

Christine Froula, in an essay entitled "The Daughter's Seduction: Sexual Violence and Literary History," makes an analogy between Homer's silencing of Helen and Freud's discrediting of his hysterical patients. "As the *Iliad* tells the story of a woman's abduction as a male war story, so Freud turned the hysterics' stories of sexual abuse into a tale to soothe a father's ear . . . Freud undertook not to believe the hysterics not because the weight of scientific evidence was on the father's side but because so much was at stake in maintaining the father's credit: the 'innocence' not only of particular fathers—Freud's, Freud himself, the hysterics'—but also of the cultural structure that credits male authority at the expense of female authority."[11] In switching from an alliance with the daughters to an alliance with the fathers, Freud had to translate the "truth" of abuse into the "beauty" of psychoanalysis. At this point we might conclude after Molière, "Et voilà pourquoi votre fille est muette."

But perhaps she is mute because she knows that neither of these accounts is quite right. While it is true that Freud's paradigmatic model of incest seems to switch from the father's desire for the daughter to the son's desire for the mother (thus letting the father

138

off the hook and granting the son the privilege of perversity), it is also true that by crediting the inside/outside, guilt/innocence opposition, critics of psychoanalysis have lost sight of Freud's understanding of the daughter's desire. Why does the father's guilt have to be tied to the daughter's innocence? Can't the daughter's capacity for perverse desire coexist with the fact of abuse?

Now I would like to explore all these issues as they play themselves out in a recent film and in a series of responses to it. The film, written and directed by Jane Campion, is called *The Piano*. The heroine, Ada McGrath, played by Holly Hunter, is mute. Her "voice" is a piano. It could be said that the piano in the film plays, with respect to Ada, the role traditionally assigned to the Muse with respect to the poet: it is her significant other, herself, and her missing piece. Ada has a daughter, Flora, played by Anna Paquin. Ada has been sent by her father from Scotland to New Zealand to be married to a man she has never met. When she is deposited by sailors on a deserted beach with her daughter, her piano, and a large number of other boxes, she is met by two European men—her husband-to-be, Alisdair Stewart, played by Sam Neill, and another man named George Baines, played by Harvey Keitel—and fourteen Maori men and women. Stewart decides that there are too few people to carry all the boxes plus the piano, and the piano is left on the beach while the party, with Baines translating Stewart's orders to the Maoris, makes its way through the dense, muddy New Zealand bush. Ada communicates by writing on a pad hanging around her neck and by signing to her daughter, who translates. She is enraged at the abandonment of her piano.

Shortly after a marriage which seems to take place as a photographic sitting, Stewart leaves to buy some Maori land, and Ada and Flora attempt to persuade a reluctant Baines to retrieve the piano. The three of them visit the piano on the beach, where Baines is fascinated by the emotional abandon of Ada's playing, so different from her normal resistant demeanor. Soon Baines has brought the piano to his own hut and has traded some of his land to Stewart for ownership of the piano, claiming a desire to learn to play. When Stewart tells Ada of the deal, and indicates that she is to give Baines lessons, she is outraged, writing, "NO, NO, THE PIANO IS MINE!" on her note pad. Stewart disregards her, saying everyone in the family must make sacrifices. Baines then persuades Ada that she can win back her piano, key by key, in exchange for sexual contact, which begins while she plays, but eventually, for a larger number of keys, takes place in his bedroom. His approach is gradual; her response is resistant, then hesitant. Flora is generally left resentfully outside Baines's hut during these sessions. Then Baines abruptly abandons the bargain, saying, "I am giving the piano back to you. I've had enough. The arrangement is making you a whore and me wretched. I want you to care for me, but you can't." Once the piano is installed in Stewart's hut, Ada is confused about her relation to it, and runs back into Baines's arms. Stewart follows her and peers at their lovemaking through the cracks in the hut walls. That night Stewart seems to make no response to what he has seen, but the following day he intercepts Ada as she tries to return to Baines. Stewart wrestles her to the ground and tries to kiss and touch her. Then he locks her into his hut. She plays the piano furiously, then, at night, enters Stewart's room and begins to stroke his body, not allowing him to touch hers. This is the first sexual contact of the marriage. When later Ada learns that Baines is leaving the area, she removes a key from the piano, writes on it "Dear George, you have my heart, Ada McGrath," and asks Flora to take it to him. Instead, Flora takes it to Stewart, who is working with his axe on his boundary fence. In a paroxysm of rage, Stewart returns to Ada and chops off one of her fingers, telling Flora to take it to Baines. That night Stewart hovers over Ada's feverish sleep, apologizing and then on the point of taking sexual advantage of the seemingly unconscious woman when he notices her full attention on him and stops. He then goes to Baines and tells Baines he has heard Ada's voice saying, "Let Baines take me away." Soon Ada, Flora, Baines, and the piano are loaded by Maori oarsmen onto a canoe. As the canoe leaves the shore, Ada asks that the piano be tossed overboard. When the others obey, she puts her foot in a loop of the piano rope and is pulled into the sea after the piano. Yet she does not drown but kicks herself free and returns to the canoe, to Baines, and ultimately to life in Nelson, New Zealand, as a wife and piano teacher. While Ada escapes us into banal colonial wifehood, the film ends by seeming to want to display its allegiance to the English poetic tradition of aestheticizing silence: the last lines uttered are a quotation from a sonnet by Thomas Hood called "Silence."

How are we to read Ada's muteness in the movie? First of all, like the urn's, Ada's muteness is not absolute. Not only does she both sign and write, but at the beginning and end of the film there is a voice-over that purports to be the voice of Ada's mind. Similarly,

Keats's apostrophe to the urn ensures that it never exists outside the realm of the anthropomorphic, and even then, it has to talk back in the end. Like the urn, Ada reassures the spectator that she is not really other, never absolutely beyond the reach of communication. But also like the urn, she does not directly answer the questions the spectator might ask. The speaker in Keats's poem asks the urn for names, narratives, legends; the urn answers with chiasmus, tautology, abstraction. The speaker asks for history; the urn resists with theory. Inversely, the men in the film attempt to establish an I–Thou relation with Ada, but her voice-over only links the events of the movie to the past and to the future, and does not offer interpretive guidance through the period—the time actually dramatized in the film—between the initial landing and the final departure from the deserted beach.

The voice opens the movie by saying: "I have not spoken since I was six years old. No one knows why, not even me. My father says it is a dark talent and the day I take it into my head to stop breathing will be my last." First interpretation, then: Ada's muteness is a talent, a talent as strong as life itself.

Stewart, the husband-to-be, is said not to mind the muteness before he sees her, considering that it makes her like a dumb animal, but when he meets her, he begins to wonder whether it is a sign of mental deficiency. This is not because he wants to listen to her—he disregards every explicit expression of her wishes concerning the piano—but because he worries that the merchandise he has bought might be defective. Yet it is he who ends up recognizing Ada's muteness as voice, as will, as resistance. As he reports it to Baines,

Ada has in the end said to him, "I have to go, let me go, let Baines take me away, let him try and save me. I am frightened of my will, of what it might do, it is so strange and strong." Of course, Stewart, having just chopped off his wife's finger, may well be frightened of what his *own* will might do. But at least he recognizes Ada as a center of will and desire.

That Ada's muteness is a manifestation of will is confirmed when the voice-over returns at the moment Ada frees herself from the piano rope that is dragging her under the sea: "What a death! What a chance! What a surprise! My will has chosen life!?"

But the final voice-over of the movie suggests that Ada, now married to Baines and fitted with a prosthetic finger, is beginning to pronounce syllables aloud. While the voice-over, like the urn's voice, may be read as a projection, a narrative fiction, perhaps even a prosopopoeia, Ada, at the end of the movie, is beginning to fade into the sound of common voice.

Thus, although Ada is passed from father to husband as a piece of merchandise, her muteness is not a form of passivity or objecthood. It is a form of resistance and subjecthood. But does the resistance and subjecthood of Ada's *character* outweigh the objecthood thrust upon her by the male bargains and decisions that structure the *framework* of her life? What is the movie *saying* about the muteness that articulates and confuses women's oppression and women's desire?

Reactions to this movie have been remarkably varied. "Jane Campion Stirs Romance with Mystery," wrote Vincent Canby when the film won the Palme d'Or at the Cannes Film Festival.

"Wuthering Heights, Move Over," wrote Jay Carr in one of two long pieces he published in *The Boston Globe*. Yet some viewers of my acquaintance found its pace intolerably slow and its characters and setting repulsive. Some found it fascinatingly romantic and emotionally gripping. Some consider it pretentious; others marvel at its subtlety. Before I saw it, I was told by one friend that it was a hauntingly beautiful love story, and by another that she experienced it as a narrative of rape. How can we determine whether it is about sexual awakening or sexual violence?

Here I am going to quote two representative readings of the film, both written by women. The first is a quotation from the filmmaker, Jane Campion:

> I have enjoyed writing characters who don't have a twentieth-century sensibility about sex. They have nothing to prepare themselves for its strength and power . . . The husband Stewart had probably never had sex at all. So for him to experience sex or feelings of sexual jealousy would have been personality-transforming . . . Ada actually uses her husband Stewart as a sexual object—this is the outrageous morality of the film—which seems very innocent but in fact has its power to be very surprising. I think many women have had the experience of feeling like a sexual object, and that's exactly what happens to Stewart.[12]

For Campion, then, the film is about sex and power and sexual power reversals. It is also, quite explicitly in the published stage directions, about the appeal of fetishistic displacement as sexual surprise: Baines is surprised into excitement while watching Ada play the piano; Ada is surprised into excitement while watching Baines fondle her clothing; Stewart is surprised into sexual jealousy while watching Ada make love to Baines. In these scenarios, there are only displacements and substitutions—*all* sexuality, not just female sexuality, is supplementarity and excess rather than complementarity. It is interesting, however, that Campion describes the film's depiction of sexual awakening in terms of Stewart rather than Ada. It is he, not Ada, who is the virgin in the story.

Now I would like to quote from another reading of the film, this one a long essay by Margaret Morganroth Gullette published in *The Boston Globe*. Gullette writes:

> I felt sullied by "The Piano," muted, mutilated, threatened by rape, pulled underwater and shrouded. Yes, I identified with the heroine . . . I knew I was supposed to identify as a woman with her Victorian fragility and silencing and her redirected expressiveness . . . Holly Hunter, one of the tiniest stars in American movies, is used for her anorexic vulnerability . . . She has the female body type that can be brutalized by men . . . Serious movies can still get away with torturing women in the audience by portraying them as vulnerable heroines and forcing them through a soft porn experience . . . What is staggering is how we're asked to relinquish instantly the resentment and obstinacy we've felt on [Ada's] behalf. She may fall in love right on time, by [Baines's] emotional time table, but why should we? At this point my vicarious anger turned into disbelief.[13]

Gullette's review continues in a more autobiographical vein, narrating the feeling she had that the movie, which she saw with her husband of twenty-five years, had gendered and sundered its male and female spectators, that while she was seeing women's entrapment in men's bargains and men's timetables, her husband was seeing the revelation of men's vulnerability and awakening.

The response to Gullette's review from the *Boston Globe*'s readers was astonishing. The *Globe* printed two long rebuttals and seven letters to the editor. One rebuttal protested the projection of twentieth-century feminist ideals upon a nineteenth-century woman (even though it is, of course, a twentieth-century film). Written by someone who calls herself "a feminist and a diminutive woman," the first rebuttal also protested Gullette's use of the phrase "anorexic vulnerability." The writer argues that Ada is strong, bold, vital, and in control every moment. The rebuttal ends: "*The Piano*'s subject is the empowerment of women despite difficult circumstances, and, as an extension of that, the voices women developed when silenced by a history of submission. I am curious about the time and space [the *Globe*] devoted to condemning a film like *The Piano* . . . Gullette's article would rather make Ada a victim, and it took a lot of words and, at times, twentieth-century cliches, to do an inadequate job."[14]

The second rebuttal, also written by a woman, also takes the *Globe* to task for giving so much space to Gullette's review. The writer rejects Gullette's reading of the body-for-piano-key bargain as rape, writing, "Rape is out-of-control violence: Here, in contrast, is a lover's painstaking delight in the sight, touch, texture of the beloved."[15] And the writer concludes with a portrait of Baines as sensitive and empathic, able to communicate well not only with Ada but also with the Maoris. The seven letters published in the *Globe* expressed, in less nuanced terms, their contempt for Gullette's feminism, their sympathy for her husband, and their outrage that the *Globe* had given so much space to her review.

I think these reactions are highly significant. The genius of the movie lies in the fact that it can provoke such diametrically opposed readings. Like the aesthetic tradition on which it implicitly comments, *The Piano* would seem to be about telling, or not telling, the difference between women's violation and women's pleasure. Yet the readings are not *simply* symmetrical. Those who view it as a love story and as a reversal of sexual power roles concentrate on the *characters:* Ada is strong, willful, and in control; Baines is sensitive, restrained, and in love; Stewart is surprised by emotion and made physically vulnerable. But Gullette's reading was not based on the individual characters but on their allegorical resonance, the framework within which they operated, and on the way the *movie,* not the characters, spoke. What message does it convey? she asked. It says that women can find the way of their desire within a structure in which they are traded between men like land, ebony, and ivory. It also says that "no" means "yes." Women may be angry, but as soon as men show any restraint, sensitivity, or need, women will abandon their anger, fall in love, and adapt happily to society as it is. Nothing, therefore, needs to be changed in the social *structure.* But in that *structure,* Ada does *not* have power. Stewart and Baines may both be responding to a *sexual* power that Ada does have over them (and there is nothing new in seeing women's power as sexual), but Baines, not Ada, can decide to go away, and Stewart has the power to either mutilate her body or give her to another man. By focussing on the contrast between Stewart and Baines, rather than on the relation of domination between both men and Ada, or, for that matter, between the Europeans and the Maori, the film encourages us to value the better of the two men rather than to question the whole structure. As bell hooks has noted,[16] the film reveals an analogy among sexual violence, patriarchal power, colonialism, capitalism, and violence against the earth. By romanticizing the borderline between coercion and pleasure in the sexual domain, the film implicitly romanticizes the rest of the chain as well.

While readers of the *Boston Globe* are eager to idealize Ada's muteness—to prove that Ada is *not* a victim, that her muteness is *not* silence—they are intent on producing a silenced woman elsewhere: Margaret Gullette. Calling her "hysterical" and "strident," they castigate the *Globe* for allowing her so much space. It is as though the taboo on women's speech has simply moved to a new place. Now it is possible for Ada to say both her anger and her pleasure, but not for another woman to object to the message Ada's story might convey. The *Boston Globe* has become the new, respectable father who ought to have known how to keep his daughter mute. This recourse to *institutional* power to keep a woman from speaking is precisely what Margaret Gullette was protesting against.

Interestingly, after a period of otherwise almost unanimous critical enchantment with the film, a different kind of disgruntlement began to surface after its nine Oscar nominations. *Newsweek* quoted one "well-known producer" as saying about the pre-Oscar hype, "I think it's pretentious . . .'Aren't we artsy? We're the fancy movie.'"[17] In the same week, *New York* magazine published "Seven Reasons Not to Like *The Piano*" ("Little Girl Vomits On Beach, Too Much Mud, Too Much Ironic Symbolism, Too Much Harvey, Cruelty to Pianos, Revoke that Poetic License! and Impending Appendage Trend ('Hunter receives a très chic replacement for her severed finger. If *The Piano* wins Best Picture, won't Tiffany's want to sell authorized movie-tie-in versions? And won't they be too expensive for the people who really need them?')"[18] Somehow, Steven Spielberg's multiple nominations can translate into greatness, but Jane Campion's make her look like just another spoiled woman with expensive and artsy tastes.

Women with expensive and artsy tastes *can,* of course, be idealized, but probably only if they project an image of graceful muteness. One has only to think of the outpouring of feeling around the death of Jacqueline Kennedy Onassis to realize the genius of her adoption of the role of silent image from the moment of the assassination onward. Prior to that time, the woman with a taste for French cooking, redecoration, and Oscar Wilde was a far less idealized figure in the American press. And the contrast between Jackie O's muteness and Hillary Clinton's outspokenness only served to give cultural reinforcement to the notion that grace, dignity, and class could only be embodied by a woman who remained silent.

But the claiming of silence around the film *The Piano* turns out not to be confined to women. The *International Herald Tribune,* reporting on what it called "the backlash" against the film, speculated:

One theory holds that the initial critical blast that launched the film into the stratosphere simply stunned any doubters into silence.

Slowly, timidly, the naysayers are gathering courage to speak. Most of them appear to be men. "I defy you to tell me what that film is about," said one hyper-male Hollywood producer . . . Kurt Anderson, the editor of *New York* magazine, said, "I have discovered, to my happiness, that there are significant numbers of people like me who think it has been highly overpraised." The reluctance to carp, he speculated, may have been political: "It arrives with this feminist baggage, or presumed feminist message, that probably shuts people up."[19]

So the whole thing becomes a political game of "muteness, muteness, who's got the muteness," and feminism, having been accused of privileging silence and victimhood, now becomes so powerful that it is a cause of silencing in others.

One of the political successes of feminism, indeed, seems to reside in its understanding of the power of reclaimed silence, a power that is not unrelated to the idealization of muteness found in the aesthetic tradition. It is no accident that every actress who has been nominated for playing the part of a mute woman—Jane Wyman, Patty Duke, Marlee Matlin, and Holly Hunter—has won an Oscar. Indeed, it might be said that the recent hysteria about protecting free speech against political correctness, in implicitly claiming that white heterosexual men were being silenced, was enacting its own form of muteness envy.

Feminism seems to have become reduced, in the public mind, to complaints about sexual victimization. Recent publications exemplifying this trend, many of them written by women, include Katie Roiphe's *The Morning After: Sex, Fear, and Feminism on Campus*. I would like to look for a moment at the ways in which this book intersects with what I have been saying about culture's investment in not being able to tell the difference between female victimization and female pleasure. By calling her book "the morning after," Roiphe implicitly ties that undecidability not to a silence that does cultural work but to the question of retrospective individual interpretation ("one person's rape is another person's bad night"). Much of her irritation is directed at the rituals that have grown up around "Take Back the Night" marches on college campuses, in which women who have been raped or abused testify to their experience. What particularly disturbs her is the way in which the speeches on those occasions have tended to constitute a literary genre:

As I listen to the refrains, "I have been silent," "I was silenced," "I am finally breaking the silence," the speakers begin to blur together in my mind . . . As the vocabulary shared across campuses reveals, there is an archetype, a model, for the victim's tale. "Take Back the Night" speak-outs follow conventions as strict as any sonnet sequence or villanelle. As intimate details are squeezed into formulaic standards, they seem to be wrought with an emotion more generic than heartfelt.[20]

Perhaps inevitably, the complaint about genre leads to a complaint about false rape accusations. The power of the literary form to engender fictions becomes the danger of feminism out of control.

Yet, as we have seen, control over the undecidability between female pleasure and female violation has always already been at the heart of the literary canon. Is the "Ode on a Grecian Urn," then, a meditation on date rape? Roiphe claims that contemporary campus feminism resurrects from the Victorian era an image of women as passive sexual victims, an image that her mother's generation of feminists worked so hard to overturn. "Proclaiming victimhood," she writes, "doesn't help project strength."[21] But doesn't it? Why are so many white men so eager to claim a share in the victimhood sweepstakes? Why did Petrarch, the father of the love sonnet, insist that it was he, not Laura, who was wounded, burned, enslaved, and penetrated by love? Even if this is "just rhetoric," why has it achieved such authority? Is it just the sexual equivalent of Christianity?

To speak about female victimization is to imply that there is such a thing as a model of male power and authority that is other than victimization. But what *The Piano* so convincingly demonstrates is that that is only partly true. Yes, for every sensitive man there is a man who chops off women's fingers. But *both* men are actually depicted in the movie as in some sense powerless. Jane Campion and actor Sam Neill both describe the husband Stewart as "vulnerable."[22] And the movie pivots on George Baines's wretchedness. "I am unhappy because I want you," he tells Ada in true Petrarchan style. "My mind has seized on you and thinks of nothing else. This is how I suffer. I am sick with longing. I don't eat, I don't sleep. If you do not want me, if you have come with no feeling for me, then go!" It is in this male two-step—the axe wielder plus the manipulative sufferer, *both* of whom see themselves as powerless—that patriarchal power lies.

Far from being the opposite of authority, victimhood would seem to be the most effective *model* for authority, particularly literary and cultural authority. It is not that the victim always gets to speak—far from it—but that the most highly valued speaker gets to claim victimhood. This is what leads readers of Apollo and Daphne to see Apollo's failed rape as "loss," or readers of "the voice of the shuttle" to say that there is always *something* that violates "us." If feminism is so hotly resisted, it is perhaps less because it substitutes women's speech for women's silence than because, in doing so, it interferes with the official structures of self-pity that keep patriarchal power in place, and, in the process, tells the truth behind the beauty of muteness envy.

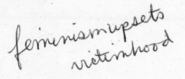
feminism upsets
victimhood

Part Three

THE "VOICE" OF
THE AUTHOR

Lesbian Spectacles: Reading *Sula, Passing, Thelma and Louise,* and *The Accused*

When I proposed this topic for a paper on "media spectacles," my intention was to push myself to try something I have never done before: to read explicitly as a lesbian, to take account of my particular desire structure in reading rather than try to make generalizations about desire as such, even lesbian desire "as such." Much has been said about the theoretical and political issues involved in what Nancy Miller calls "reading *as a.*"[1] On the one hand, to the extent that dominant discourses have used the fiction of universality to ground their authority and to silence other voices, it is important for the voices thus silenced to speak for and as themselves. But, on the other hand, just because something has been silenced doesn't mean it possesses "an" identity, knowable and stable. Speaking "as a" plunges the speaker into new questions of reliable representativity and identity, as Nancy Miller suggests. If I tried to "speak as a lesbian," wouldn't I be processing my understanding of myself through media-induced images of what a lesbian is or through my own idealizations of what a lesbian *should* be? Wouldn't I be treating as *known* the very predicate I was trying to discover? I needed a way of catching myself in the act of reading as a lesbian without having intended to.

Method

To accomplish this, I decided to look at novels or films that did *not* present themselves explicitly as "lesbian," but that could, through interpretation, be said to have a crypto-lesbian plot. I took my inspiration for such a textual category from two readings of literary texts: Barbara Smith's reading of Toni Morrison's *Sula* and Deborah McDowell's reading of Nella Larsen's novel *Passing*. I cite these critics not because they offer me examples of the act of "reading as a lesbian" (Smith does; McDowell does not) but because of the nature of the texts they read. "Despite the apparent heterosexuality of the female characters," Smith writes of *Sula,* "I discovered in rereading *Sula* that it works as a lesbian novel not only because of the passionate friendship between Sula and Nel but because of Morrison's consistently critical stance toward the heterosexual institutions of male-female relationships, marriage, and the family."[2] She grounds her reading of *Sula* in the text's description of the shared fantasies of the friends, the erotic nature of some of their games, and the ways in which the text describes them as two halves of one whole.

Deborah McDowell, who had criticized Smith's reading of *Sula* for pressing the novel into the service of a sexual persuasion, soon made her own foray into lesbian criticism, writing not as a lesbian but as a decoder of lesbian structures of desire in the text, in her reading of *Passing*.[3] After detailing the overwhelming evidence of the fact that the security-seeking, ostensibly black-identified Irene Redfield is consumed with an intense, repressed, erotic fascination with the transgressive Clare, who is passing for white even within her own marriage, McDowell concludes that the plot of racial passing is a cover for an exploration of the more dangerous question of female–female eroticism, that the sexual plot is itself "passing" as a racial plot.

In both *Passing* and *Sula,* the intensity of the relation between two women is broken by a fall into triangulation. In *Passing,* Irene imagines that her husband Brian is having an affair with the beautiful Clare. The idea comes to Irene as she looks at her husband in a mirror in which she can also see herself. That is, she projects onto Brian her own fascination with Clare. The novel ends when Clare falls, jumps, or is pushed by Irene to her death.

In contrast with *Passing,* in which there is never any proof of the affair between husband and best friend, Nel, in *Sula,* happens upon Jude and Sula in the act. She tries to howl in grief and rage but cannot until, seventy pages later, after Sula's death, she realizes that she mourns the loss of Sula, not Jude.

For me, despite Barbara Smith's excellent use of textual evidence, *Sula* does not work as a lesbian novel, while *Passing* does. My first task, then, was to explain to myself why I felt that way. Sula and Nel are certainly central to each other's lives. They achieve genuine intimacy and recognize each other's value, and the novel ends by showing how the veil of compulsory heterosexuality blinds women to the possibility of seeing each other as anything other than sexual rivals. In *Passing,* the two women remain intensely ambivalent about each other, perhaps even murderously so. Why, then, does my inner lesbometer find *Passing* more erotic than *Sula?*

I think it has to do with two things: the description of the long stare between Clare and Irene when they first meet after many years of separation, and the way in which the text is structured by Irene's constantly vowing never to see Clare again, and repeatedly going back on that vow. It is erotic to me that Irene's "no" constantly becomes a yes. The relationship is therefore overinvested and underexplained. This is what creates the effect of irresistible magnetism which is precisely *not* grounded in friendship or esteem. In *Sula,* on the other hand, while the relationship is certainly deeply invested, it is also abundantly explained. My identifying signs of a lesbian structure, then, involved protracted and intense eye contact and involuntary re-encounters ungrounded in conscious positive feelings.

To test these categories on another pair of texts, I turned to movies. I remembered my first reactions to two films, one of which has sometimes been discussed as a candidate for lesbianism, the other, to my knowledge, not. The two films are *Thelma and Louise* and *The Accused.* While *Sula* and *Passing* describe the female-female bond as existing *before* the fall into the triangulation through adultery, *Thelma and Louise* and *The Accused* both build their female-female intimacy around the consequences of rape. Because the image of the rapists is so vivid in both films, many viewers and reviewers of the films could see nothing in the films beyond a negative image of men. While I do not think that the films' critiques of male sexual violence and of patriarchal institutions are irrelevant to my attempt to view them through lesbian spectacles, I do think that to focus on what the films are saying about men is to focus on men, and thus (for me) to view the films heterosexually. Indeed, to see the films as being about the viability of heterosexuality is to make invisible the question of what is or is not happening between the women.

Thinking back to my initial reactions to the films, I remembered my very strong sense that I experienced *The Accused* as a lesbian plot while *Thelma and Louise* promised one but, for me, failed to deliver. My first justifications for these reactions might run as follows: Thelma (Geena Davis) and Louise (Susan Sarandon) hardly ever stop to look at each other—they are either looking straight down the road or Thelma's eyes are wandering toward sexually interesting men and Louise is attempting to keep Thelma's sexual appetite contained. Their intense exchange of looks and a kiss at the end comes too late to count—it is the adrenaline of death, not of desire. Their friendship is a given at the beginning, therefore there is no structure of involuntary return. My first impulse was therefore to say that their relationship was neither overinvested nor underexplained. But actually, it *is* underexplained. What are these two women doing hitting the road together? Why are they friends? What do they have in common? The point of departure of the road trip seemed to me psychologically incomprehensible, but not for that reason erotic.

In *The Accused,* on the other hand, from the moment deputy district attorney Kathryn Murphy (Kelly McGillis) picks up rape victim Sarah Tobias (Jodie Foster) in her car (and there is a lot of what Marjorie Garber calls "autoeroticism" in *both* films), the two women are intrigued by their differences, and cannot leave each other alone. The image of each woman bursting into the house of the other uninvited feels like an echo of the sexual violence around which the film is structured. That Murphy is centrally accused by Tobias of having silenced the victim she was supposed to be defending places her in a male role from which she must spend the remainder of the film redeeming herself. The long looks between the two women are looks across class, education, profession, and size. They fill each other's screen as objects of fascination, ambivalence, and transformation.

After I had finished the first draft of this paper, I looked through the literature to see whether there had not, in fact, been other lesbian interpretations of *The Accused*. The essay that sounded most promising, entitled "Up Against the Looking Glass! Heterosexual Rape as Homosexual Epiphany in *The Accused*,"[4] turned out to be a reading of the film as an indictment of heterosexuality and a confrontation for the *male* spectator with the homosexual nature of *male* spectatorship in the film. But I also found out more that I bargained for, and I'm not sure what to do with it. It seems there were rumors of an alleged affair between Kelly McGillis and Jodie Foster during the filming of *The Accused*. Was this what I was seeing in the electricity between the two actresses? Or was their alleged affair itself an *interpretation* of what was happening on the screen? In a film that from the beginning blurred the relation between art and life— McGillis herself had been raped, and Foster pursued by a psychotic literalizer of one of her previous films—it is hard to pin down the origins of a reading–effect.

However these overdeterminations may be factored in, what does it mean to say that for me *The Accused* "works" better as a lesbian film than *Thelma and Louise?* On some level, this reading does not make sense. For while Thelma and Louise eventually really get beyond any return to legal patriarchal heterosexual pseudoprotections, *The Accused* ends up validating the legal system, and Murphy and Tobias separate at the end, presumably never to meet again, each returning to a life of presumptive heterosexuality. What is lesbian about this? Isn't Murphy in the place of the one good cop in *Thelma & Louise,*[5] the tragic consciousness that sees the limitations of an institution to which in the end he nevertheless remains loyal? Certainly the relationship between Thelma and Louise is progressively more real than any relationship that is set up between Murphy and Tobias. If I do nevertheless feel that *The Accused* presents me with a plot that corresponds to my own fantasies, I have to acknowledge the role of the patriarchal institution not in impeding those fantasies but in enabling them. Murphy is attractive to me because she is a powerful woman turning her full attention toward another woman precisely *within* the patriarchal institution. It is transference onto the phallic mother, the woman whose appeal arises from her position in a power structure, that infuses my reading of the film, simple as that.

So much for reading with the unconscious.

I thus have to conclude that the project of making my own erotic unconscious participate in my reading process, far from guaranteeing some sort of radical or liberating breakthrough, brings me face to face with the political incorrectness of my own fantasy life. In a post-Foucauldian world it is perhaps more embarrassing to admit to the attraction of power than it is to confess to the appeal of violence in the era of Catharine MacKinnon. Any attempt to go on from this reading to theorize (my) lesbian desire would therefore have to confront the possibility of a real disjunction between my political ideals and my libidinal investments. But if the unconscious is structured by repetition and the political by the desire for change, there is nothing surprising about this. The question, still, would remain one of knowing what the unconscious changes, and what politics repeats.

Chapter Nine

The Alchemy of Style and Law

My turn. The story of one of my madnesses.
Arthur Rimbaud, "The Alchemy of the Word"

I have always dreamed and attempted something else, with the patience of an alchemist, ready to sacrifice all vanity and all satisfaction, as once they burned the contents and the rafters of their homes, to feed the furnace of the Great Work. What? it's hard to say . . . a book . . . the Orphic explanation of the Earth . . . whose rhythm would be impersonal and alive all the way down to its pagination . . . the Text would speak on its own, without the voice of an author.
Stéphane Mallarmé, "Autobiography"

From my two epigraphs, it can be deduced that my subject might be the relationship between madness and the existence of the impersonal book, between verbal alchemy and autobiography, between dream and sacrifice.

But my presentation is about to abandon the domain of the poetic. I promise that I will not mix genres. My assignment is to write an essay on the rhetoric of law.

The title of my paper, "The Alchemy of Style and Law," is an echo of the title of *The Alchemy of Race and Rights* by Patricia Williams, subtitled *Diary of a Law Professor*.[1]

What is to be understood by the word "alchemy"? Rather than answer that question directly, I would like to bring in a quotation from Walter Benjamin concerning the difference between a commentary and a critique: "The history of works of art prepares their

165

critique, and this is why historical distance increases their power. If, to use a simile, one views the growing work as a funeral pyre, its commentator can be likened to the chemist, its critic to an alchemist. While the former is left with wood and ashes as the sole objects of his analysis, the latter is concerned only with the enigma of the flame itself: the enigma of being alive."[2] This curious conjunction of an image of death (a funeral pyre) with a concept of life (the "enigma of being alive") will return in an unexpected way in the present essay. But for the moment, I would like simply to suggest that if "the work" in question is the entire edifice of American law, then it seems to me that Patricia Williams is undertaking its critique in exactly this sense.

Is my own title meant to suggest that style is to race as law is to rights? Am I, in other words, asserting a connection between race and style? No, if it means asserting a one-to-one correspondence between a race and a style—saying, for instance, that an author's race can be identified from his or her style, as though style were a natural and continuous and un-self-different emanation of a racial identity. But yes, if it means asserting that the intractability of racial misunderstanding or inequality might have something to do with style—both because conflict might arise from not recognizing the effects of different styles, and because certain styles are privileged over others. The ideology of style is a powerful reinforcer of hierarchy. This, at least, is one of the central tenets of Patricia Williams's critique. It is not that Patricia Williams's style can be identified as black or female, but that her writing possesses a logic that makes perceptible the realities of difference subordinated behind the rhetoric of neutrality and impersonality into which students of the law are inevitably inducted. In other words, the style of Patricia Williams is not the sign of her identity but the enactment of her critique.

It is not easy to give a capsule description of the style of Williams's book. It is not autobiography, or legal theory, or editorial, or allegory, but it partakes of all of these. It is a breakthrough book for the possibilities of a fully conscious historical subject of discourse who does not coincide with—indeed, has been subtly or overtly excluded from—the position defined as neutral, objective, impersonal. Williams analyzes the exclusions and costs of adopting that voice, the ways in which it has shaped distributions of power and privilege, the ways in which it has erased, oppressed, even killed. In a telling example, she describes the three successive edits to which one of her essays was subjected. The essay discussed effects of privatization on public accountability by narrating her experience of being kept out of a Benetton clothing store by a white sales clerk who would not press the buzzer to open the door when he saw her waiting outside. In the first edit, her anger was erased. In the second, the name of Benetton's was removed for fear of libel. In the third, all mention of her race was deleted because editorial policy forbade descriptions of physiognomy, and anyway, "any reader will know what you must have looked like when standing at that window." "This is just a matter of style," she was told. She concludes:

Ultimately I did convince the editors that mention of my race was central to the whole sense of the subsequent text; that my story became one of extreme paranoia without the information that I am black; or that it became one in which the reader had to fill in the gap by assumption, presumption, prejudgment, or prejudice. What was most interesting to me in this experience was how the blind application of principles of neutrality, through the device of omission, acted either to make me look crazy or to make the reader participate in old habits of cultural bias. (p. 48)

Again and again Williams punctures the mask of neutrality and impersonality assumed by others, showing, for instance, that when she interrogates the racism of some of the questions written by her impersonal and neutral colleagues for their law exams, they respond by taking it "personally." Again and again, the personal comes out from its hiding place whenever the ideology of neutrality is questioned.

The reader of *The Alchemy of Race and Rights* never forgets that its author speaks from a crossroads of discourses. Yet her analysis deconstructs the premises that would turn a black female law professor into an oxymoron. When she walks into a classroom, a clothing store, a street, an academic conference, everyone around her bristles with expectations, preconceptions, desires, fears, curiosities, defenses. This book is an attempt to keep just to one side of those expectations, to analyze them, to reread the social order in terms of them. The book is *not* written in function of known and expected polarities of black and white, private and public, male and female, academic and emotional, self and other. It is precisely a way of complicating, demystifying, confounding, rethinking such polarities. This is surely what explains the insistent allegorical presence of *polar* bears. Those bears, so white, so innocent, so caged, so violent, cannot be read in any simple way. Indeed, animals in Patricia Williams's text function consistently both as parables—beast fables—and as very real victims trapped in human systems of control. When she quotes a description from *The Economist* of the proper degree of socialization required to ensure the docility of pigs urged down a chute to oblivion, she does not need to transform the text's language at all for it to stand as a monstrous allegory. If academic writing or legal codes are defined through their exclusions and disconnections, then what Patricia Williams does is to find, explore, elaborate, and restore the connections among the bill of sale for her great-great grandmother, the lawyer and great-great grandfather who bought and impregnated the young slave, the contemporary homeless man on the street, the advertising industry, the academic conference circuit, a basketball camp in Hanover, New Hampshire, Christmas shopping, the Critical Legal Studies movement, and the United States Constitution. The madness of juxtaposition mimes the structure of the social text.

This daring, groundbreaking style is not without risks. In one of the more exquisitely ironic passages, Williams quotes a rejection letter from a law review which has sent back an essay with extensive comments. That is, she quoted it in the manuscript of her book, where I had read and noted it as a good example of how ordinary frames of reference obscure what Williams is doing. But when, in preparing to write this paper, I turned to the page in the published book on which I expected to find the letter quoted, I found the following:

> [A note to the reader: Logically, what should follow here is the actual letter of rejection; but the editors of Harvard University Press, on the advice of the Press's lawyers, informed me that I could not reprint it, even anonymously, without the authors' permission, which in the circumstances has not been forthcoming.] (p. 214)

Williams then concocts a fake letter to substitute for the original. In my frustration at not being able to quote the letter myself, I will here try to rephrase the gist of it and then offer my own commentary.

The editors see Williams's style as an evasive tactic. They note that she speaks of the high costs of daily traversing racial and gender boundaries, describes herself as schizophrenic and drowning, but yet also claims that it is "not just intelligent, but fashionable, feminist, and even postmodern" to be so. They complain that her calm and self-confidence impede their sympathy. They ask her whether she wouldn't be willing to take the risks of real self-exposure and write a more convincing piece.

Apart from the generally condescending and patronizing tone of this rejection letter, I think it stands as an exemplary misreading. The editors expect certain things that are highly revealing: that calm is the opposite of engagement, that to be convincing about anxiety one must demonstrate a loss of control. What seems to bother the editors is the *combination* of control and panic. They almost *want* the panic. There is nothing unfamiliar about the sight of a crazy black woman ("What's so new about a schizophrenic black lady pouring her heart out?" Williams quotes her sister as asking early in the book). What is unfamiliar is a black woman writing calmly about panic, situating her own discourse as intelligent, fashionable, feminist, and postmodern—having the kind of self-consciousness about style and reception, about genre and meta-discourse, that instates a *complex* narrative voice as something other than a symptom. The editors want to privatize the nature of Williams's writing, to see her control as a symptom rather than an accomplishment (they ask whether she is afraid of being perceived as unstable). Williams knows, in contrast, that impersonality, neutrality, and abstraction can themselves be the very *sign* of anxiety, but that that anxiety is not a *private* matter. She makes very clear the costs, the fragility, the victory, the sacrifice involved in her calm. But she extends the significance of all of that outward into the social construction of selves and others, into the crossroads and contradictions she—and not only she—traverses every day.

Patricia Williams repeatedly documents the revisions, erasures, and displacements her writing undergoes in its encounters with the rules of legal style and citation. Let me now digress a moment to describe my own small encounter with the ideology of law review style. In the fall of 1991 I was asked by the *Harvard Law Review* to write a commentary on an essay left unfinished at the death of its author.[3] The essay is entitled "A Postmodern Feminist Legal Manifesto," and the author, Mary Joe Frug, a law professor at the New England School of Law, was murdered, presumably by a stranger, on a Cambridge street. In presenting Frug's essay for publication, the editors of the *Harvard Law Review* preceded it with this note:

> The following commentary is an unfinished work. Professor Frug was working on this Commentary when she was murdered on April 4, 1991. The Editors of the *Harvard Law Review* agreed that, under the circumstances, the preservation of Mary Joe Frug's voice outweighed strict adherence to traditional editorial policy. For this reason, neither stylistic nor organizational changes have been made, and footnotes have been expanded but not added.[4]

What can be said about this departure from usual editorial procedures? It seems that it is only when the author is dead that a law review sees value in the preservation of "voice." Does the respect paid to Frug's text here have any relation to the long tradition of idealizing dead women in Western poetry? That is, is it possible for a woman to have authority only on the condition that she be dead? How does this preservation of voice as writing relate to the long philosophical tradition which, from Plato onward, tries to devalue writing as inert and secondary while voice conveys living human intentionality? It seems as though there are two no-win models for authorship here: an interactive editorial process through which a living author participates in the progressive erasure of her own words, and a textual respect that can occur only if the author is dead.

I had just finished writing the above remarks when I learned that, at the 1992 *Harvard Law Review* Banquet, the annual "spoof" issue included a parody of Mary Joe Frug's essay entitled "He-Manifesto Of Post-Mortem Legal Feminism," authored by "Mary Doe, Rigor-Mortis Professor of Law." It seems that to some of the members of the *Law Review* editorial board who had opposed the publication of Frug's unfinished manuscript, the author was not quite dead enough. The banquet, to which Frug's widower had been invited, was held on the first anniversary of Mary Joe's murder.[5]

Frug's essay concerns ways in which legal rules combine to maternalize, terrorize, and sexualize the female body so that heterosexual monogamy is a woman's safest life choice. Not only was her essay itself unfinished at her death; she got up to go out for her fatal walk in the middle of a sentence. Here is the sentence:

Women who might expect that sexual relationships with other women could

Then she gets up, she goes out, she dies. The sentence dangles in the middle of the essay, which continues for another nine pages.

Now my assignment is to read the text. Critics of contemporary literary theory have attacked the concept of the death of the author, especially of Paul de Man's statement that "death is a displaced name for a linguistic predicament,"[6] but here I precisely *encountered* Mary Joe Frug's death as a linguistic predicament. In my commentary, I wrote about this sentence, calling it "the lesbian gap," and asking, "How does this gap signify?" I sent my commentary to the *Harvard Law Review* for its round of editorial responses. When it came back from its first reading, the editors had changed "How does this gap signify?" to "What does this gap mean?" This is not at all the same question. "*What* does the gap mean" implies that it *has* a meaning, and all I have to do is to figure out what it is. "*How* does the gap signify" raises the *question* of what it means to mean, raises meaning as a question, implies that the gap *has to be read,* but that it can't be presumed to have been intended. The *Law Review* responded as if to question the mode or possibility of meaning was to speak a foreign language. In every successive revision that my text underwent, the *how* was again changed to *what.* From this I learned that legal editing is a resistance to opening up meaning as a question, as a non-given, as a bafflement, as the possibility that what is intended and what is readable might not be the same. The ideology of law review style attempts to create a world saturated with meaning, without gaps, and, indeed, doubtless without lesbians. It is no accident that the double gap occurs at the point at which the text would have spoken of that which Queen Victoria defined as impossible. How can two absences add up to anything legally recognizable? If lesbianism here stands as that which escapes the regime of the phallus, and if, as the privileged signifier of patriarchal relations, the phallus stands as the guarantor of meaning, then it seems all too fitting that Mary Joe Frug's text should exit the sayable precisely at this point.

"Style is the man," proclaimed Buffon in his acceptance speech to the French Academy. And Patricia Williams begins her book, "Since subject position is everything in my analysis of the law, you deserve to know that it's a bad morning." The connection between style and subject position, between subject position and subjective discourse, is both manipulated and parodied by this opening. For if subject position *is* everything in Patricia Williams's analysis of the law, it is not because of her moods. The apparatus of confession appears, but is not the place of subject position. To get at what is, I cite Lacan's rewriting of Buffon: "Style is the man, the man I am addressing." If style is thus constructed out of the other, whom might we say Patricia Williams is addressing? In a review in the *New York Times Book Review,* Wendy Kaminer criticizes Williams's style for its failures of address:

> Describing her encounters with students and deans or strangers on the street, recalling her family history and analyzing recent criminal cases, she darts from conversation to discourse. The result is an alternately engaging and tedious book with valuable insights, weighed down by the baroque, encoded language of post-structural legal and literary theory.
>
> How did it become de rigueur to protest oppression in a language of elites? If Ms. Williams believes that "theoretical legal understanding and social transformation need not be oxymoronic," why doesn't she simply say that scholars can be activists too? How socially transformative are academics talking to one another in a code that may take several years of graduate school to crack? Secret words and grueling initiation rites make sure that the power to critique power will not be freely shared. Ms. Williams defends her emotive, first-person theorizing, but that's not what troubles me. The first person invites us in but the language shuts us out, and her diary finally seems less personal than private, self-enclosed. Readers outside

a small circle of post-structural theorists may be not only be-fuddled, but too alienated by her exclusive discourse to stay with it. And that could be their loss as well as hers.[7]

While I do not think that the issues Kaminer raises here are non-issues, I want to focus on her assumptions about Williams's intentions. The reviewer clearly thinks she knows that Williams's language is the language of protest, and that what she means to say is that scholars can be activists too. This implies that Williams's main goal is to recommend action. But the quotation that is said to be equivalent to "scholars can be activists," is "theoretical legal under-standing and social transformation need not be oxymoronic." That is, Williams is talking about rhetoric, not directly about reality. Her object of analysis is first and foremost *language* and other forms of non-transparent representation, and the ways in which they allow certain things to be sayable and other things erased. The reviewer assumes that Williams is addressing—should be addressing—readers outside the academy, outside the circle of theorists. But does this mean that the academy should not be addressed? Do most legal the-orists write for the general public? If an argument has public impli-cations, must it conform to a rhetoric of the common reader? Isn't part of Williams's point that the articulations agreed upon in acade-mic and elite circles have so pervasive and yet hidden an effect on social structures that it might be well to meet them on their own ground? Of course, Williams's writing is generally no more likely to be welcomed by the legal academy than by the general public. In her repeated encounters with the way in which editorial boards and other institutions of style attempt to dictate what and how she writes, Williams lays bare the network of constraints and censorships that attempt to produce "plain, readable prose." In other words, what Kaminer seems to call for as a transparently readable style may be produced through just as much displacement and erasure as a style that displays its discontinuous multi-layeredness.

When Kaminer complains that "The first person invites us in but the language shuts us out," I don't think she is wrong. This effect of being at once open and closed, at once revealing and concealing, *is*, I think, strategically and explicitly intended by Williams. In one of her opening moves, she presents a conversation between herself and her sister, a dialogue in which neither sister hears, understands, or responds directly to the other, in which Williams gives a very clear statement of her intentions in writing this book, but in the embedded, self-parodic form of half a dialogue of the deaf. Communication is here represented as fundamentally missed. Williams describes her project as one of "writing in a way that reveals the intersubjectivity of legal constructions, that forces the reader both to participate in the construction of meaning and to be conscious of that process," but the moment the sister seems to catch on and pay attention, alert, ears pricked, nose quivering, Williams can only say to her, "My, what big teeth you have." The "intersubjectivity of legal constructions" is based not on a model of transitive communication, but on a dialogue of profound discontinuity.

What Williams means by subject position, in other words, involves the ways in which *she* displays herself *as constructed by others*. Her style becomes the style of the other addressing *her*. Almost half the book is taken up with reports of the ways in which she is read. She offers rejection letters, student evaluations, departmental memos, newspaper reports of talks she has given—the book is filled with scenes of reading like the following:

> A man with whom I used to work once told me that I made too much of my race. "After all," he said, "I don't even think of you as black." Yet sometime later, when another black woman became engaged in an ultimately unsuccessful tenure battle, he confided to me that he wished the school could find more blacks like me. I felt myself slip in and out of shadow, as I became nonblack for purposes of inclusion and black for purposes of exclusion; I felt the boundaries of my very body manipulated, casually inscribed by definitional demarcations that did not refer to me. (pp. 9–10)

The following quotation from Gayatri Spivak stands, I think, as a fitting definition of the notion of subject position as it is wielded by Williams:

> Quite often when we say "subject position" we reduce it to a kind of confessional attitudinizing. We say, "I'm white, I'm black, I'm a mulatto, I am male, I'm bourgeois." A subject position is not, in fact, a confessional self-description either in praise or in dis-praise . . . This is because the position of the subject *can be assigned* . . . and "assigned" means, I think, that it can and must become a sign; not for the person who speaks, but for the person who listens, not for the person who writes,

who can say what she likes about who she is, but for the person who reads. When, in fact, the responsible reader reads the sign that is the subject position of the speaker or the writer, it becomes the sign, let us say, of an ethno-politics, of a psycho-sexual reality, or an institutional position, and this is not under the control of the person who speaks. She cannot diagnose herself; we are given over to our readers.[8]

What Williams has accomplished in *The Alchemy of Race and Rights* is the writing of the giving of herself over to her readers and her reading of those readings.

Let us look again at Williams's parodic use of the question of subject position in the opening of her first chapter.

Since subject position is everything in my analysis of the law, you deserve to know that it's a bad morning. I am very depressed. It always takes a while to sort out what's wrong, but it usually starts with some kind of perfectly irrational thought such as: I *hate* being a lawyer. This particular morning I'm sitting up in bed reading about redhibitory vices. A redhibitory vice is a defect in merchandise which, if existing at the time of purchase, gives rise to a claim allowing the buyer to return the thing and to get back part or all of the purchase price. (p. 3)

The mix of genres and expectations has already begun: parodic self-description, parodic direct address to the reader, irrationality, official legal definition of a contract violation. The case Williams quotes further disconcerts expectations: it is an 1835 decision from

Louisiana, the merchandise in question is a human being, a slave named Kate, and the vice in question is craziness. It seems the merchandise was crazy and ran away, and that the seller knew she had the vice when he sold her. The seller counters with the argument that she is not crazy but stupid, a defect against which he did not warrant. Two things leap out of this case as a first example in a book of legal theory: the law in question involves the structure of a catch 22: if you run away, you are crazy; but wouldn't you have to be crazy *not* to want to run away from slavery? The law, in other words, can make a stance of sanity impossible. Legally. Second observation: Williams's own "irrational thought" mirrors the "craziness" of the slave. What rationality is, is clearly going to be constantly in question in this book. Williams goes on:

> As I said, this is the sort of morning when I hate being a lawyer, a teacher, and just about everything else in my life. It's all I can do to feed the cats. I let my hair stream wildly and the eyes roll back in my head.
>
> So you should know that this is one of those mornings when I refuse to compose myself properly; you should know you are dealing with someone who is writing this in an old terry bathrobe with a little fringe of blue and white tassels dangling from the hem, trying to decide if she is stupid or crazy. (p. 4)

This opening resembles nothing so much as the beginning of another text in which subject position, rationality, and madness come together:

Everything which I have thus far accepted as entirely true and assured has been acquired from the senses or by means of the senses. But I have learned by experience that these senses sometimes mislead me, and it is prudent never to trust wholly those things which have once deceived us.

But it is possible that, even though the senses occasionally deceive us about things which are barely perceptible and very far away, there are many other things which we cannot reasonably doubt, even though we know them through the senses—as, for example, that I am here, seated by the fire, wearing a winter dressing gown, holding this paper in my hands, and other things of this nature. And how could I deny that these hands and this body are mine, unless I am to compare myself with certain lunatics whose brain is so troubled and befogged by the black vapors of the bile that they continually affirm that they are kings while they are paupers, that they are clothed in gold and purple while they are naked; or imagine that their head is made of clay, or that they are gourds, or that their body is glass? But this is ridiculous; such men are fools, and I would be no less insane than they if I followed their example.[9]

The author, of course, is René Descartes. In his synopsis of the six *Meditations,* Descartes describes the usefulness of the progress of methodical doubt as the peeling away of uncertainties: "Although it is not immediately apparent that so general a doubt can be useful, it is in fact very much so, since it delivers us from all sorts of prejudices and makes available to us an easy method of accustoming our minds to become independent of the senses" (p. 71). Williams's book is, among other things, a meditation on the madness of accustoming the mind to become independent of the senses, the ways in which such a dissociation *underwrites* rather than eliminates prejudices.

It can hardly be an accident that Williams's opening mirrors and inverts Descartes's gestures of instatement of the self-present thinking subject in his dressing-gown, holding "this" paper, concluding *both* that what I cannot doubt is that I am, *and* that I who am (rational), am not mad. Williams relocates the human subject within the framework of historical, legal, and corporeal intersubjectivity. She charts the exclusions and omissions that have gone into the construction of the impersonal, neutral, authoritative—indeed, Cartesian—legal subject, just as Descartes himself does, and she makes readable her own mobile subject position as a floating signifier:

> I pause for a moment and gaze out the train window. My life, I think, has become one long stream of text, delivered on the run to gatherings of mostly strangers. It is a strange period in my life, watching the world whiz by, these brazen moments of intimate revelation to no one in particular in my declared challenge to the necessary juxtaposition of the personal with the private. In some odd way, it is as though the question with which I began—Who Am I—has become reconstituted into Where Am I. (p. 16)

Where Descartes's search for certainty leads him to conclude: I think therefore I am, Williams demonstrates again and again that I am where I am thought by, and think, the other.

The Postmodern in Feminism:
A Response to Mary Joe Frug

Author's note: the following is a response solicited by the Harvard Law Review to an unfinished essay by Mary Joe Frug entitled, "A Postmodern Feminist Legal Manifesto."[1] When Professor Frug was murdered on April 4, 1991, the Law Review decided to published the essay in its unfinished state followed by three responses.

"A Postmodern Feminist Legal Manifesto": how do the words of Mary Joe Frug's title fit together in her argument? She begins, "I am worried about the title of this article." What is there to worry about? The two words Frug immediately points to as problematic are "postmodern" and "manifesto," implicitly leaving "feminist" and "legal" as unproblematic, at least for the moment ("legal" will never become a problem in the essay, while the becoming-unsettled of "feminist" is, as we shall see, central to it). "Manifesto" causes a slight anxiety of influence (is she just copying Catharine MacKinnon copying Marx?), but "manifesto" soon ceases to chafe (the question of Frug's relation to MacKinnon, however, will return). "Postmodern" is the word that remains as a question, and that question structures Frug's argument in complex and significant ways.

Interestingly, Frug is not the only feminist legal theorist to express uneasiness about the word "postmodern." In a footnote to the introduction to her book *Beyond Accommodation,* "Writing the Mamafesta: The Dilemma of Postmodern Feminism," Drucilla Cornell writes:

> I use the word "postmodern" reluctantly. The very idea that periods of history can be rigidly separated is one I reject. More importantly, "postmodern" has become a catch-all phrase that defines very different philosophical positions as giving a similar message. As a result, we can potentially lose what is unique in the different positionings.
>
> That being said, I use the word anyway. It indicates both a longing—a longing certainly consistent with this book—that we not be fated to entrapment by the political and ethical concepts of feminism identified as modern. Those concepts fail to give significance to sexual difference as a philosophical question.[2]

Unwarranted difference, loss of difference, difference as a philosophical question: Cornell's ambivalence toward the word "postmodern" relates to its capacity both to regulate difference (by naming a periodization of before and after, by grouping together things that are distinct) and to liberate difference (by naming a project of escape from "modern" concepts that fail to see difference philosophically). But what are we to make of the "both" ("*both* a longing . . .") that is followed by no "and"? This is not the last of the gaps we will encounter.

Frug, too, worries about chronology—not about the possibility of separating before from after, but about the fear that the "after" may already be past. Postmodernism, for some readers, may be just a stale popover. On the other hand, for other readers, far from being tasty but slight, postmodernism may rather be significant but indigestible: it "may refer to such an elaborate and demanding genre" that one paper cannot hope to get it right. Caught between the dismissable and the attackable, Frug, after connecting her marginal "pm"'s to "premenstrual" and "postmenopausal" (thus playfully moving the question of periodization to the realm of the female body, on which the rest of her article will focus), decides to "note the discomfort and keep going." This gesture instates a logic of honesty, a refusal to offer unwarranted certainty, that characterizes the essay as a whole.

What, then, does Mary Joe Frug mean by "postmodernism"? She discusses three different ways of understanding it: (a) it is a certain style characterized by wordplay; (b) it is a way of seeing language as an agent of social construction; and (c) it is a way of seeing the human subject as decentered, polymorphous, and indeterminate.

Of these three definitions, the first is the one that seems least to characterize Frug's essay. Unlike Drucilla Cornell, she does not gesture toward James Joyce, Jacques Derrida, or Hélène Cixous as a stylistic influence.[3] She neither cites such authorities nor attempts to write like them. She does not, however, go so far as to see stylistic playfulness as being fundamentally at odds with feminist earnestness. "Although the flip, condescending, and mocking tones that often characterize postmodernism may not capture the intensity

185

and urgency that frequently motivate feminist legal scholarship, the postmodern style does not strike me as 'politically incorrect.'" Indeed, a style that challenges linear arguments and undermines singular, dominant interpretations may well have oppositional force. If linearity and clarity are themselves instruments of the system that enforces existing power relations in society, then stylistic experimentation might operate as a kind of guerilla warfare on the level of language. Nevertheless, Frug continues, "I don't think feminist legal activists need to adopt the postmodern medium in order to exploit the postmodern message; my point about the style is simply that it doesn't require us, strategically, to dismiss postmodernism as an influence on our work." While Frug had previously mentioned the inseparability of medium and message as one of the possible tenets of postmodernism, here she recommends that "we" (feminist legal activists) not throw out the message with the medium. Activism may require a stance of opposition based on either/or logic in most cases, but feminist activists do not have to choose to be for or against postmodernism, nor does a feminist who is "for" it have to choose to consider the postmodern "message" inseparable from the postmodern "style." Rather than looking for a position of theoretical purity, Frug gives herself the right to take what she can use.

What, then, is the postmodern "message" that feminist activists can employ? It has to do with the role of language in the construction of sexual difference: "The postmodern position locating human experience as inescapably within language suggests that feminists should not overlook the constructive function of legal language as a critical frontier for feminist reforms. To put this 'prin-

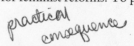
practical consequence

ciple' more bluntly, legal discourse should be recognized as a site of political struggle over sex differences." If sex differences are given by "nature," the liberatory potential of legal reform is narrowed; if legal discourse is seen as integral to the social construction of the very differences that seem most immutable, then the scope of reform is broadened. Frug focusses on the very terrain on which the social construction thesis seems the most debatable: the relationship of law to the female body.

> Since the anatomical distinctions between the sexes seem not only "natural" but fundamental to identity, proposing and describing the role of law in the production of the meaning of the female body seems like the most convincing subject with which to defend my case. In the following subsections, I will argue that legal rules—like other cultural mechanisms—encode the female body with meanings. Legal discourse then explains and rationalizes these meanings by an appeal to the "natural" differences between the sexes, differences that the rules themselves help to produce. The formal norm of legal neutrality conceals the way in which legal rules participate in the construction of those meanings.

Frug then goes on to argue that legal rules, through the wage labor market, the criminal justice system, and the patriarchal marriage system, overdetermine women's choice of heterosexuality, monogamy, and passivity through the terrorization, maternalization, and sexualization of the female body. Focussing on the case of prostitution, Frug analyzes the ways in which the "random, demeaning, and sometimes brutal character of anti-prostitution law enforcement" exploits, criminalizes, and alienates female sexuality, ensures its continued control by and for men, maximizes the insecurity of the sex worker, and contributes to many women's fear of "looking like a whore." The combined effect of defining women as weak, nurturing, and sexy, keeping women's wages low, and setting up images of the "other" woman as an identity baffle, is to produce the faithful wife and mother as the only safe identity for women.

In this central section of her argument, Frug writes in a style that is about as far from nonlinear, multivalent postmodernism as is imaginable. On the contrary, she displays a preternatural confidence in the grammar of the declarative sentence, especially the declarative sentence that begins with "legal rules" as its subject. Sentence after sentence takes the form: "Legal rules" + active verb (permit, construct, mandate, facilitate, deny, encourage, prohibit, restrict, allow, enscript, compel, assign, promote, favor, deter, influence, designate, create . . .) + consequences for women. The cumulative rhetorical effect of these sentences is to reinforce the claim they contain: by making "legal rules" the subject of at least eighty sentences in the essay, Mary Joe Frug underlines the *agency* of the law in determining the shape of women's lives.

The political force of such an argument depends on its reliance on sex differences understood in binary terms. Men are constructed one way; women another. Injustice inheres in the way in which law constructs women as different from men. Reform involves changing the workings of such constructions. But for some feminists, the social construction thesis taken to its logical extreme threatens to undermine the very grounds of intervention: "The social construction thesis is useful to feminists in so far as it informs and supports our efforts to improve the condition of women in law. If, or when, the social construction thesis seems about to deconstruct the basic category of woman, its usefulness to feminism is problematized; how can we build a political coalition to advance the position of women in law if the subject that drives our efforts is 'indeterminate,' 'incoherent,' or 'contingent'"? Once again, Frug notes the discomfort and goes on. This third definition of postmodernism, the indeterminacy thesis, is one she neither embraces nor rejects. Frug here refers to ongoing feminist debates in which it is argued that effective political action requires a determinate constituency or definable identity in order effectively to oppose the forces of oppression. If we can't define the word "woman," how can we speak of "woman's oppression"? How can women be liberated or empowered if there is uncertainty about what the word "woman" means? On the other hand, isn't it precisely the ways in which "woman" has been restrictively defined by patriarchy that have been oppressive? Is the problem with *particular* definitions of "woman" or with the very attempt to define "woman" at all? Is there any definition that fits *all* women? If not, how can the project of women's liberation be undertaken? Frug's decision not to consider the indeterminacy thesis politically disabling as such allows her to encounter the same questions in a much more productive form at the end of her essay.

If the social construction thesis is the ground on which reform can be built, what are the reforms Mary Joe Frug might recom-

[handwritten marginal note: fundamental feminist problem]

mend? It quickly becomes clear that Frug's analysis is not driven by the desire to promote any *particular* legal alteration. In the case of prostitution, she details several *different* feminist positions on decriminalization and legalization, emphasizes the promise of commonality, and does not choose:

> For me, the promise of postmodern legal feminism lies in the juncture of feminist politics and the genealogy of the female body in law. It is in this juncture that we can simultaneously deploy the commonalities among real women, in their historically situated, material circumstances, and at the same time challenge the conventional meanings of "woman" that sustain the subordinating conditions of women's lives.
>
> I do not think that the sex worker claims for legalization constitute *the* postmodern feminist legal voice. I am also unsure whether I support their position on legalization. But I believe that my analysis of the decriminalization dispute in which they are participating illustrates how postmodern legal feminism can seek and claim different voices, voices which will challenge the power of the congealed meanings of the female body which legal rules and legal discourse permit and sustain.

The tension between commonality and difference is not emphasized here, but it is readable both in Frug's uncertainty about her own position, and in her recourse to a rhetoric of challenge. It may not be clear what the feminist position should be, but the very existence of the discussion is in itself a challenge to congealed and conventional meanings of the female body. The anxiety or uncertainty about relations among women is transformed into confidence by turning it outward onto legal rules and legal discourse. This structure will repeat itself in a much more acute and self-conscious way in the example of the anti-pornography ordinance with which Frug ends her essay.

But it is also readable in a different way in the vanishing point of the essay, in what might be called the lesbian gap. In Frug's discussion of the ways in which legal rules induce women to choose heterosexuality, her text abruptly breaks off. We read:

Women who might expect that sexual relationships with other women could

[to be completed by:

economic and security incentives which make a male partner more advantageous for non-sexual reasons than a same-sex partner for women.

This passage, which so graphically marks Mary Joe Frug's death, also enacts a silence that is not, I think, absolutely contingent. Coming in the context of an argument that relies so heavily on a subject-verb structure, the fact that this fragment is missing not one but two verbs makes the gap all the more resonant. Why does the blank occur here? How does this gap signify?

It is not my intention to wonder about Mary Joe Frug's motivations, but to see this gap as one that is repeated in other forms in her argument. What goes unsaid here is an image of relations between women. What is said instead is the systemic obstacle to such relations. This is the *same* logic, in other words, as that we noted above.

The final case discussed in Frug's article is the campaign spearheaded by Catharine MacKinnon and Andrea Dworkin to enact an ordinance making it legally possible for women to recover for harm done them by pornography. Frug describes the case against pornography and the debate it engendered among feminists, including the painful effects of MacKinnon's polemical denial of the name "feminist" to anyone who opposed the ordinance. Frug also states that she does not particularly regret the anti-pornography ordinance defeat. She critiques MacKinnon for relying on an absolute dichotomy of gender and for nevertheless employing a "masculine" style of argument. But it is the intensity of the conflicts among feminists that mobilizes her attention. "The ordinance campaign fascinates me," she writes; and later, "The polarization of the feminist legal community during the ordinance campaign was terrifying to me." She concludes:

I believe the divisions the campaign produced among feminists constituted an important challenge to the polarization of the world by gender. The closing lesson I want to draw from the anti-pornography campaign about feminist organization is the observation that exploring, pursuing, and accepting differences among women and differences among sexual practices is necessary to challenge the oppression of women by sex. Only when sex means more than male or female, only when the

word "woman" cannot be coherently understood, will oppression by sex be fatally undermined.

It is precisely when the word "feminist" becomes problematic that
the essay becomes truly postmodern. In this analysis of the anti-
pornography campaign, Frug does not self-consciously dissect the
indeterminacy of woman as a theoretical issue (as she does in the
earlier section), but rather shows how in real life, as feminists split
and debate, the notion of woman—or feminist—is shown to have
more than one meaning, to be a subject of dispute in its own right.
The "incoherence" of "woman" is not posited as a theoretical
premise but *encountered* in the engagement with the heterogeneity
of "real women." Far from being at odds with material existence,
indeterminacy is what is produced by it. Indeterminacy is important not because it is an inherent problem within language but because the project of bringing about change on the basis of a category like "woman" will eventually encounter the lack of fit
between "woman" and the heterogeneous reality of women. And
it will encounter that lack of fit as a *political* problem. Indeterminacy, then, is not the property of a sign—the *word* "woman"—but
the outcome of an analysis and a politics. The multivalence of
"woman" is not a conclusion, but a place to begin the analysis
again, a political imperative to go on. At the same time, it becomes
obvious that one cannot simply "go on" without taking another
look at the logic of the language one is using to do so. The fact that
Frug's own essay combines a firm reliance on the logic of the transitive sentence ("legal rules mandate *X*") with an encounter with

193

the impossibility of continuing to formulate a feminist project in such terms ("feminists oppose pornography") makes the necessity of thinking about language and logic all the more imperative.

Does this imperative have anything to do with the "lesbian gap" that the text leaves open? I think it does, in the following sense: as long as a feminist analysis polarizes the world by gender, women are still standing *facing* men. Standing against men, or against patriarchy, might not be structurally so different from existing *for* it. A feminist logic that pits women against men operates along the lines of heterosexual thinking. But conflicts *among* feminists require women to pay attention to each other, to take each other's reality seriously, to face each other. This requirement that women face each other may not have anything erotic or sexual about it, but it may have everything to do with the eradication of the misogyny that remains within feminists, and with the attempt to escape the logic of heterosexuality. It places difference *among* women rather than exclusively *between* the sexes. Of course, patriarchy has always played women off against each other and manipulated differences among women for its own purposes. Nevertheless, feminists have to take the risk of confronting and negotiating differences among women if we are ever to transform such differences into positive rather than negative forces in women's lives.

It was this confrontation with the real differences among women that Mary Joe Frug found both "fascinating" and "terrifying" about the ordinance campaign. She noted the discomfort, the fascination, the terror, but could not go on. It is up to us to go on in her place.

Notes

Introduction

1. For an illuminating discussion of some of these debates, see Marianne Hirsch and Evelyn Fox Keller, eds., *Conflicts in Feminism* (New York: Routledge, 1990).

2. "A Conversation about Race and Class," Mary Childers and bell hooks, in Hirsch and Keller, eds., *Conflicts in Feminism,* p. 70.

3. Teresa de Lauretis, "Sexual Indifference and Lesbian Representation," in *The Lesbian and Gay Studies Reader,* ed. Henry Abelove, Michele Aina Barale, and David Halperin (New York: Routledge, 1993).

4. Joan W. Scott, "Deconstructing Equality-Versus-Difference: Or, the Uses of Poststructuralist Theory for Feminism," in Hirsch and Keller, eds., *Conflicts in Feminism,* p. 142.

5. Martha Minow, *Making All the Difference* (Ithaca: Cornell University Press, 1990), p. 21.

6. Minow, p. 23.

7. Jacqueline Rose, *Sexuality in the Field of Vision* (London: Verso, 1986), p. 5.

8. Gayatri Chakravorty Spivak, "Feminism and Deconstruction, again: Negotiating with Unacknowledged Masculinism" in *Between Feminism and Psychoanalysis,* ed. Teresa Brennan (London: Routledge, 1989), p. 209.

9. Hortense Spillers, "'All the Things You Could Be by Now, If Sigmund Freud's Wife Was Your Mother': Psychoanalysis and Race," *Boundary 2* 23:3 (1996), pp. 75–76.

10. Sigmund Freud, "An Autobiographical Study," *Standard Edition* (London: The Hogarth Press, 1959) vol. xx, p. 9.

11. Analyses of Freud's relation to Judaism are numerous and fascinating, and have been another ingredient in the current interest in "psychoanalysis and race." See Marthe Robert, *From Oedipus to Moses: Freud's Jewish Identity* (Garden City, N.J.: Anchor Books, 1976); Peter Gay, *A Godless Jew* (New Haven: Yale University Press, 1987); Yosef Hayim Yerushalmi, *Freud's Moses: Judaism Terminable and Interminable* (New Haven: Yale University Press, 1991); Sander Gilman, *Freud, Race, and Gender* (Princeton, N.J.: Princeton University Press, 1993).

12. *"Race," Writing, and Difference,* ed. Henry Louis Gates, Jr. (Chicago: University of Chicago Press, 1986), p. 19.

13. *Female Subjects in Black and White,* ed. Elizabeth Abel, Barbara Christian, Helene Moglen (Berkeley: University of California Press, 1997), p. 3.

14. Jane Gallop, "Criticizing Feminist Criticism," in Hirsch and Keller, eds., *Conflicts in Feminism.*

1. Is Female to Male as Ground Is to Figure?

1. Page references, given in the text, are to Nathaniel Hawthorne, *The Celestial Railroad and Other Stories* (New York: Signet, 1963); *The Charlotte Perkins Gilman Reader,* ed. Ann J. Lane (New York: Pantheon, 1980); and Sigmund Freud, *Dora: An Analysis of a Case of Hysteria* (New York: Collier, 1963), abbreviated, where necessary, as *Dora.* My reading of *Dora* has been greatly illuminated by Charles Bernheimer and Claire Kahane's anthology, *In Dora's Case: Freud, Hysteria, Feminism* (New York: Columbia University Press, 1985).

2. Sherry Ortner, "Is Female to Male as Nature is to Culture?" in *Woman, Culture, and Society,* ed. Michelle Zimbalist Rosaldo and Louise Lamphere (Stanford: Stanford University Press, 1974).

3. It might at first sight appear that my question ought to be asked the other way around, particularly with regard to the visual arts, where the "figure" of the woman is often at the center of a representation as the very image of beauty. I would say that the centrality of the female figure in such cases is not an indication of true gynocentrism but rather is structured like a fetish, i.e.,

the woman as idealized *object* is really a substitute for the phallus. Usually anonymous, allegorical, and pictorial, the woman as figure is very much a projection of the shaping male gaze. See Susan Gubar, "'The Blank Page' and the Issues of Female Creativity," in *Writing and Sexual Difference,* ed. Elizabeth Abel (Chicago: University of Chicago Press, 1982), for a convincing argument about the literary position of women as ground, substrate, blank slate to be written upon.

4. Douglas Hofstadter, *Gödel, Escher, Bach* (New York: Vintage Books, 1980), p. 67.

5. Sigmund Freud, "Female Sexuality," in *Sexuality and the Psychology of Love* (New York: Collier, 1963), p. 199, henceforth abbreviated as FS.

6. Joel Fineman, *Representations* 4 (Fall 1983), p. 70. Neil Hertz's essay is titled "Medusa's Head: Male Hysteria under Political Pressure." It appeared in the same issue as Fineman's reply.

7. Gubar, "'The Blank Page' and the Issues of Female Creativity."

8. Many readers have seen Aylmer's response to the birthmark as a response to female sexuality. It is instructive, however, to see the terms in which they gloss this. Simon O. Lesser, for instance, suggests that the mark "may represent female sexuality—that is, be a castration symbol" (*Fiction and the Unconscious* [Boston: Beacon Press, 1957], p. 88). If the figure is not read as recursive, female sexuality can only be read as castration.

9. See, for example, Annette Kolodny, "A Map for Rereading," in *the New Feminist Criticism,* ed. Elaine Showalter (New York: Pantheon, 1985), and Paula Treichler, "Escaping the Sentence," *Tulsa Studies in Women's Literature* 3 (Spring/Fall 1984).

10. For a truly recursive ("resisting") reading of "The Birthmark," see Judith Fetterly, *The Resisting Reader* (Bloomington: Indiana University Press, 1978), pp. 22–33.

11. It may be necessary to recall that the conference for which this essay was written took place in Normal, Illinois, in May, 1986.

12. Luce Irigaray, *Speculum* (Paris: Minuit, 1974).

13. See Gayatri Chakravorty Spivak, "French Feminism in an International Frame," and Naomi Schor, "Female Paranoia," both in *Feminist Readings: French Texts/American Contexts, Yale French Studies* 62 (1981).

14. Isak Dinesen, "The Blank Page," *The Norton Anthology of Literature by Women,* ed. Sandra Gilbert and Susan Gubar (New York: Norton, 1985), p. 1419.

2. *The Quicksands of the Self*

1. Quoted in Deborah McDowell's introduction to Nella Larsen, *Quicksand and Passing* (New Brunswick, N.J.: Rutgers University Press, 1986), p. ix. All references to *Quicksand* are to this edition.

2. Cf. Du Bois's famous formulation from *The Souls of Black Folk:* "It is a peculiar sensation, this double-consciousness, this sense of always looking at one's self through the eyes of others, of measuring one's soul by the tape of a world that looks on in amused contempt and pity. One ever feels his twoness,—an American, a Negro; two souls, two thoughts, two unreconciled strivings; two warring ideals in one dark body, whose dogged strength alone keeps it from being torn asunder" (*Three Negro Classics* [New York: Avon, 1965], p. 215).

3. Nathan Huggins, *The Harlem Renaissance* (New York: Oxford University Press, 1971), p. 236.

4. Hortense Spillers, "Notes on an Alternative Model—Neither/Nor," in *The Difference Within,* ed. Elizabeth Meese and Alice Parker (Amsterdam: John Benjamins, 1989), pp. 165–166.

5. Epigraph to Nella Larsen, *Quicksand,* in *Quicksand and Passing,* ed. Deborah McDowell (New Brunswick, N.J.: Rutgers University Press, 1986). All references to *Quicksand* are to this edition.

6. Hiroko Sato, "Under the Harlem Shadow: A Study of Jessie Fauset and Nella Larsen," in *The Harlem Renaissance Remembered,* ed. Arna Bontemps (New York: Dodd, Mead & Company, 1972), p. 84.

7. Cheryl Wall, "Passing for What? Aspects of Identity in Nella Larsen's Novels," *Black American Literature Forum* 20:1–2 (Spring–Summer 1986), p. 109.

8. Mary Helen Washington, *Invented Lives* (Garden City, N.J.: Anchor, 1987), pp. 159–160.

9. Heinz Kohut, *The Analysis of the Self* (New York: International Universities Press, 1971), p. xv.

10. Hazel Carby, *Reconstructing Womanhood* (New York: Oxford University Press, 1987), p. 169.

11. Nella Larsen, "Sanctuary," *The Forum,* January 1930, p. 18.

12. Mary V. Dearborn, *Pocahontas's Daughters* (New York: Oxford University Press, 1986), p. 57.

13. I would like to thank Beth Helsinger for suggesting this.

14. While the plagiarism episode may indeed have cast a long shadow on Larsen's writing, it is clear from Thadious Davis's biography (*Nella Larsen: Novelist of the Harlem Renaissance* [Baton Rouge, Louisiana State University Press, 1994]) that there were many other reasons for Larsen's failure to publish. She did apparently complete at least one manuscript, of which no copy survives.

3. The Re(a)d and the Black

1. Reprinted in *The Richard Wright Reader,* ed. Ellen Wright and Michel Fabre (New York: Harper & Row, 1978), p. 37.

2. Richard Wright, *Native Son* (New York: Harper & Row, 1940), pp. 391–392.

3. James Baldwin, "Alas, Poor Richard," in *Nobody Knows My Name* (New York: Laurel, 1961), p. 151.

4. Richard Wright, *Black Boy* (New York: Harper & Row, 1945), pp. 132–133.

5. See Elisabeth Bronfen, *Over Her Dead Body* (New York: Routledge, 1992).

6. Richard Wright, review of *Their Eyes Were Watching God* by Zora Neale Hurston, *New Masses*, October 5, 1937, p. 26.

4. "Aesthetic" and "Rapport" in Toni Morrison's Sula

1. Renita Weems, " 'Artists Without an Art Form': A Look at One Black Woman's World of Unrevered Black Women," in Barbara Smith, ed., *Home*

Girls: A Black Feminist Anthology (New York: Kitchen Table—Women of Color Press, 1983), p. 95.

2. Houston A. Baker, Jr., "When Lindbergh Sleeps with Bessie Smith: The Writing of Place in Toni Morrison's *Sula,*" in Elizabeth Meese and Alice Parker, eds., *The Difference Within: Feminism and Critical Theory* (Amsterdam: John Benjamins, 1989), pp. 109–110.

3. Barbara Smith, "Toward a Black Feminist Criticism," in Gloria T. Hull, Patricia Bell Scott, and Barbara Smith, eds., *All the Women Are White, All the Blacks Are Men, But Some of Us Are Brave* (Old Westbury, N.Y.: Feminist Press, 1982), p. 165.

4. Toni Morrison, *Sula* (New York: New American Library, 1973), p. 3. Further references to this text will be included parenthetically.

5. Sigmund Freud, "The Uncanny," *Standard Edition* XVII (London: Hogarth Press, 1955), p. 244.

5. Euphemism, Understatement, and the Passive Voice

1. Reprinted in *The Richard Wright Reader,* ed. Ellen Wright and Michel Fabre (New York: Harper & Row, 1978), p. 37.

2. James Weldon Johnson, *The Book of American Negro Poetry* (New York: Harcourt Brace Jovanovich, 1922; reprint, 1969), p. 9.

3. Julian D. Mason, Jr., ed., *The Poems of Phillis Wheatley* (1773; reprint, Chapel Hill: University of North Carolina Press, 1989), p. 54.

4. June Jordan, "The Difficult Miracle of Black Poetry in America or Something Like a Sonnet for Phillis Wheatley," in *On Call* (Boston: South End Press, 1985), p. 91.

6. Gender and Poetry

1. Simone de Beauvoir, *The Second Sex,* trans. H. M. Parshley (New York: Knopf, 1953), p. 237. Quoted in Elizabeth Spelman, *Inessential Woman* (Boston: Beacon Press, 1988), p. 69. Spelman's book is an eloquent critique of the functioning of white middle-class heterosexual orthopedism in feminist thought.

2. Sylvia Plath, *The Colossus and Other Poems* (New York: Knopf, 1962).

3. "Si jamais homme désira pour sa femme ou sa fille les dons et les honneurs de la Muse, il n'a pu les désirer d'une autre nature que ceux qui furent accordés à Mme Valmore. Parmi le personnel assez nombreux des femmes qui se sont de nos jours jetées dans le travail littéraire, il en est bien peu dont les ouvrages n'aient été, sinon une désolation pour leur famille, pour leur amant même (car les hommes les moins pudiques aiment la pudeur dans l'objet aimé), au moins entachés d'un de ces ridicules masculins qui prennent dans la femme les proportions d'une monstruosité. Nous avons connu la femme-auteur philanthrope, la prêtresse systématique de l'amour, la poétesse républicaine, la poétesse de l'avenir, fouriériste ou saint-simonienne; et nos yeux, amoureux du beau, n'ont jamais pu s'accoutumer à toutes ces laideurs compassées, à toutes ces scélératesses impies (il y a même des poétesses de l'impiété), à tous ces sacrilèges pastiches de l'esprit male."

4. The phrase "pour sa femme ou sa fille" is reminiscent of the opening sentence of Baudelaire's "projet de préface," drawn up at the time of the trial of *Les fleurs du mal:* "Ce n'est pas pour mes femmes, mes filles ou mes soeurs que ce livre a été écrit . . ." Desbordes-Valmore's work can be read as precisely the kind of poetry Baudelaire thought he was *not* writing. His essay about her begins by describing her poetry as being the exact opposite of all his other passions and of his doctrine. It is as though he was afraid of being contaminated by a resemblance.

5. Charles Baudelaire, "Reflexions sur quelques-uns de mes contemporains: Marceline Desbordes-Valmore," in *Oeuvres complètes* (Paris: Pleiade, 1976), vol. II, p. 146.

6. "Mme Desbordes-Valmore n'est pas une femme de lettres, puisqu'il y a de ces monstres qu'on appelle maintenant *femmes de lettres.* Nos pères, avec leur bon sens profond, appelaient *hommes de lettres* ces femmes-là, autrefois! confondant ironiquement les deux sexes dans cette dénomination hideuse et vengeresse. Elle, la simple et trop souvent la négligée, n'a jamais posé pour la *Muse.* Poser, elle! Ce qui enchante plus que le talent de ses vers, quand elle en a, c'est la plus complète absence de pose."

7. J. Barbey d'Aurevilly, *Les Oeuvres et les Hommes* (Paris: Amyot, 1862), pp. 145–146.

8. "Mme Desbordes-Valmore fut femme, fut toujours femme, et ne fut absolument que femme; mais elle fut à un degré extraordinaire l'expression poétique de toutes les beautés naturelles de la femme. Qu'elle chante les langueurs du désir dans la jeune fille, la désolation morne d'une Ariane abandonnée ou les chauds enthousiasmes de la charité maternelle, son chant garde toujours l'accent délicieux de la femme; pas d'emprunt, pas d'ornement factice, rien que l'*éternel féminin,* comme dit le poète allemand. C'est donc dans sa sincérité même que Mme Valmore a trouvé sa récompense, c'est-à-dire une gloire que nous croyons aussi solide que celle des artistes parfaits."

9. Sandra M. Gilbert and Susan Gubar, *The Madwoman in the Attic* (New Haven: Yale University Press, 1979), p. 71.

10. Jan Montefiore, *Feminism and Poetry* (London: Pandora, 1987). Montefiore critiques the feminist aesthetic, which she summarizes as follows: "Poetry is, primarily, the stuff of experience rendered into speech; a woman's poems are the authentic speech of her life and being." It is interesting that neither she nor I have found a quotable example of this aesthetic that is simplistic enough to stand as a target of our critique, even though traces of it seem to be everywhere. Whether it be Adrienne Rich, Sandra Gilbert and Susan Gubar, Audre Lorde, or Judy Grahn, the theorists of the poetic truth of women's experience seem to break out in cultural suspicion at the approach of excessive generalization, even their own.

11. This is the quarrel I would have with a book like the very interesting *Women's Ways of Knowing* by Mary Field Belenky, Blythe McVicker Clinchy, Nancy Rule Goldberger, and Jill Mattuck Tarule (New York: Basic Books, 1986). The book results from a series of extensive interviews with 135 women. "Before asking a woman to participate," write the authors, "we told her that we were interested in her experience—*and in women's experience*—because it had so often been excluded as people sought to understand human development. We told her that we wanted to hear what was important about life and learning *from her point of view*" (p. 11. First emphasis mine; second emphasis the authors'). It seems to me that by telling a woman that *her* point of view is that of *a woman,* the interviewers are inviting women to process their experience through their (culturally constructed) notions of what women's experience might be, thus potentially reproducing rather than questioning the orthopedism the study is designed to combat.

12. *Les oeuvres poétiques de Marceline Desbordes-Valmore,* ed. M. Bertrand (Grenoble: Presses Universitaires de Grenoble, 1973), vol. I, p. 49. All parenthetical page references are to this edition. All translations mine.

13. "A vingt ans, des peines profondes m'obligèrent de renoncer au chant, parce que ma voix me faisait pleurer; mais la musique roulait dans ma tête malade, et une mesure toujours égale arrangeait mes idées, à l'insu de ma réflexion.

"Je fus forcée de les écrire pour me délivrer de ce frappement fiévreux, et l'on me dit que c'était une élégie.

"M. Alibert, qui soignait ma santé devenue fort frêle, me conseilla d'écrire, comme un moyen de guérison, n'en connaissant pas d'autre. J'ai essayé sans avoir rien lu ni rien appris, ce qui me causait une fatigue pénible pour trouver des mots à mes pensées."

14. Quoted in C.-A. Sainte-Beuve, *Portraits contemporains,* t. II (Paris: Michel Levy, 1869), pp. 100–101.

15. "Le poète mourant," in Alphonse de Lamartine, *Oeuvres poétiques complètes,* ed. Marius-François Guyard (Paris: Pléiade, 1963), p. 147.

16. "Mon père m'a mise au monde à Douai, son pays natal (20 juin 1786). J'ai été son dernier et son seul enfant blond. J'ai été recue et baptisée en triomphe, à cause de la couleur de mes cheveux, qu'on adorait dans ma mère. Elle était belle comme une vièrge, on espérait que je lui ressemblerais tout à fait, mais je ne lui ai ressemblé qu'un peu: et si l'on m'a aimée, c'était pour autre chose qu'une grande beauté."

17. "Elle conçoit pour un homme de lettres, Henri de Latouche, un amour ardent qui la fera souffrir, mais la soutient d'abord parmi les soucis de sa carrière et exalte son âme chaleureuse; les échos de cette passion retentiront longtemps dans ses vers. En 1817 elle épouse l'acteur Valmore, et quitte le théatre en 1823. La vie fut dure pour cette créature sensible et passionnée: difficultés matérielles, peines du coeur, deuils cruels (elle perdit quatre enfants), rien ne lui fut épargné; mais elle trouva sa consolation dans la poésie."

18. André Lagarde and Laurent Michard, *XIXe Siècle* (Paris: Bordas, 1969), p. 282. It is interesting to note that the two poems chosen by Lagarde and Michard to represent Desbordes-Valmore's poetry are poems addressed to paternal figures, an address relatively rare in her *oeuvre*. One of the poems, indeed, is cut in half: the maternal half is omitted.

19. Francis Ambrière, *Le siècle des Valmore* (Paris: Seuil, 1987). In this huge two-volume biography, Ambrière displays a fascinatingly complex attitude toward his subject. On the one hand, he has devoted thirty years of his life to researching her every move and word. On the other hand, he is capable of saying things like "Comme la plupart des femmes, Marceline avait une invincible propension à mépriser les règlements" (vol. I, p. 419). Or consider the incredible poignancy and blindness of taking the patriarch's point of view in describing Antoine-Félix Desbordes (Marceline's father), his daughters, and their children: "Son ainée, Cécile, venait de donner à Antoine-Félix le premier des dix-huit petits-enfants que ces trois filles mirent au monde, à raison de six pour chacune. Sur les dix-huit, douze moururent en bas age, tous, sauf un, enfants naturels" (vol. I, p. 113). By entitling the biography *Le siècle des Valmore,* Ambrière elides the very name of his subject. His afterword presents another case of the disappearing female name: "Mais par-dessus tout je suis heureux de reconnaitre ce que je dois à celle qui entre très exactement pour moitié dans la longue recherche préparatoire d'où mon livre est issu. Elle s'appelait Madeleine Fargeaud quand Jean Pommier m'a présenté à elle au printemps 1955 . . . Elle s'appelle aujourd'hui Madeleine Ambrière" (vol. II, p. 429). Needless to say, she who did half the research does not get half the credit on the book's title page.

20. There was, however, one person who *was* threatened by the sincerity of her poetry: Prosper Valmore. When he questioned her about the great lost love depicted in her poems, she replied, "Those poems, which weighed so heavily on your heart, now infuse mine with regret for having written them . . . They are impressions often observed in other women who suffered around me. I said to myself, 'I would feel such-and-such in her place' and I made solitary music. God knows!" (*Lettres de Marceline Desbordes à Prosper Valmore,* ed. Boyer D'Agen [Paris: Editions de la Sirène, 1924], p. 34).

21. Jeanine Moulin, *Marceline Desbordes-Valmore* (in the series "Poètes d'aujourd'hui") (Paris: Seghers, 1955), p. 9.

22. Jeanine Moulin, *La Poésie féminine,* 2 vols. (Paris: Seghers, 1963–1966).

23. Domna Stanton, *The Defiant Muse* (New York: Feminist Press, 1986), pp. xvii–xviii.

24. Montefiore, *Feminism and Poetry,* p. 98. It is curious that Montefiore here has decided to treat Shakespeare's sonnets as unambiguously heterosexual.

25. Susan Gubar, " 'The Blank Page' and the Issues of Female Creativity," in *Writing and Sexual Difference,* ed. Elizabeth Abel (Chicago: The University of Chicago Press, 1982), p. 77.

26. A note about theories of overdetermination: When I first read this poem, I noted the verb "toucher" (which occurs with great frequency in Desbordes-Valmore's love poetry) and thought it might be a sign of the presence of Henri de Latouche as coded countersignature. If Ambrière's chronology is correct, however, Desbordes-Valmore had not yet met Latouche when she wrote this and other "touch" poems. Interestingly, though, a poem written in 1822 (thus, after their meeting) begins: "J'étais à toi avant de t'avoir vu. /Ma vie, en se formant, fut promise à la tienne; / *Ton nom* m'en avertit par un trouble imprévu . . ." If something is overdetermined here, it would seem to be the choice of lover: it is not that the word "toucher" occurs because it is the lover's name but that the lover is loved because his name is already so central to the poetry.

27. Cf. Montefiore, *Feminism and Poetry:* "The lady of the mirror-lyrics, who is the 'passive and glorified instrument of the lover's desire, reflecting what she does not truly possess,' corresponds to Irigaray's contention that woman exists in masculine discourse only as an Other passively reflecting a masculine ego-ideal" (pp. 111–112). The internal quotation is from Frederick Goldin, *The Mirror of Narcissus* (Ithaca: Cornell University Press, 1964).

28. Mary Ellmann, *Thinking About Women* (New York: Harcourt Brace Jovanovich, 1968), pp. 8–9.

29. Petrarch, Sonnet 3, trans. Thomas G. Bergin (New York, Heritage Press, 1966).

30. Maurice Scève, *Délie* # III (translation mine).

31. Ibid., # V (translation mine).

32. Pierre de Ronsard, *Amours de Cassandre,* XI (translation mine).

33. In her brilliant article on Petrarch's use of the myth of Actaeon ("Diana Described: Scattered Woman and Scattered Rhyme" in Abel, ed., *Writing and Sexual Difference*), Nancy J. Vickers emphasizes the ways in which the description of beauty is a form of dismemberment. Her reading is meant to counteract the view of the idealization of Laura as a positive and benign attitude. If she might be said to be describing the unavowed sadism of idealization, what I am

doing here is emphasizing the unavowed masochism inherent in the image of the hunter dismembered by his own desire.

34. See Robert Sabatier, *La Poésie du XVIe Siècle* (Paris: Albin Michel, 1975): "S'agit-il de ce que Marie Bonaparte étudiant la sexualité féminine appelle 'le masochisme féminin essentiel'? En lisant les sonnets, on peut glaner une ample moisson de mots exprimant la blessure: maux, menaces, ruines, combats, crier, cruelle, sanglots, cruauté, duretés, tourment, plaie, douleur, martyre . . ." (pp. 115–116).

35. Cf. Georges Blin, *Le Sadisme de Baudelaire* (Paris: Corti, 1948).

36. Cf. Adrienne Rich: "I had been taught that poetry should be 'universal,' which meant, of course, nonfemale" *On Lies, Secrets, and Silence* (New York: Norton, 1979), p. 44.

37. "Plus d'une fois un de vos amis, comme vous lui faisiez confidence d'un de vos gouts ou d'une de vos passions, ne vous a-t-il pas dit: 'Voilà qui est singulier! car cela est en complet désaccord avec toutes vos autres passions et avec votre doctrine'? Et vous répondiez: 'C'est possible, mais c'est ainsi. J'aime cela; je l'aime, probablement à cause même de la violente contradiction qu'y trouve tout mon être.'" "Tel est mon cas vis-à-vis de Mme Desbordes-Valmore."

38. "Si le cri, si le soupir naturel d'une âme d'élite, si l'ambition désespérée du coeur, si les facultés soudaines, irréfléchies, si tout ce qui est gratuit et vient de Dieu, suffisent à faire le grand poète, Marceline Valmore est et sera toujours un grand poète. Il est vrai que si vous prenez le temps de remarquer tout ce qui lui manque de ce qui peut s'acquérir par le travail, sa grandeur se trouvera singulièrement diminuée; mais au moment même où vous vous sentirez le plus impatienté et désolé par la négligence, par le cahot, par le trouble, que vous prenez, vous, homme réfléchi et toujours responsable, pour un parti pris de paresse, une beauté soudaine, inattendue, non égalable, se dresse, et vous voilà enlevé irrésistiblement au fond du ciel poétique."

39. "Jamais aucun poète ne fut plus naturel; aucun ne fut jamais moins artificiel. Personne n'a pu imiter ce charme, parce qu'il est tout original et natif."

40. "Cette torche qu'elle agite à nos yeux pour éclairer les mystérieux bocages du sentiment, ou qu'elle pose, pour le raviver, sur notre plus intime

souvenir, amoureux ou filial, cette torche, elle l'a allumée au plus profond de son propre coeur. Victor Hugo a exprimé magnifiquement, comme tout ce qu'il exprime, les beautés et les enchantements de la vie de famille; mais seulement dans les poésies de l'ardente Marceline vous trouverez cette chaleur de couvée maternelle, dont quelques-uns, parmi les fils de la femme, moins ingrats que les autres, ont gardé le délicieux souvenir."

41. "Le promeneur, en contemplant ces étendues voilées de deuil, sent monter à ses yeux les pleurs de l'hystérie, *hysterical tears.*"

7. Muteness Envy

1. Charles I. Patterson, "Passion and Permanence in Keats's *Ode on a Grecian Urn*" reprinted in *Twentieth Century Interpretations of Keats's Odes,* ed. Jack Stillinger (Englewood Cliffs, N.J.: Prentice-Hall, 1968), p. 50.

2. Jacques Lacan, *Feminine Sexuality,* ed. J. Mitchell and J. Rose (New York: Norton, 1982), p. 144.

3. Stephen Heath, "Difference," *Screen* 19:3 (1978); Luce Irigaray, "Cosi Fan Tutti," *This Sex Which Is Not One* (trans. Catherine Porter) (Ithaca: Cornell University Press, 1985); Barbara Claire Freeman, "A Union Forever Deferred: Sexual Politics After Lacan," *Qui Parle* 4:2 (Spring 1991).

4. For a brilliant analysis of the relation between aesthetics and sexual violence in Keats's urn, see Froma I. Zeitlin, "On Ravishing Urns: Keats in His Tradition," in *Rape and Representation*, ed. Lynn A. Higgins and Brenda R. Silver (New York: Columbia University Press, 1991). The aesthetic displacement of sexual violence by both Keats and his interpreters has also been analyzed by Deborah Pope in "The Dark Side of the Urn: A Re-evaluation of the Speaker in 'Ode on a Grecian Urn,'" *Essays in Literature* X:1 (Spring 1983). Pope reads the poem as the speaker's increasingly egocentric response to the *urn*'s maidenly refusal to answer his questions, nevertheless culminating in his self-effacement before her oracular, perfectly balanced, final pronouncement.

5. Peter Sacks, *The English Elegy* (Baltimore: Johns Hopkins University Press, 1985).

6. P. Joplin, "The Voice of the Shuttle is Ours," *Stanford Literature Review* 1:1 (1984), pp. 26, 30.

7. C. Brooks, *The Well-Wrought Urn* (New York: Harcourt Brace, 1947), p. 152.

8. See C. Gilligan, A. Rogers, and D. Tolman, *Women, Girls, and Psychotherapy* (New York: Harrington Park Press, 1991).

9. Maria Torok, "The Meaning of 'Penis Envy' in Women," *differences,* 4 (1992), p. 1.

10. See J. Herman, *Father-Daughter Incest* (Cambridge, Mass.: Harvard University Press, 1981), and J. Masson, *The Assault on Truth* (New York: Penguin, 1984).

11. C. Froula, "The Daughter's Seduction: Sexual Violence and Literary History," *Signs* 11:4 (1986), pp. 626, 631.

12. Jane Campion, *The Piano* (New York: Miramax Books, 1993), pp. 135, 138, 139.

13. M. M. Gullette, "'The Piano': Imperfect Pitch," *The Boston Globe,* December 3, 1993, pp. 51, 59.

14. Jane Savoca, *The Boston Globe,* December 17, 1993, pp. 93, 102.

15. Ellie Mamber, *The Boston Globe,* December 17, 1993, p. 93.

16. bell hooks, "Sexism and Misogyny: Who Takes the Rap?" *Z Magazine,* 7:2 (February 1994).

17. *Newsweek,* March 14, 1994, p. 8.

18. *New York,* March 14, 1994, p. 28.

19. *International Herald Tribune,* March 12–13, 1994.

20. Katie Roiphe, *The Morning After* (Boston: Little, Brown, 1993), p. 36.

21. Ibid., p. 44.

22. Campion, *The Piano,* pp. 139, 147.

8. Lesbian Spectacles

1. See Nancy K. Miller, *Getting Personal* (New York: Routledge, 1991).

2. Barbara Smith, "Toward a Black Feminist Criticism," in Gloria T. Hull, Patricia Bell Scott, and Barbara Smith, *All the Women Are White, All the*

Blacks Are Men, But Some of Us Are Brave (Old Westbury, N.Y.: Feminist Press, 1982), p. 165.

3. Deborah E. McDowell, introduction to Nella Larsen, *Quicksand and Passing* (New Brunswick, N.J.: Rutgers University Press, 1986). See also Judith Butler's discussion of these issues in "Passing, Queering: Nella Larsen's Psychoanalytic Challenge, " in *Bodies that Matter* (New York: Routledge, 1993).

4. Larry W. Riggs and Paula Willoquet, *Film Quarterly* 4 (1989).

5. Played, as it happens, by Harvey Keitel, whose role in *The Piano* I have discussed in Chapter 7.

9. The Alchemy of Style and Law

1. Patricia Williams, *The Alchemy of Race and Rights* (Cambridge, Mass.: Harvard University Press, 1991).

2. Quoted in Hannah Arendt's introduction to Walter Benjamin, *Illuminations* (New York: Schocken Books, 1969), p. 5.

3. The text of my response constitutes Chapter 10 in this book.

4. *Harvard Law Review* 105:5 (March 1992), p. 1045.

5. For a more extended discussion of the violence of this parody, see Barbara Johnson, *The Wake of Deconstruction* (Oxford: Blackwell, 1994), which takes up many of the issues discussed here.

6. This statement occurs at the end of an analysis of autobiography in "Autobiography As De-Facement," *The Rhetoric of Romanticism* (New York: Columbia University Press, 1984), p. 81.

7. *New York Times Book Review,* May 26, 1991, p. 10.

8. Gayatri Chakravorty Spivak, "A Response to 'The Difference Within: Feminism and Critical Theory,'" in *The Difference Within: Feminism and Critical Theory,* ed. Elizabeth Meese and Alice Parker (Amsterdam: John Benjamins, 1989), p. 208.

9. René Descartes, "First Meditation," in *Philosophical Essays,* ed. Laurence Lafleur (Indianapolis: Bobbs-Merrill, 1964), p. 76.

10. The Postmodern in Feminism

1. Now available in Mary Joe Frug, *Postmodern Legal Feminism* (New York: Routledge, 1992).

2. Drucilla Cornell, *Beyond Accommodation: Ethical Feminism, Deconstruction, and the Law* (New York: Routledge, 1991), p. 207. Cornell's book is an attempt to articulate a deconstructive critique of feminist positions that do *not* consider sexual difference a philosophical problem.

3. In adopting the Joycean word "mamafesta" for her introduction to *Beyond Accommodation,* for example, Cornell signals her debt to James Joyce and her desire to make the transformation of language itself into a central necessity for feminism. The authors most frequently cited in her footnotes as theoretical influences on her work include Luce Irigaray, Hélène Cixous, Jacques Derrida, Jean-François Lyotard, Julia Kristeva, and Jacques Lacan, all of whom are known for their stylistic density and experimentalism.

Credits

Barbara Johnson. In *Reading Black, Reading Feminist,* ed. Henry Louis Gates, Jr. (New York: Meridian, 1990), pp. 204–211.

Chapter 6 "Gender and Poetry: Charles Baudelaire and Marceline Desbordes-Valmore" in *Displacements: Women, Tradition, Literatures in French,* ed. Joan de Jean and Nancy K. Miller (Baltimore: The Johns Hopkins University Press, 1991), pp. 163–181.

Chapter 7 "Muteness Envy" in *Human, All Too Human,* ed. Diana Fuss (New York: Routledge, 1995), pp. 131–148.

Chapter 8 "Lesbian Spectacles: "Reading *Sula, Passing, Thelma and Louise,* and *The Accused*" in *Media Spectacles,* ed. Marjorie Garber, Jann Matlock, and Rebecca L. Walkowitz (New York: Routledge, 1993), pp. 160–166.

Chapter 9 "The Alchemy of Style and Law" in *The Rhetoric of Law,* ed. Austin Sarat and Thomas R. Kearns (Ann Arbor: The University of Michigan Press, 1994), pp. 261–274.

Chapter 10 "The Postmodern in Feminism: A Response to Mary Joe Frug," *Harvard Law Review,* 105:5 (March 1992), pp. 1076–1083.

Index

Index